The Early Laps
of Stock Car Racing

ALSO BY BETTY BOLES ELLISON

The True Mary Todd Lincoln: A Biography
(McFarland, 2014)

The Early Laps of Stock Car Racing

A History of the Sport and Business through 1974

BETTY BOLES ELLISON

McFarland & Company, Inc., Publishers
Jefferson, North Carolina

LIBRARY OF CONGRESS CATALOGUING-IN-PUBLICATION DATA

Ellison, Betty Boles.
The early laps of stock car racing : a history of the sport
and business through 1974 / Betty Boles Ellison.
    p.   cm.
Includes bibliographical references and index.

ISBN 978-0-7864-7934-4 (softcover : acid free paper) ∞
ISBN 978-1-4766-1622-3 (ebook)

1. Stock car racing—United States—History.
2. Stock car racing—Economic aspects—United States.
3. NASCAR (Association)—History. I. Title.
GV1029.9.S74E55 2014   796.72—dc23   2014025284

BRITISH LIBRARY CATALOGUING DATA ARE AVAILABLE

© 2014 Betty Boles Ellison. All rights reserved

*No part of this book may be reproduced or transmitted in any form
or by any means, electronic or mechanical, including photocopying
or recording, or by any information storage and retrieval system,
without permission in writing from the publisher.*

On the cover: Dick Rathmann leads Bruce Atchley in 1952
at Occoneechee Speedway, Hillsborough, North
Carolina, © Historic Speedway Group

Printed in the United States of America

*McFarland & Company, Inc., Publishers
Box 611, Jefferson, North Carolina 28640
www.mcfarlandpub.com*

For Margaret, Steve and Alex

Table of Contents

· · · · · · ·

Acknowledgments	ix
Preface	1
Introduction	5
1. In the Beginning	9
2. Beach-Road Racing in Daytona	18
3. Whiskey Roots, Red Georgia Clay and Carolina Back Roads	25
4. Hardened Heroes	34
5. A Lily White Sport	41
6. Beer, Broads and Unadulterated Bull	49
7. NASCAR's Early Years	56
8. Dollar Signs Everywhere	63
9. Drivers' Revolving Door	72
10. The Finest Years	84
11. France Gets a Prize	91
12. Kiekhaefer Factor	96
13. Big Boys Come to Town	109
14. Whatever Happened to Marshall Teague?	118
15. Charlotte, Atlanta Join the Super Speedways	124
16. Caution Flags Everywhere	135
17. Those Dreaded Teamsters	145
18. Turner's Back	159

19. The Man NASCAR Kept Overlooking	165
20. Big Boys Return	172
21. Who Was Running NASCAR?	187
22. Eastaboga and the PDA	194
23. Not as Easy as It Once Was	205
24. Money Infusion and Restrictor Plates	213
25. A New Boss Takes Over	225
26. Total Control	235
27. Ever Evolving NASCAR Rules	244
Chapter Notes	253
Bibliography	269
Index	273

Acknowledgments

• • • • • • •

A number of people made important contributions to this book from my family to those who furnished information to the readers of the final manuscript. They all have my deepest appreciation.

This book would truly not have been possible without family support. Our son, who is certainly not a stock car racing fan, took valuable time from his busy schedule to lend assistance. Our daughter, who is a stock car racing fan, never tired of reading revisions, and our son-in-law was very supportive. The copy editing skills of our daughter-in-law were invaluable.

Friends, advisors and manuscript readers made important contributions and suggestions. They included Donna L. Gosney, Madison, West Virginia; Ken Kurtz, Lexington, Kentucky; Carl West and Edward Minten from Frankfort, Kentucky, and Greg Franklin, Glasgow, Kentucky. Carl B. Franklin, Park, Kentucky, recalled the days of Daytona Beach racing and Smokey Yunick's garage. Victor and Marjorie Flock from Buford and Stone Mountain, Georgia, were most gracious with their assistance and recollections about the racing career of their father and husband, Truman "Fonty" Flock, and his relationship with Bill France. Mike Morris, Midway, Kentucky and Jennifer Hewlett, Lexington, were always helpful.

Suzanne Wise, curator of the Belk Library's Stock Car Racing Collection at Appalachian State University, Boone, North Carolina, always had answers to difficult questions. Debra McGriff, reference librarian at the Florida State Library and Archives, answered detailed questions about Florida's early board tracks. Kate Chopin, reference librarian at the Indianapolis–Marion County Public Library, provided explicit information on early racing in Indiana. Dan Smith, archivist with the Ormond Beach Historical Trust, was helpful with data on the early beach speed trials, as was Larry Gibson, reference librarian at the Volusia County Public Library in Daytona Beach, Florida.

Laverne Zachary, from Historic Speedway Group, was most generous in providing stock car racing photographs from the 1950s. Aaron Thompson, from Rep. Andy Barr's office, was instrumental in providing access to the Library of Congress' *Look* magazine photography collection from the 1960s.

Acknowledgments

The author is indebted to scores of sports editors and reporters whose newspaper and magazine articles told the story of how Bill France used the National Association for Stock Car Automobile Racing (NASCAR) to mold the business of drivers, mechanics, car owners and, to some extent, the automobile manufacturers into a racing empire and personal fortune. A special acknowledgment is given to the hundreds, perhaps thousands, of drivers, mechanics and car owners who worked hard, raced for the love of their sport but never had a chance for great individual or financial success. Those men and women were the bedrock of the sport. They were and are the real heroes of stock car racing.

Preface

· · · · · · ·

Addiction to speed in stock car racing comes in many forms regardless of the inherent danger that rides with every driver, whether on a winding highway during a dark night or fighting for position on a high-banked oval. For those who actually participate—the vibrant winners and down in the mouth losers—the heady rush of adrenaline is worth every earth-shattering minute spent in controlling not only their powerful cars but making the critical and possibly life-saving split-second decisions.

For others, that nagging craving for speed is fulfilled by building the best and most advanced cars—especially if the results covertly circumvent the rules. Some did and do revel in exerting total control over the sport. There is even a minute amount of that adrenaline that trickles down to those of us who write about stock car racing—its daredevil drivers, track builders from all walks of life, colorful promoters and the spectators who, from the beginning, fueled the business aspect of the sport.

This book documents the organization of and the first sixty-six years of America's stock car racing history, 1908 to 1974, much of which has been overlooked. Stock car racing did not, as some authors contend, begin on the hard, white sands of Daytona Beach, Florida;

William K. Vanderbilt, Jr., staged the nation's first sanctioned stock car road race over New York's Briarcliff course in 1908. Vanderbilt, known as Willie K., believed that automobiles and drivers were best tested on highways and roads. Willie K., who swept the Ormond-Daytona speed trials in 1904, wanted American cars and drivers to become more proficient than their European counterparts and worked to achieve that end (Library of Congress, Prints and Photographs Division).

nor was it invented by William Henry Getty "Bill" France, who promoted the big beach-road race there in 1939. By that time, the sport had been around for three decades.

The man responsible for establishing the sport of stock car racing was not a southerner. He was a New York millionaire, one of the nation's earlier daredevil racers, William K. Vanderbilt, Jr. He put his own and other investors' money into racing for the love of the sport and because he wanted the U.S. automotive industry to produce equipment that would enable America's race car drivers to break, and exceed, the racing dominance then held by the Europeans.

Willie K., as he was known, staged the nation's first sanctioned stock car road race over New York's Briarcliff Course in April 1908, according to the *New York Times.* Nine years earlier Vanderbilt and his cousin, Cornelius Vanderbilt, organized the Automobile Club of America (ACA) and its promotional counterpart, Motor Car Holding Company, to sanction and promote automobile racing. Initially, their races were on New York public roads. After the American Automobile Association (AAA) began in 1902, it eventually became the giant in all automobile racing, sanctioning and promoting stock car races until 1955. From the beginning, any race the AAA sanctioned required forty percent of the gate (ticket sales) to be placed in the race purse.

From New York, stock car racing traveled south, to Savannah, Georgia, for the Grand Prize races, another Vanderbilt concept. From there it branched out across the South, Midwest and West Coast. It was in the South, however, where stock car racing found its true home. There, illegal whiskey transporters and their shade tree mechanics tinkered and tamed monster cars that outran government revenue agents as they carried their popular product to a thirsty populace while, at the same time, placing their indelible stamp on the sport.

This work reaches deep beneath the surface to find answers to perplexing events. An example is the initial race at Talladega, Alabama, on September 14, 1969. Other authors write about the horrendous track conditions, chewing up tires every few laps, which caused the popular drivers to boycott the race for safety reasons. Why would a sparkling new racetrack have such terrible asphalt problems when, three weeks earlier, it was in pristine condition?

The answer is Category Five Hurricane Camille, which swept through adjacent Mississippi on August 17–18, 1969, and carried gale-force winds extending out 150–200 miles. When LeeRoy Yarbrough and Donnie Allison tested tires at the track on August 8–9, 1969, they attained speeds of 194.87 mph and 192.5 mph, respectively, and were pleased with the faultless track surface. Bill France was so proud of his high-banked track he was bringing in buses of travelers to tour the facility. On September 12, 1969, almost a month after the hurricane, an Associated Press photograph of the track showed mounds of debris stacked on the track apron. The asphalt surface became so degraded that drivers could pick up chunks of it by hand.

The National Association for Stock Car Automobile Racing's (NASCAR) initial incorporation document, from February 18, 1948, and subsequent amendments illustrate how the organization evolved as it did. The documents bear little resemblance to the rules and regulations formally adopted by France and a group of drivers, car owners and promoters at their December 1947 organizational meeting in Daytona Beach.

The incorporation document found in the office of the North Carolina secretary of state was the only internal NASCAR document the author was able to obtain. NASCAR, privately owned from the beginning, does not open its records to the public and chooses to give access only to a few. Much of the material for this book came from archived newspaper and magazine reports of races and reporters' interviews with drivers, car builders, track owners and promoters. Their quotes along with the context and situations in which they were made are quite revealing. Some, while critical of NASCAR management, were also beneficial to the sport. Some suggestions that could have saved lives were ignored.

These newspapers and periodicals provide a glimpse of how the organization's ever-changing rules, some made upon nothing more than a whim, created hardships for car owners and promoters and, for a time, threatened the sport itself. Bill France first welcomed automobile manufacturers fielding teams in NASCAR, and then scorned them for paying their drivers a salary. He threatened drivers with a gun when they dared to organize for the representation that participants in other sports enjoyed. As NASCAR president, France consistently paid, despite drivers' protests, only ten to twelve percent of the gate into the race purses while penalizing drivers entering races sanctioned by other organizations which paid more money.

This book takes the reader on a journey from the structured Vanderbilt Cup and Grand Prize races through the exhilarating years of the illegal whiskey transporters to NASCAR's infancy and its early years. Most of all, the book enables the reader to follow the influence exerted by the flamboyant personalities who made stock car racing so different from other automobile competitions.

Introduction

• • • • • • •

Early stock cars emerged from so many builders, inventors, innovators, mechanics and tinkerers it is impossible to trace their true origins. Some of the REO Speedwagon commingled with the Apperson Jackrabbit with bits of Olds' Curved Dash Runabout, Packard's Gray Wolf, Cameron's Speedster and Sears' Motor Buggy thrown in the mix. From the beginning, there was seldom anything stock about the vehicles. A few of the cars, which differed drastically from similar models on dealers' showroom floors, evaded the watchful eyes of sanctioning organizations.

As production line automobiles became less expensive, more illegal whiskey distillers purchased them to transport their product all over the South. It was inevitable, of course—one illegal whiskey transporter challenged another as to who had the best car, and the races began. There was no organization in the beginning for this raw-bone, winner-take-all competition. Contests of speed, initially staged on hidden back roads and clay flats, moved to dusty fairground horse tracks and to beaches in the East and West as well as on the white sands of Ormond and Daytona. Spectators, tired of the dust, grit and sand, wanted to see more than just a small portion of the entire race. They sought a place where they could enjoy what they paid for without wiping dirt and grime from their faces and clothing. Concrete was too expensive and no amount of oil could contain the dust created by the cars. Motordromes sprung up over the landscape. Englishman Jack Shillington Prince developed a formula for rapidly building steeply banked wooden tracks across the nation. Board tracks, even when the wood was treated, were susceptible to fire, the elements, and termites, and required constant repair.

Businessmen scrambled to take advantage of and satisfy the public's demand for enclosed racing facilities. By the end of 1909, there were ninety-one oval tracks in the United States and nineteen road courses. Two decades later, oval tracks had increased to 542 while road courses had declined to four.

Prohibition ended in 1933, and by the end of the decade there were 1,147 oval tracks and twenty road courses. The availability of legal whiskey once again did not put illegal distillers out of business; there was a continued demand for the raw, searing, clear liquid they produced.

Illegal whiskey entrepreneurs purchased and converted their vehicles into unique conveyances that, except for exterior appearances, bore little or no resemblance to the automobiles seen in dealers' showrooms. Those vehicles, adapted to carry cargos of moonshine whiskey from isolated stills to distributors for marketing in large towns and cities, eventually began to race in cow pastures and on long, straight stretches of highways.

After World War II, stock car racing had its own greatest generation, and the vast majority of those remarkable personalities were from the South. If not southern bred, they made their way south where stock car racing was no longer the domain of the elite but was a working man's sport. Drivers, car owners, mechanics and promoters like Robert "Red" Byron, Raymond Parks, the Flock brothers, "Mad" Marion McDonald, "Rapid" Roy Hall, Lloyd Seay, Edwin "Banjo" Matthews, Louis Grier "Buddy" Shuman, Joe Littlejohn, Henry "Smokey" Yunick, Elzie "Buck" Baker, Jerome "Red" Vogt, Enoch Staley, Curtis Turner, Everett "Cotton" Owens, Gober Sosebee and countless others forever branded the sport with their colorful outlaw reputations.

Overall organization in the southern sport was lacking but participants recognized it was the next necessary step. A number of stock car racing aficionados—Raymond Parks, Red Vogt, Truman "Fonty" Flock, Enoch Staley, Bill France and others—made several attempts at organizing state and national sanctioning bodies. In December 1947, France invited stock car drivers, car builders and promoters to a meeting in Daytona Beach to discuss bringing the sport under a uniform set of rules, regulations, and technical specifications and to create a ruling body. A bare bones organization called the National Association for Stock Car Automobile Racing emerged and corporate officers were elected. France was elected president and Marshall Teague, a driver, was voted in as the treasurer. Two months later, after NASCAR's incorporation documents were filed with the Florida Secretary of State's Office, the participants from the December meeting were stunned to learn France and his lawyer, Louis Ossinsky, had thrown out most of their work, and the corporate documents clearly gave France total control of NASCAR. The name of Marshall Teague, the elected treasurer of the organization, was not found in the incorporation papers. Raymond Parks, an astute Atlanta businessman, said they suddenly discovered that NASCAR belonged only to Bill France.

France had an amazing talent for bringing people like Parks, who was promised but given no official role in the new organization, around to not only support his efforts, but provide him with needed funding. At times, it seemed that France would sink the new organization with his management bungling, but he held firm to two concepts: never relinquishing organizational control outside his family and securing purse money in escrow accounts before every race. The latter was what saved him and the organization. Drivers and car owners, while complaining about his stingy purses as the cost of building cars soared, knew they could count on the prize money.

NASCAR's corporate document gave France absolute power, and he wielded it constantly. *Charlotte News* sports editor Max Muhleman wrote, when deposed Cuban dictator Fulgenico Batista moved to Florida, that Daytona Beach had two dictators living there. France did not take kindly to the description and attempted unsuccessfully to get Muhleman fired.[1] He used his dictatorial powers to keep the big-name drivers on his organizational plantation, driving in his races and increasing his profits. NASCAR's rulebook was whatever France said it was regardless of whether a specific infraction was included in the printed regulations. If a driver drove in another promoter's sanctioned race for more money, France slapped a ban on him, and if he wanted to continue racing in NASCAR, substantial reinstatement fines, up to $30,000, were required.

When the automobile manufacturers began fielding teams in NASCAR in the 1950s, they paid their drivers a salary, whether they raced or not. The ramification of this was that France could no longer require that drivers compete only in his races. While losing his hold over his drivers, he sharpened his political skills, and he was able to borrow enough money to not only build the Daytona International Speedway (DIS) but keep it off the Volusia County tax rolls.

Safety in the early days never seemed to be very high on NASCAR's list. There was little, if any, oversight of safety requirements at tracks where it sanctioned races. Master car builder Smokey Yunick was unable to convince France to use a rubber barrier made from old tires to soften the impact of drivers hitting the thick concrete track walls, and many died from those injuries. Eventually, France allowed Yunick's rubber fuel cell to be used, but only after Fireball Roberts died from injuries received in a fiery crash at Charlotte. Before shoulder harnesses and window nets were required for cars, "Little" Joe Weatherly's skull was crushed when his car hit Riverside's concrete wall.

The 1950s to mid–1960s brought good fortune for NASCAR and France. He was making money left and right but still keeping race purses at ten to twelve percent of the gate. His old nemesis, the American Automobile Association (AAA), was out of stock car racing and France seized the prized membership in Federation Internationale de l'Automobile, which governed international motor racing. Belonging to the FIA's Automobile Competition Committee for the United States (ACCUS) guaranteed that when France staged one of the big NASCAR races, no other sanctioned international automobile racing event could be held on that day. The downside, France found, was that he had to consult the ACCUS committee before instituting major rule changes.

France was not inclined to consult with Curtis Turner, Fireball Roberts and Tim Flock when they made an unsuccessful attempt to organize drivers in the Federation of Professional Athletes (FPA) affiliated with the Teamsters Union. He threatened drivers with a gun and said he would plow up his Daytona track before permitting a union driver to race there. Then, he asked the media to help him save the country from Teamster boss Jimmy Hoffa.

During Turner and Flock's lawsuit against him, France's lawyer denied he ever made those threats. Just in case he needed them, France went looking for witnesses to substantiate that denial. France slapped Turner and Flock with a lifetime ban from NASCAR. Only when track attendance dropped to a dangerously low point, in part due to Turner's absence as well as NASCAR's ever changing rules, did France reinstate the colorful timber baron for the hefty price of $30,000.

Races in the late 1960s and early 1970s were losing their crowds. Stock car racing was rescued at that time by Junior Johnson, who recommended R. J. Reynolds Tobacco Company invest its television advertising dollars in the sport. The result became Winston Cup racing.

1
In the Beginning

• • • • • • •

Stock car racing, in the beginning, was just that—cars as they came from the dealer's showroom floor. Then, the tinkering began with engines to increase the power, sleeker bodies to reduce wind resistance, experimental tires and other alterations. The race, on and off the track, road course or beach, was to make the vehicle faster.

Drivers, mechanics and car builders pursued, at whatever the price, that seductive, elusive mistress they called speed. "You are a god among men," John Bolster wrote of the early drivers, "crouching over the wheel to cleave the wind, willing that marvelous machine to go faster, faster, faster. You are staying alive because the strength of your arms alone are keeping the wayward monster from dashing itself to pieces against trees. It's not frightening because you are drunk with the sheer exhilaration of it."[1]

Spectators were just as enthralled by automobile racing as the drivers. By the second decade of the 1900s, there were 274 oval racing tracks. That number climbed to 2,011, before a decline began in 1959.[2]

In 1910, stock car events were included in the Daytona Beach speed trials. Barney Oldfield drove a Knox to the one-mile record of 128.871 mph in the trials. Gus Grosjean won the ten-mile Southern Championship. The beach speed trials, which began in 1903, ended in 1911, according to William Tuthill, because of Bob Burman's 141.732 mph and 140.406 mph records in the one and two mile traps respectively. "We could say that it was the running of the first 500-mile race at Indianapolis [Motor] Speedway that year and all other events around the world that drew interest away from the beach. Actually, it was the shattering speed turned in by Burman that did it. At that time, 141.732 mph was just too much."[3]

For some men like Burman and others, speed was never enough.

William K. Vanderbilt, Jr., more commonly known as Willie K., was a speed maven who terrorized Newport, Rhode Island, residents with his fast driving, to such an extent that municipal authorities imposed speed limits. "Arrest me every day if you want to," Willie K., was quoted as saying, "It's nothing to pay fines for such sport." There actually was a serious side to the man who revered speed along with his alleged certificate of Honorable Dismissal from Harvard.[4]

In 1904, Willie K. and his ninety-horsepower Mercedes won seven of the nine Ormond-Daytona beach speed trials.[5] The same year, Willie K. staged the first international road race in America on Long Island, New York, highways. The event was called, appropriately enough, the Vanderbilt Cup Race, and these continued on the Long Island road course—and the

The pits really were pits, as shown in this October 1910 photograph of Vanderbilt's last stock car race on Long Island. Unable to control the vast crowds who came to see his races, Vanderbilt halted his New York events but not before he achieved his goal—the first seven cars to cross the finish line were not only made in the United States but were driven by Americans (Library of Congress, Prints and Photographs Division).

Long Island Motor Parkway he built—until 1910. In his first three cup races, a Panhard and two Darracqs were the winners. American cars and drivers won the next three races—George Robertson in a Locomobile and Harry Grant in ALCOs.[6]

A banner headline in the April 25, 1908, *New York Times* heralded the winner of the first stock car road race in America, staged by Vanderbilt's Motor Car Holding Company and sanctioned by Vanderbilt's Automobile Club of America (ACA). Lewis Strang, driving J. H. Tyson's Isotta-Fraschini, won the 240-mile International race over the Briarcliff course in Westchester County, New York. Strang averaged forty-six miles per hour (mph) and finished the race in just under five hours and fifteen minutes.[7]

The Briarcliff event was one of several 1908 stock car races held or scheduled for Lowell, Massachusetts, Philadelphia and Chicago. "For some time racing affairs have been in such a turmoil," *The Automobile* magazine stated, "so that even if races were wanted it was almost impossible to hold them with any unopposed sanctions. It was after the AAA and the Automobile Club of America (ACA) had apparently buried the hatchet and hammer and settled on a definite line of joint action that the manufacturers themselves formed the Manufacturers Contest Association."[8]

Vanderbilt, after seeing the hundreds of thousands of spectators at his New York road races and the big crowds at the beach trials, devised a plan to bring stock car racing to the South. Vanderbilt chose not to build an enclosed facility specially designed for automobile racing, preferring road courses because it was on roads and highways, he insisted, where automobiles and drivers were best tested.[9]

He called his friend, George Tiedeman, mayor of Savannah, in 1907, and asked him to send a delegation to New York with a proposal to host the Grand Prize races there. Willie K. would select the location. Representatives of larger cities—Philadelphia, Atlanta, Los Angeles and Indianapolis—were puzzled their proposals were rejected in favor of a small southern town with no experience in staging automobile races. It was all because of Willie K. He just happened to be one of the original members of the exclusive Jekyll Island Club, near Savannah, located on one of Georgia's smaller barrier islands.[10]

Frank Battey, president of the Savannah Automobile Club, boasted the races would be staged so well there would not be a single complaint. The city hosted trial races in March 1908, and built grandstands for 16,000 spectators to show they could handle such an operation. In the morning contest, Herbert Lytle won the Southern Runabout Cup race in a red Apperson Jackrabbit in just under 3:36 on the twenty-mile course prepared by the Savannah Automobile Club under the direction of the AAA's Racing and Technical Board.[11]

George Salsman, in an American-built Thomas Flyer, won the afternoon race in just under 3:02. A week later, race officials felt they were prepared for the Savannah Challenge Cup. Eight cars made up the field: Herbert Lytle in the Apperson; Louis Strang, Isotta-Fraschini; F. W. Tone, American; H. Michener, Lozier; William McCulla, Apperson; Al Poole, Isotta-Fraschini; F. W. Leland, Sterns; and M. Neusetter in an Acme. Strang won the cup race in 6:44:30, and pronounced the course the best he had ever driven.[12]

Slow-paced Savannah, with its live oaks dripping Spanish moss, lacked the accommodation for such races but that did not stop Georgia Governor Hoke Smith, Tiedeman and a virtual army of local movers and shakers from promising Vanderbilt they would run a flawless operation for the November races. They established two preliminary races: the Savannah Cup and the Tiedeman Cup.[13]

Officials rousted convicts out of their cells to build the 25.13-mile street and road course out of Augusta gravel and 80,000 gallons of oil firmly packed into the course to control the dust. The thirty-two banked turns wound past grandstands built to seat thousands. Gov. Smith directed Col. M. J. O'Leary and 1,600 members of the Georgia militia, including the Georgia Hussars, Irish Green Jaspers and Chatham Artillery, to maintain crowd order and keep people and animals off the race course, with force if necessary.[14]

The governor and the mayor were determined Savannah would have none of the crowd control problems Vanderbilt experienced in his New York races. Physicians, stationed along the banked turns, were there to render assistance in case of accidents. Each turn had a bugler to let the crowd know when cars were approaching, and 160 flagmen, at intervals around the course, warned drivers of any dangers ahead.[15] Smith and Tiedeman made a group of the Georgia judiciary honorary race judges just in case something occurred that required a legal ruling.[16]

The first Grand Prize Races, in 1908, were just about everything Smith, Tiedeman and Battey promised Vanderbilt. Twenty cars and teams were invited. Fourteen European and six American teams competed in the expanded field. The European cars included two Renaults, two Clement-Bayards, a de Dietrick, three Fiats, three Italas and three Benzes. Dr. Julian K. Quattlebaum, in his book *The Great Savannah Races,* estimated the cost of the foreign cars at $25,000 each. American entries included a Lozier, Buick, Chadwick, Acme, National and Simplex. Quattlebaum referred to the events as stock car races.[17]

Louis Wagner won the first Grand Prize Race in one of the Fiats with the time of 6:10:31 and was awarded the Savannah Cup.[18] His average lap time was 25:13. The great Italian racer Ralph DePalma, in another Fiat, set a blistering lap time of 21:16 at the beginning of the race but oil problems and a bad pit stop put him out of contention and he finished ninth.[19]

W. H. Hilliard won the first Tiedeman trophy, in an Italian Lanica, covering the 196-mile course with an average speed of 52.59 mph in the second tier race. For defeating fourteen other cars, he received $500. The trophy was named for Savannah's mayor, who sponsored the race.[20]

When a car lost a tire at the Isle of Hope, crowds of spectators rushed onto the track to get a closer look at the automobile. A militia captain and his troops had difficulty preventing them from being run down. One reporter wrote, "In one instance, the spectators became so eager to see the cars pass by that the soldiers had to thrust them back by main force."[21]

The 1908 races brought into question the use of the militia to control crowds at racing events. "Generally, Savannah's policing was totally uncompromising, more than one errant spectator was jabbed back into line by a bayonet," racing historian Doug Nye wrote. "But for the European visitors Savannah's Georgian hospitality and its magnificent race circuit were to become a glowing lifelong memory." During one race, a man attempted to drive his horse and buggy across a street that was a part of the race course and got into an altercation with soldiers. The man received a bayonet wound in the chest for his persistence.[22]

Savannah's 1911 races brought American cars and drivers the success Willie K. hoped for years earlier. Racing historian Peter Helck said that the best of the European racers were beat by and outclassed by stock and semi-stock cars and a handful of outdated specials. All except the Buicks had run in the Vanderbilt Cup race three days earlier, where the Lozier, built in Detroit, beat the Grand Prix Mercedes and the winning driver was an American, David Bruce-Brown.[23]

Owners and drivers enjoyed the amenities Savannah offered, but the Grand Prize races created problems for public officials. Crowds of 100,000 far exceeded the small town's infrastructure although city and state officials and their volunteers did amazing work. The use of convict labor to build and maintain the course created animosity. The heavy hand the militia exerted in controlling crowds and keeping streets and roads closed was a constant irritant, but they did control the spectators and avoided injuries. As more and more people purchased automobiles, they expected open public thoroughfares, and denial of their use became a political issue.[24]

The Grand Prize Races in Savannah, while a rousing success, almost overwhelmed the sleepy southern town. After the 1910 and 1911 races, the Georgians were finished. "Savannah bowed to public pressure," Nye wrote, "and the magnificently policed, beautiful southern circuit was abandoned."[25]

Vanderbilt's bringing the Grand Prize race to the South enabled Savannah to help establish stock car racing's southern roots. Those roots spread not only across the South but to other parts of the country prior to World War I.

Indianapolis businessman Carl Fisher differed with Vanderbilt and the Georgians, believing that the best venue for automobile racing was a well-built, self-contained track facility. He said spectators who paid to see road course races did not get their money's worth, as they only saw cars one time during a lap. Fisher, with three partners—James A. Allen, Arthur C. Newby and Frank H. Wheeler—built the nation's first super-speedway in 1909, where spectators could watch the entire race. Initially, Fisher wanted a three-mile track, but realized the $400,000 oval's distance had to be shortened a half-mile in order to build grandstands. The infield of the 2.5-mile facility was so large, speedway officials later said, that there was space for the Vatican City complex, the Wimbledon campus, the Roman Coliseum, the Rose Bowl, Yankee Stadium and Churchill Downs' one-mile track with room to spare.[26]

Concrete, used in 1906–1907 to build the steep-banked track for the world's most elegant racing venue—Brooklands in Surrey, England—was considered too expensive by Fisher and his partners. Their track, whose quarter-mile turns were banked at nine degrees, was composed of packed soil, topped with two inches of gravel followed with two inches of crushed limestone, a layer of tar, two inches of stone chips and another seam of tar topped with crushed stone.[27]

Motorcycle races were held at the Indianapolis Motor Speedway (IMS) a week before the big 250-mile Prest-O-Lite stock car race in August 1909, but competition was cancelled after the first day due to track conditions. The tar failed to keep the dust and stone in place and it was an indication of the tragedies to come. Headlights, the rear seat and mud flaps were removed from the stock cars entered in the August 19, 20, 21 races, racing columnist Ed Hinton wrote, and the cars' rear seats were replaced by big cylinder fuel tanks.[28] AAA regulations allowed 1909 and 1910 stock cars to enter the race and required a piston displacement of 301 to 450 cubic inches.[29]

Despite everybody's best intentions, the Prest-O-Lite 250 was a disaster that was an inauspicious beginning for the stock car track Fisher and his partners built and the AAA sanctioned.

Drivers qualified nine cars for the inaugural Indy stock car race. They included the Knox Giant driven by William Bourque; two Nationals driven by Tom Kincaid and Charlie Merz; Bert Miller, Fred Ellis and Jap Clements in three Stoddard-Daytons; and Bob Burman, Lewis Strang and Louis Chevrolet in Buicks. They were all racing for 2,000 ounces of silver, which had a melting value of $1,000. In 2012, that $1,000 in silver had the economic power of $499,000. The Prest-O-Lite silver trophy, valued at $1,500, was furnished by the automobile headlights manufacturer, hence the name of the race. More than 15,000 spectators paid fifty cents for infield seats or a dollar to sit in the grandstands.[30]

Newspapers painted accurate but bloody accounts of the race. "The new motor speedway, said to be the fastest automobile race course in the world, was dedicated here today at the cost of two lives, William A. Bourque, driver of a Knox Giant, and Harry Holcomb, his mechanic, being killed when their car crashed into a fence on the home stretch during the race for the Prest-O-Lite Trophy," the *New York Times* reported.[31]

The *Indianapolis Star* reported the track was dedicated with the blood of two of Massachusetts' brave men. "The thousands of spectators were so absorbed in the tense struggle of the motor dare devils to gain the lead in the long, grueling contest that they were shocked without warning when the big racer pitched and hurled into a ditch while going about seventy-five miles per hour. Bourque turned to look back just as he was crossing a slightly rough part of the track. It was all over in an instance. His machine rushed headlong into a ditch beside the track. The car was hurled and thrown end over end to the ground and against the fence, while two helpless men were tossed helplessly to either side."[32]

Bourque, twenty-six years old, and Holcomb, twenty-two, never regained consciousness before dying. It was a miracle that spectators and physicians, rushing to their aid while dodging speeding automobiles whose drivers' vision was clouded by dust and debris, were not killed. George A. Crane, a Knox sales representative, said, "It is simply suicide, that's all it is." Crane added that he expected Knox to withdraw from racing. The *Indianapolis Star* reported that the company carried insurance on Bourque and Holcomb for about $25,000.[33]

Bourque and Holcomb were not the only fatalities that day. Mechanic Charles Kellum was fatally injured when one of the Nationals crashed the barrier and killed two spectators, James West and Homer Jolliff.[34]

Earlier in the race, Lewis Strang's Buick caught on fire. He pulled into the pits, where the flames were extinguished. AAA race officials initially refused to allow Strang to continue racing. The driver harangued them until they relented and allowed him to return.[35]

Fred Ellis and his mechanic, A. J. House, collapsed while working on their Jackson racer in the pits. Ellis and many other drivers complained about stones breaking their goggles and injuring their eyes. Louis Chevrolet, while leading the race, was temporarily blinded by bits of stone and glass that became embedded in his eyes and face. After almost hitting the wrecked Knox, he parked on the track.[36]

Willie K. Vanderbilt was there. Although some of his road races had been bloody, nothing happened to compare to the carnage he saw at Indianapolis.[37] AAA race officials, stunned by the five fatalities, threatened to cancel the remaining two days of the race meet unless Fisher and his partners performed overnight improvements to the track. In their haste to get everything finished, the owners only oiled down the small portion of the track in front of the grandstands and neglected the track's many ruts. The AAA demanded that every inch of the track be tarred and oiled down or the race meet would be cancelled.[38]

Fisher and his partners knew the track surface had to be changed. After the initial race meet was over, they decided to lay a brick surface. In just sixty-three days, they covered the track with 3.2 million bricks, each weighing 9.5 pounds, and held in place with cement.[39]

Stock car racing continued on the brick surface for the next year until Buick attempted to enter some cars that were prototypes, not production models available to the public, in a July 10 race. The AAA threw out the race results two weeks later. Fisher was disgusted, IMS historian Donald Davidson said, when he was informed about the disqualifications. "The public deserves to know that what they've seen on the race track was the results," he quoted Fisher as saying. "If the sanctioning body [AAA] is going to throw them [race results] out two or three weeks later, then maybe we should just go to specials, where the specs are freer."[40]

The AAA made the rules for stock car racing from the early 1900s to 1955, and claimed it strictly enforced them. At the Speedway Stock Car Championships in 1910 at the Indianapolis Motor Speedway, several contestants' cars were prohibited from competing. "Strict interpretation of the stock car rules was insisted on by the Technical Committee of the AAA and its rulings caused some dissatisfaction among those who found themselves on the wrong side," the *American Motorist,* an AAA publication, reported. "On the grounds they had not been produced in sufficient quantities [for public to purchase] the committee rules out the entries of Buick's models, 16a, 106 and 100; the Jackson 30; Westcott F; Cutting 50; the American Speedster; Fuller 1911 roadster, and the Empire 1911 C."[41]

The majority of cars in the first Indianapolis 500, in 1911, were stock cars. "Thirty-two of the forty starters were pretty much the original intent—production cars, maybe modified slightly," Davidson said.[42]

Among those twelve cars was the Marmon Wasp, built and driven by a company engineer, Ray Harroun, who added a new piece of equipment to the car—a rear view mirror. The Wasp carried only one person but the AAA allowed it to race against the other cars carrying drivers and their mechanics. Harroun won the race in the Wasp in 6:42:08, with an average speed of 74.602 mph. Harroun returned to IMS in 1961 to drive the Wasp for a parade lap celebrating fifty years of the race. In 2011, IMS had 1963 Indy 500 winner Parnelli Jones return to drive the Wasp two laps around the track, but the Wasp threw a rod through the side of the crankcase and had to be retired.[43]

Open wheel racing reigned at the Indiana track but stock car racing became more and more popular. Louis Chevrolet, in his summarization of the 1909 racing season for the *New York Times,* wrote about the stock car race in Lowell, Massachusetts, where the Buicks excelled. Chevrolet won the stock car race at Riverhead, on Long Island, setting a world's record of seventy-five mph over the 138-mile course in a Buick. At the two-mile Atlanta Motordrome, Chevrolet won the 200-mile race averaging seventy-two mph while driving a Buick.[44]

The sport spread to Texas, Louisiana, Illinois, California, Iowa, and Georgia, to name a few states. Stock car races were staged as stand-alone events or in connection with other types of racing. In the span of one decade, 1909 to 1919, the number of automobile race tracks in the United States jumped from ninety-one to 274. In the same period, the number of road courses increased from nineteen to twenty-seven.[45]

In just one month, August 1910, twenty-two AAA sanctioned stock car races were held in Texas, Pennsylvania, New Jersey, New York, Ohio, Wyoming, Colorado, Minnesota, California, Illinois and Arkansas. Those races were in addition to all the hill climbs, reliability contests, speed trials and undocumented competitions.[46]

The AAA's Contest Board had stringent rules for stock cars in those races. As early as 1910, the Contest Board implemented extensive pre-race tests for motors, brakes, clutches and transmissions. No work was allowed on a vehicle after the final inspection. While replacing tires during a race, motors were kept running and penalty points were assessed for late arrivals at check points. Special aprons were allowed in front of the radiator; screens between side members of the frame, rubber bumpers for springs, rebound straps and tire inflating tanks were allowed. Special shock absorbers, covers and screens for oil boxes, magnetos and carburetors were not allowed unless they were stock items. Spare parts carried by each vehicle were inventoried, checked by officials before each event and sealed.[47]

The speed trials returned to the Florida beaches in 1919, under both the AAA and the ACA sanctions. The resumption of the beach speed trials are closely tied to stock car racing after World War I. Some of the beach drivers, mechanics and promoters later participated in stock car racing there and in other venues across the country.

Ralph DePalma, from Brooklyn, New York, brought a monster Packard with a twelve-cylinder airplane engine to the beach. DePalma and the Packard swept all the speed trials. He did the twenty-mile event in 9:20:40 as compared to Bob Burman's 1911 record of 13:11:92, despite having to swing out 792 yards in doubling back on the course. "Most of the marks against which he rode were of long standing so the intrepid Italian took particular joy in supplanting them with paces made by a car thoroughly American in design and construction," the *Reading Eagle* reported.[48]

DePalma's return led a long list of distinguished drivers, their automobiles and mechanics who returned to test on the hard white sands of Ormond and Daytona beaches. He was followed by "Terrible" Tommy Milton, from St. Louis, and his mighty Duesenberg, which hit the 156.046 mph mark in 1920. Sig Haugdahl, a former Norwegian speed skater and motorcycle competitor from Minnesota, opened a garage in Daytona the same year. Haugdahl built a Fiat, the "Wisconsin Special," that reached a top beach speed of 180.27 mph in 1922. Henry O'Neal de Hane Segrave, a former Royal Flying Corps major, brought his red, bulb-nosed Sunbeam with its 1,000 hp engine to the beach in 1927. Accompanying Segrave and the car were four engineers, six mechanics, 500 gallons of fuel, seven crates of tires and the English media. More than 15,000 lined the beach to see him set a new land speed record of 203.79 mph.[49]

Malcolm Campbell, a British diamond merchant's son, brought his Napier Bluebird to the beach determined to break Segrave's record. Pennsylvanian Ray Keech and his five-ton White Triplex, and Californian Frank Lockhart and his Stutz Black Hawk Special with the oversized wheel covers also arrived in 1928. Campbell's car, with a 900-hp Broad Arrow engine with three banks of four cylinders, reached 206.95 mph. Keech's car, with three 27-liter Liberty airplane engines, hit 210 mph before the radiator exploded. His second run set a new world land speed record, 207.55 mph. Lockhart reached 225 mph in his first run when the tires hit something in the sand and the Black Hawk catapulted into the ocean.[50]

"Dozens of men ran pell-mell into the water up to their necks and tried to pull Lockhart out of the wreck," the *Daytona Beach Morning Journal* reported. "But, the car's body had been crimped against his groin and he screamed with pain when they yanked at him. All the while, the breakers were curling again and again over the car engulfing Lockhart's head. He would have drowned had it not been for a happy-go-lucky young man named Gil Farrell."[51]

Farrell climbed on the back of the car, behind Lockhart, cupped his hands over the driver's mouth and nose when the waves came in; when they receded, he took his hands away and yelled for him to breathe as a wrecker pulled the Stutz out of the water. When the car was on firm sand, mechanics used torches and chisels to cut Lockhart out of the car. Farrell, who was later instrumental in the beach-road stock car races, came nearer to drowning than Lockhart.[52]

Lockhart, winner of the 1925 Indianapolis 500, was persistent and brought the Black Hawk back for another try at the record in April 1928. He was going an estimated 225 mph when the right tire exploded, sending the car airborne 140 feet down the beach. Lockhart's lifeless body hit the sand fifty feet beyond his car. Lockhart's legacy continued, however, when Ray Keech drove the car he had been building to victory in the 1929 Indy 500.[53]

Campbell returned to the beach attempting to reach the elusive land speed record of 300 mph. Spectators who came to see the beach speed trials, as well as the automobile manufacturers, drivers and mechanics, poured a considerable amount of money into the Daytona Beach economy. That economic bubble, however, was about to burst. Campbell built another Blue Bird, with a 2,500 hp Rolls-Royce engine, in his Brooklands garage and came back to the beach in 1935. Campbell's 276.82 mph was far short of the record. Concerned about the soft sand and lack of traction, Campbell took the same Blue Bird to the Bonneville Salt Flats, in Utah, and achieved his goal, 301.13 mph.[54]

When Campbell and the other drivers stopped using the beach in their efforts to break land speed records, the Daytona Beach economy suffered. The loss of tourist revenue and the money the testing teams spent there presented a problem for city officials. A veteran of the earlier beach speed trials gave city officials some advice about the future of automobile racing there. Wintering in Florida like many of his peers, including Willie K. Vanderbilt, Ransom Eli Olds advised city officials to begin stock car racing on a beach-road course. "It possesses the necessary attributes to become a permanent event at Daytona Beach," he told them.[55]

2

Beach-Road Racing in Daytona

....

Years before the speed trial events ended, a Daytona Beach resident had the same idea as Ransom Eli Olds for beach-road racing. Gilbert T. Farrell, the automobile salesman who saved Frank Lockhart's life in the first Black Hawk wreck on the beach, incorporated the Daytona Beach Speedway Association in July 1931. No evidence of an automobile race conducted under that name was found. An earlier entity, Daytona Beach Racing Club, was incorporated in March 1931. However, that incorporation document listed no names of an agent or officers. The only connection between the two corporations was that they were both dissolved on the same day, December 14, 1936.[1] Farrell, over the next decade, played important roles in beach-road races, as did many other Daytona Beach residents along with some northern snowbirds.

Louis Jerome "Red" Vogt, an early master of the mechanics of building whiskey and stock cars, headed south in 1929 and stopped in Atlanta when his money ran out. The Washington, D.C., native, who grew up with Bill France, said he had four cents in his pocket. "We needed to pay our hotel bill and we were out of food," he recalled in a 1974 interview. "I'd always heard the place to borrow money was a bank, so that's where I went. The banker, a Mr. Bergstrom, said he'd be glad to lend me a $100 and asked about collateral."[2]

"I told him my assets were a wife and car; he didn't seem too impressed," Vogt added. Bergstrom was apparently impressed with Vogt because he lent him the $100 backed by the banker's personal note. "Top pay then was $27.50 a week for a real good mechanic—ten hours a day, six days a week. I didn't have any trouble getting a job or paying back the bank."[3]

Vogt became so successful that he had his own garage, which was open twenty-four hours a day.

France, a Washington, D.C., mechanic tired of the cold Eastern winters, arrived in Daytona Beach in 1934 with his wife Anne, a nurse, and son, William Clifton France, in a Hupmobile. France said he had been interested in speed since he sneaked his father's Model T and attempted to drive it on the board track Jack Prince built in Laurel, Maryland. "I would try to make it ride up on the banking but it wouldn't stay there," he said. "Dad would complain about how his tires wore out so fast. He'd take it back to the dealer and complain and I couldn't say a word.[4]

"I just started thinking if I was going to have to work all the time fixing automobiles, I might as well fix them where it wasn't snowing," he said. "I really didn't like going out start-

2. Beach-Road Racing in Daytona 19

ing all those frozen automobiles, fixing dead batteries, working on them, laying on my back on the cold ground. I decided I might as well go on down to Florida to work on them where it was warm and comfortable. When I saw Daytona Beach, I thought it was the prettiest place I'd ever seen."[5]

"We stopped at Daytona because it was the place we wanted to live and I got a job as a mechanic at Sax Lloyd's Buick-Pontiac-Cadillac garage." France recalled seeing Malcolm Campbell's last beach run in his Bluebird in 1935. "It was quite a sight seeing Campbell go 276 mph," France recalled. He was impressed with the Rolls-Royce airplane engine Campbell used in the car. "The crew on Campbell's car was made up of aircraft mechanics instead of automobile mechanics," he said.[6]

France said Sig Haugdahl came up with the idea for incorporating the beach and the adjacent highway into the beach-road course. Haugdahl was the first man to reach three miles a minute in the beach mile speed record.[7]

Haugdahl was another major player in the beach-road races. He began racing in events promoted by J. Alex Sloan in his International Motor Contest Association (IMCA), which the AAA classified as an "outlaw" organization. Haugdahl was IMCA champion from 1927 to 1932. He built the "Wisconsin Special" using an aircraft engine from a World War I airplane and drove it on the beach in April 1922, to the world-land speed record of 180.27 mph, which the AAA refused to recognize. Haugdahl, according to the *Dallas Morning News,* was responsible for laying out the famous Daytona racing course that was half beach and half road in 1936.[8]

The City of Daytona Beach organized the Daytona Beach–Volusia County Racing Association to stage the beach-road race using the course Haugdahl laid out along the beach and Highway A1A, which ran parallel to the shore, for the 3.2-mile competition. Haugdahl was asked by the city to promote and organize the race with a purse of $5,000, with $1,700 going to the winner. Strangely enough, the AAA, which refused to recognize Haugdahl's earlier beach speed record because of his association with Sloan, agreed to sanction the event although he was the promoter. AAA sent in Ted Allen, supervisor of their Contest Board, to oversee the race. Cars in the race had to be stock and built in 1935–1936. According to Buz McKim, a NASCAR historian, Haugdahl was assisted in the 1936 race by attorney Millard Conklin, and Bill France, a local service station operator, was a consultant. Contrary to the accounts of France and the *Dallas Morning News* report, McKim maintained that France, not Haugdahl, laid out the beach-road course.[9]

Everything that could go wrong with the race did. In the measured mile format, a car made nine-mile passes up and down the beach with no other vehicles about. It was an entirely different situation when scores of cars plowed through the beach every few seconds roiling up sand and debris. The beach part of the course was a total disaster as the sand turns at each end became impassable.

United Press correspondent Henry McLemore said the course was so bad it would cause a horse to balk. "A driver is stuck at the bottom of the south turn," he wrote. "He's right in the middle of it and is out digging away the sand with a shovel. He's crazy to be standing there for the other drivers are missing him by inches as they bounce and slide and spin through the sand."[10]

McLemore wrote that a driver, whom the crowd called "No Brains" Elmore, was leading the race at one point but, since he had almost wrecked nearly a dozen times, the reporter did not expect him to win. McLemore was correct. Elmore finished second.[11]

When the race was called after seventy-five laps, Milt Marion, Canadian dirt track champion from St. Alban, New York, was in the lead and pocketed $1,700. Tommy Elmore, from Jacksonville, was second, $1,000; Ben Shaw, AAA Eastern Dirt Track Champion, was third, $700; and Sam Purvis, winner of the 1935 Jacksonville road race, was fourth, $500. Fifth was Bill France in a Ford owned by Glen Brooks, from Daytona Beach, and he won $375. Prize money was paid through tenth position. Shaw and Elmore protested the decision to call the race but to no avail. When the race was called, only ten of the twenty-seven entries were still running.[12] The confusion was so great the AAA left town thoroughly soured on Daytona's brand of stock car racing.[13]

The AAA continued to sanction stock car races in the South at other venues like the Carolina Speedway, a board track in Charlotte that drew 27,000 for its inaugural event in October 1924. "Terrible" Tommy Milton won the race with an average speed of 120.2 mph and took home $10,000 out of the purse of $25,000. Multi-millionaire automobile dealer C. C. Codding was one of the investors in the $300,000 bowl-like facility that, a year later, was drawing crowds of 50,000.[14] Those were crowds the Daytona Beach promoters only dreamed about.

The Daytona Beach Elks Club promoted the 1937 beach-road race. After that, things become rather murky about France's involvement in the beach-road races the next two years. In their book *Inside Sports Magazine NASCAR Racing*, Bill Fleischman and Al Pearce describe how Haugdahl and France became fast friends during the first race and talked the Elks into promoting the 1937 beach-road race on Labor Day with a $100 purse.[15]

Actually, the Daytona Beach Elks Club began sponsoring beach races a decade earlier. In April 1927, the Elks sponsored races on the beach course along with trap shoots, parades and street dances as they hosted the first Tri-State Convention of the Benevolent Order of Elks ever held in the South.[16]

Race results again created a controversy in 1937. C.D. "Smokey" Purser, a native Georgian who made a lot of money during prohibition in bootlegging, and who owned the New Yorker Bar and Grill in Daytona Beach and was a prominent figure in the local numbers racket, came in first. (Purser was later named as one of four gamblers who attempted to bribe state officials in Tallahassee with $40,000.) Pre-race and post-race inspections were required of the cars. At stake was the purse containing a bottle of rum, and cases of beer and motor oil. While waiting for his turn for inspection, Purser drove away. There were claims after the race that Purser changed an engine part. When he returned at the appointed time for his inspection, Purser found he had been disqualified by a vote of the drivers. Purser questioned why his car had to be inspected after the race when a pre-race inspection had been made. Disqualifying Purser made France the second place winner. Since France was involved in some part of the race management, the third place driver, Lloyd Moody, was given the booty but France kept credit for the win and took second.[17]

Dan Pierce wrote in his book *Real NASCAR: White Lightning, Red Clay and Big Bill France* that France was the race official and promoter and a driver in the 1937 race.[18] If the 1937 beach-road race was anything like the first beach event in 1903, there were twenty-eight people actively involved in staging the race.[19] Thirteen years later, Daytona Beach sports writer Bernard Kahn continued the company line as he waxed poetically about Bill France and the 1937 beach-road race. "The nation's first smashup derby was run on the hammer hard sands of the beach here in 1937 under the direction of Bill France who is promoting the race this weekend," he wrote.[20]

The Elks had had enough and declined to sponsor the 1938 race. Haugdahl returned to his garage to build engines. With Haugdahl out of the picture, France was hailed as the savior of the beach-road races. Fleischman and Pearce wrote, "France was the last real hope to keep racing alive in the Daytona Beach area." The authors stated that Ralph Hankinson, whom they described as a wealthy hotel owner but was actually the largest promoter of auto races in the nation, had refused to take France's collect telephone call in connection with promoting the 1938 race. Unable to reach Hankinson, France turned to Charlie Reese, a local restaurateur, who agreed to put up $1,000 for the purse. France ran the race and their collaboration continued to run the races through 1941.[21]

Hankinson was nearing retirement but was still promoting races. In October 1941, Hankinson, along with his acolyte, Sam Nunis, staged a 100-mile stock car race for the Spartanburg (South Carolina) State Fair. The cars had to be 1938–1942 models conforming to factory specifications.[22]

Hankinson, an innovative race promoter, had bought a Florida hotel to enjoy his retirement. In the early lean years, the Kansas native staged auto-polo events, where cars pushed a huge ball across the opponent's goal line at fairs, expositions, even in Madison Square Garden. Drivers liked the Hankinson-promoted races because he was honest, his deal money was good and he had excellent dates. Most of all his races paid well, the forty percent of the gate that AAA demanded when it sanctioned races. Eventually, AAA claimed he ran afoul of its rules by staging a race in Minneola, New York, the organization did not sanction, and it demanded he pay a $500 fine. There may have been a conflict of interest—Hankinson owned the Langhorne Speedway and regularly put 40,000 spectators in the stands.[23]

"It is my belief, which can hardly be challenged," Hankinson said, "that in the period 1926–1941, I paid more revenue to the AAA Contest board for sanctions and licenses than all other promoters combined, including the Indy 500."[24]

William P. Lazarus, in his book *Sands of Time,* wrote that Hankinson wanted $10,000 from city officials to promote the 1938 race and they turned him down. When Hankinson declined to accept France's collect call, Lazarus quoted him as saying, "That's when I called Charlie Reese, it [the call] wasn't a toll call. I decided to promote the race myself." Lazarus echoed the idea of France as the driving force saving the beach-road races. Lazarus worked for the Frances at International Speedways Corporation (ISC). Even more important, the copyright for his book *Sands of Time* was held, not by the author, but by NASCAR and its sister company ISC.[25]

Bill France's biography, prepared by NASCAR for his 1990 induction to International Motorsports Hall of Fame, understandably gave him credit for promoting the beach-road races. The biography describes how the City of Daytona and the Elks Club lost money on the races. "Since racers gathered at France's service station, he was asked if he would like to help promote the next event. He tried to enlist the help of an Orange City, Fla., promoter but his 15-cent collect call was refused. France decided to do it himself. France was successful and branched out to other races."[26]

In later years, the Daytona Beach newspapers became virtual public relations organs for France and NASCAR, especially through the columns of sports editor Bernard Kahn. France once bailed Kahn out of jail for failure to pay a parking ticket. In 2003, the *Daytona Beach Morning Journal* reported, "By 1938, Bill France was very much in charge of staging the annual beach-road race, which eventually began showing signs of national success."[27] France's exact involvement is not quite that clearly documented.

When entries closed for the July 1938 beach-road, twenty-one cars had entered the 150-mile event, staged by the Daytona Beach Racing Association. Lloyd Moody was the expected winner because he had a Sig Haugdahl motor in his car. Around 5,000 spectators saw Smokey Purser win the race and first place money of $240.[28] Danny Murphy, of Ormond Beach, won the Labor Day 1938 beach-road race with an average speed of 69.6 mph. The attendance was described as fair.[29]

In interviews with small newspapers in the South, Bill France insisted that he and Charlie Reese ran the 1938 beach-road races. "Charlie Reese and I ran the race in 1938. We charged .50 cents for admission and 5,000 people showed up. We divided a $200 profit. A month later we ran another race and increased the price to $1 and just as many people turned up."[30]

There was no doubt France drove in the 1938 beach-road race. A Daytona newspaper reported that he was scheduled to drive a car owned by Charlie Reese. However, the newspaper stated that Bill Jesse was the race manager for the July 4 race.[31]

France went to great lengths to emphasize his managerial involvement in the 1938 event. The *Lewiston Daily Sun* reported, "One day in 1938, Daytona Chamber of Commerce officials stopped by his service station and asked if he knew anyone to promote a race." France said, "One of my associates said he'd finance the races if I would put them on. I ran one in 1938 and I've been running them ever since.'"[32]

The *Milwaukee Journal,* in a 1971 article, quoted France, "I got the idea of organizing in 1938, but I couldn't get the promoters to go along with [me] and other organizations that were sanctioning racing didn't seem to be interested in stock cars."[33]

In February 1939, the Daytona Beach Chamber of Commerce and city officials met to discuss outdoor events for that year. The group included Millard B. Conklin, who was involved in the 1936 beach-road race, and automobile dealer J. Saxton Lloyd, in whose dealership garage Bill France had once worked. The events included a major golf tournament, automobile and motorcycle races, regattas, possibly an air show and other events. The same month, Jaycees (Junior Chamber of Commerce) met at Charlie's Grill and Hi-Hat Club with Charlie Reese, the owner and president of the Daytona Beach Racing Association, to plan the beach-road stock car race.[34]

There was no mention of Bill France running the holiday beach-road race other than he might have been driving in it. However, it was possible he may have promoted some less publicized beach-road races on other dates.

The *Daytona Beach Morning-Journal,* on March 3, 1939, reported there were forty-eight entries for the beach-road race scheduled for March 19. If more entries came in, the newspaper stated, "Charlie Reese, president of the association, is going to have to run his March 19 event in heats like a trotting horse race." The article quoted Reese, not France, with providing information on qualifying dates, erection of a new grandstand, the public address announcer, Johnny Whitmore, and other details.[35]

Reese's involvement with that beach-road race was reinforced by another Daytona Beach newspaper. In an article recalling events that occurred fifty years earlier, the *Daytona Beach News-Journal* described how a group of Jaycees met with Reese, head of the Daytona Beach Racing Association, on February 4, 1939, to plan the annual beach-road stock car race.[36] At that time, France was picking up rides in races wherever he could find them. "Bill

France even raced for Parks," Neal Thompson wrote, "when, for an example, Roy Hall was in a courtroom or behind bars."[37]

Hall, in jail or out, was Parks' star driver. In late 1939, he won four consecutive races including a 100-mile event in Salisbury, North Carolina, where he beat France. "Hall beat the best of me," France admitted. The two met again in France's first big beach-road race the next year. "If I can't beat him here, I never will," France said. "Hall held the lead for the entire second half of the race," Thompson wrote, "finishing more than a mile ahead to the nearest competition. France finished fourth, getting spanked in his own backyard."[38]

For whatever reason, the Jaycees appeared to have dropped their sponsorship of the beach-road races after 1939. Bill France did promote the 1940 and 1941 holiday beach-road races for a most unusual sponsor, the Central Labor Union (CLU) of Daytona Beach. CLU was unique among labor organizations due to its involvement in and promotion of civic activities. It was a strange association, as Bill France later publicly disparaged labor organizations. There were complaints after the July 4, 1940, race about the inequalities of the cars' engines. For the Labor Day race, France came up with specifications that no car could cost more than $1,100, have less than 120 hp, or have special rear end, valves or heads.[39]

His co-promoter for some of the beach-road races was none other than C. D. "Smokey" Purser, who was once his rival driver. Purser was much more than a race car driver. He was a gambler and, according to accounts in the *Daytona Beach Morning Journal*, was arrested for allegedly running a numbers operation in Volusia County where Daytona Beach was located.[40]

France may have had connections to draw drivers to the beach-road races but he lacked promotional funds, and the CLU certainly was not going to furnish him with unlimited funds. Smokey Purser had the money to promote the races. A February 1940 article in a Daytona newspaper stated, "Bill France and Smokey Purser were so eager to participate in a beach-road race that, impatient with the delay in finding a backer for the stock car classic, they'll put it on themselves March 10 over the regular course."[41]

The day before the race, the same newspaper predicted that the race would be seen by many spectators. "Bill France and Smokey Purser, who are putting on the races, will have a press box for the first time since the beach-road classic was inaugurated. They think they have the best field of cars (of some of the best makes) to date."[42]

France and Purser not only promoted the July 1940 beach-road race but they drove in the event. At least thirty cars were expected to enter. By then, Gil Farrell, who had once promoted the event, was the course superintendent. Farrell, a newspaper article said, was making repairs to the grandstand and applying calcium chloride to the turns to prevent a recurrence of the flying dust which made spectators uncomfortable at the March race.[43]

France promoted the race for CLU under his new organization, National Stock Car Racing Association (NSCRA). Joining France in the new racing organization were Bruce Thompson of Charlotte, North Carolina, Joe Littlejohn of Spartanburg, South Carolina, and Frank Funk of Winchester, Indiana. While promoting the beach-road race, France stated NSCRA would promote three more stock car races in 1940 in North Carolina in September and November. France said he organized NSCRA in an attempt to bring all stock car racing under one main governing body.[44]

Prior to the 1940 Labor Day 150 mile beach-road race, France decided to hold a twenty-five mile race for women. One of the drivers was his wife, Anne Bledsoe France, but she did not place in the money. Evelyn Reed, of Daytona Beach, won the race at a respectable 68.4 mph. For winning the race she received $50, a home permanent kit and some other prizes. Virginia Atkins, also of Daytona Beach, was second. Margaret Treadmill, of Atlanta, finished third, and Mrs. Fred Crowe, from Daytona Beach, was fourth.[45]

In March 1941, France promoted the Frank Lockhart Memorial beach-road race. Purser won the $600 purse with a course record of 76.19 mph. Roy Hall, in a car owned by Raymond Parks, was second, Joe Littlejohn was third and Skimp Hersey came in fourth.[46]

Whether Smokey Purser joined Bill France in the promotion of the July 1941 beach-road race was not clear. France, by that time, had accumulated enough influence with the locals that he managed to have twenty officers from the National Guard, Volusia County Sheriff's Office and the Daytona Beach police assigned to patrol the beach-road course.[47]

A Daytona Beach newspaper reported that both France and Purser, along with Red Vogt, from Atlanta, drove in the race. Fifty cars from at least eight states entered the race. France decided to limit the field to thirty-three cars, which meant all had to qualify. Neither France nor Purser was able to qualify. Therefore, as he would do many times in the future, France changed the rules and expanded the field to thirty-five to include himself and Purser. After Hall, Lloyd Seay and Fonty Flock knocked each other out of the competition, the race was won by Bernard Long, a moonshiner from Dawsonville, Georgia.[48]

In an August 1941 beach-road race, Seay, from Atlanta, won the event, leading from start to finish with a record speed of 78 mph. The previous record, 76.19 mph, was set by Purser in March 1940. Seay won $432. Joe Littlejohn, from Spartanburg, was second; Harvey Taylor, from Atlanta, was third; and William Snowden, from St. Augustine, was fourth.[49] According to the *Miami News,* a crowd of 10,000 watched Seay win the race.[50]

After the Japanese attacked the U.S. Naval installation at Pearl Harbor, Hawaii, on December 7, 1941, organized automobile racing was halted until after the war. Even before World War II began, the popularity of stock car racing far exceeded existing facilities. Beach-road courses, in Florida and elsewhere, and horse tracks could not contain a sport that needed specific tracks and accommodations. Hill climbs had lost some of their charm and endurance races and speed trials were giving way to the excitement of watching races in one specific area. Lurking beneath the surface was a more elemental, primal form of racing.

3
Whiskey Roots, Red Georgia Clay and Carolina Back Roads

·······

Distilling and transporting illegal whiskey, along with the miserable economic conditions of the Great Depression, were vital factors in the evolution of southern stock car racing, a different kind of racing from the sophisticated road course events in New York and the tightly structured, militia-controlled Grand Prize Races in Savannah.

The Georgia officials, who used convict labor to build their racing course and threw grandiose spreads for their guests, represented vestiges of the old, aristocratic South where the accent was as thick and languid as the Spanish moss flowing over live oak trees. Grand Prize racing, with either imported European vehicles or expensive American stock cars, was too fancy and too costly for southerners who made their whiskey at home and drank it straight from the dipper.

When the moonshiners were able to afford an automobile to distribute their illegal whiskey, they created their own style of racing, which was as unnamed as it was unscripted. The word *redneck* was applied to them. Merriam-Webster's dictionary defined the word as meaning a poor white person from the rural laboring class of the South.[1] Rednecks were, however, so much more than that.

Bands of sunburned skin above those men's shirt collars were badges of honor indicating they diligently worked hard to meet their family obligations. Many were honest, almost to a fault, in their business dealings. Firm handshakes sealed their agreements and they considered them as binding as if they had signed a formal written contract. Their accents contained a southern drawl but it was laced with the Old English phrases of their ancestors. They were just as proud of their origins in the hollows, hills and mountains as their lowland brethren were. There were, of course, some scoundrels among them who lived up to the stereotype of being too inbred, too trifling and too lacking in ambition to better themselves by seeking legitimate employment.

Make no mistake, distilling moonshine whiskey was no idle occupation; it was hard work. In addition, guile, intelligence and ingenuity were required to not only manufacture the liquor but to evade revenuers and figure out how to transport their product to market. Many had the ambition, fortitude, quirkiness, courage and determination that led them to make an eventual move from whiskey running to a loosely structured form of racing. They established their own brand of stock car racing as a unique American sport. The connections between illegal distilling, the South's shattered economic conditions created by the Civil War and furthered by Reconstruction, the appearance of affordable automobiles to haul whiskey, and early stock car racing were inseparable. Combined, those entities gave added definition and identity to a raw type of southern automobile racing. For hundreds of thousands of southern families, illegal distilling was their only income. For others, the extra income enabled them to become more affluent.

Robert Glen Johnson, Jr., better known in the stock car racing world as simply "Junior," described making moonshine as a handed-down occupation from generation to generation in Wilkes County, North Carolina, where he grew up. "It was hard, dangerous, scary work," Johnson said. "It was how we made our living back then."[2]

Johnson said his father dropped out of school in the third grade but was the smartest man he ever knew. "He wanted to make sure his family was taken care of and he didn't care if he went to the penitentiary doing it. As a kid, you don't appreciate things like that until you are older. Then, you appreciate things like that."[3]

Revenue agents in the South admired the honest, reliable moonshiners such as Johnson, who had a high moral code, except for their proclivity to break the law with their illegal distilling activities. Many felt the government had no right to tell them how to dispose of their corn crops.[4]

Robert Glenn Johnson passed his values on to his children. His teachings were put into practice when Junior ran out of gas while making a whiskey run on a dark Carolina night. He found a farmer's tractor filled with gas, siphoned out the fuel and filled his tank. There was no such thing as stealing in Junior's lexicon. Legend has it that he left the farmer $200 on the tractor seat.[5]

Moonshiners were able to purchase the less expensive vehicles as early as 1910–1912, and adapt them to the special needs of distributing their whiskey. Drivers in Georgia, the Carolinas and elsewhere learned to make their vehicles more powerful by tinkering with the engines, not only to carry heavier loads of whiskey but also to escape lawmen waiting for them on the back roads. As more and more illegal distillers acquired cars, it was inevitable one driver bragged about his car's speed only to be challenged by another.

Motorized whiskey vehicles gave the illegal distillers more control of their sales to retail outlets such as barbershops, grocery and drug stores, bars and garages. Automobiles also allowed them to sell their product in bulk to large distributors. Soon a vehicle was as essential to moonshiners' business as the corn from which they made their whiskey.

From 1910 to 1920, according to the federal government's statistics, revenue agents were destroying approximately seventy-five gallons of whiskey with each still they seized. By that time, the business of illegal distilling in the South was so large the moonshiners hardly missed the estimated $1.6 million in whiskey government agents seized and poured out each year.[6]

Illegal distillers received another big boost to their business from temperance reformers' efforts to turn American into a dry nation. Moonshiners knew all about dry territories; most of them had been living in them since 1862.

The reformers won their battle in 1920 when Congress wiped out the nation's seventh largest industry, the distilling and brewing of alcoholic beverages, by passing the Eighteenth

Amendment prohibiting such activity. Congress, under the guise of creating an enforcement mechanism, approved the Volstead Act, which contained sufficient loopholes to insure an adequate supply of alcohol for a thirsty populace. Temperance forces finally lost the war in 1933, when Prohibition was repealed.

Moonshiners were unable to make and deliver whiskey fast enough to satisfy the demand during Prohibition. Consequently, it was no longer feasible to haul the illegal liquor in glass jars or tin containers in the small cars of the day. Cars were altered by adding 150-gallon tanks extending from the back of the drivers' seats into the trunk area. Their drivers, called transporters, wheelmen and trippers, were piloting potential fire-bombs on wheels. Moonshiners had the resources to purchase and install expensive parts that enabled their engines to carry the heavier loads of whiskey while eluding revenue agents.

Making alterations to these vehicles were the South's famed shade tree mechanics, some of whom were also moonshiners. They were so-named because, at first, their garages were areas under the shade trees in their yards. Their workbenches, often sawed-off tree trunks, held meager supplies of tools. Shade tree mechanics were some of the most inventive and imaginative people in the world. The repairs they could make with pieces of hay-baling wire were amazing.

Henry Shelton, who lived in Grimsley, Tennessee, like his counterparts all over the South, had the skill to tear an automobile engine apart and put it back together without diagrams or sophisticated tools. The vehicles Shelton repaired and rebuilt provided service far beyond that intended by their manufacturers. Shelton, like many of his brother mechanics in the South, passed his talents on to his sons, who raced a battered old Chevrolet with "Blue Moon" painted on its side at local tracks.[7]

For successful shade tree mechanics, like Shelton, the next step was a shed near their house where they worked on one vehicle at a time. Advancing to a two-bay garage meant they had it made. If the automotive grease and grime under their fingernails was still visible after they washed their hands, it was a proud mark of their advancement.

Moonshiners' first big boom since the Civil War was not to last. Historian Herbert Asbury called the thirteen years of Prohibition the Era of the Big Lie. "The Drys lied to make Prohibition look good," Asbury wrote. "The Wets lied to make it look bad; government officials lied to make themselves look good and to frighten Congress into giving them more money to spend, and politicians lied through force of habit."[8]

Who lied about Prohibition made little difference when the nation was plunged into a deep depression. After the stock market tanked on October 29, 1929, personal incomes fell twenty to fifty percent and unemployment rose from 3.1 percent in 1929 to 25.2 in 1933. Most moonshiners were accustomed to living off the land. They had their home canned fruits and vegetables to sustain them through winters. Milk cows produced dairy products, hogs and wild game provided meat, chickens gave eggs and the whiskey the moonshiners sold provided for the other necessities of life.

Transporting illegal whiskey to a thirsty populace not only kept many families from starving during the 1920s and 1930s, but also further established automobile racing in the south. The Flock family, from Fort Payne, Alabama, was literally saved from starvation by the business of transporting illegal whiskey. The Flocks became the first family of southern stock car racing. Their father, Lee Preston Flock, was a bicycle racer in Germany and later an Alabama taxi driver. "I think that seeing our daddy walking a tightrope [strung up in their back yard] is really what started the Flock clan into different daring things," recalled Tim Flock, the 1952 and 1955 NASCAR Grand National champion.[9]

A sister, Reo, became a parachutist and airplane wing walker. Another sister, Ethel, drove race cars along with brothers Tim, Bob and Fonty. Their brother, Carl, was a hydroplane racer.[10] Before the family achieved racing fame, they struggled to survive after their father's death in 1929.

"There were nine of us, counting Mama, having to live on nine dollars a week she made working in a hosiery mill," Tim Flock recalled. "It was one of the awfullest times we were in. We had an uncle named Peachtree Williams, named after a street in Atlanta, who was the biggest bootlegger who ever lived in Georgia." Flock said his maternal uncle, after discovering his nieces and nephews were starving and didn't have clothes to go to school, began to bring the family to Atlanta. Williams first took Carl, the oldest, and taught him the business. "One by one, he got us kids out of Alabama, Bob, Fonty and me and he put us in school to help Mama. After a year or so he got Mama and the rest of the family and that's where we grew up.[11]

"We would haul liquor after school," Flock recalled. "I was too little to drive so I would ride with my brothers and help. Fonty was sixteen when he got started. We would go to the still and pick up the liquor and put it in a '34 Ford. My job was to keep the bottles from getting broke. You made forty bucks a run if you got back with it. You could make two runs a day if you were lucky. You'd go up to Dahlonega, Georgia, which was about sixty or seventy miles up in the mountains. You had one of those special cars that had heavy springs that, when empty, would sit up real high and looked like it was running on its nose.[12]

"Those old sheriffs knew when you were going by. They watched you go through the little towns with the tail end of your car hiked up. Then you come back the other way and it was level. They knew you had nothing but a bucket seat in that car and the rest was for storage—180 gallons in a car." Flock said the altered 1934 Fords had bucket seats before anyone ever heard of bucket seats.[13]

Flock talked about the sheriffs' efforts to catch them. "It was like a race, you know, only we had the best cars by far. We had the money, the know-how and the sheriffs didn't. We got hot-rod parts from California for our bootleg cars." Sheriffs, Flock said, would attempt to catch them on the return trips, loaded with moonshine, as they slowed going up hills. "So, they come up with these cowcatchers on their bumpers.... They'd run up behind you and pinch onto the bumper and hold you.... So, we come up with putting the bumpers on the back of our cars with coat hanger wire. They'd run up and grab on, then we'd give it the gas and it would break loose and roll up under the front of their car and get all tangled up. By the time they got loose, we were long gone."[14]

Flock said the sheriffs received half of the money when the confiscated whiskey cars were sold on the courthouse steps. "They tried to catch every car they could," he said. "The cars back then would sell for $350 or $400 and they had beautiful engines in them. Red Vogt was building then in Atlanta and most of the time the bootlegger would try to buy the car back because he couldn't replace it with that kind of money.[15]

"I tell you, to get that load back to Atlanta safely you would do anything in the world but try to hurt somebody. We used oil spills, smoke screens, bootleg turns where we spun a 180 [degrees] and went the other way. We cut through this one cow pasture so much the cows quit giving milk."[16]

3. Whiskey Roots, Red Georgia Clay and Carolina Back Roads   29

Drivers of the moonshine-loaded cars were the kingpins because they always had money, Flock said. He said his brother, Bob, one of the best of the early stock car drivers, helped create a Georgia dirt track where the whiskey cars could race. "In the mid-thirties, in a cow pasture in Georgia, that's where racing began. We didn't have no tickets, no safety equipment, no fences, no nothing. Just a bunch of these bootleggers who'd been arguing all week about who had the fastest car would get together to prove it."[17]

The term *bootleggers* is used interchangeably but not always correctly with the word *moonshiners*. Bootleggers, for the most part, brokered and sold the moonshiners' illegal whiskey as well as legal liquor.

"Thirty or forty of these bootleggers showed up in this cow pasture at Stockbridge about fifteen miles outside Atlanta," Flock continued. "They made a track by running around and digging their wheels in the ground in about a half-mile circle. These guys would run and bet against their own cars, betting who had the fastest car. About fifty people saw this dust cloud and came up to see what was causing it. Next time, a hundred would show up. Then, three or four hundred would show up. Then, three or four thousand would show up."[18] Flock said they passed around an old football helmet among the crowd to collect nickels, dimes and quarters for admission. The admission money, along with side bets, made up the purse. "Pretty soon, they raced every Sunday. Five or six thousand people started showing up."[19]

While the Flock family was tearing up the red Georgia clay hauling illegal whiskey and racing, the Petty family was burning up the back roads in North Carolina's Piedmont region with their cars. Taxi driver and trucker Lee Petty and garage owner Julian Petty were addicted to speed. Lee's son, Richard, provided the best description. "All of this was leading Daddy and Uncle Julie closer to the tracks themselves," Richard Petty said. "They had been going to races all over the area—even up to Martinsville, Virginia—for a long time and you could see them getting the bug. I guess they were filing away everything they saw from the grandstands, putting it back there in the memory banks for future use."[20]

Richard Petty said there was something special about the power in the cars his father built and drove. "You could feel it in the seat of your pants first. When he stood on it, there was a heavy vibration that started on your bottom and worked its way up your spine. By the time it got to your shoulders, the hair on the back of you neck was standing up."[21]

"I think the only thing that kept him from jumping right into the roundy-round racing deal was the fact that he was becoming the king of back-road racing around the Piedmont." Lee Petty was beating the local competition around Randleman, North Carolina, and other racers, from Raleigh, Charlotte and Atlanta, who came to challenge him. "There were good stretches of road around our part of the country, sections where you could really open up a car. There was one down toward Asheboro, for instance, that had a straightaway that must have been five miles long," Richard Petty said.[22]

Lee Petty was winning as much as $1,000 on those back road races. He won so many races he had to repaint his car often so his competitors would think he was driving a different car. Most of Lee Petty's back roads racing competitors were whiskey transporters. "Many of the best drivers to come out of the South in those days were guys who learned their skill behind the wheel of a car hauling moonshine," Richard Petty said. "These 'wheelmen' could drive wide open on about any kind of road. You can imagine what some of those races between them and Daddy were like. It's a shame they couldn't have raced in some arena, where a lot of people could have watched, because there was more skill displayed in those races than in any thrill show that ever was."[23]

"You may have heard about a lot of those moonshine runners in later years because some of them became famous as race drivers but there were others nobody ever heard about again," Petty said. Otis Walker, from Virginia, was one such wheelman Petty talked about admiringly. He heard stories about Walker from a retired revenue agent who came to his uncle Julian's garage.[24]

One night, the revenue agent was chasing Walker, in his fully loaded Ford coupe, when four state troopers set up a running road-block with two cars in front of Walker and two behind. The revenue agent saw two balls of smoke from behind Walker's rear wheels. "I knew what he had done," Petty quoted the revenue agent as saying. "He had caught second gear and he was headin' for the front two cars. He hit the one on the right first and then he hit the one on the left. Well, they had been driving about four feet apart so they could use up all the road and, when Otis hit them, one went in one ditch and one went into the other. It was the damnedest piece of driving I've ever seen. I figured right then that if a man's good enough to do that, damn if I run him until he's crippled."[25]

When the revenue agent saw Walker pull into a side road, he accelerated and the other two troopers, who had been following Walker's car, suspected he was also transporting and began chasing him. A short time later, the revenue agent stopped and identified himself as a lawman also chasing Walker. The revenue agent saw Walker a few days later. "I really 'preciated that," he quoted Walker as saying. "You know, when I slid in that side road, every tire was cryin' a different tune." Petty said he never saw Walker race because he died when the drive shaft dropped out of his car at 120 mph.[26]

"The wheelmen built fast cars," Petty said. "The feds built fast cars. The wheelmen drove the back road at night with their lights off. The feds learned to drive with their lights off. And, when a runner didn't have a load of 'shine, the feds left him alone. It was a respect competitors hadn't had for one another since the time of the World War I fighter pilots. But just let the feds see sagging rear springs and the chase was on. And, if they caught them, they went to prison."[27]

"This whole deal of moonshiners and back-road racing gives you some idea of exactly where stock car racing was at this point," Petty said. "They had their own code. Call it the 'law of the West,' call it what you want but they had an honor about them."[28]

Another wheelman Petty admired was Louis Grier "Buddy" Shuman, of Charlotte, whom he called one of the first great drivers to become famous after World War II. Shuman was driving on some of Charlotte's back roads one day when a deputy sheriff drove up behind him. Shuman began speeding, not because he was transporting moonshine, but because he had left his driver's license at home. Shuman would have outrun the deputy if he had not taken a road that had a bridge washed out. "The deputy was shaking like a leaf," Petty said, "and Buddy smiled a great big smile at him. But, the deputy pulled a pistol, stuck it right up to Buddy's throat and pulled the trigger. Nobody could ever explain it but the bullet didn't hit any arteries or anything."[29]

"They put Buddy in a chain gang and he served the time," Petty continued. "He could have gotten off because he had a lot of influential friends around—he was a popular race driver, everybody knew him—but he didn't want anything to do with probation. He wanted to serve his time and be completely free when he got out."[30]

3. Whiskey Roots, Red Georgia Clay and Carolina Back Roads

Those "wheelmen" who turned from transporting illegal whiskey to racing were some of stock car racing's most colorful and talented drivers and owners: the Flock brothers, Raymond Parks, Bobby Isaacs, Elzie W. "Buck" Baker, Roy Hall, Lloyd Seay, Gober Sosebee, Curtis Turner, "Buddy" Shuman, Carl D. "Smokey" Purser and Wendell Scott. They were the bedrocks of southern stock car racing.

None of those drivers marched as defiantly to their own drumbeat as Junior Johnson, who followed it through the heavily timbered landscape of Wilkes County, North Carolina. Johnson and his friends, Willie Clay Call and James W. Shew, initially used superchargers and larger pistons shipped from California to create the powerful whiskey cars needed to escape revenuers. Later, they made their own parts. "I never seen [an engine] that I couldn't make better," Johnson said. He is credited with inventing the 180-degree bootleg turn to avoid being caught by the law while hauling whiskey.[31]

Johnson said while in a close race with revenuers, he would drop the car into low gear, cut the wheels hard, spin around and head back toward his pursuers. "Whoever had the most guts made it," Johnson recalled. "I usually went right between 'em. Doing a 180, if you messed up with that, they got you."[32]

Other drivers were behind the wheels of some of the fast whiskey cars built by Louis Jerome "Red" Vogt in his Atlanta garage. Bill France raced some of the cars he built for Raymond Parks in his Atlanta garage. The sign in front of the building, "Open 24 Hours, 'Red' Vogt Garage," indicated the demand for his talents.[33]

Jack Etheridge, in an interview for the Georgia Racing Hall of Fame, talked about those early days in Atlanta. "I raced for Airline Auto Service, over on Spring Street, some of the time," he said. "A bunch of us guys would be there or over at Red Vogt's garage on West Marietta Street. All the trippers and drivers and mechanics had some links with both places. They always worked on trip cars at Vogt's and it just overflowed over to Airline. Trippers and racers were in those days much one and the same."[34]

Etheridge said he and Raymond Parks agreed that the best whiskey transporting car was a 1932 Ford. "It would carry 128 gallons ... best trip car there was in my mind." Etheridge described how the trippers carried their whiskey from the north Georgia mountains into Atlanta without too much trouble. "Trippers usually came out better when they filled up their cars [with whiskey] in the mornings to blend in with the morning traffic going to Atlanta," he added. "They called it sneak traffic."[35]

Robert "Red" Byron, who won NASCAR's first Grand National Championship in 1949, gave Vogt credit for his success. "You can't win a horse race without a good horse and you can't win a stock car race without a good car. What the trainer is to the horse, a mechanic is to the car and I've got the best mechanic in the business. Red Vogt is the reason I win. He puts those motors together like a watch. When other mechanics learn his secret gear ratio, there won't be any stragglers in a race. They'll all travel."[36]

When he was fifteen, Parks, who once served three months in jail for illegal whiskey possession, left his home in Dawson County in the north Georgia mountains to work for a moonshiner in Athens transporting illegal whiskey to Atlanta.[37] After Prohibition ended, Parks went into the legal end of the business with a chain of liquor stores, ran a novelty machine company and accumulated large blocks of property in downtown Atlanta. However, he continued his interests in racing as a driver and car owner and, together with Vogt, fielded some of the best race cars in the South. "I don't remember anybody back then racing cars like he [Parks] did," former driver and car owner Cotton Owens said. "He did everything first class. The cars had showroom finishes every race. There was never a bent fender that wasn't replaced."[38]

In March 2005, the Georgia Senate passed a resolution honoring Parks: "Mr. Raymond Parks was one of the first people to realize the potential of auto racing to become a major spectator sport and he spent great sums of his own time and money to make it happen; he owned a fleet of beautifully prepared race cars driven by the most talented drivers of his time." Since the state was celebrating the Atlanta Motor Speedway at the Capitol, "it is only fitting and proper that the remarkable achievements of this hometown racing legend be appropriately recognized on this grand occasion ... and honor his legacy as a founding figure in the sport of auto racing."[39]

Always well dressed in a business suit, shirt and tie and a hat, Parks was easy to spot at races. He did shed his coat and hat once when he helped change a tire on "Red" Byron's car at Darlington's first Southern 500.[40]

Parks-owned and Vogt-built cars were driven by many drivers in the 1930s and 1940s. They included Robert "Red" Byron, Bob, Fonty and Tim Flock, Glenn "Fireball" Roberts, Gober Sosebee, Curtis Turner, Jack Smith and Bill France.

Since the distilling and transporting of illegal whiskey did not stop with the repeal of Prohibition, it was not possible for the practice to escape France's notice as he raced against whiskey trippers around the South. Certainly, he had to be aware of Parks and Vogt's backgrounds, since he drove some of their cars and hung around Vogt's garage.

Driver Frank Mundy recalled an incident when he and France were hanging around Vogt's garage and a couple of bootleggers arrived. They began arguing over territories and one of them pulled a gun. "When France and I saw the gun," Mundy recalled, "we ducked down underneath the car."[41]

When Sylvia Wilkinson interviewed France for her book on early stock car racing, she asked him about "Red" Vogt being famous for building liquor cars. France avoided the question. "He told me not to his knowledge but any good 'tuner-upper' might end up working on one." Wilkinson continued, "He tells me there are all kinds of 'con men' out there who'll try and take away a good thing." Wilkinson said she felt like she was not getting information but a lecture from France.[42]

In a 1965 book, *The Racing Flag: NASCAR—The Story of Grand National Racing*, written by Bloys Britt and France, all references to illegal whiskey were circumspectly avoided. In the section on drivers, Junior Johnson's biography was carefully worded to avoid any mention of his previous occupation. "His life has been as colorful as his driving," the entry read. "*Esquire* published an in-depth profile on him this year and his legend among the mountain folks of North Carolina is firmly established as one of the great ones."[43]

In the introduction to the book, France wrote, "We're proud at NASCAR that no hint of scandal has ever touched our sport of stock car racing. You may be assured we'll keep it that way."[44]

Junior Johnson was an impeccable source who easily punctured France's denial of the moonshine connection. Johnson said he first met France when France talked to some of his moonshine friends about France's efforts to get a handle on racing. "I was young," Johnson said, "but I was old enough at the time to remember him talkin' to them about wantin' them to get involved in his racin' organization."[45] Johnson, who had a talent for yanking Bill

France's chain, later said, "We had the money and the fastest cars and Bill France wouldn't leave until he got our money and our cars."[46]

France was more than willing to have the moonshine trippers participate in his races, knowing their reputations would help draw bigger crowds. When the sport became more established, France attempted to shove his association with the trippers under the rug, but facts kept getting in the way.

France drove with Parks' cousins from Dawson County, Roy Hall and Lloyd Seay, who were both trippers. In November 1938, Seay drove a Parks-Vogt car to victory at the old Lakewood Speedway in Atlanta. Hall won the March 1940 beach-road race, which France promoted, constantly smoking a cigarette while driving. Not only could Hall drive, but he had an excellent pit crew. The *Gainesville Sun*, writing about the July 1940 beach-road race, reported Hall's pit crew looked like a group of trained monkeys who got him in and out of the pits in forty seconds.[47]

The *Georgia Encyclopedia* credited Hall and Seay with dominating southern stock car racing with the vehicles Vogt prepared for Parks in the late 1930s and early 1940s. Hall was memorialized in the Jim Croce song "Rapid Roy, the Stock Car Boy." The team of Vogt, Parks, Hall and Seay came to an abrupt end in September 1941 when Seay was shot by his cousin, Woodrow Anderson, during an argument over a shipment of sugar for their moonshine whiskey business, just after he won a 100-mile race at Lakewood.[48] Anderson, convicted of murder, received a life sentence.[49]

Seay's tombstone is shaped in an outline of a 1939 Ford with his picture, on porcelain, attached to the side window.[50] Seay's death broke up the "Georgia Gang." Parks, drafted into the Army, fought in the Battle of the Bulge in Belgium. Vogt repaired trucks from southern military bases and according to Neal Thompson, Hall, without Parks to keep him halfway straight, descended deeper into a world of criminal behavior and finally went to prison.[51]

4

Hardened Heroes

•••••••

Robert "Red" Byron was emblematic of the greatest generation of stock car drivers who served in World War II, from 1941 to 1945, and returned home to resume their racing careers. Byron began racing at the small dirt tracks around Talladega, Alabama. Like many others in the 1930s, he moved to Atlanta, where he prepared his race cars out of his own garage.

During the decade of the 1930s, Atlanta, due in part to the prolific business of transporting illegal whiskey in from the north Georgia mountains, was the Mecca of garages in the business of building moonshine-hauling vehicles which doubled as racing cars.

Byron flew fifty-seven missions as a B-24 tail gunner before being shot down over the Aleutian Islands. He spent twenty-seven months in a military hospital having his left leg rebuilt. In a February 1946 race at the Seminole Speedway near Orlando, Florida, Byron drove a Raymond Parks owned and "Red" Vogt built car to victory over Bob and Fonty Flock, "Mad" Marion McDonald, Roy Hall and Bill France. What made his victory unique was Byron drove with his left leg in a steel stirrup bolted to the clutch.[1]

Another racing veteran was Henry "Smokey" Yunick, a motorcycle-car racer from Philadelphia. Yunick wanted to be a pilot but had difficulties joining the Army Air Force. A priest helped him obtain a birth certificate needed for enlistment. The Army Air Force required either a college degree or the ability to pass college level tests for skills and knowledge to become a pilot. Yunick said he spent twenty hours a day, seven days a week, studying during his three months of flight school. "The math, physics, military code and chemistry were all way out of reach for me," Yunick said. "I decided to try and memorize the stuff I was totally lost in. I found I could hold it for a day or two. They always tested within forty-eight hours." Yunick won his wings and flew B-17 Flying Fortresses, B-25s and B-29s in Europe, China, Burma, India, Africa and the Pacific theaters.[2]

Yunick, who began racing in 1938, used his mechanical and aerodynamic talents to aggravate Bill France as he creatively circumvented NASCAR rules for years. France occasionally implemented Yunick's changes into his rulebook, but more often specifically prohibited them.[3]

Yunick, his sister-in-law, Judy Judge, recalled, chaffed at restrictions. She said he would fly his helicopter from his Daytona Beach shop, known as "The Best Damn Garage in Town," across the river and land at his home for lunch. So many people complained that their pool furniture and landscapes were being damaged that the city council prohibited helicopter landings except at the airport or pier.[4]

Bill France, left, presents the Edward Knowles Rayson Trophy to Robert "Red" Byron, center, for winning the Modified race on the beach-road course in Dayton in 1947. Louis J. "Red" Vogt, right, built Byron's 1939 Ford for car owner Raymond Parks. France later penalized Byron for driving in races other than those of NASCAR (State Archives of Florida).

"Smokey thought that was a direct hit at him, which it was," Judge said. "So, Smokey would fly over to his house but instead of landing he would hover. We'd all run out in the backyard and wave hello and then he would fly off. He wasn't allowed to land but he did more damage than ever and it was on purpose."[5]

When he was not aggravating local authorities, Smokey's favorite target was Bill France. He labored in vain to convince France to replace the heavy jacks used to raise cars in the pits with the pneumatic jacks Indy cars used. Racing columnist Ed Hinton recalled asking Smokey if the pneumatic jacks would work for the heavier stock cars. "A fellow I know took a Pontiac to Darlington in 1960 with pneumatic jacks. NASCAR told him never to bring it back and to forget it. I've still got those pieces of aluminum tubing lying around here somewhere."[6]

Yunick and Junior Johnson were responsible for many of the innovative technical advances in stock car racing's earlier days. Yunick's eighteen inventions, eleven of which he patented, included the pressure vent, hot vapor engine, fuel conditioning apparatus and method, and the Smoketron for testing internal combustion engines.[7]

Johnson-built cars in the 1960s enabled Junior to lap the field at the Hickory (N.C.) Speedway, then a ⁵⁄₁₀-mile dirt track, and at a 200-mile race at the paved track at Bowman Gray Stadium in Winston-Salem. Johnson purchased cars from dealers' showrooms and implemented his changes. "Me and the boys working for me turned it into a race car, changing the chassis, the suspension and building a good strong engine," he said. Johnson was particularly proud of his 1963 Chevrolet's chassis. In 2006, he estimated that ninety-nine percent of the cars racing in NASCAR still used the same chassis he perfected decades earlier.[8]

Aside from his records as a driver and car owner, Johnson's lasting contribution to stock car racing was bringing the R.J. Reynolds Tobacco Company into NASCAR in 1971, when support for stock car racing was faltering.

Elzie Wylie "Buck" Baker, a South Carolina native who had worked for the Civilian Conservation Corps (CCC) planting trees, served in the U.S. Navy. While stateside in Maryland, in his spare time, Baker returned to his old occupation of hauling moonshine for his fellow swabbies. After leaving the Navy, Baker took a job as a Trailways bus driver in Charlotte. On one trip, he and his passengers decided to stop for a big square dance in Chester. When Baker and his bus failed to return on time, the highway patrol began looking for them. Baker finally pulled into the station, hours behind schedule with a bus full of happy, drunk, singing passengers who persuaded the supervisor not to fire him.[9]

Baker was known for being combative. When he decided to change car manufacturers, Baker wanted to keep it quiet. Racing columnist George Cunningham wrote about it. When he confronted Cunningham, the columnist told him he reserved the right to write about anything he wanted. Baker replied, "And I reserve the right to whip your ass."[10]

Another moonshine whiskey transporter, Virginian Curtis Turner, also served in the Navy. Turner claimed he hauled his first load of whiskey when he was nine years old. In his father's Oldsmobile loaded with whiskey, he could not recall whether he was supposed to pass a slow moving vehicle on the left or right. He chose the right and went off the road into a fence. But, he learned and later demonstrated his expertise. Turner lined up two rows of whiskey jars on the road, ten feet apart. Then, got into his car, sped toward the containers, did a 180-degree turn and slid backwards between the glass receptacles without touching them. "No point in wasting good whiskey," he said. Aside from his off-the-track antics of hard living, hard partying and hard drinking, Turner was a successful timber broker and was one of the first stock car drivers to fly his own plane.[11]

Turner's friend, Joe Weatherly, was from Norfolk, Virginia. He served in the U.S. Army and was wounded in the face by a sniper in North Africa.[12] Weatherly eventually bought his own plane.

Another Virginian and former moonshine tripper, Wendell Scott, served in the U.S. Army as a mechanic. After Scott came home, he drove a taxi and delivered whiskey until he lost his chauffeur's license after accumulating thirteen speeding tickets. When Danville, Virginia's new race track opened, promoters were looking for black race drivers. They consulted the experts, lawmen, to find out who was the best tripper and were told Scott was the only one they could never catch. Scott's work as an Army mechanic served him well in later years when he operated his own garage and built and repaired his own race cars.[13]

France did not serve in the military during World War II. Instead, he worked in the Daytona Beach Boat Works, which made parts for naval vessels. His wife, Anne, ran their service station, whose business suffered from scarcity of gas and tires, which were rationed during the war.[14]

France was once charged with violating World War II rationing laws governing the use of gasoline and automobile tires, implemented by the Office of Price Administration (OPA), in connection with his beleaguered service station business.[15] In March 1946, France was arrested by U.S. marshals in Jacksonville, Florida, fingerprinted and charged with conspiracy to violate OPA laws. He posted a $1,000 bond and was released.[16]

The incident came to public light when Yunick's book, *The Best Damn Garage in Town,* was published in 2001. A year later, CNN-SI reporter Mike Fish did a television program on France and NASCAR, which included a Federal Bureau of Investigation (FBI) background report on France when he was under consideration for an appointment in President Richard M. Nixon's administration. Nixon did not give France an appointment. France told the agents, at that time, about being involved in the sale of gasoline in violation of OPA's rationing regulations. France said the case was dismissed "because the government was unable to produce any witnesses" against him.[17]

France's FBI background report stated, "No additional record or disposition is available in the files of the Identification Division and no record was found in the records of the United States District Court, Middle District of Florida, Jacksonville, Florida, concerning this charge."[18] Business associates and friends, according to the FBI report, described France as "a man of even temperament ... an upright citizen ... a great patriot ... a person of high integrity ... a highly competent professional."[19]

Yunick had a different opinion of France's character as well as what happened to the federal charges. Yunick's father-in-law, Daytona Beach lawyer William Judge, was France's attorney in the government's case against him on the rationing charge.[20]

"Turns out," Yunick wrote, "during World War number two tires and gas were hard to get (both were rationed). France, for whatever reason, didn't spend any time killing Germans or Japs. He stayed home. (I used to call him a holy-roller draft dodger.) While at home, he apparently pissed the government off by selling stolen government merchandise: hot rationing stamps for tires and fuel. They wanted to penalize him with a lengthy stay in prison.[21]

"I guess by the time Billy got to it, the government had a 'done deal' and France's ass was mud," he continued. He said Judge convinced the government that nothing really bad happened and got France off. France promised to send the lawyer a check for his bill of $1,500, but Judge said he was never paid. "This one thing might have canceled the whole NASCAR adventure," Yunick wrote.[22]

Yunick said he had first-hand knowledge about France selling counterfeit tire ration coupons. "Guess who bought counterfeit tire rationing coupons from Bill France?" he wrote. "Ray Fox, Cliff Whaley and I did."[23]

When asked about France's arrest during a 2002 CNN-SI program on the sport, NASCAR Vice President Jim Hunter floundered in an effort to provide a reasonable answer. "I wonder if they had something to do with one of those early beach races," Hunter said. "My guess is with rationing gas and not knowing how it worked, if maybe Bill needed gas to run the races on the beach?"[24]

The early beach-road races Hunter mentioned during the CNN-SI program, that France was involved with, ended when war was declared in December 1941. Neither gasoline nor tires were rationed until after the war began. The beach-road races resumed after the war, in 1945, when tires and gasoline were no longer rationed.[25]

Bob Latford, in his book *NASCAR: A Celebration,* wrote rather boastfully about France's work at the Daytona Boat Works during World War II, and described the financial problems at his service station during that time. Latford talked about France's recollections of his service station during the war but failed to mention his arrest. "He thought, too, of his little gas station where he had toiled to support his family and his racing; of the rationing during the war which had concluded two years earlier and cut so badly into the station's business; his work during the war years at the local boat works where he had utilized his mechanical skills to build submarine chasers as part of the war effort."[26]

Hunter praised France's devotion to his country in the CNN-SI report. "One of the things I remember about Senior is his being a truly patriotic guy. He was military."[27] Neither of France's two sons were named for him but NASCAR officials and the media constantly referred to him as senior and his oldest son, William Clifton France, as junior.

"He [France] and Mendel Rivers, when Mendel Rivers was chairman of the House Armed Forces Committee, were good friends. Mendel, for a period after he retired, was NASCAR's commissioner." Hunter added, "Senior was very warm. He was a communicator, sort of like President Ronald Reagan. He connected with people."[28]

South Carolina Congressman Mendel Rivers certainly had political clout. He was a Democrat member of the powerful Armed Services Committee for thirty years (chairman 1965–1970). Both France and Rivers were supporters of Alabama Governor George Wallace's bid for the presidency in 1968. Mendel Rivers was also an early supporter of Sen. Strom Thurman's "Dixiecrat" movement.[29]

After the war ended, France lost no time in returning to stock car racing.

Germany formally surrendered on May 4, 1945. Aboard the USS *Missouri*, Japan agreed to cessation of hostilities on September 2, 1945. Three days later France wrote *Daytona Beach Morning Journal* sports editor Bernard Kahn that he had just returned from a race in Atlanta. The content of the letter indicated France was there as a driver, not a promoter. "I just got back from Atlanta and a stock car race there," France wrote. "Everything went all right and the only trouble was that proportionally to the crowd the purse was small. The pre-race publicity was the strangest yet. There is a reporter on the *Atlanta Constitution* who thought it a shame that rum runners be allowed to participate in race competition on a city owned Atlanta track."[30]

France was referring to the Lakewood Speedway, a one-mile dirt oval built around the Poole's Creek Reservoir in 1917. Known as the largest track south of Indianapolis, Lakewood drew more than 15,000 for its first race. The AAA sanctioned the July 4 races there and IMCA staged the races during the annual fair dates. Other Lakewood races were promoted by Central States Auto Racing Association, International Stock Car Racing Association, Atlantic States Racing Association and Gulf States Auto Association. Some of those events drew as many as 30,000 to 35,000 spectators.[31]

France's letter continued, "He [the reporter] wrote several nasty editorial pieces about Lee Roy Hall and two or three other drivers. This reporter, whatever his name is, appealed to the decent people of Atlanta not to attend the race. There must not be many decent people in Atlanta because everybody was at the race and those who couldn't crowd in looked through the fence."[32] France realized there was more money to be made in promoting races than being a driver.

In 1946, France organized the National Championship Stock Car Circuit (NCSCC), which he operated out of his house in Daytona Beach.[33] This was his second organizational effort.

4. Hardened Heroes

While attempting to garner publicity for a NCSCC race at the old Charlotte Fairgrounds, France bragged to the *Charlotte Observer* sports editor the race he was staging would be for a national championship. Wilton Garrison, accustomed to promoters' ploys of boasting every race as a national championship, asked him which drivers he had signed for the race. France replied that Buddy Shuman, John "Skimp" Hershey and Roy Hall were in the race.[34]

Garrison said he might call it a southern championship with those men driving. "There's no way it's a national championship race," he told France. Garrison suggested that, if France wanted to stage national championship races, he needed the following: an organization to supervise the races where all the rules were the same, make sure the rules were enforced, and set up a points system to decide the annual winner. Garrison told France, if he wanted to stage national championship races, he should talk to the AAA Contest Board, the sanctioning body that then controlled American automobile racing, including stock car events. France did and the AAA turned him down.[35]

Retiring from behind the wheel to give his full attention to promoting NCSCC races, France's success as a driver was rather cloudy. Authors Bill Fleischman and Al Pearce believed France's driving achievements were stellar although their facts were vague. "He left an impressive driving resume, two victories and six other top fives in sixteen beach/highway races, plus several other major victories throughout the southeast, mid-west and northeast. He was declared the 'unofficial' national champion in 1940, well before any sort of points system came into play."[36] France switched to promoting races, usually on a shoestring budget.

According to the entry of Raymond Parks' biography in the Georgia Auto Racing Hall of Fame, the Georgian had spent $30,000 by the middle of the 1947 season to race in helping prop up France's faltering NCSCC organization. In twenty-first century money, that was well over a half million dollars.[37]

Parks' bankrolling France's racing efforts was partially confirmed by Neal Thompson in his book *Driving with the Devil*. Thompson, whose book was based on Parks' recollections and his vast compilation of racing material, wrote that France needed a back-up source of money in case the ticket revenue failed to produce enough cash to pay the purse. "Neither Parks nor France acknowledged their arrangement but there were signs," Thompson wrote.[38]

Thompson pointed to an instance when Parks gave driver Gober Sosebee a locked briefcase to deliver to France at Daytona and said neither Parks or France ever admitted the practice existed. "But a few of Parks' relatives and friends were aware of the arrangement and have since confirmed its existence," Thompson added.[39]

"My dad and Raymond Parks gave him [France] money over the years," June Wendt, Red Vogt's stepdaughter, said in January 2003. "There was another man here [in Daytona Beach] who owned a bar who sponsored him in the early days."[40]

France, for a short time after the war, also promoted races as the Stock Car Auto Racing Society. In a sport as dangerous as automobile racing, having a sanctioning body with the acronym SCARS was perhaps not well considered. SCARS was a short lived entity.

At the same time in North Carolina, Bruton Smith, a young car salesman, was having some success sanctioning races under the banner of the National Stock Car Racing Association, at Concord Motor Speedway and the Charlotte Fairgrounds, a dirt track built in 1926. Smith wanted to drive a race car and bought one when he was seventeen. His mother objected. "She didn't just put her foot down, she started praying on it," Smith said. To placate his mother, Smith gave up driving race cars and began promoting races after a short stint at a local hosiery mill.[41]

Few, if any, of stock car racing's sanctioning bodies in the South had the same rules. They included, in addition to those of France and Smith, the AAA, National Auto Racing League, United States Stock Car Racing Association and the American Stock Car Racing Association.

Car owner Raymond Parks realized that stock car racing desperately needed direction, organization and a uniform set of rules and did something about the situation. The businessman chartered the National Stock Car Racing Association, Inc., on March 25, 1947, in Georgia. He planned to bring some order to the rapidly growing sport and install some basic rules and regulations. The corporation was not dissolved until 2001.[42]

France was probably concerned that Parks, whose cars he had driven, had advanced a plan to organize the sport. He also knew that Parks had the money to make such an organization happen. Enoch Staley talked about organizing a race group in North Carolina. Truman Flock and another group of drivers and mechanics had the same idea in Atlanta.

While promoting races in 1947, France was busy pushing his own plans for organizing an automobile racing sanctioning body. Enoch Staley, France's partner in the Occoneechee-Orange Speedway, near Hillsborough, North Carolina, recalled a meeting with France. "After our fall race in 1947, we had a meeting in the old Wilkes Hotel in North Wilkesboro," Staley told the *Greensboro News and Record* in April 1995. "Some of the early promoters such as Joe Littlejohn, Alvin Hawkins, Clay Earles, France and I drafted some plans for the organizational meeting at Ormond Beach the following February."[43]

William Tuthill, a Connecticut racing promoter, and Edward Otto, a racing promoter from New Jersey, also had ideas for organizing stock car racing. Truman "Fonty" Flock, and others, put together an organization to regulate stock car racing. Marjorie Flock, his widow, recalled their meeting in an Atlanta garage in 1948. She said there were six or eight drivers and mechanics at the meeting including Flock, Carson Dwyer, Ed Samples and Buckshot Williams, and she kept the minutes of the meeting. "I sat on that cold garage floor and wrote down everything that was discussed, by-laws and all," she said.[44]

"Later, Fonty told me Bill France came to see him and said he heard he was talking about organizing stock car racing and wanted to see the minutes," she said. "Fonty gave the meeting minutes to Bill France and that was the last we saw of them."[45]

The stock car racing community was small and, even in the 1940s, was well connected. How Bill France knew about Fonty Flock's plans to organize the sport was a mystery until an article in the July 16, 1974, *Daytona Beach Sunday News-Journal* revealed the answer. During an interview with sports reporter Brad Wilson about his retirement, Red Vogt mentioned he had heard about some race car drivers in Atlanta meeting to form a stock car organization to protect their interest. "I called Bill in Daytona Beach and told him," Vogt said. "He said to gather them up and bring them down to Daytona."[46]

As various people talked about organizing the southern sport of stock car racing, little attention was paid to either the accomplishments or the inclusion of black race drivers.

5
A Lily White Sport

•••••••

The AAA refused to sanction races with black drivers, although they had been racing almost as long but without the advantages their white counterparts enjoyed. Racial prejudices not only in the South but in the Midwest hindered black race drivers from competing. On the West Coast, it was somewhat easier for those drivers to enter and compete in races. Even in California, black drivers were exceedingly careful in the early days about acknowledging their race.

Black drivers resented methods the AAA used to keep them out of their races: physicals exams, finding fault with their equipment, and instigating other requirements. Mel Leighton, a talented black driver, said in 1948 of his chances to advance in the sport, "The only thing that might stop me is the unwritten lily-white clause of the American Automobile Association."[1]

Many black drivers whose race entries were accepted by promoters drove cars they built themselves. A great number were master mechanics but not many were as successful as Charlie Wiggins, who lived in Indianapolis. Few in automobile racing would recognize the name of Charlie Wiggins had the Colored Speedway Association (CSA) not been established in the 1920s. Due to his mechanical talents, his refusal to be dismissed because of his race and his persistence in attempting to enter the Indianapolis 500, Wiggins eventually became the face of the CSA.

The CSA, in turn, inspired William "Wild Bill" Jeffries and William Bottoms to organize the Chicago Colored Speedway Association in 1924. There was the Negro Stock Car Racing Association in the Atlanta area in the late 1940s. The Dixie Racing Circuit, established by the National Sports Syndicate, out of New York, held races that included black drivers in New York, the District of Columbia, North Carolina and South Carolina, Virginia and Florida. The Dixie Racing Circuit's logo was two crossed flags, one a Confederate and the other a checkered flag.[2]

Charlie Wiggins, "Wild Bill" Jeffries, Gen Smith, Malcolm Hannon, A. J. "Speedball" Russell, Jack "Long Shot" Sargent, Eustice Williams and countless other black drivers had the opportunity to compete in these races because William Rucker, who worked for the Cincinnati, Indianapolis & Western Railroad (CI&W), and other prominent black businessmen organized the CSA in 1924. They were backed by an investment of $50,000 from Harry A. Earl and Oscar E. Schilling, white CI&W executives. Earl also owned the Walnut Gardens Speedway in Mooresville, Indiana, where he and Schilling promoted races.[3]

The CSA's first race was on August 2, 1924. They advertised in black newspapers throughout the Midwest boasting that the "World's Fastest Colored Drivers" would compete in the race at the State Fairgrounds. There would be fireworks, a parade and other events. Admission was $1 for the grandstand and $2.50 for reserve seating.[4]

Pathe News, that produced news events for movie theaters, agreed to cover the event. Rucker's best promotional idea was contacting Frank A. Young, sports editor of the *Chicago Defender*, whose syndicated column was the most widely read of any black sportswriter. When Young learned that the AAA refused to sanction CSA's first race, he pledged his support.[5]

Young did more than support the CSA, he gave the series its name, the Gold and Glory Sweepstakes. "This auto race," Young wrote, "will be recognized through the length and breadth of the land as the single greatest sports event to be staged annually by Colored people. Soon, chocolate jockeys will mount their gas-snorting, rubber-wheeled speedway monsters as they race at death defying speeds. The largest purse will be posted here and the greatest array of driving talent will be in attendance in hope of winning gold for themselves and glory for their race."[6]

Malcolm Hannon, a chauffeur for Indiana Billiards Parlor owner George Graham, was the first driver to sign up for the Gold and Glory Sweepstakes. Rucker and Earl, determined to find Hannon a good car, secured a Barber-Warnock Ford Special, the car that finished fifth in the 1923 Indianapolis 500. To attract attention to the race, Rucker parked the car outside Harry Dunnington's billiards parlor on Indiana Avenue. The car and sign publicizing the race attracted vast crowds every day.[7]

When the parade down Indiana Avenue was over on race day, Rucker had street cars lined up to carry spectators, men in suits and ties and women in their best dresses and hats, to the State Fairgrounds. Some drove from Pennsylvania and Minnesota to see the race and the accompanying activities.[8]

There were forty applicants for the fifteen slots in the first Gold and Glory Sweepstakes. Among them were Jack "Long Shot" Sargent, from St. Louis, and William Walthall, from Indianapolis. Sargent attached a rope to the front bumper of his Shields Special and towed it more than 250 miles with his Model-T. The American Giants Garage, in Chicago, and the *Chicago Defender* paid Wathall's $50 entry fee and obtained the loan of a Marmon, similar to the car that won the first Indianapolis 500.[9]

Others, such as William "Wild Bill" Jeffries, had no problem with paying the entry fee or obtaining a competitive car. Jeffries, a Chicago bail bondsman and real estate broker who operated a fleet of delivery cars that carried illegal liquor to the city's black neighborhoods, paid $12,000 for a Frontenac-Ford to enter in the race. Noted for his tailored suits and gold jewelry, Jefferies employed a chauffeur to drive his personal fleet of Stutz cars.[10]

Charlie Wiggins, acknowledged as Indianapolis's finest mechanic, was not in the first Gold and Glory Sweepstakes. Wiggins, born in Evansville, Indiana, was noticed by a garage manager shining shoes outside his building and offered him an apprenticeship. In 1924, Wiggins reached a personal plateau when he purchased Louis Sagalowsky's auto repair shop, where he had worked for three years. For a twenty-seven-year-old black man who raised his orphaned younger brothers, owning his own shop was a dream come true and more. Roberta Wiggins said, "He was floating high and nothing was going to take him down."[11]

But, something did.

Charlie Wiggins attempted to enter the Indianapolis 500 a number of times and was always rejected by the AAA, despite the fact that his speeds, in his Wiggins Specials, on dirt equaled those of drivers on the paved track. "He just wouldn't give up," Roberta (Sullinger) Wiggins, a former model, said. "Race after race, he kept on entering his car. And, race after race, they kept turning him away. But, he was proving a point. He was exposing their prejudice. The white drivers all liked Charlie but those promoters would have nothing to do with him. Truth be told, I think they were kinda scared of him—the chance that a Colored man might win their race. I think that scared the hell out of them."[12]

It was Rucker's decision not to allow Wiggins to enter the race. The mechanic was just five and a half feet tall and weighed only 100 pounds and the promoter was concerned he might not be able to control his car.[13]

More than 12,000 watched Malcolm Hannon and the Barber-Warnock Ford cross the finish line first in the CSA's first Gold and Glory Sweepstakes with a speed of 63.5 mph. He received $1,200 for first place. John Simmons, second in a Frontenac-Ford, got a check for $500. Gaston and Arthur Chevrolet built the engines for the Fords driven in the race at their Frontenac Motor Plant in Indianapolis. Eventually, the company name was shortened to Fronty-Fords and their cars continued to race into the 1940s.[14]

Leon "Al" Warren, an Indianapolis grocery delivery truck driver and racer who competed in some of the CSA races, described what the series meant to black race drivers. "To drive out there will all those folks cheering was a feeling I just can't describe," he said. "We could never ride with the white boys. Now, we were finally getting a chance to compete in a sport we loved. We were representing ourselves as drivers and representing all of us as a people. The feeling of accomplishment was really something, just overwhelming really."[15]

Not only did they know how to race, they also knew how to celebrate afterwards. Former heavyweight boxing champion Jack Johnson presented Hannon with a large silver trophy at the Gold and Glory Ball. More than 600 hundred danced to the music of Kioda Barber's Ten Jazz Kings.[16]

"Wild Bill" Jeffries, admiring what Rucker had accomplished with the July Gold and Glory Sweepstakes, decided to hold a similar race, the Dreamland Derby, in Chicago, on September 2, 1924. Jeffries signed a contract with John Owens, president of the National Motor Speedway Association to allow the Chicago Colored Speedway Association (CCSA) to hold their race at Hawthorne Speedway on the city's southwest side. Jeffries took some pages from Rucker's promotional book. He parked his Frontenac-Ford in the lobby of the Dreamland Ballroom and Café and furnished the *Chicago Defender* with plenty of copy.[17]

CSA officials worked with their Chicago counterparts until they discovered that both promoters, Jeffries and his partner, William Bottoms, planned to enter the race. Jeffries was driving his Frontenac Ford and Bottoms had a $10,000 Duesenberg. CSA officials, suspecting the promoters might control the outcome of the race, withdrew and many of the Indianapolis drivers cancelled. The race went on as planned. Rucker was among the 15,000 attending.[18]

Neither Jeffries nor Bottoms won the race. The winner was William Carson in a Beck Special.[19]

Black journalists referred to Jeffries as the "Black Ralph de Palma," comparing him to the Caucasian driver noted for his sharp attire and high speed race cars. Always the showman, Jeffries waved at the grandstand each time he passed until a rock severed his car's water line, forcing him into the pits.[20]

Not everybody in Indiana was happy with the Gold and Glory Sweepstakes being in Indianapolis, much less using the State Fairgrounds facilities.

In 1925, more than half the male population of Indiana belonged to the Ku Klux Klan (KKK) led by D. C. Stephenson, the Klan's Grand Dragon. Stephenson staged the largest KKK rally in the nation that drew 200,000 people to Kokomo, Indiana. When the KKK held a parade, they demanded that all men remove their hats in deference to the white sheet–clad marchers.[21]

The KKK attempted to enclose black Indianapolis residents into a contained area, burned crosses in front yards and intimidated the media. In 1924, Republicans, backed by Stephenson, swept statewide offices and the Klan decided to make an example of Charlie Wiggins. They tore down his garage signs, broke the building's windows and physically attacked him. Roberta Wiggins' tears were mixed with water as she washed her husband's bloody clothes.[22]

Stephenson's reign of terror was short-lived but deadly. At Gov. Edward Jackson's inaugural ball, Stephenson met Madge Oberboltzen, a state employee who did not return his attentions. Stephenson, not taking rejection very well, allegedly kidnapped and repeatedly raped her. Ashamed of being raped, she swallowed mercury and, before she died, named her rapist. Stephenson was charged with second degree murder, was tried, found guilty and sentenced to thirty-one years in prison. After realizing that his friend Gov. Jackson, whom he had helped elect, was not going to pardon him, Stephenson spilled his tale of political fraud. The governor was indicted for corruption along with a raft of Republican Party officials, including Indianapolis mayor John Duvall. A number of Marion County (Indianapolis) commissioners resigned after being accused of taking bribes from the Klan and Stephenson, who once declared, "I am the law in Indiana."[23]

Regardless of the Klan, the 1925 Gold and Glory Sweepstakes went on as scheduled and Charlie Wiggins was in the race. The winner that year was Bobby Wallace, in a Trey of Hearts Special with an average speed of 64.9 mph. He received a check for $1,250, not that he really needed the money. Bill Carson was second in a Lyons Special. Wiggins, in his Wiggins Special, finished just out of the money with engine problems.[24]

Bobby Wallace had such a light skin tone that he later rode in the 1934 Indy 500 as Deacon Litz's mechanic and the ever vigilant AAA failed to notice. Wallace, the son of an A.M.E. minister, transported illegal whiskey out of Chicago during Prohibition for Walter and Ollie Kelly, allegedly part of Al Capone's organization. Wallace was one of the wealthiest black race car drivers in the Midwest.[25]

The 1926 Gold and Glory Sweepstakes was special for a number of reasons. After two years of staging the race, the Colored Speedway Association had a successful promotional formula. The attendance increased. The circuit's most popular driver won the race. More than 15,000 spectators filled the State Fairgrounds. A band played patriotic music, barnstorming pilots performed acrobatics and there was special music from the Atlanta Gospel Chorus.[26]

Charlie Wiggins won that race in his Wiggins Special with a speed of 66.7 mph. Ben Carter led the other drivers in a Fronty-Ford. Wiggins carefully prepared his car, testing it at the Walnut Gardens Speedway to avoid his engine blowing up as it did the previous year. He used a special mixture of motor oil and castor oil for his engine and low-grade airplane fuel. Pacing himself, Wiggins lagged behind the rest of the field. Other drivers stopped for tires and fuel but Wiggins was able to drive the entire 100 miles without a pit stop. When

"Wild Bill" Jeffries stopped for fuel on lap seventy-five, Wiggins passed him in front of the grandstand as spectators screamed their support.[27]

"'Wee' Charlie Wiggins, that plucky young mechanic from Indiana, had to build a special seat on his chassis to boost his tiny body so he could reach the gears of his home-made creation," Young wrote. "But at the end of this grand Gold and Glory event it was not the mechanics that mattered but the mechanic himself. As he crossed the finish line well ahead of the pack, a wild burst of applause greeted him from his home-towners, some of whom lost their heads and ran across the track, despite yells from cooler heads warning them that other drivers were pushing their metal steeds for second place honors."[28]

Realizing that potential disaster was imminent, CSA official Harry Earl grabbed the checkered flag and sprinted to the fourth turn to stop cars before they reached the crowd gathered around Wiggins on the track. Those cars and drivers were awarded their proper finishes although they did not quite complete the 100 miles.[29]

Charlie Wiggins was the man of the hour that night at the Gold and Glory Ball at Trinity Hall. "They put up posters all over Indiana Avenue," Leon "Al" Warren, recalled. "Everywhere you'd go, you'd see Charlie's picture with the title 'National Champion.' He was a local boy, the guy everyone in the neighborhood knew. His victory was like a victory for all of us. We could all relate to it, whoop it up, just like we'd done it ourselves."[30]

CSA sponsored nine races in 1926, and Charlie Wiggins won seven of them: Dayton, Chicago, Cleveland, South Bend, Keokuk (Iowa), Langhorne (Pennsylvania) and Detroit. After the Detroit race, the usually reticent Wiggins spoke to the *Chicago Whip* about the AAA's segregation racing policies. "We have the desire and the skill to compete with the nation's best," he said. "The AAA folks just don't want to see that. That's why we must work to prove our ability within our own ranks so that we can show the rest of the world we belong."[31]

Historian Richard Pierce pointed out the differences in the newspaper coverage of the Gold and Glory Sweepstakes. Black newspapers, such as the *Indianapolis Recorder,* he said, carried long front page articles and photographs of the 1926 race while the *Indianapolis Times* and the *Indianapolis Star* wrote little about the race. He inferred the difference in the newspapers' coverage was due to AAA influence.[32]

Todd Gould, author of *For the Gold and Glory: Charlie Wiggins and the African American Racing Circuit,* wrote, "The AAA did not simply attempt to discredit the Gold and Glory Sweepstakes. They went even further. They wanted all traces of Charlie Wiggins and the Colored Speedway Association to be erased from existence, at least in any racing capacity." The AAA considered any racing event not sanctioned by their organization to be outlaw races.[33]

Speeds declined in the 1927 annual race, when Bill James in a Graham Fronty-Ford Special won the race with an average of 56.723 mph. "Wild Bill" Jeffries was second in a Fronty-Ford in a field of fifteen drivers. Jeffries won the 1928 race over twenty-one other drivers. Rodney Morris was second in an M & M Special.[34]

The Colored Speedway Association not only flourished in Indiana but expanded to sponsor races in Ohio, Wisconsin, Illinois and Michigan. Barney Anderson led the field in the 1929 Gold and Glory Sweepstakes in a Model-A Ford with a speed of 67.22 mph. Wiggins was second. In 1930, the race was won by Gene Smith with a Boyle Valve Special at 60 mph and Hugo Barnes was second in a Barnes Special.[35]

The Great Depression dealt a severe blow to the Gold and Glory Sweepstakes. In 1931, the CSA moved the race from the State Fairgrounds to the Walnut Gardens Speedway, owned by Harry Earl, one of the series' original backers. Charlie Wiggins won again in his Wiggins Special with an average speed of 58.2 mph. Bobby Wallace was second in his Chevrolet Special.[36]

The 1932 race returned to the State Fairgrounds and it was a financial disaster. Only 600 spectators paid the admission price of two dollars each, leaving the $2,000 purse eight hundred dollars short. Initially, drivers refused to race but finally agreed to a shorter distance, twenty miles, with a winner-take-all purse. Wiggins captured the pole with an amazing speed of 80.4 mph, and his race average of 70.5 mph left the other twenty-six drivers in the dust. Bobby Wallace was again second.[37]

Appreciative for the mentoring he received as a youth, Wiggins helped other young men. One, known as Johnny, hung around Wiggins' garage. Wiggins invited him to watch his race practices and to come to the track when he was testing his cars. In 1933, Wiggins opened his newspaper one morning and, to his amazement, there was Johnny's picture. The newspaper identified the man as John Dillinger.[38]

Walnut Gardens Speedway, twelve miles outside of Indianapolis, was again the site for the 1933 Gold and Glory Sweepstakes. Harry Earl rented the CSA the track for one dollar plus a portion of the gate receipts. The Elks sponsored the race. Charlie Wiggins was again the winner but under unusual circumstances. He was late arriving at the track and missed the preliminary heat. Then, he was assessed a five-lap penalty for ignoring a yellow caution flag. His brother, Lawrence Wiggins, was second.[39]

There was no Gold and Glory Sweepstakes in 1934, but Charlie Wiggins did get into the Indy 500 that year, in a manner of speaking. Driver Bill Cummings, who called Wiggins one of the greatest mechanics he ever knew, wanted him on his race crew but the AAA only allowed blacks to be hired as janitors, not mechanics. Wiggins swept floors by day and worked on Cummings' car at night after AAA officials left the track. Cummings won the Indy 500 while Charlie Wiggins watched from the colored section of the grandstands.[40]

The CSA moved the race back to the State Fairgrounds in 1935. However, it made the mistake of bringing in a promotional team from Dayton, Ohio, to run the event. The Ohioans left with the purse money. No record of the race was located.[41]

Charlie Wiggins' life would have been much better had there been no 1936 Gold and Glory Sweepstakes. Dust was so thick on the fairgrounds track that fourteen cars collided in a massive wreck on the second lap. Wiggins was injured in the pile-up and lost his right leg. The race, shortened to fifty miles, was won by Bill Carson in a Boyle Valve Special at 57.69 mph. Summer "Red" Oliver was second.[42]

For the next forty years, Wiggins built and repaired cars and trained generations of mechanics. He made himself a wooden leg but recurring infections created medical bills that consumed his and Roberta's savings, leaving them nearly penniless when he died in 1979. He was buried in Crown Hill Cemetery in Indianapolis.[43]

When the Corporation for Public Broadcasting produced a documentary on the Gold and Glory Sweepstakes and Charlie Wiggins in 2003, one of the entities providing grant money was the Indianapolis Motor Speedway that had allowed Wiggins to work there only as a janitor. The documentary transcript stated that Wiggins was buried in an unmarked grave. However, a November 10, 2009, telephone call to the Crown Hill Cemetery revealed that Wiggins' grave indeed had a marker.[44]

Charlie Wiggins's efforts were not forgotten.

Like Wiggins, Dewey "Rajo Jack" Gaston, was another of those master mechanics. However, he went to excessive lengths to conceal his ethnic origin. He would often tell race promoters that he was Portuguese or an American Indian. In addition, he avoided having his photograph taken at race tracks. Often in the winner's circle, his wife Ruth would come down from the grandstands, in a prearranged agreement with the promoter, and present him with the trophy instead of the usual Caucasian beauty queen. Gaston claimed he never attempted to enter AAA races because of a health issue: he lost the use of one eye in a motorcycle stunt.[45]

The nickname "Rajo Jack" came from Gaston being the top West Coast salesman for Joe Jegersberger's Rajo cylinder head for the Model T Ford. He raced under that name as well as others.[46]

Gaston began racing in the early 1920s in Vancouver, Washington. A 1925 match race against Francis Quinn resulted in a lifelong friendship between the two men. Racing under the name Jack DeSoto, Gaston neared the finish line when the seat fell out of his car. Gaston later joined Quinn's Legion Ascot racing team.[47]

In his early racing days, Quinn, like most drivers without a lot of money, drove a Fronty-Ford, considered by some as inferior to the Miller Motor Speedsters. When Quinn accumulated enough money, he was the 1930 AAA Pacific Southwest Champion, and he built a Miller Marine of his own design. Out of contention for the 1931 championship, Quinn decided to enter the Miller in the season's last race, December 14, at Oakland. He wanted to compete with the great Eastern AAA drivers, Mauri Rose, Ralph Hepburn and Louie Meyer, who were going to be in the Oakland race.[48]

Anxious to meet his fellow racers, Quinn and his mechanic Claude French left Los Angeles for Oakland in Quinn's Model-A roadster towing the Miller. Near Merced, they learned the race was cancelled due to rain. They headed back to Los Angeles when a truck hit the roadster head on. Quinn died on the roadside, French suffered minor injuries, the roadster was demolished but the Miller was undamaged.[49]

After Quinn's death, his family gave Gaston his 225-cubic-inch Miller. In April 1939, the Miller was scattered over Gaston's Los Angeles garage floor, in the midst of installing new bearings, when he heard about a 100-mile race the next day at the Oakland Speedway. Gaston and his wife Ruth carefully wheeled the Miller's parts into the bed of his truck. While she drove to Oakland, he rebuilt the Miller and they reached the track in time to qualify third. Gaston and the Miller finished the race in second place.[50]

Racing in California for Charlie Curreyer's American Racing Association, Gaston won two 250-mile stock car races, at Mines Field in Los Angeles in 1939 and at Ascot in Los Angeles the next year. Curreyer later promoted Bill France's first NASCAR race in California at Riverside in 1958.[51] After leaving racing, Gaston owned a cartage fleet. He died in February 1956 of an apparent heart attack while driving one of his trucks from Los Angeles to San Francisco.[52]

While not as successful as Gaston, Joie Ray made his contributions as a black driver in a different manner.

Louisville, Kentucky, native Joie Ray was the son of a banker and real estate agent. He began racing in the 1940s in the Midwest Dirt Track Racing Association (MDTRA) organized in the 1930s by Dan Sheek, Jr., from Greenwood, Indiana. The races were known as the

"Kerosene Circuit" because most of their races were run in the hinterlands of Illinois and Indiana.[53]

Ray also raced in the Central States Racing Association (CSRA). In 1948, he was fifth in MDTRA standings and twentieth in the CSRA. In his sixteen years of racing, he won three races. "His biggest career accomplishment was how many friends he made," said his biographer, Pat Sullivan. "I don't know a soul who didn't like Joie Ray. He was a great ambassador for racing and a great ambassador for African Americans."[54]

In 1949, Joie Ray decided to leave midget racing and passed his AAA sprint car driver's test, breaking their color barrier and running his first race April 8, 1947, a week before Jackie Robinson made his Major League Baseball debut.[55] In 2003, Ray drove the pace car for the Indianapolis 500.[56]

Wilbur Gaines, apparently the only black driver in Andy Granatelli's Hurricane Racing Association in Chicago, had longevity in the sport as he continued to race into his sixties. Gaines told *Ebony* magazine in 1951 that he never made over $3,000 to $6,000 in a year from racing and received a bonus for stunts. He recalled that drivers in the 1920s could pick up as much as $200 if they rolled their cars over during races.[57]

A photograph in *Jet*'s March 6, 1952, issue showed Gaines, at age sixty-three, in his race car wearing glasses and a battered helmet. The Chicago native raced in the 1929, 1930, 1931 and 1936 Gold and Glory races.[58]

The August 5, 1950, issue of *Time* magazine described the Hurricane Racing Association as a stable of professional drivers who raced five nights a week at Soldiers Field in Chicago. They also raced in Granatelli promoted events in Rockford, Illinois, and Milwaukee and Waukegan, Wisconsin. Drivers received $35 whether or not they won races. Granatelli promoted hot rod racing under the Hurricane Racing Association.

In Granatelli's biography in the National Business Hall of Fame, Barbara E. Mathews, M.D., wrote, "Using his penchant for showmanship, Andy single-handedly created a series of hot rod and stock car racing events that were held in 1947 in Chicago's Soldier Field, packing in an all-time record of 89,560 fans."[59]

Granatelli's ties to the early days of stock car racing apparently reached back to the speed trials on Daytona Beach. Mathews wrote that Granatelli built and sold engines for the flathead Fords used by illegal whiskey transporters as well as the cars that ran in the early beach competition.[60]

6

Beer, Broads and Unadulterated Bull

∙ ∙ ∙ ∙ ∙ ∙ ∙

Bill France held his stock car racing organizational meeting in the Ebony Lounge of the Streamline Hotel, in Daytona Beach, on December 12, 1947. Sports columnist Bernard Kahn indicated that France was part owner of the bar. "They hammered away at the 'idea meeting' at the Streamline roof bar in which the local filling station operator and part-time race promoter and driver France owned the principal interest," Kahn wrote.[1]

In addition to France, those attending included Joe Littlejohn, a Spartanburg, South Carolina, driver who later promoted his own races; Red Byron, an Atlanta driver; Tom Gallan, a New York promoter; Harvey Tattersall, a New Yorker who later ran the United Stock Car Racing Club; Frank Mundy (whose real name was Francisco E. Mendenez), another Atlantanian who became the 1955 AAA stock car racing champion; William Streeter and William Tuthill, New York promoters; Alvin Hawkins, who promoted races with France at Bowman Gray Stadium in Winston-Salem, and Louis Ossinsky, France's Daytona Beach attorney and service station customer.[2]

Others at the meeting were Marshall Teague, a Daytona Beach driver who later left NASCAR after a split with France over the division of race purses and found success in AAA and United States Automobile Club (USAC) racing; Sammy Packard, a Rhode Island driver who later worked for France; Raymond Parks, a former moonshine transporter turned wealthy car owner and sometime driver, from Atlanta; Red Vogt, the famed Atlanta car builder; Bob Richards, an Illinois driver; Ed Samples, another Georgia driver; Fonty Flock, from the original Alabama gang; Buddy Shuman, a former moonshine transporter from Charlotte; Enoch Staley, a France ally and founder of the North Wilkesboro Speedway in North Carolina; E. G. "Cannonball" Baker, a former motorcycle and automobile racer from Indiana; Bernard Kahn, and Jim Quisenberry, from *Speed Age* magazine.[3]

France's biggest racing rival, the AAA, the largest organization sanctioning stock car races at that time, was not represented at the meeting. The AAA emphasized it would only sanction stock car races if they were limited to automobiles of the strictly stock status. In addition, the AAA required that forty percent of the gate had to go into the race purse.

The AAA was correct about France's style of racing, there was nothing stock about the vehicles. However, the organization's failure to recognize what was becoming a popular sport in the racing world eventually opened an international door for France and he quickly took the advantage. Stock car racing, France confessed to those assembled, was his whole life.[4]

France was well prepared with plenty of distractions when he held the organizational meeting. Beer and whiskey flowed freely and good Cuban cigars were available. France brought in a batch of beautiful women from a "modeling" agency. The women, in the middle of the day, were dressed in bathing suits and circulated among the drivers, car owners and track promoters.[5] Some of the men stayed in the lounge with the models and never bothered to attend the meetings.[6]

France said he placed advertisements in various publications inviting men from the North, East and South to attend a meeting to "discuss plans for the formulation of an association that would encompass drivers, track operators and car owners."[7]

By the time of the meeting, France had eliminated most of his promotional competition in the South, with the exception of Sam Nunis and Bruton Smith. France, according to Marjorie Flock, had the meeting minutes from Fonty Flock's group for organizing the sport.[8]

Enoch Staley and Clay Earles, race track owners and promoters from Virginia and North Carolina respectively, France assumed would support him, as he had worked well with them. Raymond Parks, who had the Georgia charter for the National Stock Car Racing Association, Inc. (NSCRA), was another matter.[9]

If Raymond Parks seriously considered following through with his recently incorporated organization in Georgia, he would have been formidable opponent. Bill France, however, had an enormous gift of persuasion and the talent to know when and how to use it.

The group gathered in the Ebony Lounge was an eclectic mixture of racers, car owners, promoters and mechanics. France ran the meeting, appointed committees and told those assembled that stock car racing could become a nationally recognized sport, if managed properly. Some of those attending were concerned about France's intentions; it appeared as if he intended to rule the sport. "By the end of the first night, sufficiently lubricated by free booze and beautiful women, the soon-to-be founders of a new sport seemed ready to follow France's lead," Neal Thompson wrote in his book about Raymond Parks.[10]

France droned on about drivers being duped by shady promoters who supposedly vanished with purses before the end of races and promised that would never occur in his organization.

In 2002, Sammy Packard, one of the last surviving of those who attended, was still following the France party line of crooked promoters. He said those in racing wanted to get away from the fly-by-night promoters who absconded with the race purses. "What we discussed was getting money put in a bank before a race, so the promoter wouldn't skip out on us. That seemed to be one of the main problems we were having. We'd get done running somewhere and the promoter would skip town with the money. It happened to me several times."[11]

Packard, originally from Rhode Island, came to Daytona for the beach races, decided to stay and worked for France.[12] Joe Littlejohn, who had extensive experience with race promoters and was one himself, saw things differently. He estimated that only two or three percent of the promoters left the races with the purse money and he had considerable experience as a driver. Raymond Parks, who also had broad experience in racing, said he had never heard of promoters leaving with the purse money before the race was over.[13]

Nevertheless, crooked promoters absconding with the purse before races were over became a litany France uttered for decades when he found himself boxed in a corner over some unpopular rule or his small race purses.

Packard and many of those attending the organizational meeting enjoyed the kegs of beer France made sure were always available during the three-day event. According to Ben A. Shackleford, who had access to NASCAR's organizational meeting minutes for his Ph.D. dissertation at Georgia Tech, wrote that France opened the meeting recounting his resume and emphasizing how racing mass produced automobiles could become a "respectable and profitable sport for drivers, mechanics, car owners and racing promoters alike."[14] NASCAR, sixty-four years later, is allowing access to those meeting minutes only to a chosen few and refusing to make them available to the public.[15] Being a privately held corporation, they certainly have that right.

France told those in the meeting room that they were there to lay groundwork for a new organization. He proceeded to outline his plans for creating a national championship racing series much like those suggested to him earlier by *Charlotte Observer* sports editor Wilton Garrison. Under such a plan, France said, drivers could travel to all regions of the country and still race under the same set of rules and technical requirements. France advocated "maintaining standards that prevented technology from providing an obvious advantage and accounting entirely for victory."[16]

France made it clear that the rules adopted at the meeting would reflect regulations which would provide entertainment rather than the testing of mass produced automobiles.[17] That concept was tossed out, and much else added, after the meeting and before the organization's articles of incorporation were filed with the Florida secretary of state's office in February 1949.

France talked about a two-tiered racing series with both funded on a percentage of the prize money. That phrase, "percentage of the prize money," caused considerable problems for France in the years to come, but its vagueness was exactly what he intended. He said that each region could play host to the traveling 'first tier' of drivers from across the country. Shackleford wrote, "Because both levels of championship would be funded on a percentage basis from prize money offerings, and prize money was pulled from gate receipts, funding the championship would cost no money up front. Promoters would pay fifty dollars per $1,000 of prize money into the regional championship fund and $100 for each thousand into the national championship fund."[18]

Technological advantages, he told those in attendance, would be controlled through deliberate and arbitrary distinctions between cars selected for the sport and which parts owners would be allowed to use. France would countenance no one, not even Detroit, to define a stock car.[19] France joined those gathered in the lounge after the first session and took one of the models on his lap.[20]

Portions of the December 1947 meeting minutes and sections of other early minutes Shackleford used indicated France counted on building a base of paying customers through their identification between the vehicles they owned and those running on the tracks. France emphasized, like Raymond Parks' high standards for his vehicles, that race cars must present a respectable public appearance.[21]

France sought and got just what he wanted out of the Ebony Lounge meeting. There would be uniform rules; near equal specifications for cars; a single national authority; three divisions—modified, roadsters and strictly stock; competition money would be paid deeper into the field, including the first twenty-two finishers; drivers could not compete in another series within 200 miles of a NASCAR event and then would have to have permission from

France; portions of the profits from each race would pay drivers' bonuses and national championship points fund; and there would be a benevolent fund for injured drivers.[22]

Driver Red Byron suggested the organization be named the National Stock Car Racing Association and the group approved the name. Mechanic Red Vogt was said to have later suggested another organization name, the National Association for Stock Car Automobile Racing, and that name stuck.[23]

France was elected the NASCAR president and William Tuthill, a New York racing promoter, was the secretary. Byron suggested a governing body of a president, secretary, two promoters, two drivers, two car owners and two mechanics. Byron and Buddy Shuman were elected to represent the drivers. Red Vogt and Marshall Teague were to represent the mechanics. The group elected Teague as the treasurer. E. G. "Cannonball" Baker was named the high commissioner.[24]

Marshall Teague and his Fabulous Hudson Hornet won the 1952 beach-road race at Daytona, as he did the previous year. Teague, from Daytona Beach, was elected NASCAR treasurer at the organizational meeting in December 1947, but the formal incorporation documents, filed in February 1948, listed Bill France as president and treasurer. Teague, in a disagreement with France over purse monies, left NASCAR and piled up records and trophies in AAA racing. In 1959, France offered Teague, whom he had banned from racing in NASCAR, $10,000 to break the closed circuit record of 177.04 mph at his new Daytona superspeedway. Teague was killed in his effort prior to the first race there in 1959 (State Archives of Florida).

Regardless of Bryon's suggestion and the group's elective choices, France had other plans and only Tuthill made the cut. Marshall Teague was never going to be the treasurer—nobody was going to handle money but Bill and Annie France. The idea of having a NASCAR governing body, to make final decisions, was never taken seriously by France.[25]

Although the Ebony Lounge meeting was held the middle of December, NASCAR was not incorporated until February 18, 1948. The lawyer handling the incorporation procedure was Louis Ossinsky, a cash customer at France's service station. Tuthill told France democracy would never control such a raucous group of individuals and suggested the new organization needed a dictator, not an elected president.[26] France was more than happy to comply.

However, since France and Ossinsky incorporated NASCAR as a private entity, no one outside of those two, and Tuthill, were knowledgeable of the corporate structure, or exactly how the shares of stock were split. Neal Thompson wrote that relatives and friends of Vogt and Parks told him that those two men, along with Joe Littlejohn, were supposed to have been either officers or stockholders in the corporation. There was no mention of the three men in the incorporation document. Thompson understood that Ossinsky received ten shares, Tuthill, forty and France the other fifty. "By this point, the NASCAR board that was elected back in December had become largely inert and apparently no one questioned France's distribution of stock shares—at least not openly," Thompson wrote.[27]

The gradual shift in control of NASCAR, Shackleford stated, began soon after the formation meeting, but he described neither that control nor a division of the corporation's stock.[28]

France and Ossinsky, without any interference or oversight from the other organizers, had plenty of time to draw up the incorporation document just the way they wanted. "He used his lawyers to draw up legal papers giving him all rights to our organization. The next thing we know, NASCAR belongs to Bill France," Raymond Parks said.[29] Parks' assessment came close to the reality of what had happened. In time, France would own NASCAR in its entirety.

The author, while researching incorporation documents in the North Carolina Secretary of State's office in April 2010, found a copy of the original NASCAR incorporation document. France and Ossinsky had used the document in the process of establishing a North Carolina agent, CT Corporation System, to transact NASCAR business in that state, including the sanctioning of all branches of auto racing and automobile testing.[30]

France told the Ebony Lounge group that the new organization would have little to do with testing. Racing was only for entertainment. France included testing in the corporate document as a NASCAR satellite operation. In all probability, it was Ossinsky, not France, whose brilliant legal mind created the far-reaching implications of the organization's corporation structure.

NASCAR's general nature of business, according to the incorporation document, was "To engage in the advancement of automobile racing in all its branches; to sanction and supervise auto racing in all its branches. To promote auto racing. To hold or arrange auto races and other matches and competitions and offer and grant, or contribute toward provision of prizes, awards and distinctions."[31]

The language here differed from that of the organizational meeting, which specified the amounts of money promoters would put into the fund for end of season NASCAR awards.

"To sanction and supervise speed trials of all kinds and in all its branches," the document continued. "To sanction and supervise economy and/or endurance trials of all kinds in all its branches. To provide auto racing grounds or tracks and to lay out and prepare such auto racing grounds or tracks for auto racing and other purposes of the corporation and to provide pavilions, lavatories, refreshment rooms, refreshments, bleachers, grandstands and other conveniences in connection therewith."[32]

NASCAR could join with other similar organizations, acquire real and personal property, raise money by subscription, and sanction fees and memberships. It would promote safety and cooperate with traffic authorities and safety organizations.[33]

The two men, France and Ossinsky, envisioned NASCAR could manufacture and control automobile parts used in the racing vehicles and even construct the cars themselves. That section of the corporate document read: "To manufacture, buy, sell, license, lease, deal in and deal with automobiles, auto trucks, auto cars, trailers, house cars and any and all other forms of auto conveyances and trailers and any and all supplies, materials, parts or accessories connected therewith or that may be useful, convenient or incident to the manufacture, sale or handling thereof."[34]

"To manufacture, purchase, own lease, license, construct, install, use, sell and dispose of wheels, rims, tires, axles, batteries, dynamos, generators, compressors, pumps, motors, engines, machinery, structures, apparatus, instruments, springs, fixtures and appliances for the manufacture, production, generation, distribution, use supply and application of electricity, compressed air, steam, oil, gas, gasoline or other power either singly or in combination thereof."[35]

Did France have plans to require car owners and drivers to buy their parts from him? NASCAR was authorized by the incorporation document "to manufacture, buy, sell, license, lease and deal in and with any and all kinds of wheels, springs, axles, gears, differentials, carburetors, bearings, motors, engines, radiators, machines, machinery, tools supplies, materials, parts and apparatus for assembling or manufacture of operation of automobiles, auto cars, motor trucks and other vehicles and any and all other supplies, apparatus, machinery, appliances or equipment, mechanical and mercantile specialties, utilities, devices, castings, implements and tools of any kind or character which may be used in connection therewith."[36]

NASCAR, if France so chose, could buy, sell, lease, hire, rent, import, export, deal in remodel and repair of automobiles, taxicabs, trucks or any other kind of vehicle. The organization could carry on the business of mechanical and electrical engineers, toolmakers, machinists, founders, metal workers, smiths, builders, fitters, cutlers, merchants or any similar business "to render profitable any of the company's property or rights or conductive to any of the company's objects."[37]

William C. and James C. France, Bill France's sons, were directors in a firm called Daytona Parts, Inc., that was incorporated on January 1, 1977. Whether the firm was ever active in the business is unknown. Daytona Parts, Inc., was voluntary dissolved December 28, 1982.[38]

The NASCAR articles of incorporation had the usual boilerplate items concerning borrowing money, contracting debts, owning, leasing and mortgaging property and establishing offices.[39]

The total authorized capital stock of NASCAR was ten shares, "all of which shall be common stock without a nominal or par value," the document directed. The capital with which NASCAR began business was $500, and the principal place of business was to be in Daytona Beach, Volusia County, Florida. The number of corporate directors was limited to three, which partly explained why Park, Vogt and Littlejohn were not named to the board of directors.[40]

NASCAR's first three directors were Bill France, William B. Tuthill and Louis Ossinsky. The directors' terms were staggered at one, two and three years. Nothing changed when the corporation's officers were named. France was the president and treasurer, Ossinsky was vice-president and Tuthill was secretary. Marshall Teague, who was elected treasurer at the organizational meeting, was not mentioned in the incorporation documents.[41]

Although the corporation documents called for ten shares, the actual division was only half of that. France and Tuthill had two shares each and Ossinsky had one share. Presumably, the remaining five shares were held in reserve for corporate expansion. The NASCAR board of directors, on October 26, 1953, voted to reduce the authorized capital stock from ten shares of no par value to eight shares of no par value. That action was attested to by both France and Ossinsky. On September 29, 1956, the NASCAR board of directors voted another change. Ossinsky certified that "the authorized capital stock of the National Association for Stock Car Auto Racing, Inc., be changed from eight (8) shares of no par valve to three hundred thousand (300,000) shares of the par value of one ($1) dollar each so that the total authorized capital stock of this corporation shall be divided into three hundred thousand (300,000) shares, all of which shall be common stock with a par value of one ($1) dollar each instead of eight (8) shares of no par value as heretofore."[42]

The corporate change in the stock shares occurred before France began building the Daytona International Speedway, and was an early indication that both NASCAR and the speedway, which later became International Speedways Corporation, were controlled by France.

NASCAR was not the only entity Bill France incorporated in the late 1940s. On December 19, 1949, he incorporated the National Racing Corporation (NRC). France was the registered agent and president of the corporation. His address was listed at 714 John Anderson Drive in Daytona Beach. His sixteen-year-old son, William C. France, and his five-year-old son, James C. France, were the other officers. Just what France intended to do with that corporation was not clear. The NRC incorporation document was annulled in September 1977 for non-payment.[43]

Bill France was so anxious to begin his first NASCAR season in 1948 that he scheduled the organization's first race, on the Daytona beach-road course, before the organization's papers were signed and notarized.

7

NASCAR's Early Years

• • • • • • •

Bill France did not begin NASCAR's first season in 1948 on a high note.

Although the corporate structure of NASCAR gave him total control of the organization, France was short on money. NASCAR's capital was only $500, and the list of competing racing stock car promoters and organizations was expanding. There was Sam Nunis, at Atlanta's Lakewood Speedway, Alf Knight, in Chattanooga; Bruton Smith, in Concord, North Carolina, with the National Stock Car Racing Association, Joe Littlejohn and his South Carolina Stock Car Racing Association and the Atlanta Stock Car Club for black drivers. Ed Otto organized the New England Stock Car Racing Association. Bill Barkheimer was promoting stock car races in California. John Marcum ran the Midwest Association for Racing Cars from Ohio.[1]

Jack Higgins, operating as Florida Speedways, jumped ahead of France in promoting a stock car race at the Pompano Race Track in early 1948. Higgins announced he had secured Fonty Flock, Buddy Shuman, Ed Samples, Marshall Teague and Bill Snowden for his race.[2]

In addition to Higgins' stock car race in his own back yard, France had complications with his old standby, the beach portion of the road course. After the war, new construction sprung up along the beach portion of the course where homeowners, who hated the noise, wrecks and car parts left behind by the races, demanded the races be moved. In addition, the winter's high tides had changed the contours of the beach and washed out the turns.[3] Consequently, France had to find a new beach-road course for his first NASCAR modified race on February 15, 1948.

With the help of municipal officials, France leased, from the city, county and private owners, land south of Daytona Beach in order to build the 2.2 mile course over the beach that connected with the road portion, Route A1A.[4]

The south turn, said to be two blocks wide, was mushy and the sand was not packed down like the old course. Concerned about a massive pile up from fifty-six modified cars starting at the same time, France staggered each row of four vehicles at one-second intervals. France posted a warning signs about rattlesnakes to keep non-paying spectators out. He charged the 14,000 spectators $2.50 each for tickets, collecting approximately $35,000, if all the tickets were sold.[5] France also collected entry, membership and various and sundry violations fees in addition to the gate, concessions and parking revenue.

That was not a bad gate for NASCAR's first race, the Rayson Memorial. France had a proclivity for naming his races for dead drivers. British Royal Air Force pilot Theodore Rayson, a former Grand Prix driver, was killed in November 1939 crash in Wiltshire, England.[6]

Since the race occurred six days before NASCAR was legally incorporated, it was not known if the race was conducted by NCSCC rules, those of the new organization or a combination. As would become the case, the rules were whatever France stipulated.

France announced that the sixty-two drivers, from twelve states, would compete for $3,500 in prize money for the seventy-lap race.[7] France had no intentions of placing forty percent of the gate into the race purse as AAA sanctioned races required. The Rayson Memorial was his race, sanctioned by his organization and, as became the norm, the purse was determined by France alone. Consequently, France established a purse precedent of paying drivers approximately ten percent of the gross gate generated by ticket sales. That is not to say France pocketed the remaining ninety percent. He had expenses of land rental for a portion of the course, insurance, race day personnel, tickets and promotional posters. Much of his advertising came free through the news columns of Daytona Beach and other newspapers. There is no doubt that he made a tidy profit.

Red Byron, in his Red Vogt prepared car, came in first. He was followed by Marshall Teague and Bob Flock. Only twelve of the fifty-six cars finished the race and they were all 1939 Ford V-8s.[8]

A week later, France staged another modified race at Speedway Park in Jacksonville. Fonty Flock won that race after the steering wheel of his 1939 Ford broke. Flock steered the car with the wheel stem across the finish line.[9]

Instead of complaining that France hijacked their racing organization, Joe Littlejohn did something about it. He began the South Carolina Stock Car Racing Association (SCSCRA) and started holding regular races at Greenville-Pickens Speedway, built in 1940 at Greenville, and at Piedmont-Interstate Fairgrounds, built in Spartanburg in 1937. Littlejohn's organization had a points system and the high point man at the end of the season would receive the new Oldsmobile 68 club sedan he purchased from Stafford Motors in Spartanburg.[10]

On April 14, 1948, Littlejohn, operating as Hub City Speedways, staged his second race of the month at Piedmont-Interstate with $2,000 in prize money. Drivers expected included the three Flock brothers, Red Byron, Ed Samples, Jack Smith, Gober Sosebee, Buddy Shuman, Glenn Dunaway, Buck Baker, Fred Mahon, Bill Snowden and Cotton Owens, all regulars from France's races.[11]

Littlejohn guaranteed $2,000 purses for his races. He often held "powder-puff" derbies as preliminary races featuring drivers such as Sara Christian, from Atlanta, for the July 4, 1948, event at Piedmont-Interstate Fairgrounds. Littlejohn's admission fees were $1.50 and $1.75.[12]

Some of France's drivers—Ed Samples, Bob Flock, Fred Mahon and Joe Eubanks—were in the field for SCSCRA's first race on April 2. Samples' win in that race placed him atop the association's standings.[13]

France opened the NASCAR season in North Carolina at the Lakeview Speedway, near Lexington, on April 11. The five-eighth mile dirt oval's grandstands accommodated 5,000, while the grounds could handle 20,000 spectators. The local newspaper printed NASCAR's news release. "Already installed as race director is Bill France, of Daytona Beach,

Florida, the nation's foremost stock car race manager and a former driver and two times national champion driver." Forty drivers, including Bob Flock, Buddy Shuman and Ed Samples, were expected. If paying customers reached peak capacity, the return ranged from $30,000 to $35,000, if France charged his usual $2.50 admission, plus parking, program and concessions profits.[14]

France, during one week in April 1948, staged races at Lakeview, North Wilkesboro and Greensboro.[15] Some of the other races France promoted that April covered three states, Alabama, Georgia and Virginia, in addition to the North Carolina tracks. They included one in Birmingham, a joint operation with Ben Tucker; another in Danville, Virginia, that Bob Flock won; and another in Columbus, Georgia, where the grandstands seated 6,000.[16]

Despite his reassurances at the NASCAR organizational meeting the previous December that he envisioned the sport as a weekend occupation for drivers who had regular jobs,

The one-mile Occoneechee Speedway, also referred to as the Orange Speedway, was originally a horse racing track in a bend of the Eno River, near Hillsborough, North Carolina. The track is one of the few facilities from the 1940s that has been preserved, and that was through the efforts of the Historic Speedway Group. NASCAR's third Strictly Stock race was held there in 1949 and was won by Bob Flock in a Frank Christian Oldsmobile. The last Grand National race there, in September 1968, was won by Richard Petty in a Plymouth. Occoneechee's Grand National race date was transferred to Talladega the next year by track owner Bill France (Historic Speedway Group).

France was promoting races wherever he could. Smaller purses and scheduling his drivers for races in different states soon presented big problems for France.

By early May 1948, it became obvious that some of NASCAR's regular drivers, due to minuscule purses, were looking beyond France's plantation and the South. Buddy Shuman, Frank Mundy and Bill Snowden headed for New York's Fronda Fairgrounds Speedway, where they raced under the lights in a stock car race promoted by Jack Knochman with a purse of $2,400.[17]

Littlejohn promoted a 1948 Memorial Day 100-lap race at the Piedmont-Interstate track. Ed Samples, Fred Mahon and Joe Eubanks finished in that order. Bob and Fonty Flock drove in the race.[18]

In June 1949, an estimated 10,000 spectators saw Bob Flock win the inaugural race at Occoneechee Speedway, a new one mile dirt track in Hillsborough, North Carolina. France and his partners raked in an estimated $25,000, not including any profits from concessions, programs and parking.[19]

Another new track, the Columbus Speedway, near Midland, Georgia, opened on June 20, 1948. The half-mile dirt oval, built in forty-five days by local investors, cost $50,000. The new track's grandstands could seat 6,000. If France charged his usual admission fee, $2.50, his gate was $15,000. It was difficult to determine how much Bob Flock, won as record keeping for that year was incomplete.[20]

However, the "Flying Flocks" were the big story that day. Along with Bob's win at Columbus, Fonty Flock beat Billy Carden, from Mapleton, Georgia, in the Birmingham Fairgrounds race and Tim Flock won his race in Greensboro, North Carolina.[21]

Bill France staged races all over the South that year with two exceptions: one was in Langhorne, Pennsylvania, and the other in Dover, New Jersey. On the same day, he scheduled races at three tracks in different states. The previous month France had races scheduled for three states on the same day, May 23. Gober Sosebee won the Macon, Georgia, race; Bill Blair, from High Point, North Carolina, was first in the Danville, Virginia, contest; Johnny Rogers, from Trenton, won the competition in Dover, New Jersey.[22]

To keep a schedule like that, France had to delegate a lot of authority to his staff. Safety, for drivers and spectators, was not a high priority. Eventually, something was going to go terribly wrong.

It did.

On June 25, France again was promoting two races on the same day, one at the Columbus Speedway and the other in Greensboro, North Carolina. Sam Nunis and NSCRA were also staging a race in Chattanooga. Suspecting some of his drivers might defect to Nunis' race with a larger purse, France went to Greensboro, where he could check on his regular drivers. He also wanted to advertise a race he was promoting in two weeks at the Lakeview Speedway, near Lexington, North Carolina.[23]

France left the details of the Columbus Speedway race to a crew that included "Lucky" Sauers, a former driver from Rosman, North Carolina. The odor of fresh sawdust from the newly sawed lumber used in the grandstands and posts mingled with gasoline fumes from the cars. Approximately 3,000 spectators, many of them from nearby Fort Benning, were enjoying the event until two laps from the end of the feature race. Bill Carden was attempting to pass Red Byron when Byron blew a tire.[24]

Charles Jenkins, from Columbus, had just advised his wife and her friend to move back from the fence to the bed of a pick-up truck to watch the end of the race from a safer distance. "As Red came flying into the turn, you could hear his engine breathe briefly," Jenkins said. "At that moment, I recall his right tire exploding." Jenkins said Bryon did everything possible to control the car and avoid the crowd.[25]

"I remember the car going through the fence," Jenkins continued. "The people were pressed so close his car just raked along doing damage. I remember a huge wooden post flexed enough from the impact that it 'head-popped' the little boy that later died at the hospital. The child's father picked him up and put him in the family car and left. He did not wait for the ambulance. People were lying around everywhere."[26]

When all the debris settled, seven-year-old Roy Brannon was dead. Sixteen other spectators had injuries ranging from an amputated leg to a fractured pelvis to broken limbs. Billy Carden won the race.[27]

Bill France was not faring much better at the Greensboro race. Near the end of that race, Bill "Slick" Davis, from Concord, North Carolina, rolled his car and was ejected onto the track. Four drivers were unable to avoid hitting Davis' car, which, in turn, hit the unprotected driver lying on the track. Davis died of his injuries later that evening.[28]

On the same day, NASCAR experienced what could only be described as carnage at the two tracks, lacking the barest of safety precautions, where the organization sanctioned races. France immediately went into damage control saying that Byron's accident was unavoidable. Greensboro authorities went along with his assessment listing Davis' death as an occupational accident.[29]

France again staged a memorial race in August 1948, over the new beach-road course, but the event was not named for Slick Davis killed in the Greensboro race. This time the race was named for Buck Mathis, a driver fatally injured in an October 1947 race at an Orlando track when his car collided with that of Al Bignal, from Jacksonville. France announced he expected a thirty-car field to compete for $3,500 in prize money. He said Bob and Fonty Flock, Red Byron and Curtis Turner were scheduled to drive in the race.[30]

In October 1948, Littlejohn's SCSCRA was promoting races, somewhat differently from those of France, at the Piedmont-Interstate Fairgrounds' track, but he was still attracting NASCAR drivers. Ed Samples, Bob Flock, Gober Sosebee, Billy Carden and Roscoe Thompson signed up for the race. Littlejohn ran a Wednesday-Saturday program at the track. The Wednesday feature was for black drivers. The local newspaper quoted Littlejohn as saying, "A section of the stands will be reserved for white spectators at the Wednesday speed circus." Littlejohn offered a $1,500 purse for the thirty-five lap race.[31] Littlejohn put up $2,000 in prize money for the Saturday race.[32]

NASCAR's first season, with the modified races, ended about the way it started, fraught with confusion. An estimated 2,000 fans arrived for the November 7 race at the Columbus Speedway. France flew up from Daytona Beach to make sure all seventeen of his drivers showed up. Only Red Byron and Fonty Flock and four others were there. Byron and Flock were in a tight race for the first championship. The other drivers France expected chose to drive in a Sam Nunis race at the Lakewood Speedway in Atlanta for a larger purse. Flock's engine died in a qualifying lap and that left Byron far outclassing the rest of the field.[33]

France decided to postpone the race until the following week. He told the crowd, over the public address system, there had been a scheduling error among the other drivers. He then made a mistake by asking them if they wanted to see the race or come back the next week for the free event. The crowd wanted to see a race that day but France cancelled the event and fled amid their howls of protest.[34]

France held the race on November 14. Byron was the winner, by about fifteen feet, over Flock and won the championship. It must have been a bittersweet win for Byron at the track where his accident killed little Roy Bannon and injured sixteen others. The final championship calculations were remarkably close: Byron 2,966.5 points to Flock's 2,963.75; Byron won eleven races and Flock fifteen; Byron's race earnings were $13,150 and Flock's $14,385.[35]

The top five modified drivers for 1948—Byron, Bob Flock, Tim Flock, Curtis Turner and Buddy Shuman—had average winnings of $8,799. Their share of the end season points fund, $2,700, brought their annual average race earnings to $9,339. The 1948 Indy 500 purse was $1,721,075 and winner Mauri Rose's share was $42,800.[36]

NASCAR's modified cars division ran a fifty-two race schedule on dirt tracks in 1948.[37] If each of those modified races had a conservatively estimated $2,000 purse and France was paying the drivers one-tenth of the gross, then his gross racing revenue that year was approximately $1,040,000 or more. Subtracting the purses and allowing for his expenses, he possibly pocketed between a half to three-quarters of a million dollars.

Author Neal Thompson wrote that France took in $64,000 in ticket sales for 1948 and put $5,000 in the end of season point fund. Thompson did not indicate if the $64,000 figure was gross or net or if it included profits from the races' parking and concessions. Thompson cited NASCAR related sources for that figure.[38]

The $64,000 ticket sales figure, divided by fifty-two races, produced average ticket revenue of $1,231, which was much less than most of France's purses. Newspaper accounts of those modified races clearly indicated he was paying purses from $2,000 to $3,600. Consequently, his gross ticket sales had to total more than $64,000.

Figures compiled by the auto editors of *Consumer Guide* also disputed the $64,000 figure. According to their tallies, the amount of the purses France paid to the top fifty modified NASCAR drivers in 1948 was $90,890.[39]

Ed Hinton, in his book *Daytona, From the Birth of Speed to the Death of the Man in Black,* recalled that sportscaster Chris Economaki told him about stopping by France's bungalow after one of the early beach-road races. France, usually cordial and hospitable, did not invite Economaki inside. "On this evening he was very nice but he stood in the doorway with the door opened only a couple of feet," Economaki was quoted as saying. "I got a glimpse inside. There were stacks of money—cash—everywhere on the floor. And in the middle of all that money sat Annie B. [France] counting."[40]

In his biography of Curtis Turner, Robert Edelstein described how France and Turner jointly promoted races. He said Ann Turner's job at those races was to collect the money from the ticket sellers and turn it over to Annie France, who made sure the money and the ticket stubs came out equal. The next day France and Turner would also count the money and take it to the bank.[41]

With all the NASCAR receipts being in cash, probably only one person knew exactly how much money they were making, Annie France. Ed Hinton, in an ESPN article, wrote that Annie France kept two sets of books: one containing the real numbers and the other she showed her husband, "who was a profligate spender."[42] Hinton quoted their granddaughter, Lesa France Kennedy, CEO of International Speedways Corporation, "There was the real set and then she had one she would show my grandfather."[43]

Drivers had no access to either set of books but they saw France wheeling and dealing, buying into race tracks and flying around the country, and they naturally wondered why the race purses were not increasing. Bill France kept a hectic pace to schedule modified races, at an average of one a week in 1948, plus other divisions. Where was all the money going from the 1948 modified races, as well as the 248 other events France promoted that year under the NASCAR banner? That was what Marshall Teague and other drivers wanted to know.

8

Dollar Signs Everywhere

•••••••

After promoting a schedule of fifty-two modified and 248 other races in the initial 1948 NASCAR season, France saw dollar signs everywhere he looked. In addition to sanctioning NASCAR races, he placed his promotional businesses in Bill France Enterprises, Inc., in 1949.[1]

Bill France Enterprises evolved into Bill France Racing, Inc., in 1953. Bill France Racing, Inc., continued until 1957, when it became Daytona International Speedway Corporation. In 1968, that entity became International Speedway Corporation (ISC).[2]

France, after the organization's first season, reveled in the private ownership of NASCAR, which sanctioned the races and determined entry fees and purses, coupled with the control of race track promotions through Bill France Enterprises. This far-reaching idea was clearly set out in NASCAR's articles of incorporation in 1947. It was a brilliant concept that even today guides the vast fortunes of NASCAR and ISC.

France's 1949 racing season saw the evolution of NASCAR's top tier of racing change from Modifieds to Strictly Stock, that later became Grand National, which grew into the Cup series. However, he continued to stage the Modified, Roadster, Convertible, Sportsman races plus various other series.

Decades old modified coupes were not drawing the crowds who wanted to see the sleek post World War II cars that were coming off the assembly lines in Detroit. Promoters Lysle May and Johnny Wohlfiel staged one of the earlier races using the new stock automobiles at the Owosso Motor Speedway, in Owosso, Michigan on July 4, 1948. The Michigan race was sanctioned by the Central States Racing Association (CSRA). The CSRA appeared to agree with the AAA on vehicle standards for stock car racing. According to the local newspaper, "The 'stock car' label signifies exactly what the term states, cars of regular manufacture with no alterations or changes whatever in the mechanical construction. They run at only the maximum speeds for which they are constructed as they come off the assembly lines. Front and rear bumpers and bumper brackets must be removed."[3] Glen Northern set a track record in that race covering the half mile in 20.28 seconds. There was no indication as to the make of his car.[4]

The switch from Modifieds, mainly 1939–1941 models, to Strictly Stock cars increased car owners' cost considerably. Drivers and owners continued questioning the size of race purses France was awarding them. Other promoters, some of whom were raiding drivers from his plantation, were paying larger purses and drawing bigger crowds. France decided he needed to buy into or lease more tracks.

France opened the 1949 NASCAR racing season with a 200-mile Modified beach-road race over an expanded 4.3-mile course on January 16. France bragged about the new course, "With such long straightaways, the full 200 miles will be run in practically the same time that it required to run 150 miles over a shorter course. The boys can open up on those long straight runs as they don't have to slow down so often for turns." He predicted that new records would be set. Marshall Teague won the race with an average speed of 88.23 mph. Arthur B. "Speedy" Thompson, from Monroe, North Carolina, was second.[5]

Tommy Moon, from Jacksonville, Florida, was overcome by carbon monoxide fumes, a safety problem NASCAR managed to ignore for decades, and had to leave the race. An estimated 9,000 spectators watched the race. If France charged his usual $2.50 admission, his gate was around $22,500, plus parking, programs and concessions.[6]

After the beach-road race, it was discovered that Marshall Teague had an oversized gas tank. His thirty-six gallon tank was the reason he made no pit stops during the race and had twelve gallons of gas in his tank at the end of the race. France decreed, after the Broward race, that car owners, mechanics and drivers had to use only the tank manufacturers placed on the car.[7] From all indication, France neither fined nor penalized Teague.

A week after the beach-road race, France flirted with a Strictly Stock race at the Broward Speedway, a two-mile, round, paved track over what was part of the Fort Lauderdale–Davie Airport. He billed the fifty-mile race as a contest of mechanics between Red Vogt, from Atlanta, and Joe Wolfe, from Reading, Pennsylvania. France also threw in a ten-mile Sportsman's contest and a four-mile ancient models race.[8]

France staged another race at Broward Speedway in Fort Lauderdale. In February, he promoted at least two roadster and sports car races at Daytona Beach and Fort Lauderdale. France added a ten-mile Strictly Stock race at the Fort Lauderdale track. Benny Georgeson, from Fort Lauderdale, in a 1947 Buick, won the feature.[9] France was searching for larger facilities and increased crowd numbers.

Sam Nunis was pulling in crowds, estimated at 35,000, at the Reading, Pennsylvania, track with his AAA sanctioned "big car" races. Nunis was also doing something that France would not do for decades. In 1949, Nunis met with television representatives to discuss selling them the rights to televise the races he promoted.[10]

Alfred Knight, in Chattanooga, Tennessee, and other promoters were successfully staging NSCRA races in the South.[11]

NSCRA was an interesting collection of 250 individuals, some of whom had nothing to do with stock car racing. The president of NSCRA was Delmar Jones, who headed the Georgia Bureau of Investigation and was noted for his expertise in catching escaped convicts. Association members involved in racing included Weyman Miller, who promoted races in Macon and Atlanta; Harold Hill, a Columbus, Georgia, promoter; Gene Wilson, a Chattanooga, Tennessee, promoter, and a young, energetic promoter from Oakboro, North Carolina, Ollen Bruton Smith.[12]

NSCRA attracted some of France's drivers, including Jack Smith, Ed Samples, Gober Sosebee, Bob Flock, Billy Carden, Buddy Shuman, Red Byron, Curtis Turner and Speedy Thompson.[13]

Joe Littlejohn promoted a March 19, 1949, race for his Hub City Speedways at the Piedmont-Interstate half-mile track, before an expected crowd of 10,000. Littlejohn ticket prices were lower than France's: general admission $1.25 and grandstand $1.75, but the purse,

$1,800, was also less. Drivers expected included Marshall Teague, Ed Samples, Buddy Shuman, Buck Baker, Bill Snowden, Bob and Fonty Flock, Cotton Owens, Red Byron and Jack Etheridge, all from France's plantation.[14] Littlejohn had no objections to the drivers racing in events he promoted as well as in NASCAR.

Regardless of the competition, France was making money and saw a chance make even more as an Indy car owner. He wanted to enter a car in the 1949 Indianapolis 500. He contacted Joe Wolfe, from Reading, Pennsylvania, who had built the car Fonty Flock was having so much success with at Winston-Salem and Fort Lauderdale tracks and the Daytona beach-road races. Wolfe said France asked him to assemble an engine and build a car for Flock to drive in the 500-mile race. The lease on his garage in Reading had expired and Wolfe only had ninety days to find a new location. He was unable to accommodate France.[15]

The Indianapolis 500 was sanctioned by the AAA, which earlier refused to have anything to do with France and his brand of stock car racing.

France discovered an old plan for NASCAR to make new money. He resumed the measured mile runs on Daytona Beach. In one test, the new Hudson Commodore reached 95.605 mph. "This was the first supervised one mile straightaway stock car time held in the United States in recent years," France bragged. He added that NASCAR was available to supervise similar time trials.[16] "Now that we have the city's expensive electric timer back here—it was recently recovered from Bonneville Flats where AAA officials were using it—we have the only such racing timer clock in the United States," he added.[17]

France and Alvin Hawkins leased the track at the municipally-owned Bowman Gray Stadium in Winston-Salem. They held weekly, sometimes semi-weekly, races at the quarter mile paved track around the football field used by the Winston-Salem State University football team.[18] The Bowman Gray grandstands seated 17,000. If France and Hawkins sold all their tickets at $2.50, they had gross gates of $42,500, per race.[19]

NASCAR drivers defecting to other racing organizations continued to trouble France. In October 1948, Red Byron left to win a NSCRA race at the old Charlotte Speedway. In fact, Ed Samples was the 1949 NSCRA champion.[20] In March 1949, Teague and Billy Carden drove in Joe Littlejohn's Hub City Speedway race at the Piedmont-Interstate Fairgrounds.[21]

Teague was not the only driver asking questions about the increasing difference between the gate revenue and race purses. He was joined by former whiskey transporters Ed Samples, from Dawsonville, and Buddy Shuman, from Charlotte, and brothers James and Alfred "Speedy" Thompson, from Monroe, North Carolina, in asking France to end the practice of a specifically stated purse amount and pay forty percent of the gate to the drivers as the AAA and other racing promoters did. France refused.[22]

Shuman, the 1948 NSCRA champion, took his case for increasing NASCAR purses public through a Charlotte newspaper.[23] Shuman pointed out that drivers, at a recent race not sanctioned by NASCAR, were paid forty percent of the ticket sales at Midland Speedway, about $2,700, while France promoted an event at the same speedway with a $2,000 purse. Other drivers began to follow Shuman. A racing publication editorialized that paying drivers a purse of forty percent of the paid admissions appeared to be a good idea.[24]

William Tuthill, NASCAR secretary, attempted to defuse the situation by telling the drivers and media that he and France were not lining their own pockets. His denial indicated the drivers made that accusation. Author Neal Thompson wrote that France "felt that he had sacrificed his own racing career to take on the leadership role that none of the others wanted. As he saw it, he had done all the spadework. So if he got rich in the process, well, he deserved it." Tuthill said if he and France started a successful organization, then they deserved their money.[25]

Some did not think France's racing career was so stellar. "Then, when I seen him drive in a race at Langhorne, I gave him a one star rating on a scale of one to five," Smokey Yunick wrote.[26]

Certainly, there was no lack of capable men to lead stock car racing. There were Raymond Parks, Joe Littlejohn, Walter "Bud" Moore, Glen and Leonard Wood, Everett "Cotton" Owens, Bruton Smith and Sam Nunis to name a few, who were more than competent to lead NASCAR. Ossinsky's incorporation documents clearly set up Bill France as the sole head of the organization. Parks was exactly right when he said they suddenly discovered that NASCAR belonged only to Bill France.

France, according to Thompson, told the drivers, when they asked for higher purses, that NASCAR racing was supposed to be only a weekend hobby. He informed them that forty percent of the gate was too much money to put into purses.[27] France's 1948 Modified and other races, estimated to be 300 reaching from Florida and Georgia to Pennsylvania and New Jersey, were scheduled during the week as well as over the weekends.[28] For drivers, who had other jobs, it was impossible for them to make all of the races held during the week. France looked at all those dollar signs and decided it was time to keep the drivers on his racing plantation.

France sent the complaining drivers telegraphs saying, "Drivers who fail to race exclusive for NASCAR will be barred ... for a period of one year." Independent and defiant, Shuman, Teague, Curtis Turner and Bob Flock signed up for an NSCRA race at North Wilkesboro.[29]

France, however, was not finished with his errant drivers. He charged that Shuman, Samples and Speedy Thompson had scattered thumbtacks on a track before some previous NASCAR race. He banned those three along with Teague and Jimmy Thompson from NASCAR for a year. France was sure he could lure these drivers back with larger race purses.[30] In addition, France intended to charge them hefty fines for reinstatement. France appeared to give Turner a wide berth in the infractions accusations.

Bruton Smith, and his mentor, Sam Nunis, announced in early 1949 that NSCRA would hold a strictly stock race for post World War II cars at the Lakewood Speedway in Atlanta. A municipally owned one mile dirt track facility, Lakewood had drawn as many as 35,000 for automobile racing events. The stock car race was set for June 19, 1949.[31]

France immediately announced that Bill France Enterprises would also be staging a race for thirty-three Strictly Stock cars, on the same date on a three-quarter mile dirt track, the Charlotte Speedway, built two years earlier by the infamous moonshining and bootlegging Harvey brothers, Pat and Charles. France announced that the purse would be $5,000, with $2,000 going to the winner and $1,000 to second place. That was $2,500 to $3,000 more than his usual race purses.[32]

Smith countered by simply dialing his Lakewood race day back a week to June 12, which enabled some of France's star drivers to compete. The race drew a crowd of 15,000. Ed Samples won the feature event followed by Jack Smith, Red Byron, Billy Carden and Bob Flock.[33]

The Lakewood and Charlotte races were pivotal points in the evolution of southern stock car racing. Smith's success at Lakewood indicated there was room for more than one successful southern promoter in the sport. France discovered racing fans were more likely to part with their hard-earned cash to see cars similar to those they drove in a race, especially if the cars were driven by the infamous moonshiners, bootleggers and trippers. A successful race would help keep his drivers in check and away from other promoters' races. The race also led to a lawsuit resulting in the first of many favorable court decisions for France and NASCAR. Those events helped cement France's efforts to keep drivers on his plantation and the race purses small.

France took no chances with the Charlotte race. He was the supervisor in charge; flying about promoting the race. He announced the field would be composed of the thirty-three fastest stock cars and advertised the race in the *National Speed Sport News*. On race day, crowds clogged the single lane road to the speedway. Some parked miles away and walked to the track. They all wanted to see the new Buicks, Lincolns, Hudsons, Fords, Olds, Cadillacs, Chryslers and Kaisers and their drivers.[34]

All five of the drivers France had banned for a year—Shuman, Samples, Teague and the Thompson brothers—asked to be reinstated. France required them to appear individually before a panel made up of NASCAR commissioner "Cannonball" Baker, the former motorcycle racer, William Tuthill, NASCAR secretary, and France's attorney, Louis Ossinsky. France, of course, was in the hearing room at the Selwyn Hotel. The panel exonerated Speedy Thompson due to lack of evidence that he dumped tacks on the track during an earlier race. The other four could return to NASCAR racing only if they paid fines ranging from $50 to $150, and would be on probation for a year.[35]

The Thompson brothers sued NASCAR but the judge refused to hear their case. Daniel Pierce wrote in his book *Real NASCAR: White Lightning, Red Clay and Big Bill France* that the reason France suspended Shuman, Samples and the Thompson brothers was they signed forms to drive in a NASCAR race and did not show up.[36]

Teague, in three years of NASCAR racing, had earned $10,060 and he was tired of Bill France's miserly purses. He moved to the AAA stock car circuit in 1952. In three years of AAA racing, where the purses were forty percent of the gate, he earned $27,512. By 1953, Teague had bettered eighteen of the twenty-nine AAA track records and nine of eleven national records, and started in the eighth row of the Indianapolis 500. After the AAA left stock car racing in 1955, Teague turned to USAC where, in two years, he earned $16,102.[37]

France was just as inconsistent in holding his drivers to a rigid standard of only driving in NASCAR races as he was with his ever-shifting interpretation of the rules. On June 6, 1949, France staged Frank Mundy Day at his race in Winston-Salem. Mundy, while driving in NASCAR races, was also a ramp-to-ramp driver in Jack Kochman's Thrill Shows and competed in the NSCRA events.[38]

Bob Flock and Red Byron drove in Bruton Smith's races and France allowed them to drive in his first Strictly Stock race on June 19, 1949. Bob Flock sat on the pole for the Charlotte race. Other drivers qualifying included Tim and Fonty Flock, Buck Baker, Curtis Turner, Red Byron, Herb Thomas, Lee Petty, Sarah Christian, Jim Smith and Jim Paschal.[39]

The Charlotte race did something else that would haunt NASCAR for the decades the Frances spent attempting to refute the sport's relationship with illegal whiskey transporting. Most of the drivers and car owners in the race had, at one time or another, connections to either the distilling, selling or transporting of illegal whiskey. Many of the cars in the race were trippers' vehicles.

The race allegedly had three leaders but the track was so dusty it was difficult, not only for the spectators, but the officials to determine who was leading. Bob Flock, in his Hudson, led the first five laps. Bill Blair, in a Lincoln, led laps six through 150. Glenn Dunaway, in a Ford, led the remaining laps and finished three laps ahead of the second car, a Lincoln driven by Jim Roper, from Great Bend, Kansas.[40]

Perhaps it was Dunaway's margin of victory that resulted in NASCAR's chief technical inspector Al Crisler's careful examination of Hubert Westmoreland's winning car. Westmoreland had used the car to transport whiskey. Crisler found a wedge in the rear springs, used to balance the car when it was carrying heavy loads of moonshine. Tuthill nervously hovered around Crisler during his inspection, while reporting back to France in his Charlotte hotel room by telephone. Crisler said it was possible that Roper's Lincoln was the only car in the race that had not been illegally modified. Were all cars or even the top five examined? No. France disqualified Dunaway's win, placed Roper in first and had to contend with Westmoreland's $10,000 lawsuit.[41] It was almost a foregone conclusion that Westmoreland would lose his lawsuit since NASCAR rules clearly stated such modifications were not acceptable. Greensboro, North Carolina, Judge John J. Hays decided in France's favor.[42]

Some sources said there were approximately 13,000 spectators at the Charlotte race who paid from $2.50 to $4 for their tickets. Newspapers in Virginia and Missouri quoted a NASCAR official as estimating the Charlotte crowd at 22,500. If $3.25 was the average ticket price and the 22,500 figure was approximately correct, then France's gate was around $73,125. "But, France, who was mindful that drivers and the tax man were watching, quickly readjusted it [the crowd figure] to 13,000," the *Daily Press* reported.[43]

For some reason, the *Daytona Beach Morning Journal* was still attempting to correct the attendance at that Charlotte race fourteen years later. France was carefully protected through the efforts of the newspaper's sports editor, Bernard Kahn, and editorial writer Eddie Pappis. Pappis moonlighted for Houston Lawing, a former Greensboro, North Carolina, sports editor, who had headed France's public relations efforts since 1947. In describing the first Strictly Stock race in Charlotte, the *Daytona Beach Morning-Journal* article said, "Bill France Enterprises promoted it. The purse was $5,000. France said they had about 13,000 paying customers not the variously reported 19,000 to 20,000."[44]

Using the smaller figure of 13,000 paying spectators, times the average ticket price of $3.25, France's gate would have been approximately $42,250. Either way, after deducting the purse, track rental, race personnel, insurance and sundry other expenses, France made a lot of money that day.

He lost no time in scheduling another Strictly Stock race for July 10, at the Daytona beach-road course over 166 miles. A much smaller crowd, around 5,000, turned out for the race that Red Byron won by passing Gober Sosebee, who lost a tire with six laps remaining. Tim Flock was second and his sister, Ethel Mobeley, finished seventh ahead of their brothers, Bob and Fonty.[45]

On August 7, 1949, France replaced the scheduled modified race at Occoneechee Speedway in Hillsborough, North Carolina, with a 200-mile stock car event. Over 17,000 spectators watched a wreck take out Red Byron, Bob Smith, Felix Wilkes and Sara Christian while Bob Flock won the race in a 1948 Olds. Gober Sosebee, in a 1949 Olds, was second and Glenn Dunaway was third, this time in a 1949 Olds.[46]

A grandstand was built at Occoneechee, whose name was changed to Orange Speedway. Sidney Cruze, in a 2004 *Carolina Country* article, described the grandstands as being filled

8. Dollar Signs Everywhere

Gene Hobby of Henderson, North Carolina, with his pristine 1964 Dodge at the March 14, 1965, race at the Occoneechee Speedway. After flipping five times on the front stretch, Hobby's M. E. Whitmore Dodge was out of action (courtesy Historic Speedway Group).

with 17,000 screaming fans while other climbed trees across the Eno River to watch the race. People also watched from a hillside fenced from the track. France's purse for the race was again $5,000. Since France had graduated his previous admission prices from $2.50 to $4, it was safe to use the medium figure of $3.25. The gate for the Occoneechee race was in the neighborhood of $55,250, plus concessions, programs and parking. Subtract the race purse, insurance, promotion and race personnel costs and France and his partners probably split just under $50,000.[47]

France's take grew even larger on September 11, 1949, at the Langhorne (Pennsylvania) Speedway, where 20,000 spectators turned out for his fourth Strictly Stock race. Using the same average ticket price, $3.25, France's gate was approximately $65,000. The race purse was $6,000, less than ten percent of the estimated gate.[48]

By this time France had a well-oiled NASCAR public relations machine, led by Houston Lawing. A Missouri newspaper printed a September 22, 1949, news release. "NASCAR now pays more than $500,000 a year in prize money. In each sanctioned event, $50 of each $1,000 in prize money is held in escrow. The top 20 [drivers] at the end of the year receive this as a bonus. The number one driver gets twenty-five percent. Last year, Red Byron pulled down $10,000 from this pot, won $15,000 additional for a $25,000 take."[49]

Lawing's news release not only raised a number of questions, but left out some essential elements. First, Byron kept only a portion of his winnings; the remainder went to his car owner, Raymond Parks. Second, Byron's 1948 NASCAR Modified earnings were $13,150. His bonus for winning the championship was $1,250 for a total of $14,400, considerably below the $25,000 figure Lawing cited.[50] If Byron had additional earnings from sponsors, that money did not come from NASCAR.

The more important question was the amount of purse money put in escrow for the end of season awards.

NASCAR's sanction application that track officials filled out and returned described the location, size of the track, type of surface, seating capacity, proposed race date, time trial dates, specific rain date, race distance, starting time, hours for time trials, amount of public liability insurance and agent's name. There were lines for purse and points fund totals, for sanction and official fees and a total for all those lines.[51]

Tracks agreed to specify "NASCAR Sanctioned" in all advertising. The first thing the representative NASCAR appointed to be in charge of the race did was to collect the purse, points fund money, sanction and officials fees and provide the track owner with a receipt. NASCAR agreed to provide benefit coverage for all competitors, print and distribute entry blanks, provide a scoring system, inspectors and other necessary officials, distribute the prize money and "conduct the above contest in accordance with NASCAR rules."[52]

Regardless of how much money promoters gave France to put in such an escrow account, the amount actually awarded drivers at the end of the seasons was entirely up to him, according to NASCAR incorporation documents. Subsection Four, Part Two of the incorporation document read, "To hold or arrange auto races and other matches and competitions and offer and grant, or contribute toward the provision of prizes, awards and distinctions."[53]

France's race purses lessened in the next Strictly Stock races. Most of the point contenders did not enter his race in Hamburg, New York, on September 18. Jack White, from Lockport, New York, won the race in a Lincoln and collected $1,500 for first place.[54]

From New York, the Strictly Stock series shifted to H. Clay Earles' half-mile Martinsville (Virginia) track on September 25. Despite Earles tamping down the track with chemicals and oils and watering the dirt before the race, he said there was a cloud of red dust ten feet high after the competition began. Red Byron made his way through the dust to beat Lee Petty by three laps to win first place money of $1,500.[55]

A week later, France had his gaggle of drivers at the three-quarter-mile Heidelberg Speedway, near Pittsburgh. Lee Petty drove his Plymouth to a win over Dick Linder, from Pittsburgh, in a Kaiser.[56] The 1949 Strictly Stock season closed out with an October 16 race at North Wilkesboro, where Bob Flock, in an Olds, came in first.[57]

For his first Strictly Stock season, France paid out $39,630 in purses to the top fifty drivers, an average of $4,403 per race.[58] For whatever reasons, the purses appeared to decline toward the end of the season. Regardless, Bill France Racing probably grossed far over $500,000 that year from just the nine Strictly Stock races, plus parking, programs, concessions and the income from the Modified, Sportsman, Roadster and Convertible divisions.

Red Byron's points of 842.5 and earnings of $5,800 won him the top driver award over Lee Petty's 725 points and $3,855. Also in the top five were Bob Flock, third, with 704 in points and $4,870, in earnings; Bill Blair, 567 points and $1,180, and Fonty Flock with 554 points and $2,015. Fonty Flock was also the 1949 Modified champion.[59]

After the North Wilkesboro race, France went after the really big money and joined Sam Nunis in promoting a 150-mile Strictly Stock race at the Lakewood Speedway outside of Atlanta. The race attracted 33,452 spectators and France was convinced that stocks were in NASCAR's future.[60]

It was possible that Nunis and France grossed approximately $117,000 from the race. France decided to change the name of the Strictly Stock series to Grand National for the 1950 season. Grand National is best known in the sporting world as the National Hunt Horse Race first held in 1839 at the Aintree Racecourse in Liverpool, England.[61]

9

Drivers' Revolving Door

• • • • • • •

Marshall Teague drove in few 1950 Grand National races. By the end of that season, not only his name but also those of competitors Buddy Shuman, Ed Samples and Red Byron were missing from the end of the season standings of the top fifty drivers. According to Bernard Kahn, sports editor of one of the Daytona newspapers, NASCAR also reorganized itself in 1950, arranged insurance for drivers and sanctioned 395 races.[1]

Teague's relationship with Bill France was, when he entered the February 1950 Daytona beach-road race, rather tenuous. Teague was still questioning the small purses as the gate continued to grow. France predicted that Teague's 1949 beach-road record of 88.23 mph would be broken and he was right. Harold Kite, a former U.S. Army tank driver from Marietta, Georgia, won the race in a Lincoln with an average speed of 89.894 mph.[2]

France's traveling crew of stock car racing officials was ready for a new season. It included one of his speedway partners, Alvin Hawkins. Hawkins and Joe Epton, both from Spartanburg, were starters. Two former bootleggers and race track owners, Enoch Staley and Charlie Coombs, from North Wilkesboro, were pit stewards. Al Crisler, Henry Underhill and Bill Middlebrook, all from Charlotte, were inspectors. Epton spent decades as the series' traveling race timer-scorer.[3]

The Grand National schedule continued with April races at Charlotte, won by Tim Flock, and in Langhorne, Pennsylvania, by Curtis Turner. Marshall Teague, meanwhile, was racing on quarter-mile tracks, like the one in Daytona Beach, promoted by W. R. Creeden at Memorial Stadium.[4]

After the Pennsylvania race, there was a month's gap in the Grand National schedule. France stirred up interest in the Carrera Panamericana, a 2,135-mile road race over what was supposed to be Mexico's newly completed portion of the Pan American Highway.[5] Sections of the road were more reminiscent of some of the trails traveled during the Peking to Paris race in 1907, instead of a transcontinental highway built more than four decades later. It was unclear if France knew anything about the race other than seeing it as a promotional opportunity for NASCAR, and the $17,000 winner's purse was most attractive. He pushed the idea among his owners and drivers.

Both large and small cars of all descriptions, from Grand Prix racers to slope-backed American sedans, competed in the first Mexican road race. In subsequent races, cars were divided into three and four different classes.[6]

The Mexican government provided $28,900 for the race promoted by Mexico City Pontiac dealer Antonio Cornejo. While not officially sanctioning the race, the AAA assisted the promoter with public relations and sent copies of the rules and entry blanks to 600 of their registered race car owners, drivers and mechanics.[7]

Raymond Parks outfitted a 1949 Lincoln coupe for Red Byron and himself. Bob and Fonty Flock borrowed a Lincoln from an Atlanta dealer. France arranged with a Nash dealer in El Paso, Texas, for a car. France and Curtis Turner flew to El Paso in France's plane. They joined the 132 other two-man teams from twelve countries.[8]

The Flock brothers cracked their engine block halfway through the race. An hour from the finish, Byron collapsed over the steering wheel and he and Parks were lucky to escape with their lives when the car crashed.[9]

As the race progressed, France became increasingly wary of Turner's driving methods. In his biography of Turner, Robert Edelstein provided the following account of what happened when they came upon a sharp turn with no room to spare to avoid plunging into a 500-foot chasm below. "Turner slams on the brakes and throws the car into a broadside, heading to the right. The Nash spins around, treading backwards, with the passenger side (where France was sitting) heading toward the precipice. Turner slams the brakes again and turns the wheel, trying to hug the car against the cliff side. The tires spin and dirt flies but in a moment, the Nash comes to a quick halt, with three tires on level ground."[10]

Edelstein described how France grabbed onto Turner using the driver's body to haul himself out of the car and hitting the dirt with a thud. Glaring at Turner, France said, "I have a wife and kids at home and I'd like to *see* them again." With France out of the car, Turner managed to get all four tires back on the road. Later, when France was driving, he decided to take a short cut off the course, crashed and punched a hole in the radiator. The night before the last leg of the race, France and Turner met another Nash driver, Roy Pat Connor, a Corsicana, Texas, automobile dealer, who was also tired of the race.[11]

Turner took over Connor's car with his co-driver, Robert Owens. Connor and France headed back to Texas. Turner managed to pass the leader, Piero Trauffi, in an Alfa Romeo on the last part of the race and blew a tire. Trauffi passed them and Turner and Owens finished third, for a while. Seems Turner had neglected to change ownership of the car from Connor's name into his name. At that, he and Owens fared better than many of the teams. Only fifty-two teams made it to the finish and six drivers were killed.[12]

Hershel McGriff, from Bridal Veil, Oregon, won the race in an Oldsmobile with an average speed of 74.421. McGriff, who raced in NASCAR on and off for four decades, said he paid about $1,900 for the Olds and took home first prize of $17,000.[13]

It must have been almost mundane for the Flocks, Byron, Parks, Turner and France to return to the Grand National schedule at Martinsville, where Turner won in an Olds. Meanwhile, Teague and Byron raced in NSCRA. Samples and Shuman raced in NSCRA, USAC, midgets and on short tracks.

It was Curtis Turner the stock car racing fans flocked to see. Bill France was too good a promoter not to utilize Turner's talents to the maximum. As Turner's popularity grew, France appeared to withdraw from the driver. It was as if he sensed possible competition in the charismatic Turner, who was also a successful timber broker.

Curtis Turner's six-foot, two-inch tall frame contained a trim 200 pounds with curly dark hair, blue-gray eyes, an infectious, naughty smile, a calculator for a brain and the firm conviction that he could accomplish anything he attempted. He was NASCAR's first legendary driver, the first stock car racer to be on the cover of *Sports Illustrated*. It was not the fact that he won more than 350 races; it was the fact that he did it easily, so convincingly, even recklessly, while engaging spectators' rabid support. If he failed to win, fans still wanted to see him race because as Smokey Yunick put it, "He drove southern style, belly to the ground, ears and tail straight back." In gauging his impact on the sport, Yunick said, "There would have never been a Dale Earnhardt without Curtis Turner." Asked what made Turner a legend, actor James Garner, a friend of Turner's, replied, "He knew he was a legend and therefore, he lived it."[14]

France's long-time director of public relations, Houston Lawing, recognized what Turner meant to stock car racing. "Woe to the promoter who advertises that Curtis Turner is going to drive in a race and fails to produce Turner," he said in a 1957 interview. "The fans can get real nasty when that happens. Especially, if it is Turner. Although Turner never won a season title until he took the Convertible Division last year, he is the best drawing card we've ever had and has been for a long time."[15]

Although France still had Turner, the Flocks and a newcomer, Glenn "Fireball" Roberts, he was short about half of his southern stars. Roberts' nickname, Fireball, came not from racing but his fastball pitches for the University of Florida baseball team. The shortage of southern drivers might have been the reason that nine of the nineteen 1950 Grand National Races were held in New York, Pennsylvania and Ohio that year.[16]

Or, France may have used those races to line up tracks for future races and to attract more drivers. Regardless, when September arrived, France had bigger problems. Sam Nunis announced he would be promoting a 500-mile stock car race at Atlanta's Lakewood Speedway for the 1950 Labor Day event. Nunis was accustomed to crowds of 25,000 to 30,000 at races he promoted for AAA.[17]

Reacting to Nunis' announcement, France began searching fast and furiously for a facility for a 500-mile stock car race. He doubted that stock cars were durable enough to last that distance but if Nunis could stage such a race so could he. Bowman Gray, Lakeview, Charlotte, Martinsville and Occoneechee were out for one reason or another: too small, too isolated or too dusty. Nunis had a fifteen-year lease on Lakewood. For some reason, the only facility he might have used, Daytona's beach-road course, apparently was not considered.

France discovered somebody in South Carolina was building, of all things, a paved race track. Harold Brasington, a Darlington, South Carolina, earth moving contractor, began construction on a 1.25 mile, banked, asphalt speedway on seventy acres of farm land in 1949. As the story goes, Brasington, at their weekly poker game, remarked to Sherman Ramsey that they ought to build a race track on the land Ramsey owned on Hartsville Road. Brasington, who had raced on the beach in the 1930s, wanted to not only pave his track but bank it like some of the New England board tracks he had seen.[18]

Brasington had been nursing an idea of building a track at Darlington after attending the 1933 Indianapolis 500, but could never raise enough money. He told sports columnist Mac MacLeod he never considered that Darlington had only a quarter of the population of Indianapolis. "I never thought of it that way," Brasington said, "I just thought if people would go up there to watch a race, why wouldn't they come here to watch a race?" When the earth moving contractor had raised $25,000, he convinced Sherman Ramsey to trade land for stock in the company.[19]

"I got a road grader and bulldozer and went to work," Brasington recalled. "Sherman went to Florida and while he was there had a change of mind about the race track but when he got back I had already moved enough earth that he couldn't change his mind. He told me that what I started, he wouldn't make me tear down but I couldn't use any more of his property. That's one reason the track is shaped the way it is, bigger in turns three and four than it is in one and two."[20]

Brasington found other investors and continued building the track. He asked Paul Pacillos, who owned the local concrete business, to design turns so that the straightaways would blend in with the high bank.[21]

Construction began in the fall of 1949 with Brasington and his crews working nights and weekends to meet his goal of holding a 500-mile race on Labor Day in 1950. He originally intended to build a true oval track but Sherman's refusal of providing any more land turned the track into an egg-shaped configuration. The banking on the turns was twenty-three to twenty-five degrees and on the straightaways it was eight degrees. The front and back stretches were 1,229 feet.[22]

By May, when the Grand National cars were racing in Canfield, Ohio, media reports indicated work was progressing well on the new paved race track in Darlington: 250 entries were expected for the Labor Day race; the steel and concrete grandstands would seat 14,000, and the infield could accommodate 30,000.[23]

Brasington, in his haste to build the track, lacked an organization to sanction or promote the race. When he approached the AAA in its Washington, D.C., office, about sanctioning the stock car race in South Carolina, Brasington said the officials laughed at his proposal. He signed a contract in 1949 with Central States Racing Association (CSRA) and Norman Witte to promote the Labor Day race.[24]

CSRA, a Midwest sanctioning body, had problems attracting drivers for a South Carolina race. Brasington, having sold $25,000 in tickets, was desperate. He asked France for help. Sports columnist Ed Hinton wrote that France agreed to promote the race if CSRA would agree to co-sanctioning billing. Witte was demoted to the race publicity post and ended up sharing that with France's director of public relations, Houston Lawing.[25]

France not only arranged the qualified cars three abreast, like Indianapolis, as Brasington requested, but spent two weeks holding qualification laps of ten miles.[26] The higher number of qualifying races a promoter staged, the more money he made, and the more chances drivers would wreck their cars.

Some of the drivers shared France's apprehensions of a 500-mile race. However, France dug into his bank account to post a purse of $25,000, with $10,510, plus lap money, going to the winner. The driver entries poured in to the track. Buck Baker did not know what it would take to race 500 miles. "A lot of us rigged containers of something to drink," Baker said. "One guy took beer. After only a few laps of racing on that banking, with the car jerking and pitching around violently, that beer foamed up. The car had so much foam pouring out of it that it looked like a washing machine was overflowing inside it."[27]

"I decided to take a jug of tomato juice—figured it would keep me hydrated and give me a little energy," Baker continued. "Well, then I wrecked. The tomato juice spilled all over me and I was slumped over in the seat. When the emergency crew got there, one of them looked inside and hollered to the others, 'There ain't no way of helpin' this 'un! Po sumbitch has done got his head cut off.'"[28]

By Sunday, September 3, the invasion of approximately 30,000 racing fans into the small county of Darlington, population 50,916, began. South Carolina law prohibited the selling of race tickets on Sunday. Darlington, situated along the Pee Dee River, had only one motel, with twelve rooms. People slept in their cars, on the hoods of vehicles parked along city streets, on the grass and even on the steps of the chamber of commerce building. Some of the residents put up cots in their front rooms and rented them out. France opened the track and allowed fans to sleep in the infield. At first light, he chased them out.[29]

Nights in the Darlington infield had little to do with the race. "You look around and some people are preaching and some are shooting craps," Brasington said. "People can let their hair down and get the good times rolling."[30]

Some of those good times included drunken binges, fights, knifings, rock music competing with country along with hidden pleasures. According to Darlington lore, local madams brought hearses into the infield to provide privacy for their clients. There was the story of a wife who became angry because her husband visited his girlfriend in the infield. To embarrass him, she fired up his motorcycle, zoomed past the gate guards and onto the track. The husband, along with the guards, began chasing her. Hundreds of wide-eyed admirers cheered the woman as she roared past them on her husband's motorcycle naked.[31]

The 30,000 fans, for the first Southern 500, paid an average of $5 for each ticket. Track officials took in so much money, an estimated $150,000 from tickets alone, that they ran out of envelopes and brought in peach baskets to hold the money, according to Harold King, a Darlington native who helped count the baskets of money.[32]

While he expected a crowd, Brasington said he had no idea that that many people would show up for the race. "We found money in paper sacks months after the race was over," he said.[33]

King recalled that first Southern 500 as being a demolition derby. He said the starting grid of seventy-five cars—led by Curtis Turner on the pole, with Jimmy Thompson and Gober Sosebee filling out the front row—covered about three-quarters of the track.[34]

Marshall Teague, along with Herb Thomas, was responsible for Pure Oil's involvement in providing fuel for the first Darlington race. Teague carried the company's logo on his race car. Dick Dolan, manager for automotive events for the oil company, recalled that Teague and Thomas persuaded Pure Oil to bring in a tanker truck to provide fuel for the race.[35]

Tire companies had no tires specifically designed for the asphalt track and they were wearing out after twenty to twenty-five laps on the Darlington asphalt. King said race crews went into the crowds buying spare tires from cars in the parking lots. Raymond Parks even took the tires off his personal Cadillac to help his driver, Red Byron, whose car had about thirty blowouts.[36]

Rubber was the story of the day at the first Darlington race and overshadowed the maneuvering of France, Curtis Turner, Alvin Hawkins and Hubert Westmoreland, the bootlegger whose car France disqualified in the first Strictly Stock race in Charlotte the previous year. The Nash that Turner and France drove in the Mexico road race was entered, probably by France. The car was driven by Ebenezer "Slick" Smith, from Atlanta, who finished twentieth out of the twenty-six cars still running at the end of the race. A photograph of the Nash from the Darlington race showed this lettering on the side, "Driven by Bill France and Curtis Turner in the Carrera Panamericana."[37]

Aside from France's co-sanctioning and promoting the race, Hawkins being the starter

Stock car racing's first national superstar, Curtis Turner, right, is shown with driver Jack Smith at the 1952 beach-road race at Daytona. Turner, a successful Roanoke, Virginia, timber broker, began driving as a youngster transporting his father's illegal whiskey. Bill France banned him from NASCAR in 1961 for attempting to unionize drivers in order to have input in scheduling, driver benefits and increased purses. France was forced, by track owners, to lift the ban four years later and reinstate the popular driver (State Archives of Florida).

and Turner driving another car in the Darlington race, they were also co-owners, along with Westmoreland, of a competing car driven by Johnny Mantz, from Long Beach, California. Mantz qualified thirty-fifth in a six-cylinder Plymouth owned by the group. France met Mantz in Mexico and invited him to drive in the NASCAR series. Neal Thompson wrote that in later years France and his cadre of co-owners and race officials stuck to their story that Mantz and his mechanic did not take the Plymouth's engine apart but just tuned it up as it came off the showroom floor.[38]

Thompson differed, "But after qualifying, Mantz and Westmoreland took the Plymouth to Westmoreland's garage in North Carolina and began souping it up." The race lasted six and a half hours and Mantz's Plymouth came in first, leaving his nearest competitors, Byron and Fireball Roberts, eleven miles behind. Other car owners and drivers, incredulous that a car with a six-cylinder engine had beaten the more powerful eight-cylinder cars, demanded that chief NASCAR inspector Al Crisler tear down the winning car's engine while they

Herb Thomas, at the Occoneechee Speedway in Hillsborough, North Carolina. The track, originally constructed for horse racing, was built in a bend of the Eno River. Thomas, from Olivia, North Carolina, won the October 1951 Occoneechee race in his number 92 Fabulous Hudson (Bill King Collection, Historic Speedway Group).

watched. France, being one of the car's owners, could hardly deny the examination and kept in contact by telephone from his hotel room. The fact that no illegal parts were supposedly found could have been the result of a bootlegger's ingenious mechanical ability or Crisler's inadequate examination. The Plymouth's winning strategy was attributed to the hard rubber tires Mantz brought with him from California, which were not illegal in the NASCAR rule book.[39]

Mantz got the first place money of $10,510, but the car owners, France, Hawkins, Turner and Westmoreland, received the majority of the purse. Roberts received $3,500 for second and Byron $2,000 for third.[40]

What Brasington built at Darlington was not just a track in humid, sultry South Carolina but something unique in all of stock car racing. Bigger, more elongated tracks, whose grandstands would hold more spectators, would be built but none had the mystique, the quirkiness, of Darlington. South Carolina Senator Strom Thurmond, on the fiftieth anniversary of the track, described the Darlington experience from the floor of the United States Senate. "These cars rumble past at well over 100 mph with only inches between their bumpers and as they go through the turns the earth literally shakes under one's feet and the air is thick with the deafening roar of the engines and the fumes of high performance fuel."[41]

Master car builder Henry Hyde, from Brownsville, Kentucky, described his first sight of Darlington. 'I've never seen such a gosh-awful place in all my life. No two turns are just alike. Turns one and two take one chassis set-up but three and four take something different. You work to be good at one end and hope you survive at the other."[42]

If anybody came close to conquering the quirky track, it was David Pearson with ten wins. Pearson said he thought listening to the race on the radio, that the track announcer was crazy talking about the drivers hitting the wall. "When I got here, I found the drivers were the crazy ones," Pearson said in a 1989 interview. "It was tougher back then before they changed three and four. To make time, you had to lay your right side on the rail and ride it through three and four. It would sound like the whole right side was coming off but it wasn't so bad."[43]

After the Southern 500 at Darlington, Brasington and France were quite pleased with the baskets of money the race brought them. A month later, Brasington announced they would promote a 200-mile race for Indy cars sanctioned by AAA in December, and a varied track schedule for 1951. The December race purse would be $2,000 or forty percent of the gate for the AAA race, whichever was greater. The promotional agreement was interesting, as AAA officials had previously refused to be associated with France. Feature attractions of the race were Indianapolis greats Johnny Parsons, Bill Holland and Wilbur Shaw. France and Brasington were listed as co-directors of the race.[44]

Rain washed out the Saturday race and the event was rescheduled for Sunday. That was a problem in South Carolina because they could not sell tickets on a Sunday and racing on the Sabbath was a questionable activity. The Carolinians prized their Blue Laws. Brasington was even chastised by his church congregation for working on the track's construction on Sundays. The two men pulled the correct political strings. Lawing announced that State Supreme Court Justice D. Gordon Baker had signed a restraining order to prevent local law enforcement officers from stopping ticket sales and the race.[45]

The rain abated and the judge's order was obeyed, but only 8,000 spectators showed up to see Johnny Parsons win the race. It was not a good day for Brasington and France.[46]

The 1951 Darlington schedule Brasington announced included a motorcycle race on Memorial Day, a 250-mile "big car" AAA race on July 4, and the stock car race on Labor Day.[47]

Before the Grand National race in Vernon, New York, France decided to experiment with short track racing on the circuit. He staged a twenty-five mile race on Buffalo's quarter mile Civic Stadium track. The event was won by Bobby Courtwright, from Butler, New Jersey.[48]

In late October, Red Byron drove in the NSCRA sanctioned race at Lakewood Speedway instead of the final Grand National race in Hillsborough, North Carolina. At that time, Byron was sixth in Grand National standings with 1,315.5 points. Because Byron drove in the NSCRA race, France stripped him of his Grand National Points. The names of Byron, Marshall Teague, Buddy Shuman and Ed Samples were absent from the 1950 Grand National top fifty driver standings. Although Johnny Mantz's purse for Darlington's Southern 500 was nearly $11,000, the average purse for the top fifty drivers in the nineteen races in 1950 was $4,831, from a total of $91,795 in prize money.[49]

France just knew there was even more money out there waiting for him but Bruton Smith, tutored in promoting races by Nunis, and NSCRA were cutting into his profits. Smith recalled that France asked him to dinner in 1950 to discuss a merger of their two organizations. "I was so doggone young," Smith said, "I didn't know anything about merging or anything like that. But it didn't sound like a bad idea."[50]

There was no merger. Smith was drafted into the U.S. Army in January 1951, during the Korean Conflict, and Nunis had problems keeping NSCRA going without him. When

Smith returned to civilian life two years later, stock car racing was firmly in France's control.[51]

In 1951, without Nunis, Smith and NSCRA to worry about, France expanded the Grand National schedule to include fifty races from California and Arizona to Connecticut and from Michigan to Alabama and Florida. However, the average race purse, for the top fifty drivers, plunged from $4,831 in 1950 to $2,786 in 1951.[52]

Marshall Teague was back in NASCAR for the February 1951 Daytona beach-road race and finished first in his Hudson Hornet. France held up Teague's $1,200 winning check because NASCAR failed to have the manufacturer's specifications to check against Teague's car. When France got the specs, Teague's car passed inspection and he received his money.[53]

France's revolving door of banning drivers when they defied him and consequent reinstatement—including fines—when he needed them had a deleterious effect not only on his relationship with them but on the sport itself. Teague started in fifteen races that year and won seven of them. Buddy Shuman started in seven Grand National races and Ed Samples drove in four.[54] An increase in race purses would have kept those drivers in NASCAR.

France needed every driver he could corral in May of 1951. He knew the celebration of Detroit's 250th founding anniversary was an opportunity for him to showcase NASCAR with a Grand National race and establish the close relationship he wanted with automobile manufacturers.[55]

France contacted the Detroit Festival of the Great Lakes, Inc., the entity charged with conducting the event, and convinced them to let him stage a 250-mile race at the Michigan State Fairgrounds dirt track. The festival organization began in December 1949 and sold 30,000 shares of stock at $100 each to raise $3 million to pay for the celebration. Without a doubt, France got a piece, however small, of that $3 million. He asked automobile manufacturers to enter at least one car in the race.[56]

Fifty-nine cars were in the race that had a purse of $12,500. Tommy Thompson, from Louisville, Kentucky, in a two-tone green, Hemi-powered Chrysler won the race and $5,000. Joe Eubank, from Spartanburg, South Carolina, was second in an Oldsmobile and took home $2,000.[57]

While France's maneuverings proved successful in Detroit, they were costly to Darlington's Fourth of July race card, resulting in a financial hit for the track. Brasington's expertise was in earth moving, not in promoting stock car races. "The AAA said that, under an agreement with its Contest Board, Darlington Raceway will stage a 250-mile national championship race every year beginning in 1951, on July 4," *The Dispatch* stated.[58]

After promoting the exceedingly profitable Labor Day Grand National race at Darlington the year before, France convinced Brasington to piggy-back a July 3 NASCAR race on to the AAA holiday event. AAA officials were furious and demanded that Darlington Raceway officials cancel the Grand National race. They did. AAA officials, while known to ignore some things, did not hold France in high regard. They held the 1951 July 4 race but cancelled any future Darlington races, saying they did not wish to be associated with NASCAR.[59]

Although the Darlington track was successful, those annual AAA races would have increased its value. According to media reports, the Darlington track's debts were paid off in two years and it was operating at a profit. About that time, the Raceway's board of directors shoveled Brasington out the door and installed Bob Colvin, a former peanut broker and track secretary, to run the track.[60]

France had his drivers racking up about as much mileage on highways as on the race tracks. In July 1951, he scheduled a month's races in this order: Grand Rapids, Michigan, July 1; Bainbridge, Ohio, July 8; Heidelberg, Pennsylvania, July 15; Weaverville, North Carolina, July 29; and Rochester, New York, July 31. Fonty Flock won the Weaverville race and Lee Petty won the Rochester event.[61]

For the second Southern 500, at Darlington on Labor Day, France loaded the paved track with 82 cars. Although that was the Raceway's second year of operation, the track had no pit wall—just a wide expanse of asphalt. The only separation between the track and pit row was a white line painted on the pavement. Herb Thomas won the race in a Hudson. Marshall Teague, owner of Thomas' car, also drove in the nearly seven-hour race.[62]

In September 1951, Norman Witte and Central States Racing sued Harold Brasington and the Darlington Raceway for $200,000, claiming a violation of his December 6, 1949, contract to promote the Labor Day Darlington race in 1950. Witte alleged that his contract was ignored and, since then, other individuals took over the promotion.[63] Witte was referring to Bill France, who promoted all the Darlington races. According to Buzz Rose, an author and authority on Central States Racing, the lawsuit was quietly settled out of court.[64]

France and Teague had more disagreements over the reduced size of the purses. In the early 1950s, Teague was driving in AAA races in California, Connecticut, Wisconsin, Illinois, the Indianapolis 500 and the Mexico road races. Frank Mundy, another of France's revolving door drivers, and Johnny Mantz also drove in some of those races.[65]

Mantz drove in five Mexican road races from 1950 through 1954.[66] France, who would later penalize Teague for driving in the Mexico road race, rewarded Mantz, who drove in more of the Mexico road races than Teague. In January 1951, France appointed Mantz to be the NASCAR regional director in California.[67]

The last six races of the 1951 Grand National season were an example of the erratic scheduling France put together. He held races on the same dates in April, September, October and November. The October 21 race was in North Wilkesboro. The next week the race was in Hanford, California. Then it was back to Jacksonville and Atlanta. The November 11 race was in Gardena, California, and the season's finale was in Mobile, Alabama.[68]

Herb Thomas, from Olivia, North Carolina, started in thirty-five of the races, won seven and was the season's champion with $20,850 in winnings plus $2,264.50 from the season's points fund. Grand National purses increased for the top fifty drivers, from $139,305 in 1951 to $154,475 for 1952, for an average of $4,543.[69] In all divisions, NASCAR announced it awarded over $500,000 in purses that year and distributed $23,000 in bonus money for drivers.[70]

France's scheduling was, to some extent, the result of reduced purses for the 1951 Grand National Season. All of the thirty-four races in the 1952 Grand National series were in eleven states east of the Mississippi River and in Canada.[71] The first eight races that year were clustered in the South. Florida had three, two were in Georgia, and the other three in Virginia and North and South Carolina.

During Daytona Beach's Speed Week in 1952, Tim Flock, the eventual Grand National champion that year, ran afoul of Bill France. Flock won the Modified and Sportsman race that France had loaded with 118 cars on the beach-road course. Flock was disqualified because technical inspectors found his roll bar was made out of wood, not metal.[72]

Flock, in an interview with author Sylvia Wilkinson, admitted that his roll bar was made from wood but said the material was supplied by France. Flock said he was ready to race when France told him he had to have a roll bar. "I never heard about a roll bar," he said. Some track workers were erecting a fence to keep spectators back from the racecourse and Flock asked France if he could make a roll bar out of two by fours. "He said, 'Damn right you can borrow the wood,' and the carpenters sawed me some boards and nailed them in there and they didn't move," Flock recalled.[73]

Flock said after he won the race, another driver, Jack Smith from Sandy Springs, Georgia, protested that his roll bar was made of wood, not metal. "Bill France disqualified my car," he added. "Cost me a lot of money. Just another one of the quick change rules in NASCAR. And, he loaned me the damn wood."[74]

NASCAR's first effort at Grand National racing outside the United States in July 1952, at Niagara Falls, Ontario, was not a resounding success. The 200-mile race was apparently the idea of Ed Otto, the newest member of France's inner circle. Stamford Park Raceway was a horse racing venue whose surface was so rough that only six of the seventeen cars finished. Buddy Shuman went in front with his Hudson on lap seventy-one and led the remainder of the race with an average speed of only 45.620 mph. He won $1,000 out of the $3,315.99 purse. More than 4,000 paid an admission price of $1.75 each. The gate was at least $7,000, plus any profits from parking and concessions. After expenses, NASCAR's profits, if any, were small.[75]

On May 10, France decided to stage a 200-mile race for late model big cars at Darlington. Buck Baker won the race in a Cadillac with an average speed of 95.09 mph and took the $2,000 first place prize. Twenty-one starters entered the race for the $10,000 purse. The event drew 6,000 spectators. In those days, France's admissions were running around $3.50, which translated into a gate of about $21,000. Paying about fifty percent of the gate was an abnormality for France. Media reports called the race the first for NASCAR's new division, Speedway. Buck Baker was the Speedway Division Champion in 1952. The division was another France idea that was short lived.[76]

To boost attendance, France coupled the 200-mile event with a 100-mile Grand National race. Dick Rathmann, from Alhambra, California, won that race in a Hudson, which was rapidly become the division's most dominant car.[77]

Due to the success of this approach, France applied it to the July race at Darlington. He hurriedly inserted a modified race into an already crowded schedule prior to the July 4 Grand National event. The AAA was holding an Indy car race at the new, paved, one-mile Southland Speedway at Raleigh, North Carolina, on the same day.[78]

The hurriedly inserted Darlington race produced tragic results. Spartanburg driver Rex Stansell died the next day in a Florence, South Carolina, hospital from injuries he suffered in a race collision with Fred McConnell, from Kannapolis, North Carolina. McConnell, who sustained only minor injuries, blew a tire in the middle of the first turn and Stansell hit his car. Curtis Turner won the race and $1,000 in first place money.[79]

France slightly increased the purse for the 1952 Darlington Labor Day race to $25,750, and he had no co-promoter. Brasington was simply listed as the track's general manager. Fonty Flock not only won the race in an Oldsmobile and received $9,500, but defied the standard uniform to wear Bermuda shorts and a short sleeved shirt. After crossing the finish line, he parked his car on the front stretch, climbed on the hood and led 32,000 spectators in a rousing rendition of "Dixie."[80]

Judges spent over an hour trying to decide who came in second. Finally, they decided Johnny Patterson, from Huntington, West Virginia, was second and he received $3,000; Herb Thomas, Olivia, North Carolina, third, $1,500; Bud King, Corbin, Kentucky, fourth, $1,200; and Banjo Matthews, Miami, fifth, $900. A newspaper account of the event made reference to a large number of accidents and noted the drivers spent a good part of the race driving on a rain-slick track.[81]

Another NASCAR driver died at the Langhorne Speedway race on September 14. Larry Mann, from Yonkers, New York, suffered massive injuries when his Hudson overturned near the end of the race. Lee Petty won in a Plymouth.[82]

In the last race of the season, at West Palm Beach, Tim Flock flipped his Hudson, slid across the finish line with the car upside down and finished twelfth to the race winner Herb Thomas. Regardless, he closed out the season 106 points ahead of Thomas. "I bet I'm the only guy who ever won a championship while on his head," Flock said.[83] Flock's Grand National championship earned him $22,890, plus end of season bonuses.[84]

10

The Finest Years

• • • • • • •

Without a doubt, the mid to late 1950s were Bill France's finest years. He pulled off the slickest deal of the decade by pitting Daytona Beach against West Palm Beach in an attempt to get public financing assistance and tax-free status for the super speedway he wanted to build.

Only half of NASCAR'S capital stock, ten shares, were assigned: France held two shares, Tuthill had two and Ossinsky was allotted one. That left five shares for France to use to raise money. According to NASCAR's incorporation documents, the remaining five shares could be paid for in property, labor or services as well as money.[1]

A new player, Edward Otto, a New Jersey automobile and motorcycle race promoter, entered the NASCAR hierarchy. Edgar Otto, a Boca Raton medical products inventor and entrepreneur, wrote that his father purchased half of Tuthill's stock of NASCAR in 1953, when he was named vice-president.[2]

In discussing an article in the November 23, 1953, issue of *National Speed Sport News* that reported his father had been named NASCAR vice-president, Otto wrote, "No mention was made of Bill Tuthill and, although a few outside the inner circle knew it, he and Bill France were about to have a parting of the ways. The following year, Tuthill would leave NASCAR and transfer his remaining twenty percent of NASCAR stock to Otto, who in 1954 would then own forty percent himself—the same amount as Bill France held."[3]

Before Tuthill left NASCAR he was involved with France's dealings in the Daytona Beach–West Palm Beach ploy. Where Tuthill appeared to be blunt in his public utterances, France was more subtle, a much smoother operator. The biggest problem France then faced was the very real possibility of losing the beach-road course.

Post war construction continued to gobble up beach front properties in Daytona. Homeowners were no longer interested in having two months or more each year taken up with the noise, odors and crowds that gathered for the measured mile trials, automobile and motorcycle races and the trash they left behind. France, without a doubt, was wearing out the beach.

Racing on the beach was cheap when compared to building expensive tracks. The tides often presented difficulties. Bernard Kahn firmly believed France knew just how to work the tide charts. "Big Bill," he wrote, "had no problem with the tides interfering with his races for twenty years." As Kahn explained it, France studied the tide charts to find out which Sunday in February would have the lowest tide. Then, he scheduled his race date for the low tide Sunday which closely followed the new moon that preceded the full moon. When Kahn asked the U.S. Weather Bureau for their assessment of France's calculations, they told him it was a bunch of malarkey.[4]

France was absolutely packing the beach-road course with activity and it was no wonder beach-front property owners were complaining. He reinstituted the measured mile trials on the beach in 1952. A glitch occurred when the city's $10,000 Gaertnac timing device failed and the replacement timing device also broke down. On the same day, he had new speedway type cars racing on the beach part of the course while the stock cars held acceleration tests on the paved portion.[5]

A Daytona Beach newspaper advertisement for the February 1952 beach-road races featured France's photograph and copy that read, "Stock Car Auto Races, all late model stock cars, America's top drivers, under the personal direction of Bill France Famous President of the National Association for Stock Car Auto Racing; Florida's greatest races."[6]

The advertisement went on to say 100 drivers were expected for Saturday's 100-mile race for Modified and Sportsman cars that had a purse of $3,500. Sunday's Grand National race had eighty drivers in the field for the 200-mile race with a $6,500 purse. Admission for the Saturday races was $2; for the Sunday race, $3, and there were 13,000 seats in a reserved grandstand for $4 each.[7]

Actually, 118 cars were entered in the Modified and Sportsman race on Saturday and sixty-three in Sunday's Grand National event. The Sunday race, which had 20,000 spectators, had to be shortened to 150 miles due to a late start and a rising tide that narrowed the beach course.[8]

A total of the gross revenue for that Grand National race, less the amounts from parking, programs and concessions, further indicated France was still placing just over ten percent of his gate into the purse. Grandstand ticket revenue was around $52,000. General admission was approximately $21,000, for an estimated gate total of $73,000.[9]

France's purse was just under nine percent of those figures. At the Daytona beach-road races, France had few track expenses, only personnel, security, insurance, advertising and promotion. NASCAR netted an estimated $60,000, which would help toward building the new super speedway France wanted.

France and Tuthill got their wires crossed on whether or not to move NASCAR headquarters, Speed Week activities and the Victory Dinners from Daytona Beach to West Palm Beach. Ossinsky's position never came into question; he always stood with his client. France knew exactly how he wanted Daytona Beach to subsidize his racing plans while Tuthill utilized no subtlety in the matter. Otto appeared to be waiting to see what was going to be successful. A February 1952 Daytona Beach newspaper editorial was tailored to France's plan. "The cost of ocean front property will grow and, unless provision is made soon, the day will come when no permanent track and probably no racing will be possible," the editorial stated.[10]

In March 1953, Tuthill, NASCAR secretary, spoke to the Halifax Mutual Apartment Association at the Princess Issesa Hotel, where the Victory Dinners were held. He reminded his audience that the advertising and promotion money the organization spent brought a lot of visitors to the city of Daytona Beach. Those visitors, in turn, spent a lot of money with local businesses. Tuthill painted a gloomy picture of NASCAR's finances. He told the audience the organization had shown a deficit for the last three years and unless the city showed NASCAR more cooperation, no more races would be held there.[11]

Tuthill's deficit claim was counterproductive to France's plans. If NASCAR was so badly managed that it carried a three-year deficit, why would local officials shell out all the goodies France wanted in order to keep the races in Daytona Beach? Why would West Palm Beach be interested in such an unsuccessful organization?

In 1951, NASCAR paid out $139,305 just to the top fifty Grand National competitors.[12] If France continued to pay other divisions' drivers only ten to twelve percent of their gates, he was probably grossing in the millions of dollars.

France purchased a house at 42 Peninsula Avenue for $18,000 from Dr. Robert L. Beckwith. The imposing residence became NASCAR headquarters.[13] The purchase was an indication that France expected to keep NASCAR in Daytona Beach.

On October 14, 1953, eleven prominent West Palm Beach elected officials and businessmen came to Daytona Beach to make a presentation to NASCAR officials on moving the entire operation to their city. The proposal did not just come out of the blue. Newspaper columnist Bob Galfe wrote, "This city didn't make a move to get Speed Week [activities] until NASCAR sponsors revealed that changes in the Daytona set-up made a transfer possible."[14]

West Palm Beach authorities had already made far-reaching arrangements, with state and federal officials, for NASCAR to use part of the Boca Raton airfield for Grand National races in November and February. The airfield was used at the time for transitional flights from the Palm Beach International Airport. The group proposed that the Modified championships be held at the quarter-mile dirt track in West Palm Beach.[15]

On October 17, the media reported that the four members of the NASCAR board of directors—France, Tuthill, Otto and Ossinsky—went to West Palm Beach to hear the official presentation and look at the facilities. They were feted at a bountiful breakfast hosted by the West Palm Beach chamber of commerce, a lavish luncheon by the Boca Raton chamber of commerce and were told that, within a fifty mile radius, the area had a population of one million that doubled during the winter season.[16]

France was quoted in the newspaper, "Your proposition is the nicest thing that has ever been offered to NASCAR." The same newspaper said Tuthill admitted he was impressed by the offer but reminded West Palm Beach officials that he lived in Daytona Beach. Ed Otto was quoted as saying Speed Week should be moved to West Palm Beach. Ossinsky, as usual, said nothing.[17]

France said that he would make no immediate decision on the West Palm Beach proposal. "I gave my promise to City Commissioner Dan Warren that I would not take any action on moving the speed program away from Daytona Beach today," France said on October 21. France agreed to a board vote on the presentation. He claimed a change of mind occurred after he received a call from Daytona Beach insurance agent Dotti Niver informing him that she had finally been able to secure liability insurance for the beach-road races. What happened was that Warren promised France if he gave Daytona Beach a year's reprieve officials would work on a plan to build him a new speedway.[18]

France held a closed door meeting with Ossinsky, Tuthill and Otto and issued a statement saying, "The decision on the races has never been a question of the lack of cooperation. It has been the lack of facilities for handling the tremendous crowds." He added that the size of the West Palm Beach Speedway was also a factor.[19] Of course, the fact that the West Palm Beach Speedway was only a half-mile dirt track remained a factor. Bill France wanted a paved track that was bigger than Darlington.

On October 28, 1953, the NASCAR board of directors met. The result was the reduction of shares from ten to eight. The amendment, attached to the organization's article of incorporation, making that change was signed by only two people, France and Ossinsky. Previous NASCAR legal documents had been signed by France, Ossinsky and Tuthill.[20] Bill Tuthill was out of NASCAR and Ed Otto was in, for a while.

Five years later, Bill France admitted that he never intended to move NASCAR from Daytona Beach.[21] Of course, he did not plan to leave since Daytona Beach was his power base.

Over the next three years, that power base faltered as first one idea and then another for a new speedway bit the dust. In 1954, the Daytona Beach Race and Recreational Facilities District (DBRRFD) voted down a $3.5 million plan for the Daytona Beach–Volusia Speedway that began with an original estimate of $1.75 million. Part of the increased cost was for a covered grandstand and all the other extras France wanted somebody else to provide. J. Saxton Lloyd, the commission chairman, said the estimate was too high and suggested giving more attention to improving the beach-road course.[22]

Then, there was the idea to sell revenue bonds to build the speedway. The DBRRFD employed the Cincinnati firm of Westheimer and Company to prepare and sell the bonds in 1955. There were two stipulations regarding the leasing of the $3 million facility: the annual rent would be about $200,000, and a rental payment of two years in advance was required. The cost of the speedway was $2,028,268, with $500,000 in reserve and the remainder of the $3 million to be used for fiscal agents, architects, engineers and lawyers' fees.[23]

With the possibility of using the public's money, Bill France had grandiose ideas for the proposed speedway. One of them was to build a football field inside the track, much like Bowman Gray Stadium but on a larger scale. In 1956, he admitted that the football field would have to wait but he envisioned holding National Football League championship games in the track's infield. "Three million dollars just won't go that far," he said.[24]

According to Tom Cobb, DBRRFD secretary-treasurer, that particular contract called for Bill France to lease the speedway facilities for six months out of the year, pay $225,000 plus a percentage of the net profits in rents and the district could lease out the facility the other six months for non-racing uses. There were many problems beginning with the initial layout of the proposed track. Whoever drew up the plans had a portion of the race track extending over one of the runways at Daytona Beach Municipal Airport. Cobb said the district did not anticipate any problems in the selling the bonds.[25]

Despite Cobb's assessment, the speedway bonds did not sell for three years. In fact, the bonds did not sell at all. Money in the mid–1950s was in short supply due to the Korean Conflict having drained public funds and the Federal Reserve's tightened monetary policies to control inflation.[26]

The NASCAR board of directors voted on September 29, 1956, to change the capital stock structure of the organization.[27] One way or another, France was determined to build his race track.

The stock change certificate was signed by Louis Ossinsky, as NASCAR vice-president–secretary, but, for some reason, it was not filed with the Florida secretary of state until March 29, 1957, six months after the board vote.[28]

An October 1957 editorial in the *Daytona Beach Morning Journal* urged that France be allowed to build a more modest track. "It would not have been the first time promoters of Daytona Beach had had to settle for less than the best, nor would it be likely to be the last," the editorial concluded.[29]

On November 7, 1957, the DBRRFD abandoned its efforts to sell $3 million in bonds to finance the speedway. At a meeting in Chairman J. Saxton Lloyd's office, the district also voted to lease the site to Bill France Racing, Inc. Lloyd and Arnold Vincent, France's attorney, scolded district members for their inaction, saying that "Bill France had become tired of waiting for the nebulous rumors of private speedway financing to materialize."[30]

The lease France signed was far different from the lease that accompanied the proposed bond sale arrangement and was much more to his advantage. The fifty-year lease was very generous to France and had a renewable option for an additional twenty-five years. Property rent began at $6,000 for the first year and gradually climbed up to $10,000 by the end of the fiftieth year. If the option was renewed, the rent went up to $20,000. France was required to pay a $25,000 advance deposit on the rent to allow the purchase of an additional forty acres for the speedway site. The extra acreage enabled the track to be built without intruding on the airport runway.[31] "The contract guarantees racing in Daytona Beach and the resulting economic impact and that's all it does," Lloyd said. "It isn't what I want at all and it isn't what you want."[32]

It was exactly what Bill France wanted. The contract exempted his facility from the Volusia County property tax rolls. Eleven days later, France, who had been operating his stock car race promotions as Bill France Racing, Inc., incorporated the Daytona International Speedway Corporation. France was the president, and H. Muse Womack, president of Womack Asphalt Paving, in Daytona Beach, was vice-president.[33]

France certainly deserved credit for rousting up money to build the speedway, along with assistance from local public entities. In an early 1980s interview with author Sylvia Wilkinson, France recalled, "I raised the money the hard way, borrowing a lot of it to get the track built like it is. I guess we sold 300,000 shares at a buck a share and I borrowed another $600,000—thanks to Clint Murchison and Howard Sluyter. I had met Clint, who now owns the Dallas Cowboys (among other things) and he and Howard came to my rescue on the construction, otherwise it might have ended up as a conventional track."[34]

Sluyter, a Dallas associate of Murchison, was also a director in one of France's incorporations. On November 7, 1958, while he was building the Daytona speedway, France incorporated the River-Ocean Development Corporation. France was the president and the other director was Sam Fletcher, a Fort Wayne, Indiana, industrialist. William S. LaRue, Daytona Beach, was the corporation's registered agent. Fletcher later fielded a car Turner drove at Darlington in 1965. River-Ocean was involuntarily dissolved as a corporation on December 5, 1979.[35]

Murchinson and Sluyter owned a portion of the Lamar Life Insurance Company, in Jackson, Mississippi, that made the $600,000 loan. France's son, William C. France, later said it was that loan which made the Daytona International Speedway possible.[36]

The Murchison family may have assisted France in other ways. In June 1959, while the speedway was being built, Clint Murchison, Jr., and his brother, John, announced plans to build a $12 million development on six Boca Ciega Bay islands, two miles from St. Petersburg. Sluyter also had an interest in automobiles, as he began importing MGs and Jaguars from England in 1950.[37] If the Murchinsons did more than just invest money in the project, they could have assisted France with machinery and technical expertise.

Speedway stockholders, in addition to Murchison and Sluyter, included W. G. Holloway, Jr. of Grace Steamship Lines; popular bandleader Paul Whiteman; Walter Briggs, former owner of the Detroit Tigers; Donald Kendall, Pepsi-Cola; Harley Earl, General Motors; Norman Curtis, a retired oil executive; and more than 1,800 others.[38]

No one, not even the France family, owned as much speedway stock as Claude S. Brinegar, president of the 76 Division of the Union Oil Company. Brinegar, whom President Richard Nixon nominated to be secretary of the treasury in 1972, allegedly owned a million shares of the International Speedway Corporation, twenty-five percent of all the shares. France supposedly took out a second mortgage on his home to raise more money.[39]

France told author Sylvia Wilkinson that he could not have built the speedway without the help of Pure Oil officials Ray Sturgis, Leo Spanuello and Harry Moir.[40]

Charles Moneypenny, Daytona Beach's city engineer, was taxed with finding a location with a substantial base to accommodate the high-banked track France wanted. Most sites had too much sand to support a structure of that size. Moneypenny found a suitable location near the airport where the ground had a high content of marl gravel underneath the subsoil. Moneypenny, however, had never built a race track and could find no instructive manuals on the subject. He used his own judgment and assistance on the turns and banking from the engineers at the Ford Proving Grounds in Detroit. France purchased slag, which contained fine iron filings, from the Bethlehem Steel Mills in Birmingham to mix with the asphalt for track adhesion.[41]

Womack, the Daytona Beach asphalt company executive and speedway vice-president, was in charge of construction. Moneypenny was the supervising engineer and was credited with the layout where every grandstand spectator could see the entire track. Just clearing the site took from December to May 1958. Originally, grandstands would seat 17,000, including 6,880 chair seats.[42]

Removing dirt from the infield for the steeply banked turns created the 3,000 foot long, 700 foot wide and nine foot deep Lake Lloyd that Florida Fish and Game officials filled with bream and bass. France envisioned holding motor boat races on the lake, named for J. Saxton Lloyd.[43]

The Miami News explained the trouble in surfacing such a steeply banked track. "The difficult problem of leveling and surfacing the two 31 degree banked turns in the west and east ends of the track has been conquered with the use of extra heavy machinery moving over the asphalt maintenance road circling the [top of the] track with cables extended to the machines actually engaged in working on the steep turns, laying the surface, spreading and packing."[44]

In the spring of 1958, France was still maintaining he could build the speedway for between $800,000 and $900,000. He said $100,000 would be used for a NASCAR headquarters building at the track entrance. As was his usual habit, France low-balled the cost of the track.[45]

In January 1958, he asked the Racing and Facilities District to allow him to use his leasehold of city and county land as security for a $250,000 loan to be repaid within twenty years. A year later, France was back again asking them to approve another loan. This time he wanted to mortgage the existing grandstands, either those he owned on the beach-road course, those already built at the track or both, and his lease with the city to refinance the remainder of a short term $500,000 loan that was soon due.[46]

The speedway's opening racing date was only a month away and France had to have funds available to pay track expenses, advertising and promotion and the purses for his opening card of races. Beginning February 20, France was staging a Modified race followed by a late model Convertible contest and a Grand National race. He planned, according to newspaper reports, to take the forty fastest cars from the Convertible and a like number from the Grand National race to stage the first Daytona 500.[47]

There was opposition to his request to use the grandstands for collateral. City attorney Paul Raymond told the commissioners that the speedway was owned by a private, profit-making corporation and Daytona Beach should get a decent return on its investment. In addition, Raymond said the city had "blundered" in granting the original lease and should hold out for a share of the track's earnings. France and his attorney either made a powerful argument or the commissioners felt they were in far too deep to refuse. France's request for further financial assistance was approved.[48] France asked Clarence Cagle, supervisor of racing for the Indianapolis Motor Speedway, to come to Daytona Beach and help with the crowd and traffic flow.[49]

More than 40,000 spectators got their money's worth at the first Daytona 500. The race, at the finish line, between Johnny Beauchamp, from Harlan, Iowa, and Lee Petty, from Randleman, North Carolina, was too close to call. Four days later, after milking the event dry for national publicity, France finally decided Lee Petty won the race and first place money of $19,050 from a race purse of $67,760.[50]

11

France Gets a Prize

• • • • • • •

Despite the problems involved with building the Daytona International Speedway and two drivers' deaths on the track during its opening events, the 1950s brought Bill France a multitude of favors.[1] The AAA, once his biggest foe, gave him the biggest prize.

The AAA decided to leave racing in 1955. USAC made a weak attempt to take over the AAA racing program and become the United States' member of the Federation Internationale de l'Automobile (FIA), the Paris-based body that governed the world of motor racing. France saw his opportunity and did not hesitate to grab the chance to claim the AAA's former position on the FIA's Automobile Competition Committee for the United States (ACCUS).[2]

That association gave NASCAR an international presence that led to the protection of France's product. When he conducted one of his important 500 or 600 mile races, those dates would be protected by FIA, as no other internationally recognized racing event could be held on that day.

The decade of the 1950s also saw the automobile manufacturers pour millions of dollars into stock car racing. Cars that previously carried the driver's, owner's and mechanic's names and maybe that of a local garage became rolling billboards for car manufacturers and accessory products. The same decade saw those manufacturers, due to the carnage of highway deaths that many said was caused by the excessive horsepower under the hoods, publicly withdraw their support. The manufacturers, however, surreptitiously continued their maintenance of stock car racing. Sixteen drivers lost their lives on NASCAR tracks and scores were injured during the decade.

Meanwhile, France was flying around the country hunting for tracks to sanction NASCAR races. By 1955, France had upgraded his aircraft to a twin-engine plane. When he promoted events at tracks owned by others, he paid them a facilities use fee. In addition, he collected unknown amounts from track owners for sanctioning NASCAR races. He continued to be tightfisted with race purses although NASCAR had expanded into nine divisions—Grand National, Short Track, Modifieds, Sportsman, Convertibles, Hobby, Sports Car, Midgets and Drag Racing.[3]

France's Grand National race purses began the decade with an average of $2,099 per race purse and, in 1959, reached $6,572, which included the big purse that year for the first Daytona 500. For the entire decade, the Grand National purse average, for the top fifty drivers, was $4,660, which meant some of the race winnings were rather slim.[4]

NASCAR kept all the money from membership fees, which at that time were $20 a year and everybody—car owners, drivers, mechanics, pit crews—in the organization had to pay their membership dues. If a racing official's decision was questioned, the protester had to pay a nonrefundable fee, usually $200.[5]

France's hot and cold attitude toward his drivers in general and Marshall Teague in particular continued. Teague won the 1951 and 1952 Grand National beach-road races. Before he could enter the 1952 beach-road race, France penalized Teague $575 for driving in the 2,000-mile Mexican road race the previous year. There was no evidence that Curtis Turner, Red Byron, Raymond Parks, Bob and Fonty Flock, or France himself, were ever fined by NASCAR for driving in the Mexican road race. The entry fee for the Mexican road race was $575. Teague paid the fine, led all but the first two laps and collected $1,500 first place money plus his Hudson and Pure Oil endorsements.[6]

Teague knew the $6,500 purse was just a fraction of the gross receipts for the Sunday Grand National beach-road race. More than 17,000 spectators, according to a newspaper estimate, watched the 1952 race and paid admissions of approximately $65,000. That figure did not include receipts from concessions, programs and parking. That attendance was almost doubled, 30,000, at the Saturday Modified race that Tim Flock won. The Modified race purse was $3,500. France probably grossed in the neighborhood of $105,000 from the Modified gate alone.[7]

The Palm Beach Post reported that the 1952 beach-road race was shortened from 200 to 150 miles because a late start resulted in a rising tide that narrowed the beach portion of the course. That newspaper estimated the Grand National race crowd to be 20,000 on Sunday. At an average ticket price of $3.50, the gate with that attendance would have been approximately $80,000.[8]

Certainly, France had personnel, promotional and insurance expenses for those races. He grossed around $170,000 from the gates alone for the two races while paying combined purses of $10,000. In addition, he received fifty-five percent of the profits from all concessions sold at the beach-road races, and probably had a like percentage from parking and all revenue from programs.[9] Then, there were the drivers' entry fees.

For the 1952 beach-road Modified race, France loaded the course with 118 automobiles that resulted in massive wrecks. Tim Flock was the Grand National champion that year, a season that first saw roll bars and two-way radios used in NASCAR races. Fonty Flock played radio music in his car.[10]

It was apparent that France's staff was too small to keep up with the rapid expansion of NASCAR. Promoters were complaining they were not informed about which drivers had entered their races. Without those names, which drew the crowds, it was difficult for them to advertise and promote the races. Rather than centralize the problem at NASCAR headquarters, France sent drivers two entry forms, one to send to promoters and the other to NASCAR headquarters in Daytona Beach.[11]

Prior to beginning the 1953 season, Eddie Pappas, one of France's public relations representatives, wrote a news release bragging that NASCAR, at the Victory Dinner, had distributed $56,000, plus another $10,000 from manufacturers, for the previous year. "After each race," Pappas wrote, "promoters send in specified sums to the 'Points Fund.'"[12] If the $56,000 was divided equally among NASCAR's nine divisions, each tier had only $6,222.22 to divide among their drivers.

Pappas added that NASCAR sanctioned 1,029 races and awarded a total of $1,208,609 in prize money.[13] Grand National was supposed to be NASCAR's premier division. In 1952, the top fifty Grand National drivers were paid $154,475, including points fund monies, for their efforts.[14] Other NASCAR divisions were eclipsing the Grand National in profits or NASCAR was inflating the prize money figure.

Before the 1953 NSACAR season began, France filed a lawsuit in Pittsburgh federal court against John Marcum, from Toledo, who had been his NASCAR representative in Pennsylvania and Ohio, and three associates. France claimed they were staging unofficial races in NASCAR's name and keeping the $40,000 profits. In the suit, France professed that NASCAR had paid out cash prizes of $1,208,609 to drivers the previous year and had a membership of 6,000 in the United States, Canada and Hawaii.[15]

Henry Alan Sherman, France's attorney, alleged that the races staged by Marcum and Ralph Quarterson, from West Middlesex, Pennsylvania, and Harry Maynor and Frank Canale, from Toledo, were damaging NASCAR's reputation by failing to adhere to the organization's standards and ethics. France asked not only for the money to be returned but all records associated with the races in question.[16]

Marcum and France eventually mended their fences. Marcum's Midwest Auto Racing Club (MARC) became the Automobile Racing Club of America (ARCA). In 1964, the ARCA 250 was made part of Daytona's Speedweek activities.[17] It was not unusual to find former opponents in France's fold.

However, there was one man in NASCAR's history who was never subservient to Bill France or anybody else. Sylvia Wilkinson, in her book on early stock car racing, recounted a conversation that took place between France and a popular young driver. France was pressuring the driver to run all the season's races but the driver had decided to run only a partial schedule. France insisted the driver was committed; the driver maintained he was only involved. Wilkinson quoted the driver as explaining, "Bill, you've just got all the words wrong. Now, listen. If you sit down to breakfast tomorrow to bacon and eggs, the chicken is involved. The pig is committed."[18]

The driver told the story again when he was one of the first five men inducted into the NASCAR Hall of Fame in May 2010. The driver was Robert Glenn Johnson, Jr., who drove in the 200-mile Modified-Sportsman race at Darlington in 1953. The entrance of the young man from Ronda, North Carolina, into the sport would forever change the face of NASCAR racing.[19] From that point forward, when the name Junior was mentioned, everybody knew it was Junior Johnson, the master car builder, the astute driver and independent car owner.

Race winnings for the top fifty Grand National drivers barely varied from the thirty-four races in 1952 with an average of $4,543 to an average of $4,526 for thirty-seven races in 1953. Herb Thomas was the 1953 Grand National champion with winnings of $22,890. The Grand National schedule of thirty-seven races in 1954 returned an average purse of $4,798 to the top fifty drivers.[20]

The 1954 Grand National beach-road race was won by Tim Flock, from Atlanta, in a 1952 Oldsmobile sedan with a two-way radio communicating with his pit crew. Before Flock could collect $1,700 first place money, the post race inspection revealed illegal soldering on one of the screws in the carburetor. Lee Petty, from Randleman, North Carolina, was elevated to first place with Buck Baker, from Charlotte, in second. Flock car's was owned by Ernest

Woods, from Winchester, Kentucky, who said, "This Flock boy never saw the car till he came to Daytona Beach to drive it for me. He is absolved of all blame." Woods added that all the work on the car was done in Winchester.[21]

There was public backlash from France's disqualification of Flock. Spectators left the Daytona Beach thinking Flock was the winner. Then, they heard about a different winner from newspapers, radio and television. When France and NASCAR announced an illegal carburetor was found in Flock's car and Lee Petty was the winner, there was immediate suspicion that spectators had been duped. One racing fan sent a letter to a newspaper asking why go to a race if you have to wait a week to find out who won. A Los Angeles sportswriter wrote, "We won't print any more NASCAR results."[22]

Flock was furious and blamed France for his disqualification and loss of 800 points, and charged that NASCAR changed the rules whenever they wanted. Flock maintained that he would have won the championship that year if he had not lost those points. Flock finished the season in fourteenth place with 458.5 points and, even with the 800 points he lost, would have finished no better than seventh.[23]

The real reason Flock lost the championship was probably the concussion he suffered before a July 4 race at Piedmont Interstate Speedway in Spartanburg. While he was sleeping in the infield, a vehicle ran over his head and he was out of racing for some time.[24]

The Grand National gate for the 1954 beach-road race was approaching the $100,000 mark. More than 27,000 people, according to one media report, saw the race. Multiply that number by the average ticket price of $3.50, and the result was a $94,500 gate. The race purse was $9,000, following France's usual practice of paying ten percent, or less, of the gate. France announced after the race that the course lacked the facilities to handle the increasing crowds and he did not plan to race on the beach in 1955. The beach portion of the course was littered with wrecks because he loaded the Grand National field with 136 cars.[25]

Without a doubt, France was wearing out the beach part of the course and probably the highway also. For the February 1954 Speed Week events, France conducted acceleration tests on the beach for twenty-four cars, qualifying events for the Friday, Saturday and Sunday races and the three races themselves.[26]

Again, France was running his drivers from one end of the country to another. After the July 4, 1954, race at Weaverville, North Carolina, and before the Labor Day race at Darlington, France's Grand National schedule took drivers to Willow Springs, Illinois; Grand Rapids, Michigan; Morristown, New Jersey; Oakland, California; Charlotte, North Carolina; San Mateo, California, and Corbin, Kentucky, in that order.[27]

In an August 1954 interview, France boasted that NASCAR would sanction 2,000 racing events at 100 American tracks, seen by eight million spectators who would pay between seven and ten million dollars to watch the competition. Eight million spectators, if they paid his average 1954 beach-road race ticket price of $3.50, would have paid $28 million at the gate.[28]

France announced 4,000 drivers would race stock cars in his organization. Of that number, he predicted, four would probably earn $25,000 in prize money, twenty or more would earn $15,000, and some would rake in $20,000 from personal appearances. "We feel that we have given an incentive to mechanically minded kids who want a chance to make a little money and win national recognition and, of course, this also keeps them off the highway," he said.[29]

11. France Gets a Prize

A crowd of 28,000 braved the sweltering 100-degree temperature to watch the 1954 Southern 500 at Darlington Raceway. The crowds came for the week-long festival of parades, beauty contests, concerts and the camping in the infield as well as the racing. Drivers began referring to the track as being too tough to tame and most left the Raceway with the famous Darlington stripe on their cars. "You never forget your first love whether it's a high school sweetheart, a faithful old hunting dog or a fickle race track in South Carolina with a contrary disposition," seven-time Cup champion Dale Earnhardt said. "And, if you happen to be a race car driver there's no victory so sweet, so memorable as whipping Darlington Raceway."[30]

There was big news even before that year's race. Herb Thomas and his car builder, Smokey Yunick, would part company because of money problems. Yunick later praised Thomas as being a hard worker whose sense of balance and desire to win were unexcelled. He said Thomas was an unusual driver who did not drink or chase women. "When the Hudson deal wore out, end of '54, I really didn't give a damn whether I raced or not," Yunick said. "I finally woke up that those first seven years of NASCAR were a Bill France benefit performance."[31]

Thomas finished a close second to Lee Petty for the 1954 Grand National Championship. Actually, Thomas won the most money, $30,975 to $21,127 for Petty. There was a slight increase in the earnings of the top fifty Grand National drivers, an average of $4,798 for each purse for the thirty-seven races.[32]

It was the mid–1950s and the top fifty Grand National drivers had yet to break into $5,000 race purse averages, but that would soon change.

It was possible the Sportsman Division may have been more profitable than the Grand National, with the exception of the beach-road and Darlington races, but no figures were available to make a comparison. In 1954, NASCAR sanctioned 2,200 races in the United States and Canada and only thirty-seven of those were Grand National events. In April 1955, France was in Pennsylvania, where he signed agreements with Lincoln, Lancaster and Susquehanna speedways to sanction Sportsman races.[33]

France had a new car owner who was willing to pour hundreds of thousands of dollars into numerous cars for NASCAR races and initially welcomed him with open arms. That owner's money and success prompted the automotive manufacturers to direct more funds, expertise and equipment into stock car racing. With such an infusion of money, Bill France's control of NASCAR was threatened.

12

Kiekhaefer Factor

• • • • • • •

Carl Kiekhaefer, a Wisconsin native who had earned an estimated $2 billion from the sales of his Mercury outboard engines, took NASCAR by storm in 1955 and 1956 with his powerful, pristine Chryslers. He changed the mechanics of stock car racing, giving the sport an entirely different perspective.

Kiekhaefer fielded multiple teams; placed his drivers in identical white uniforms; paid them salaries while allowing them to keep the prize money they won; took his cars back to his Wisconsin factory for post race inspections that resulted in innovations benefiting American-manufactured automobiles; and created a marketing and advertising program Bill France could only dream about. Kiekhaefer's entry into NASCAR destroyed the drivers' plantation system France had so carefully developed, nurtured and controlled.

Had Carl Kiekhaefer's personality been different, his influence on stock car racing might have rivaled or exceeded that of France. Kiekhaefer was a perfectionist and a workaholic and expected the same from his employees. To inspire his sales staff, he once built a bonfire with his competitors' engines and danced around the flames. He fired top executives and then berated them because they were not at their desks. Once, Kiekhaefer threw an employee's tools out a factory window and the workman followed soon thereafter. He attempted to fire truck drivers who did not work for him because they were standing around while their trucks were being unloaded at his Mercury plant.[1]

Kiekhaefer's work ethic and intellect made him a multi-millionaire. At nineteen, he began working for Nash as a design detailer in 1925. In 1939, he paid $23,000 for an out-of-business outboard motor plant in Cedarburg, Wisconsin. By 1941, he had filled orders for 45,000 of his Mercury outboard motors. During World War II, Kiekhaefer created more than fifty engine applications for the Army and Navy, ranging from two-man power saws to power plants for radio-controlled aircraft.[2]

Kiekhaefer sucked all the publicity out of France's carefully planned 1955 Speed Week when his white trucks, with "Kiekhaefer's Mercury Outboard Motors, The Most Powerful Name in Outboards" painted on the sides, rolled into Daytona Beach. Jeffrey L. Rodengen, Kiekhaefer's biographer, described their entrance, "When Carl and his entourage pulled up people just couldn't believe their eyes." Rodengen said mechanics, with greasy wrenches, stopped working on their cars to watch in amazement as Kiekhaefer's crew, in spotless white uniforms, opened the truck's door. "Then, down the ramp it came," he wrote. "It was a platinum white and gleaming new 1955 Chrysler C300, all 4,005 pounds of it.³

"Though it was professionally lettered with the Mercury name and the number 300, to most it looked like a luxury touring car, complete with an (unthinkable) automatic transmission handle poking ostentatiously out of the dash. It looked as out of place as a beached whale, or as one journalist commented, 'He might just as well have been an Egyptian pharaoh arriving by barge.'"⁴

Rodengen wrote that before Kiekhaefer left Wisconsin for Daytona Beach, the Chrysler was disassembled and modifications made according to the NASCAR rules. "Using parts from Chrysler's inventory of heavy duty taxicab and light truck accessories, the Kiekhaefer crews beefed up suspensions, brakes, axles, steering systems, chassis components and exhaust systems," he wrote. Everything was checked and rechecked before the Chrysler left the Mercury research facility in Oshkosh.⁵

Kiekhaefer arrived in Daytona Beach without a driver. He put Tony Bettenhausen, an open wheel driver, in one of the Mexican Road cars and entered him in an AAA sanctioned stock car race in Milwaukee and he won the race before 32,000 spectators. Bettenhausen,

One of the mighty armada of cars Kiekhaefer fielded in NASCAR, a Dodge driven by Fonty Flock, leads a group of racers around Daytona's crudely constructed beach-road course in August 1956. Disabled and abandoned cars are seen scattered about that portion of the beach (State Archives of Florida).

due to NASCAR-USAC rules, was unable to drive the Chrysler at Daytona. Both Buck Baker and Herb Thomas turned Kiekhaefer down when he initially offered them the ride.[6]

Tim Flock, not having much success with his Atlanta service station after he departed NASCAR, let some friends talk him into going to Daytona Beach for the February 1955 races. Flock said he was standing on the beach when one of Kiekhaefer's Chrysler 300s came by and he casually remarked he could win the beach-road race with the car. "The man standing next to me was Tommy Haygood, Mercury outboard dealer in Orlando, [who] said, hey buddy, I know the man who owns that Chrysler 300," Flock recalled. Haygood took Flock to meet Kiekhaefer, who hired him to drive the car. Flock said he told Kiekhaefer that it would be difficult for a car with an automatic transmission to win the race because it would take the engine too long to regain speed emerging from the turns.[7]

It was not clear who paid the driver's $1,000 reinstatement fine for him to drive in the beach-road race, Flock or Kiekhaefer. Once the fine was paid, Flock was immediately able to race in NASCAR.[8]

Flock not only qualified the car first in the straightaway beach run but set a new beach record of 130.293 mph. Flock came in second to Glenn "Fireball" Roberts in the 1955 beach-road race. Flock said he and Kiekhaefer got into a shouting match because he lost the race. He explained to Kiekhaefer that the problem was the car's automatic transmission. The next day they learned that Roberts' car had been disqualified because it had shortened pushrods. Consequently, Flock got the win. Flock said Kiekhaefer got on the telephone with Chrysler and they built a stick shift car for him in a month.[9]

To celebrate his first victory in NASCAR, the car owner did something else unusual in NASCAR. Kiekhaefer threw a big party for his crew in Cypress Gardens, where his company supplied outboard motors for their ski shows and where he had a testing facility.[10]

More than 28,000 watched the beach-road race amid all the hype France could generate. By 1955, France was charging $2.50 general admission and $5 for reserved seats for the Modified-Sportsman race, and $3 and $6.50 for the Grand National race. The beach-road course grandstands seated 13,000, and spectators numbered 28,000. France collected around $122,000 in admissions from the Grand National race and approximately $56,250 from the 15,000 who watched the Modified-Sportsman race. The purse for the Modified-Sportsman race was $8,300 and the Grand National was $13,950. In addition to the gate, parking, concessions and program revenue, France collected $14,050 in entry fees from the 281 drivers entered in the beach-road races.[11]

The combined admission totals for the two races was approximately $178,250 and France paid out $22,250 in race purses, eight percent of the approximate amounts he collected at the gates.

The regimented life Kiekhaefer demanded of his drivers, who eventually included Buck Baker, Herb Thomas, Tim and Fonty Flock, Jack Smith, Speedy Thompson, Norm Nelson, Lee Petty and even Junior Johnson, was excessively restrictive on the free spirits of the good old southerners.[12]

Tim Flock described what his life was like working for Kiekhaefer. Flock said he rented an entire Daytona hotel for his drivers to sleep in rooms on one side and their wives on the other side. "He would watch the rooms to make sure you didn't sneak over," Flock said. "At six o'clock in the morning, he would blow a whistle and you would march to breakfast."[13]

There was another side to Kiekhaefer's multifaceted personality. Despite his rages,

Flock said he was the only owner he ever heard of who gave his drivers the entire race purse and, as a bonus when he was pleased with their performance, would slip his drivers three or four hundred dollars. Some of Kiekhaefer's drivers were on salary for as much as $40,000 a year and drove only in those races selected by Kiekhaefer.[14]

In 1954, Herb Thomas was the top money-earner in Grand National racing with $30,975, for thirty-four starts. Lee Petty, the Grand National Champion, was second with $21,127 for thirty-four starts.[15]

Aside from winning Grand National stock car races, Kiekhaefer's brilliant mind made considerable contributions to automobile manufacturing. Dirt tracks were sucking all the power out of the Chryslers. Their filters were unable to keep the dirt out of the engines. Kiekhaefer went to work and, with the help of Purolator, devised a dry paper filter, a type of which is still used today.[16]

With the filter problem solved, Kiekhaefer's cars began to win races again until they came up against a real quirk in NASCAR rules, which mandated every part of a car and accessories had to be stock available to the public from the manufacturer. Kiekhaefer's crew noticed the Buick that Herb Thomas drove in the August 20, 1955, race at Raleigh made no pit stops for tires during the 100-mile event. That was the Buick Kiekhaefer's Chryslers had been beating all season. Tim Flock came in second.[17]

Kiekhaefer discovered that France allowed Thomas to use experimental Firestone tires on his cars. After a similar incident at an AAA race in Milwaukee, where Marshall Teague won without changing tires, Kiekhaefer went back to the drawing board. In addition, he pressured France to mandate parity and Firestone to accelerate its production of the new tires.[18]

Kiekhaefer did everything he could to make France follow his own rules. Rodenger wrote that, in retaliation, France had his inspectors tear down Kiekhaefer's cars more than any other entries in post-race inspections, ensuring they would find infractions. "But Carl played by the book and remained within both the letter and the spirit of the rules," Rodenger wrote. "His ingenious methods, though, often concentrated on what the rule book *didn't* say as often as on what it did say."[19] France told a Winston-Salem newspaper, "Carl is a dynamic, energetic man, one who 'needs' to have problems to overcome, and when problems don't exist, he'll make them."[20]

France let his vice-president, Ed Otto, have a shot at Kiekhaefer in the middle of the racing season. Kiekhaefer wrote a letter five days after the June 2 Charlotte race, which Flock won. He did not mail the letter but used it to make points with Otto during a telephone conversation in which he apparently reamed out the NASCAR official. Otto had given an interview on June 23 to the *Pittsburgh Press* in which he suggested Kiekhaefer, whom he described as a millionaire playboy, could sell more outboard motors if he stayed out of stock car racing and criticized him for painting the name of his product on his race cars.[21]

Neither France nor Otto had a clue about how to handle Kiekhaefer.

He accused Otto of using the reporter, Chester L. Smith, to get coverage for his opinions of Kiekhaefer and pointed out that NASCAR permitted Pure Oil, Champion Spark Plugs, Firestone and other manufacturers to paint the name of their products on cars they sponsored. "If the attention cannot remain commercial and is getting over into the personal, I will have to withdraw my contracts with the Flock boys and others," he wrote. "If I am to be nettled and needled out of NASCAR it will hurt people like the very nice Flock boys more than it will hurt me. We could probably find other endeavors in the sporting field."[22]

Kiekhaefer cars dominated the forty-five Grand National races in 1955, winning twenty-seven races, and Tim Flock won the championship. Still, Kiekhaefer was not happy and the object of his rage this time was Junior Johnson. The man who brought the whiskey tripping style of racing back into NASCAR was not exactly the kind of fellow to make mad. Racing writer Ed Hinton described what happened. "In a six week stretch of May and June 1955," he wrote, "Johnson won five races. After the first win at Hickory, North Carolina, Kiekhaefer pissed off Junior something fierce by throwing a hissy, demanding an inspection of the '55 Chevy, claiming nobody could have beaten the fleet of mighty Kiekhaefer Chryslers legally. So in the remaining four victories, Junior just by-god lapped the entire field, including the Kiekhaefer armada."[23]

The Kiekhaefer armada was not exactly invincible. Herb Thomas, in a Chevrolet, won the Southern 500, and $7,560, before 50,000 cheering Darlington fans. Those fans gave France a gate of about $250,000 while he bragged that the $35,000 purse was the largest in stock car history.[24]

Johnson finished sixth in the points that year behind Flock, Buck Baker, Lee Petty, Bob Wellborn and Herb Thomas.[25] Meanwhile, Marshall Teague was winning races in Wisconsin, New Jersey, Arizona and California. In 1954, he was the AAA stock car national champion.[26]

His former racing associate, Buddy Shuman, was not so fortunate. Shuman, an exceptional mechanic, had left driving, spent some time as NASCAR's chief inspector and then joined Ford's stock car racing program. In 1955, he was preparing cars not only to compete with Kiekhaefer's Chryslers but, took a page from his promotional plans to grab additional publicity. Shuman painted his cars purple and called them "Wild Hogs." The drivers selected to race the Fords, Curtis Turner and Joe Weatherly, certainly fit the publicity profile of the cars.[27]

Shuman died on November 13, 1955. Some say he was exhausted from working overtime; others speculated he decided to have one last cigarette. After he fell asleep, ashes from that last smoke ignited the bed sheets and Shuman died from smoke inhalation in a hotel room in Hickory, North Carolina.[28] Turner held one of his famous parties in honor of Shuman and vowed, along with Weatherly, to win the Southern 500 in tribute to their friend.[29]

The 1955 Grand National season ended with the top fifty drivers collecting $206,368 in purses for an average of $4,586 per race.[30]

Another little known collaboration occurred that indicated France needed all the help promoting races he could get, even if it meant joining forces with a former rival. Pat Purcell, who had several titles in NASCAR but was better known as France's enforcer, signed a contract with former promotional rival, Bruton Smith, to sanction fifteen races in 1955 at the Rock Hill Speedway in North Carolina. Smith, according to newspaper advertisements, was staging Sportsman and Modified races.[31]

Kiekhaefer's successful 1955 season brought Ford and Chevrolet roaring back into NASCAR with big bucks. Ford's $2.5 million racing team operated under the umbrella of Peter de Paolo Engineering. Winner of the 1925 Indy 500, de Paolo was the nephew of the great early race driver Ralph de Palma. Chevrolet sent $2.6 million into a similar racing operation under the direction of Mauri Rose, a multiple Indy 500 winner.[32]

All the money Kiekhaefer, Ford and Chevrolet were pouring into his sport was diluting, to some extent, France's power and certainly grabbing the headlines from his public relations machine operating out of Daytona Beach and Greensboro, North Carolina. Media coverage was concentrated on the racing teams, their equipment and their sponsors. NASCAR and France were relegated to secondary status. France attempted to retain control by his rules and regulations that he could impose as he saw fit.

In 1956, Kiekhaefer was back with his mighty Hemi-powered Chryslers, winning twenty-two of the fifty-six Grand National races. Ford won fourteen, Dodge, eleven, and Chevy only two.[33]

Bill France, that year, instituted a new NASCAR division, Convertibles, which became very popular with the fans because they could see the drivers' expressions and how they steered their cars. The Convertible Division was short lived, as France deactivated the division in 1959 (though convertible events continued at some tracks, including Darlington, until 1962). Pop Eargle, crew chief for Joe Weatherly's car, owned by Bud Moore, summed up the complaints of the Convertible Division. "It's too much unnecessary work," he said, "when you have to put the top back; it takes time to do it right."[34] Many of the same cars ran in the Convertible and Grand National races.

With the Kiekhaefer, Ford and Chevrolet invasion of NASCAR, the small, independent owners such as Bud Moore began to leave the sport, as they simply could not compete. Race attendance began to drop since fans knew only a small group of drivers were going to win. Bud Moore, from Spartanburg, explained what was happening. He said, "All of a sudden we

Marvin Panch's Pontiac convertible, owned by Ray Fox, at a pit stop during a Rebel 300 race at Darlington. Fans enjoyed a close-up view of the Convertible Division drivers, especially Curtis Turner, who excelled in that division. The division lasted from 1956 to 1959 (State Archives of Florida).

were running fifth, sixth and seventh to Kiekhaefer. We couldn't compete. We were racing for about $125 for fifth place. I just parked my team and, first thing you know, eight or ten more teams did that."[35]

Moore said France flew to Spartanburg, came to his garage and asked him why he was not racing. Moore said he replied, "Well, France we have a problem. We can't run for fifth place. I can't outrun Dodge and Kiekhaefer. How do I do that?" In his 2010 interview with Fox News, Moore did not elaborate on the financial details he worked out with France, but his cars returned to the tracks.[36]

The Daytona beach-road course was a disaster for 1956 Speed Week events; rough winds had created a wash-board effect, with water slicks on the sand. France had to postpone the measured mile speed trials, which cut into his profit. There were more problems. The night before the Grand National race, more than 2,000 rowdy, drinking teenagers decided to hold their own drag races. After their races were finished, the teens marched into Daytona Beach's Main Street where they broke windows, slashed tires, threw bottles and committed mayhem in general.[37]

Barton MacLane, an actor from Columbia, South Carolina, usually cast as a movie villain, was drinking at one of Daytona Beach's nightclubs. He decided, given his on screen persona, he could handle the situation. MacLane went outside, climbed on a bench, introduced himself to the crowd as a Hollywood bad guy and bellowed, "Now, you punks get out of here and go home."[38]

The rioters, when they recovered from laughing, launched a barrage of beer cans and bottles in MacLane's direction and the chase began. The actor fled with the crowd hot on his heels. MacLane, weaving in the front doors and out the backs of various bars, managed to reach the safety of his motel five blocks away. Reporters found him in his room with a fresh Scotch and soda. MacLane, who later played Gen. Peterson in the television series *I Dream of Jeannie*, informed the reporters that he was getting ready to mobilize the motel owners on the beach. "We will counterattack in twenty minutes," he said. In twenty minutes, MacLane was in his car heading south. Daytona Beach police and firemen were unable to quell the riot and 100 National Guard troops answered the city's call for help. Even after the troops fired their carbines in the air, it took five hours to restore order. Seventeen were injured including three policemen and firemen, and three police cars and two fire trucks were damaged.[39]

Regardless of the riot, France had twenty Fords, eighteen Chevrolets, fifteen Dodges, six Buicks and six Chryslers qualify for his big race.[40] Kiekhaefer entered three teams, Tim Flock and Frank Mundy in their 1956 Chrysler 300 Bs. Mundy, the 1955 AAA stock car champion, had to post a $1,000 bond and swear he would be a good fellow, obey the rules and only drive in NASCAR races thereafter. Buck Baker and Norm Nelson drove 1955 Chrysler 300s, and Fonty Flock and Al "Speedy" Thompson were in D-500 Dodges.[41]

The Ford drivers included Glenn "Fireball" Roberts, Curtis Turner, Joe Weatherly, Ralph Moody, Joe Eubanks and Bill Widenhouse. Herb Thomas, Jim Reed, Bob Wellborn, Gwyn Staley and Al Keller drove Chevrolets.[42]

When the sand settled back down in the rutted beach, only thirty-nine cars were still racing when Tim Flock crossed the finish line and took his share, $4,025, of the $13,950 purse.[43] Flock also won the Modified race in a 1939 Chevrolet, built by Joe Wolfe, the Reading, Pennsylvania, mechanic France asked to build him an Indy car. His average speed was 89.16 mph.[44]

The initial Convertible race proved so popular that France posted a $13,450 purse, almost a match to the Grand National purse. Curtis Turner won the rough and tumble Convertible race. Promoter Bruton Smith, later a partner of Turner's in the Charlotte Motor Speedway, called Turner the best driver he had seen. "He could do more with a car than anyone I've ever seen," he said. Smith recalled a dirt race when Turner and Fireball Roberts were racing on the last lap. Turner, he said, knew that Fireball had the faster car and was going to pass him before they reached the finish line. "So, as soon as Fireball got to his quarter panel, Turner just throws it sideways in front of him and Fireball pushed him across the start-finish line."[45]

That Convertible race had another talented driver. Bob Pronger, from Blue Island, Illinois, had won 148 feature stock car races at Raceland Park in Chicago. According to newspaper accounts, Pronger later drifted from racing into illegal chop shop operations.[46] In 1971, he disappeared and authorities thought he might have been one of the victim in the fourteen murders involved in the "Chop Shop Wars." An unidentified body later found near Griffin, Indiana, was thought to have been that of Pronger.[47]

Two months later, Tim Flock won his third race of the season at North Wilkesboro and promptly announced he was leaving the Kiekhaefer team. Flock said the frantic schedule and his boss' management style were killing him. He cited an incident in July 1955 when Kiekhaefer wanted him to race twice the same weekend: a 100-mile race in Syracuse, New York, and a 250-mile race in San Mateo, California, the next day. "So, I won in Syracuse, a 100-miler, set on the pole and led every lap," Flock recalled. "At eight o'clock we get on a big old airplane he's got chartered and I still got dirt in my teeth. Fonty had qualified my car on the pole in California. We flew all night and, would you believe, I got in that car on Sunday and led the whole race, 250 miles. I was just dead, blisters, whiskers, hadn't even had a chance to shave. That's what you call demanding. He ruined my health."[48]

Flock said, after his weight went down to 130 pounds and he developed ulcers, he decided to quit the Kiekhaefer team. Despite the demanding schedule he had to follow, Flock later said he liked Kiekhaefer and got along with him. Flock had no problem picking up a ride with the Mercury team of Bill Stroppe, from Long Beach, California, who later headed Ford's racing program and built cars for the great Parnelli Jones. Tim Flock won only three Grand National races in 1956, two of them were the Daytona beach-road races and the Elkhart Lake Road event.[49]

There may have been other reasons Flock left Kiekhaefer's team. Flock later said, "I lost a lot of friends because Mr. Kiekhaefer tried so hard to win." Flock did not elaborate on who those friends were. In a draft letter from Kiekhaefer to NASCAR officials dated May 1, 1955, found by his biographer after his death, there was a hint that perhaps France preferred Tim Flock to drive for another team. The letter, written before Flock left his team, complained of his driver being manipulated by the pace car in a race to put him several laps down when he was in second place before the caution flag came out. "When this unfriendliness and biased attitude extend to the officials, it can mean only one thing—that Tim Flock must drive a car of some other make to please the officials," he wrote. Kiekhaefer pointed out that Flock's car could pick up two seconds a lap and for that he was being penalized.[50]

Another incident, Kiekhaefer wrote, had to do with blocking Tim Flock's entrance to the pits by flipping over a junker car. "Fortunately, Flock had enough fuel for several more laps until this Studebaker (which qualified at a ridiculously low speed) could be pulled away from the entrance," he wrote. "It was also obvious that when the Studebaker spun in front of the (pit) entrance, the driver was apparently free of the car at a moment's notice without anyone unbuckling his door. There can be no question about his intent of preventing Tim's pit entrance. If it was not intent, it was certainly a very off coincidence. Of course, such things as razor blades slashing tires can always be expected. This too was found not only at one race but several."[51]

Kiekhaefer, however, did not miss a beat and gave Buck Baker Flock's ride.

Baker, a more combative personality than Flock, jumped at the chance to drive for Kiekhaefer. "Carl took me out of the kitchen eating hamburger and put me in the dining room eating steak," he said. "He put me in a financial bracket I didn't hardly know how to handle."[52]

In October, Ralph Moody, from Taunton, Massachusetts, driving one of the de Paolo Fords, broke the Kiekhaefer teams' sixteen race winning streak at the high banked, 1.5 mile Memphis-Arkansas Speedway, in Lehi, Arkansas. During the race, Cotton Priddy, from Louisville, Kentucky, was critically injured when he collided with another car and was thrown on the track. Priddy died less than an hour later at Crittenden Memorial Hospital in Memphis. Less than twenty-four hours earlier Clint McHugh, from Biloxi, Mississippi, was injured when his car flipped at the same speedway and rolled down a fifty-foot embankment into a lake during time trials. Spectators pulled McHugh from the water but he died later at a Memphis hospital.[53]

Public opinion against automobile racing became intense. Bill Vukovich's death in the 1955 Indy 500 reminded the public, who reminded their elected representatives, that Vukovich was the forty-sixth fatality at the speedway. In November 1955, a month before the event was scheduled to start, the Mexican road race was cancelled due to the ever increasing number of racing deaths.[54]

Back in NASCAR, the Grand National sniping continued as Kiekhaefer contested Fireball Roberts' July 4th win in the 250-mile race at Raleigh Speedway. Kiekhaefer maintained the flywheel in Roberts' car was of an improper weight. It was another instance where NASCAR was caught up short. Race officials had no scales on which to weigh the flywheel. One of the racing officials took the flywheel to a local fish market to use their scales to determine the weight. Roberts' win was upheld.[55]

Strange things happened during the 1956 NASCAR racing season. At a September 30 Convertible race at Asheville-Weaverville Speedway, Curtis Turner was declared the winner of the 100-mile event when the other twenty-three cars either crashed or had mechanical difficulties. Turner's buddy, Joe Weatherly, stayed with him until lap 176. Race officials finally called the race five laps later since there was only one car left running.[56]

Anomalies continued to plague NASCAR. In the August 3, 1956, Grand National race at the Oklahoma State Fairgrounds in Oklahoma City, the dust was so thick the drivers were blinded. Lee Petty stopped his car a third of the way into the 200-lap race on the half-mile dirt track, grabbed a red flag from the starter and began flagging down cars. His actions caused a near riot of the 6,000 spectators.[57]

Jim Paschal, from High Point, North Carolina, won the race, the only Grand National event held at the Oklahoma State Fairgrounds. Lee Petty finished fourth behind Ralph Moody, Fireball Roberts and Herb Thomas. Of the twelve cars that started the race, only seven finished.[58]

Charlotte was a good market for stock car races so France and Enoch Staley leased the three-quarter mile Charlotte Speedway and held four Grand National races at the improved dirt track that season.[59]

Finally, after all those years of being shut out of the facility, France signed an agreement with Lakewood Speedway, in Atlanta, to stage NASCAR races in 1956. After NSCRA folded, USAC sanctioned stock car races at Lakewood.[60]

France's fortunes took a nose dive when he lost one of his star drivers. Junior Johnson, after a successful 1955 season, signed to drive for Ford. Johnson, in both the Modified and Grand National divisions, drew big crowds to watch the former whiskey tripper race. Before dawn one morning, Johnson built a fire under the family still. A normal process was to fire the still during darkness so the smoke could not be seen by revenuers. By morning's first light the fire had died down, the mash was cooking and the smoke was not visible. However, revenue agents had been watching the family still figuring they would again capture Glenn Johnson, but it was his famous son they caught.[61]

Racing writer Ed Hinton described what happened next. "When word reached Daytona Beach, Bill France scrambled to fight the setback. He tried to intervene—sent a telegram to a federal judge promising a high-paying, legal job for Johnson as a race driver, if only he were put on probation. But the judge had the prize Johnson of them all and wasn't about to let him go. France's brightest budding star, the one who'd captured the imagination of the public faster than any other driver was gone."[62]

By the mid–1950s, traffic deaths, as well as racing deaths, had reached alarming heights. In addition to Vukovich's death, Formula One champion Alberto Ascari was killed at Monza. The most traumatic of all racing fatalities occurred at Le Mans when Pierre Levegh's Mercedes spun and plowed into the crowd, killing him and ninety spectators and injuring over 100 others. From the Revolutionary War to the Korean Conflict, the United States suffered 1,009,750 causalities. From 1900 through 1953, automobile accident deaths reached 1,050,000. Newspapers all over the nation clamored for action against automobile manufacturers, which, they said, were building faster and more powerful cars and using racing as an advertising avenue to sell those vehicles. State and federal officials were criticized for not doing enough to stop the highway carnage.[63]

Sen. Richard L. Neuberger, Democrat from Oregon, told the Senate it was time for Congress to prohibit the "bloodshed" of automobile racing. Neuberger, a *New York Times* reporter before his election, excoriated the sport, saying, "Deaths on the highways are sad and tragic but at least they are not staged for profit and for the delight of thousands of screeching spectators."[64]

From 1951 through 1959 in the U.S., 357,802 people lost their lives in traffic accidents.[65]

The public relations war against automobile manufacturers and racing organizations was increasing. Earl Sache, executive secretary of Wisconsin's Legislative Council, had a suggestion. "If you license cars at a dollar per horsepower, you might slow down the horsepower race," he said. *The St. Petersburg Times,* on the other hand, suggested drivers had slow reflexes, poor depth perception and inadequate knowledge of the vehicles they drove. Another newspaper editorialized that manufacturers should disassociate themselves from automobile racing.[66]

A Pontiac display advertisement in the *Los Angeles Times* touted their automobile breaking the NASCAR endurance and speed records at Bonneville, Utah.[67] Whether Bill France approved or not, the Detroit manufacturers, not just Kiekhaefer, were using NASCAR to tout the speed and power of their products.

In 1953, President Dwight D. Eisenhower signed into law the National Safety Council (NSC) in an effort to lessen highway deaths. By 1955, traffic deaths had increased so much the NSC refused to make any traffic safety awards.[68]

While local, state and federal officials argued about the connection between automobile racing and highway traffic deaths and what to do about it, the 1956 Grand National season began to wind down. After Buddy Shuman's death, John Holman, a trucking company businessman with racing interests, took over the Ford operation that was moved to Charlotte. The Southern 500 at Darlington was set to be the showdown between the Fords and Kiekhaefer's Chryslers. There was a crowd of 70,000 to see stock car racing's answer to the Indy 500. Curtis Turner and Joe Weatherly remembered their pledge to win the Southern 500 for Shuman. Their Purple Hogs gleamed in the sunlight. At the 375-mile mark, Turner was ahead by four laps and he decided to back off and save his car. It was an unusual tactic for him to employ, as he usually drove flat out. After taking the checkered flag, racing fans mobbed Turner and took the Hog's oil dipstick and sparkplugs for souvenirs. The celebration went on into the night and it was de Paolo, not Turner, who yelled, "Let's have a party."[69]

A North Carolina race signaled the beginning of the end of Kiekhaefer's time in NASCAR.

Buck Baker, in a Kiekhaefer Chrysler, won the Grand National race at Newport, Tennessee, in early October, and was 246 points behind the series leader, Herb Thomas. Thomas had joined the Kiekhaefer team in June, found he was unable to work for such a domineering boss and left a month later. Most media accounts of exactly what happened at the 100-mile Grand National race in Shelby, North Carolina, on October 23 were lacking in specific details. Both Buck Baker and Speedy Thompson were driving Kiekhaefer's cars. Herb Thomas was driving his own Chevrolet. There were only three races left in the season, at Martinsville, Virginia, and Hickory and Wilson, North Carolina. If Thomas won the Newport race, Baker would have a difficult time catching up.[70]

But, Baker won the race after his Kiekhaefer teammate, Speedy Thompson, triggered a six car pile up that took Thomas out of the race and almost cost him his life. Unconscious for days, Thomas suffered severe head injuries and almost lost his right arm. Baker collected $950 for first place and Thompson $675 for second. Ray Fox, Thomas' mechanic for the race, observed, "There was a lot of hanky panky on the short tracks but you didn't expect to cripple somebody."[71]

Whether it was genuine remorse or a public relations ploy, Baker told the media he would not be in the next race at Martinsville unless Thomas was also in the race. "Should Baker hold to this decision, the national title would go to Thomas because no other driver is close enough in the points standings to win the title," the *Herald-Journal* observed.[72]

Apparently, Kiekhaefer had a discussion with Baker and he did drive in, and win, the Martinsville race in a Dodge with his fellow team drivers, Thompson and Lee Petty, second and third. Baker and Thompson split the season's last two races and they finished first and second in the championship points with Thomas third. Thomas attempted a comeback but drove in only two races the next year.[73]

Actions, however, have consequences. Race fans pilloried the three men because they thought Kiekhaefer had ordered Thompson to wreck Thomas so Baker could not only win the race but the championship. It was never proven. Kiekhaefer saw the criticism as so damaging to his Mercury outboard business that he closed down his automobile racing teams and vanished from the NASCAR scene.

Earlier in the year Kiekhaefer had threatened to pull out of NASCAR. He said he could not compete against France's rules and regulations as well as the cars sent out by the manufacturers.[74] Kiekhaefer, however, had achieved what he intended with his superior methods, cars, drivers and two Grand National Championships, and had made lasting contributions to automotive advances. The exposure afforded him in NASCAR racing enabled him to increase outboard motor production at his Fond du Lac plant by fifty percent the next year. In August 1956, he was selected as "Outboarding's Man of the Year" by the American Power Boat Association.[75]

Grand National drivers finally reached a plateau in 1956, with the fifty-six races producing an average race purse of $5,438.[76] After the 1956 season was over, France held a December 30 Grand National road race over the 1.6 mile course at the Titusville-Cocoa Speedway. The race counted in the 1957 statistics. More than 10,000 turned out to watch just fourteen stock cars compete. As the course covered parts of an airport runway, it was a good gate, around $35,000, for France. Fireball Roberts won the Indian River Gold Cup with Curtis Turner second and Marvin Panch, Gardenia, California, third.[77]

Grand National racing in 1957 experienced a number of changes. Spectators, weary of the dust and grime of the dirt tracks, were either staying home or crowding into the paved tracks such as Darlington. Richard Petty described what it was like to race on the dusty dirt tracks. He said he started wiping off the dust from the outside of his windshield and then had to wipe off both sides. "You finally just had to take your goggles off, because the dust would get on the inside and you'd sweat and that turned it to mud."[78]

He recalled what happened to him one night on a dusty short track. He said he was following Herman Beam, from Johnson City, Tennessee, and could not see to pass him. "Herman was going so slow that everybody called him 'Turtle,' so I figured I would be safer following him than getting run over in the groove. When I thought it was safe, I pulled out to the right to pass and get back in the thick of things. I didn't know how low we were. I hit a light pole. Herman was driving in the infield."[79]

North Wilkesboro and Weaverville paved their tracks as did Martinsville two years earlier. Five-hundred-mile races, once a rarity in Grand National racing, were increasing. Road course races at Watkins Glenn, New York; Willow Springs, California; Raleigh, North Carolina; and Titusville, Florida, were added.[80]

H. Clay Earles was experiencing financial difficulties with his Martinsville track, even though he turned all his poker winnings back into its operations. He bought out his partners and then sold half interest to Bill France. Earles, who built the track in 1950 with moonshiner and bootlegger J. Sam Rice, also from Martinsville, said his attendance for the first seven years averaged only about 3,000. When Earles suggested to his partner that they pave the speedway, Bill France made fun of the idea. Earles said he insisted, paved the track and their attendance jumped up to 12,000.[81]

The partners also disagreed on the viability of running a 500-mile race on a half-mile track. France said the track was too short. Earles argued they could and added a retaining wall; 15,000 came to see the first Virginia 500. France was no fool; he was aware of Earles' background and knew he was a man one did not want to cross. Earles said he always went to the Martinsville races fully dressed—he carried two pistols—since there was always a fight breaking out in the pits after a race.[82]

Earles, like many of the great race promoters, had a soft spot for drivers and car owners down on their luck. "We used to make deals, maybe $100 or $150, with car owners—especially the independents to run in our races," he said. "I'd also give those who had a particularly bad day a little extra after the races."[83]

France was more interested in building his new paved Daytona track than dabbling in dirt tracks. Sports editor Bernard Kahn wrote, "France announced in 1955 that the famed beach-road races were ended here but continued the national sports event in 1956 and this year on a stop-gap basis at the request of civic leaders in the Halifax area who are working on speedway plans."[84]

France made excuses for the condition of the beach but that certainly did not stop him from loading the course with events. "The beach is not in the best condition but it is better than it was on opening day last year," he said. Aside from the usual Modified, Sportsman and Grand National qualifiers and races, Measured Mile trials, Century Races for various classes of cars that could reach 100 miles or more, and amateur and antique runs, he did not let beach conditions stop him from adding an experimental auto race for cars not classified as factory production. France had to postpone some of the Measured Mile activities resulting from poor beach conditions but not before Bill Korkett, from Chicago, was badly burned when his Ford Thunderbird overturned at 130 mph and caught fire. Peter de Paolo, driving a 1930 Duesenberg in the Measured Mile, was an added attraction. In addition, France staged three days of midget racing at Memorial Stadium with seven races each day.[85]

Kiekhaefer's departure was probably welcomed on the Grand National circuit, but he certainly left his mark. "We never went up against somebody so completely organized and well staffed," Smokey Yunick said. Yunick, who at that time was building cars for Fireball Roberts, said things NASCAR crews did in four or five weeks Kiekhaefer's did in four or five days. "He had engine men, chassis men, brake men," Yunick said. "We never experienced anything like that and he would sometimes come with four or five cars. But, he was a tough s.o.b., and he worked hard himself. And, he was ruthless. He had enough money to pay anybody he wanted but he made us all become more professional. Up until then, we were part-time racers."[86]

13

Big Boys Come to Town

·······

Along with thousands of racing fans, a gaggle of automobile executives, and their minions descended on Daytona Beach for the 1957 Speed Week activities, Measured Mile trials and races to continue the good times from the previous years.

In 1955, Bill France imported Tom McCahill, the automotive editor of *Mechanix Illustrated,* to direct the Measured Mile trials on the beach for about any vehicle on four wheels whose owner paid an entry fee. Sports editor Bernard Kahn bragged about how McCahill was courted by automobile manufacturers to endorse their products, as he was the first man responsible for testing and recording performances of American automobiles.[1] Kahn drooled about Cahill's warm friendship with "Bill France, NASCAR's pin-up president."[2]

The sports editor was equally enthusiastic about the attention automobile manufacturers gave Speed Week, France and all of Daytona Beach in 1956. He described it as "a special Valentine time—15 days—during which the automotive world gives us an eight cylinder hug and a shower of mash notes that go out in the form of international publicity for the international speed trials on our beach."[3]

Kahn said in recent years the automobile giants from Detroit had been aloof to the Measured Mile trials. "Today though the entire automotive industry's attitude toward high speed and safety performances has undergone a radical change since last year and nearly all the billionaires Detroit operators are in the race," he wrote. "And the public interest has more than kept pace and NASCAR's racing cult today has millions of addicts from coast to coast and overseas."[4]

Everywhere one looked, Kahn wrote, there were factory engineers and representatives, public relations agents, advertising directors, drivers and automobile executives.[5]

Kahn neglected to mention the embarrassment France suffered in 1956 when deteriorating beach conditions caused the postponement of some of the Measured Mile trials. The same thing happened in 1957, when France's friend and automobile dealer J. Saxby Lloyd cut the ribbon for the Measured Mile trials. It appeared the trials for the experimental cars would have to be rescheduled. Experimental cars, according to France's definition, were vehicles not currently classified as factory production. France planned to hold the trials the next day.[6] Bad beach conditions also caused the postponement of the family sedan class in the Measured Mile trials for several days.[7] Meanwhile, there were parties to attend.

Jane Merrell wrote in the February 17, 1957, *Daytona Beach Morning Journal* there was no truth in the rumors that NASCAR would present a special award to those who managed to make all the cocktail parties and buffet dinners. NASCAR, she said, opened the social whirl with a press party at the Ellinor Village Country Club, which was the site of numerous similar events.[8]

The country club was the site of the Chevrolet party honoring driver Betty Skelton who was driving their Corvette in the Measured Mile trials. Skelton, a professional pilot who soloed when she was twelve, was never able to break into NASCAR and Indy racing, although she was competitive with male drivers. The club was also the scene of the extravaganza the J. Walter Thompson Advertising Agency threw for NASCAR, and Ford and Chrysler's parties.[9]

Another big party was held at the New Smyrna Beach Yacht Club for drivers, car owners and mechanics. Merrell quoted an automobile executive's wife as saying, "I just don't think I can stand much more of this fun."[10]

While France, along with his family, reveled in the social events and welcomed all the automobile manufacturers who paid him fees to compete on Daytona's public beach Measured Mile trials and all his races, he became uncomfortable. Automobile manufacturers were using the speeds attained in the trials and races to advertise their products whenever they won events. Publicity from the trials he was unable to control, but the races were NASCAR operations that belonged to only to him.

On December 5, 1956, France notified the Detroit automobile manufacturers they were in violation his 'pure advertising law,' which stated that no points awarded owners for performances could be considered official until after NASCAR released them. If NASCAR was peeved at a particular manufacturer, their 'official' news release of an event could be delayed for weeks. Media coverage often included owner points awarded and the current standings the day of, or the day after, trails and races.[11]

France's letter said, in part, "NASCAR is of the opinion that if these advertising rules are adhered to the public will be able to purchase vehicles equipped as advertised, as the advertisers are bound by legal and ethical requirements governing the advertising media."[12] France denied he was attempting to tell the automobile manufacturers how to build or sell their cars. "NASCAR is endeavoring to better serve the public as well as the competitors in NASCAR sanctioned events," the letter continued.[13] The *Daytona Beach Morning Journal* hailed France's letter as a history-making event.[14]

Sports editor Kahn accused Ford of violating France's edict by advertising that Joe Weatherly won the 1957 Convertible beach-road race in a Ford and three other Fords placed in the top ten of the February competition before the news was officially released by NASCAR. In May, three months after the event, the newspaper quoted France as announcing all points accumulated by Ford in the Convertible Division through February 19, 1957, were disqualified on the grounds the car maker's advertising agency had failed to comply with NASCAR's regulation on official records.[15]

However, United Press International sports writer Jim Lockenkemper said the split between France and the automobile manufacturers came from the Measured Mile trials, not the beach-road race. "Only time and inspection of the advertising and promotion of the auto firms will tell whether they'll continue to hold the line against exploiting the vice for speed to the American public," Lockenkemper wrote.[16] "That was certainly true after the Daytona Beach stock car speed tests last winter [when] the advertising claims of Ford, Mercury, Chevrolet and Pontiac made it seem they'd all won and that NASCAR, the sponsoring body, had said so."[17]

France hastened to say his ruling did not apply to drivers' point accumulations, only to the car owners. The *Daytona Beach Morning Journal* article concluded by saying, "The disqualification of Ford's points marked the first time in the history of stock car racing that an advertising code has been enforced."[18]

By the beginning of Speed Week in 1957, politicians, editorialists and the public were clambering for ways to lessen automobiles' speed and decrease traffic accident fatalities. The automobile executives maintained that speed tests from racing were vital to the continued development of the automobile and attempted to present a united front.

John Mills, executive assistant to Ford President Benson Ford, reinforced that idea: "The interest displayed by the executives of the automotive industry is an example of the importance they place in the tests which automobiles receive in racing competition." Mills was careful to include France, "The entire automotive activities here are a credit to Bill France, the NASCAR president. France has indeed brought national prominence to Daytona Beach."[19]

The automobile executives may have been looking at the Daytona Beach trials and races for testing, but what they got was speed. Paul Goldsmith, from St. Clair Shores, Michigan, ran the Measured Mile in a 283 hp Chevrolet in a record 131.062 mph. His speed was an average of two runs. Tim Flock won the Convertible Division race with an average speed of 101.32 mph over the 4.1-mile beach-road course.[20]

Beach conditions and wrecks claimed nine of the twenty-eight Convertibles entered in the race, but automobile manufacturers had no shortage of cars. More than 17,000 spectators paid between $4 and $5 per ticket, giving France a gate in the neighborhood of $80,000 to $85,000. The race purse was $14,500, and Flock collected $3,750 of that amount. Two other Mercury drivers, Joe Weatherly and Billy Myers, from Germanton, North Carolina, finished second and third, and won $2,450 and $1,500 respectively.[21]

More than 37,000 turned out for the Grand National beach-road race, which had a purse of $15,000. That meant France's gate was in the neighborhood of $165,000, and the drivers got their usual purse of ten percent, or less, of the gate.[22]

Laboring as hard as he ever worked in his life, France expected to regain the title of the undisputed dictator of stock car racing once again.[23] Kiekhaefer had left and it looked as if he had those suits from Detroit, who built the automobiles and poured millions of dollars into his sport, on the run.

On June 3, 1957, the Automobile Manufacturers Association (AMA) unanimously recommended that their members not only withdraw from automobile racing, or other events involving speed, but refrain from referring in their advertisements to the speed and power capacities of the vehicles they produced. The AMA board acknowledged the public interest in increasing the safety of highway travel and agreed not to advertise or publicize any aspects of their products that suggested speed.[24] Automobile fatalities decreased 1,033 from 37,965 in 1956 to 36,932 in 1957.[25]

Sports editor Kahn saw the move as a victory for France. "The withdrawal of Detroit factory teams, if anything, will produce a healthier climate for good racing competition. Stock car racing would have been better off if they'd outlawed factory teams when they first appeared in 1955. By 1956, they had already exercised a monopoly on racing competition and by 1957 they had driven off almost all of the independents who brought the sport to the national forefront."[26]

According to Kahn, the National Safety Council objected to factory sponsored teams, the factories themselves, and "objected to the NASCAR 'truth serum' advertising regulations which forbid hetaerism and misleading information about racing results."[27]

Kahn concluded, "Since the factory drivers will take over the cars which have been 'set up' by Detroit for racing, they'll probably continue to set the 1957 pace. But, in 1958, the factory influence will disappear—barring secret assistance or indirect help which some factories might try to get away with."[28]

In addressing the AMA announcement, France said their withdrawal "will put automobile racing back as more of a sports affair than it was prior to the manufacturers entering the field." France continued, "I think that while the industry was actively competing in racing it learned a lot about handling and about performance, in fact, more about its own cars than it had ever known before although it built them. Consequently, I think the industry's participation will reflect favorably on cars to come ... the industry sure did play hard while it was playing."[29]

Kahn was right about the remainder of the 1957 Grand National racing season. Drivers continued to use the same Detroit equipment and speeds did not decline.[30] Nor did the sport's practice of ignoring the bump and grind style of driving.

After the Southern 500 at Darlington, Smokey Yunick sent Bill France a tongue-in-cheek letter about the race and Lee Petty's style of driving. Petty put Curtis Turner, in one of Yunick's Fords, into the fence. "Dear Bill," the letter read, "This is a request that you look into/investigate the Curtis Turner crash at the 'Cotton Picker's 500.' I did not see the accident but Curtis Turner and about 200 other people have told me that, during and after the combination Hell Driver's Thrill Show and part-time race, it appeared as though Lee Petty, America's favorite driver (in an Oldsmobile), had a hell of a dislike for black and gold Fords with 31s on them and kind of crashed it into the fence...."[31]

"Let me explain just how Lee's attitude has affected my whole life. To start with, everyone said that if I took my cars to Darlington September 2, there would be a race there and that I would win from $12,000 to $20,000. So, after months of work and quite a bit of money spent, we arrived at the racer's paradise. There we had to sweat out the gnats, inspectors, a dirty hole called 'inspection station' and the local female cotton pickers. After many anxious moments at the inspector station, I finally won the title of the biggest cheater, not to say anything of the mental hell we were going through as we staggered to our beds at the motel."[32]

Yunick said he was so sure he would win the race, with Turner and Paul Goldsmith driving his cars, that he had started spending the money. Yunick noticed one of his cars was missing. "Finally I see it staggering around the bend, like a bow-legged Memphis beauty queen, just hit by a train on the way to the Town Park Motel. I rush to the window and Mr. Turner is purple and hollers, 'Lee put me into the fence!' I notice you don't stop the race and wait for me to fix the car.... Last year we had much better luck. Paul and Herb Thomas were well wrecked long before the halfway mark."[33]

Yunick said it was impossible for him to work when he returned to Daytona Beach due to people calling and visiting his garage to talk about the race and the wrecks and, in addition, he was reduced to walking since he drove a black and gold Ford. "Any time I drive near an

Oldsmobile the damn Ford runs into a ditch and stops. If you care to discuss this with me any evening you can find me around Second Avenue getting a reversing treatment as this is the fourth time this has happened."[34]

Yunick said he received the following reply from Pat Purcell. "Dear Smokey: Your very elucidating letter of September 7, 1957, to Bill France has finally reached its resting place on my desk and is now enroute to the files for a very honorable response. I must congratulate you on the rhetorical value, as well as the pertinent information contained therein. I have written to Lee Petty requesting his version of this episode and it is my ardent wish that the final washing will not lead to complete ruination of your life; you are much too lugubrious a character to pass from the racing scene. Sincerely yours, Pat Purcell, Executive director."[35]

Buck Baker repeated as the 1957 Grand National champion with Marvin Panch, Speedy Thompson, Lee Petty and Jack Smith rounding out the top five drivers. The average race purse, $5,408, for the top fifty drivers was just a few dollars less than the preceding year. The points fund, distributed at the annual Victory Dinner, totaled $71,000 plus $60,000 in industry awards. Champion Spark Plugs instituted the Buddy Shuman Award to be given annually to the person who most exemplified the attitude and devotion the late racer held regarding NASCAR, which, at one time, banned him from racing. Herb Thomas was the first recipient of the Buddy Shuman Award.[36]

France opened the 1958 Grand National season by announcing that he had signed a contract with George Hamid, George Hamid, Jr., and Sam Nunis to stage a 500-mile race at the one mile, paved Trenton (New Jersey) Speedway. USAC had previously sanctioned the race. France boasted that NASCAR now had five big events: Daytona, Martinsville, Raleigh, Darlington and Trenton. "There is another real big event in the making on the Pacific coast," he added. The Trenton 500 race, he said, would pay a $20,000 purse with an additional estimated $5,000 from accessory firms. The Hamids, through several fairgrounds operations, controlled automobile racing in New Jersey. They owned the famous Steel Pier in Atlantic City, theaters and insurance companies, and were major investors in the Miami Dolphins football team.[37]

After the Trenton 500 race announcement, France gave an in-depth interview, printed the day of the Grand National beach-road race. Kahn asked him what NASCAR had done for stock car racing. "Prior to 1948," France said, "car drivers received no national recognition. They were not guaranteed any purse."[38]

National, regional and local newspapers carried news about Vanderbilt stock car road races and Grand Prize races for stock cars as well as the 1909 Prest-O-Lite Special and 1910 Speedway Stock Car Championship at Indianapolis. *Billboard* magazine and a host of industry publications regularly carried stock car racing schedules, results and the amounts of purse money.

France's statement that drivers were not guaranteed any race purses before 1948 was patently untrue. Promoters like Willie K. Vanderbilt, William Morgan, Ralph Hankinson, Sam Nunis, Bruton Smith and Joe Littlejohn would never have stayed in business without guaranteeing race purses. As noted earlier, many of those promoters paid their drivers forty percent of their gate, not the stingy ten percent or less that France handed out.

France pointed out that drivers had "no insurance. They had no protection. NASCAR established guaranteed purses, hospitalization and insurance and set up safety regulations for each track before it could acquire a sanction [from NASCAR]."[39] He did not address how the 1957 Southern 500 at Darlington managed to get a sanction is spite of the track's condition or the lack of safety measures, such as softer walls, that Smokey Yunick and others suggested would reduce racing deaths. France also neglected to mention the dangerous wind and rain conditions at his Daytona track when he refused to cancel or postpone races.

He did address friendlier issues. "By organizing promoters, car owners, mechs and drivers, we were able to schedule events with some degree of continuity," he said. "In other words, NASCAR just made a respectable sport out of it."[40]

Kahn asked France if there was any gambling on NASCAR races. "No one makes book on stock car drivers," he replied. "Millions follow the sport but there is no bookmaking, thank goodness. The integrity of stock car racing is 100 percent and we'll fight to keep it that way."[41]

There had been bookmaking on stock car competition since the early 1900s beach trials. Dan Pierce and Daytona Beach newspaper articles indicate that the area was a hotbed of illegal gambling operations and part of it involved France's former promotion partner, Smokey Purser.[42] If somebody wanted to make book on the outcome of NASCAR races there was nothing Bill France could do about it. France did not mention that he sanctioned races in Canada, where pari-mutuel betting was legal and, of course, there was betting on the results of those races.[43]

Two weeks after France's initial interview with Kahn, something occurred that caused the columnist to unload big time on the Detroit automobile manufacturers. A year after pandering to the executives who came to Daytona Beach in droves, following their every move, detailing all the social events they attended and running countless photographs of them, Kahn complained the executives were giving France gastric pains. "In 1958, stock car racing throughout the U.S. is suffering from a hangover acquired from the two year reign of Detroit's automobile manufacturer," he wrote.[44]

Initially, Kahn said, everybody thought automobile racing and the factories that produced the cars were made for each other. But, he noted the factories' aim was to sell cars. NASCAR, he pointed out, was organized by promoters and its success was determined by stock car racing being seen as a legitimate sport producing ticket revenue. Kahn painted a picture of 'big bad' Detroit pouring millions of dollars into NASCAR, signing the best drivers, using the best parts and equipment and confusing the public and racing fans. "After the Daytona Beach speed trials and races last year," he wrote, "the advertising claims of Chevrolet, Plymouth, Ford, Mercury and Pontiac made it seem they'd all won and that NASCAR, the sponsoring organization, said so. You couldn't escape the feeling that there must be something wrong, not to say rotten."[45] Kahn went on to say that Detroit wasn't really interested in NASCAR as a sport but was just using stock cars racing to sell their products.[46]

Of course, France was unhappy with the automobile manufacturers. Along with Kiekhaefer, they had temporarily usurped his control of stock car racing. For more than a decade, he had kept drivers on his plantation by paying them ten percent, or less, of his gates. Then, Detroit came along and actually paid the drivers a salary and, in some cases, allowed them to keep all of the money they won. Some owners even gave them cars.

Detroit was enriching top drivers, Kahn wrote in his column that ran across the top of the sports page of the *Daytona Beach Morning Journal*. He accused Detroit of introducing unprecedented hoopla and ballyhoo to stock car racing.[47] "Finally," he continued, "NASCAR clamped down on the hucksterism and threatened to expose any manufacturer who misled the public with false advertising claims. NASCAR issued an official news release berating two major Detroit manufacturers for false advertising claims."[48] What Detroit did was scare the hell out of France, who saw the possibility that his gravy train might end before he got his new speedway built.

Kahn claimed that the National Safety Council and President Dwight Eisenhower threatened to rake Detroit automobile manufacturers over the coals for their conduct. In Kahn's opinion, two things happened after Ford, Chrysler, General Motors, Nash-Hudson and Packard left stock car racing: Bill France put out the word that Detroit was trying to kill stock car racing, and when the manufacturers left there was a vacuum for independent car owners to fill. "All that was left after last June 6 were the used cars and tools left behind by Detroit."[49]

France's charges against Detroit automobile manufacturers amounted to a drop of water in the Atlantic Ocean. Along with establishing the interstate highway system, which would facilitate even higher automotive speeds, President Dwight D. Eisenhower created an advisory council to the NSC and named newspaper tycoon William Randolph Hearst as the chairman. Hearst used his newspapers and magazines to not only inform the public about the rising toll of traffic deaths, but to urge them to contact their elected officials to do something about it. From October 1952 through December 1955, Hearst newspapers printed approximately three million lines on highway fatalities and injuries and how to reduce the death toll.[50]

There were other fallacies in Kahn's assumptions. Detroit's efforts to kill stock car racing when, even after their departure, the sport remained a marketing tool for their sales by its very nature made no sense. The association between the automobiles racing fans drove and those on the track was one of the foundation of NASCAR. Independent car owners such as Bud Moore began to return to NASCAR before Detroit pulled out because France subsidized them. As for the cars the manufacturers left behind, they were state of the art racing vehicles, as were the parts and tools they also left.

France's hand was visible long before the end of the column. France repeated from his Ebony Lounge speech of December 1947: "The main thing I never want to lose sight of is the fellows NASCAR started out to take care of, the little independent fellows, they're the backbone of stock car racing and we want to keep them going ... during the past couple of years when Detroit spent vast sums on factory racing crews, it took over the winner's circle and froze out the independents."[51]

France could not have asked for a better ending to the beach-road race saga than the 1958 Grand National race. Paul Goldsmith, in a Smokey Yunick prepared 1958 Pontiac, and Curtis Turner, in a 1958 Ford, battled down to the last second. Turner was driving the same car in which he won the Convertible race but with the top bolted down. As 35,000 spectators held their collective breath, the two took the checkered flag. Goldsmith finished two seconds ahead of Turner.[52] Of the forty-nine cars that entered the race, thirty-one finished.[53]

Otherwise, the beach-road races ended in the usual fiscal manner. France paid out $38,500 in purses for the Modified-Sportsman, Convertible and Grand National races while taking in approximately $226,500 from the three gates, in addition to his fifty-five percent cut of concessions plus parking and program revenue.[54]

In May 1958, NASCAR executive manager Pat Purcell worked with Sam Nunis, the Trenton Speedway director, to promote the first Northern 500. The $20,000 Grand National

Memorial Day race purse was more than Bill France was accustomed to paying for races except for the Southern 500 at Darlington. The amount certainly exceeded the $15,270 purse France posted for the Grand National beach-road race.[55]

Nunis, when he was promoting stock car and Indy car races for the AAA, was accustomed to directing forty percent of the gate into the race purse. The fiscal advisability of staging a 500-mile stock car race in New Jersey on the same day as the Indianapolis 500 was questionable.

An incident at the Northern 500, and another at the Southern 500 at Darlington indicated that NASCAR was truly what Smokey Yunick described as a seat-of-the-pants operation as far as consistent rules enforcement was concerned. Frankie Schneider, from Lambertville, New Jersey, won the pole for the Northern 500. He asked Pat Purcell, who was helping Nunis promote the race, if NASCAR could buy him a set of tires. Purcell informed Schneider that promoters could not give any favors to entrants and took away his pole position for even asking the question. Schneider protested. Purcell told him he could get his pole position back if he returned his car to the track, where the cars were impounded, and resubmitted it for mechanical inspection. Or, Purcell told Schneider, if he did not return his car and submit it for re-inspection, he would be suspended immediately for unsportsmanlike conduct.[56] It was easy to see why many in and around stock car racing referred to Purcell as France's enforcer.

The Northern 500 gave NASCAR a shot in the arm, publicity wise. Junior Johnson, who won five races in 1955 and was sixth in points, had returned to racing from an enforced stay, eleven months out of a two-year sentence, in the Chillicothe (Ohio) Federal Prison. Johnson was driving a Ford owned by Syracuse automobile dealer Paul G. Spaulding in the Trenton race.[57]

Johnson did not win the Northern 500 but he came in second to Fireball Roberts. Lee Petty was third. Only fifteen of the thirty-five cars finished the race before a sparse crowd of 5,000. "To say promoters dropped a bundle is putting it mildly because the purse for the race was more than $28,000," *Herald-Journal* sports editor Jim Foster wrote. Foster pointed out that there were three races, one of which was a NASCAR event, staged on the West Coast the same weekend, and combined attendance for all three barely topped 12,000. "Promoters estimated a loss of close to $50,000 on those three races," Foster added.[58]

The longevity of the contract France signed with Nunis and the Hamids to use the Trenton track was not known but, in the beginning, France hailed it as a NASCAR victory over USAC. However, Nunis was promoting USAC car races at the Trenton Speedway in August 1959.[59]

Just how much money France and his partners lost on the New Jersey race over the Memorial Day weekend was not known. However, the purse at the next Grand National 500-mile race at Martinsville on June 3 was much less than the Northern 500 purse. The Old Dominion 500 winner, Fireball Roberts, received $3,150 out of the $13,675 purse for his win.[60]

Kahn, in the *Daytona Beach Morning Journal,* pointed out a few weeks later that NASCAR's purse money was based on track size, location, seating capacity, attendance and type of race meet. He hastened to add the people in NASCAR who handled the money for the races were bonded.[61]

Just about all of the big money races in 1958 were won by Fireball Roberts. He took first in the Raleigh 250 over the Fourth of July before 15,000 spectators. The race was a combination of Grand National hard tops and convertibles. Of the fifty-five cars entered, only thirty-two finished. France must have had high expectations for the race because the purse was $19,000.[62]

The next big money race, with a purse of $60,000, was the Southern 500 at Darlington Raceway over Labor Day. If the expected crowd of 75,000 showed up, the gate was in the neighborhood of $450,000.[63] Twenty-two of the fifty cars were Fords but that made little difference to Roberts and his 1957 Chevrolet. When Fireball crossed the finish line five laps ahead of the second car driven by Buck Baker, he had averaged 102.590 mph. Roberts' winnings, plus lap money, came to $11,450.[64]

Again, there was a problem with the Darlington track. The first turn became so slick that three cars went through the guardrail and down a thirty-foot embankment. Eddie Gray, from Gardena, California, was probably in more danger after the wreck than during. First aid attendants were giving him oxygen while mechanics were using torches to cut away the wreckage of his car in order to remove him. Don Kimberly, from Tyrone, Pennsylvania, ripped off his gas tank when he hit the guardrail but escaped the burning car. Eddie Pagan, the race's pole sitter from Lynwood, California, blew a tire in the same turn, went through what was left of the guardrails and down the embankment. He crawled out uninjured.[65]

All fifty cars in the Southern 500 were furnished a free set of tires by Darlington Raceway with the approval of NASCAR.[66] The NASCAR rules on free sets of tires had changed between the Memorial Day race in New Jersey and the Labor Day race in South Carolina.

Although Fireball Roberts won the most money, $32,219, during the 1958 Grand National season, Lee Petty won the championship and earned $25,565. Regardless of some of the high purses, such as the $60,000 payout at Darlington, the fifty-one Grand National races averaged $5,259, slightly less than 1957, for the top fifty drivers.[67]

14

Whatever Happened to Marshall Teague?

• • • • • • •

Speed Week 1959 in Daytona Beach was much different from the previous years. Instead of being all about the visiting automobile executives, all the promotion was built around the hastily finished Daytona International Speedway, which France envisioned would eclipse Darlington. Safety did not hinder NASCAR officials' agenda, as they had cars driving practice laps before all the guardrails were installed on the high-banked track. France even crossed his own forbidden line of mixing NASCAR and USAC events in order to pull the biggest crowds, get the most national publicity and make as much money as possible. To build publicity for the big race, the Daytona 500, France wanted a driver on his new track to break the closed circuit speed record of 176.818 mph set by Tony Bettenhausen, from Tinley Park, Illinois, at Monza, Italy, in a Novi Special in 1957.[1]

He had the driver in mind that might have a chance to break Bettenhausen's record, Marshall Teague, who had been setting records and winning championships in USAC.

Smokey Yunick described Teague as "A real good human, a damn good driver and one of the top three mechanics in racing in the thirties and forties." While he chose to put his own World War II experiences behind him, Yunick said Teague, who he described as one of the founders of NASCAR, talked proudly about being a flight engineer on a B-29.[2]

The $10,000 bait France dangled before Marshall Teague to persuade him to break the closed circuit record was too tempting for the driver and his family to pass up. Teague, along with Buddy Shuman and others, had been constant thorns in France's side about constantly changing rules and his race purses in relation to what they knew his race gates produced.

All that aside, there were a number of reasons France selected Teague. He knew he needed the money. Mitzi Teague said her husband talked about having a big business deal in the works. She said he told her, "One thing's certain, now we can send Patricia to college."[3]

Teague was exceedingly popular in Daytona Beach; he had gone to Seabreeze High School there and was always a big favorite in the beach-road races. His car owner, Chapman J. Root—a millionaire who made his money from glass Mason jars, often used to hold moonshine whiskey, and the distinctive green Coca-Cola bottles—spent the winters in Ormond Beach.[4]

If Teague broke the closed circuit speed record, France would reap world-wide publicity for his track. France, who already had the beach course packed with races, refused Root's request to test his car on the beach. He would gain more publicity, and money, from a test on his new high-banked race track.[5]

In addition, Smokey Yunick said France promised to let Teague back into NASCAR if he broke the world record. Yunick was concerned about Teague's safety because he said the Sumar Special was not only seven or eight miles short on speed but it had bad aerodynamics. "It wants to fly the nose," Yunick wrote. There was a close association between the two. "Marshall Teague was the first driver I ever worked with," Yunick said.[6]

Yunick, after Teague asked for his help with the car, said he told him the car's body was all wrong, it would have to be rebuilt. Teague said there was no money to do that. Teague did a practice run at the speedway and was clocked at 171.82 mph in the Sumar. The car was not exactly an Indy car, as it was more streamlined and had a canopy over the driver's cockpit. "We were not geared for the speedway," Root said of Teague's practice run. "The mechanics will change the gears tonight for a Tuesday run. It looks to me as if someone will do over 180 mph here." John Blouch, the chief mechanic for the Sumar from Terre Haute, said, "We miscalculated on the centrifugal force here, so we are making changes."[7]

For the media, Teague jumped through all the hoops. "Comparing Daytona to Monza is like comparing a highway to a country road," he said. "The Daytona course is smoother and vision is not as bad as it is in Monza because the turns are not as sharp."[8]

On Tuesday night before the speed trial on Wednesday, February 11, Teague was apprehensive about the car. "We're trying to get the gears and the weight adjusted and everything set up proper for this speedway," he said. "This is the finest track in the world. It's deceptive, though. When you are going 165 mph you just feel like you're coasting at about 135."[9]

Both Teague and his wife were concerned about the car. Mitzi Teague said she did not accompany her husband to the speed trial because she was afraid he would sense her fear. "You can do that, you know, you can make someone else feel it. And, I stayed away," she said. Teague had his own doubts and called Yunick around 7:00 on the morning of his official run and asked him to come to the track to help him. "I can't help you," Yunick told Teague. "Get the hell out of the car and quit it." Concerned that he could not talk Teague out of making the run, Yunick wrote about his efforts to stop the speed race, "I call France at 8:30 a.m. chew his ass out and ask him to go to the track and tell Marshall the 'deal's off' but okay his return to NASCAR. It don't happen, France tells me to 'mind my own god-damned business.'"[10] Bill Cannon, Teague's mechanic, was also very concerned. "I tried to get him not to go out today ... but he wouldn't hear of it."[11]

A United Press International (UPI) article in the Sarasota newspaper contained a stunning observation. "The front of the car appeared to be sagging when Teague took it out of the pit on Wednesday," the article stated. "Then, tragedy struck on the west turn of the International Speedway course."[12]

Joe Epton, NASCAR timer, clocked Teague at 160.25 mph before he crashed on the third lap of the trial. Teague's car went into a slide on the high bank west turn. The Sumar flipped five times, traveled 500 yards (the length of five football fields) from the point where the slide began, the engine separated from the chassis, parts flew everywhere and the seat, with Teague still strapped in, landed 150 feet from the chassis.[13]

Marshall Teague, thirty-seven years old, was dead and the world of stock car racing was in shock. Bill France gave a tepid explanation of the accident, "There's no indication of tire or mechanical failure. It could have been physical failure or something like that."[14]

Buck Baker said, "I always feel that there has to be a reason for a fellow with the experience like Teague when he cracks up. Something went wrong with the car and I can't figure it out."[15] Fireball Roberts, tears pouring down his face, said, "Marshall is the guy who started me out in racing."[16]

"No one knows for sure what happened," Tom McCahill, auto editor of *Mechanix Illustrated,* said. "The car was in the dead center of the course as it entered the approach of the turn. Then it dipped down. I don't think it was driver failure. An experienced driver such as Teague would have been able to overcome it if it wasn't for equipment failure somewhere."[17]

His accident was more than adequately covered in the Daytona Beach newspaper with a front page full of articles, photographs and interviews, but the publication went further. Reporter Mabel Norris Reese went into the Teague home on Terrace Avenue and described his grief-stricken widow prostrate on her bed sobbing uncontrollably as relatives and neighbors urged her "to let it all out ... it's the best for you." The reporter also described Mitzi Teague's halting speech as she stood in the trophy-filled den of their home.[18]

In the garage behind their home, Teague had been building a Chevrolet Impala for Montreal native Dick Foley to drive in the Daytona 500. Bill France had agreed for Teague to set the car up under NASCAR rules and enter as an owner but not as a driver. Red Vogt, Joe Wolfe and Fireball Roberts decided, in tribute to Teague, they would gather up other mechanics and finish the car. "We're going to talk to Mitzi and see if she wants us to finish the car," Vogt said. "We'd like to go ahead and run it under his name. The tuning and set-up is about done. A lot of the best mechanics in the business have volunteered to get that Teague running as fast as we can for the championship races. The decision is up to Mitzi, of course."[19]

Marshall Teague's friends finished his car and entered it in the Daytona 500 under his name as owner. Dick Foley finished thirty-second in the fifty-nine car field, winning $150.[20]

Yunick and his other close friends knew that Teague was a near mechanical genius. But, most in racing were unaware of what Teague did the previous season when he was not racing. Marshall Teague was working on what was then a little known government project up the Florida coast at Cape Canaveral.[21]

"They named a grandstand after him and put him in a couple halls of fame," Yunick said. "He was finally back in good standing with NASCAR. The day I helped carry Marshall his last foot horizontally, and then six foot down, I started to feel a smoldering resentment toward France." He added that resentment did not go away until he discovered France had been suffering from Alzheimer's disease during the last decades of his life.[22]

Recalling Bill France's last visit to his shop under the watchful eye of a male nurse, Yunick said it dawned on him that life was like a race. "Skill and brains could set up a victory but the ultimate challenge of the variables of life itself dictated the winner or the loser," he said. "I also learned it's very difficult to really know if you won or lost. Did the man who lived to be ninety and was sick the last twenty-five years of his life or did the man who dies at thirty-five doing what he wanted to do win?"[23]

There was speculation about whether France paid his widow the $10,000 Teague died trying to earn. Pat Purcell compelled all drivers at the track to take a physical examination given by a team of doctors at the speedway's infirmary. The previous month, Purcell announced that before any driver could even practice on the new speedway, he had to undergo a rigorous physical.[24] If Teague underwent a physical before his trial run, it was never made public.

Whether Chapman Root provided Teague's widow and daughter with any compensation, since both Root and the mechanics admitted the car was not initially set up properly, was not known.

It only took Bill France two days after Marshall Teague's death to blame Teague for the accident that took his life. He was quoted as saying, "He saw no indication of tire or mechanical failure—it looked like he lost control." USAC chief steward Harlan Fenger, from Dayton, Ohio, agreed with France's assessment.[25]

In an effort to stave off critics of his new race track, France said, "We think the track is designed for the utmost safety. We can see no more possibilities of other fatalities than there would normally be." There would be twenty-five other fatalities at the Daytona International Speedway between Teague's death and that of Dale Earnhardt on February 18, 2001. One of those fatalities was that of Dr. Bernie Taylor, who died in a powerboat race on Lake Lloyd, in the infield of the track, on June 14, 1959, four months after Teague's death.[26]

Bill France had defenders in Teague's tragic death. One was Bill Robinson, a sports reporter for the *Atlanta Journal-Constitution* who covered NASCAR. After he retired, Robinson wrote that Teague was "a dear and personal friend of Bill France. Big Bill reportedly wept when he found out that Teague had died."[27]

Marshall Teague's death on the new speedway did not deter either NASCAR or USAC from staging an Indy-type race there on April 4, 1959. France worked out an agreement with USAC through Thomas W. Binford, from Indianapolis, the president, and Henry Banks, director of competition, and the FIA in Paris. France further agreed that USAC cars could practice at Daytona.[28]

On the last lap of the USAC 100-mile race, the Bowes Seal Fast Special driven by George Amick, from Rhinelander, Wisconsin, hit the track's outer guardrails at 170 mph, flipped end over end and disintegrated. Amick, considered one of the best speedway drivers in the nation, was killed instantly. Amick had qualified for the race at 176.887 mph. "I had no idea I was going that fast," he said. "I might be able to squeeze a little more out of the car but not much."[29]

Dick Rathmann, whose brother, Jim, won the race, said he thought Amick lost it coming out of the west turn. "There was so much junk in the air I could hardly see to pass on the inside of Amick's car." Rathmann said. Amick's car was crumpled like a paper wad, the front wheels were torn off and the vehicle broke off eight guardrail posts. The car was owned by Robert M. Bowes, II, from San Francisco, whose company made tire accessories, lug nuts, air gauges and air hoses. George Bignotti, who won the Indianapolis 500 in 1961 and 1964 with A. J. Foyt, was Amick's chief mechanic.[30]

After Amick's death at Daytona, France circled the wagons to protect himself and his track. Banks, holding his credit, investigated and announced DIS was absolved of any blame in Teague's accident and death. USAC officials wanted to get away from Daytona as fast as they could. Racing director Henry Banks, from Indianapolis, announced the 300-mile Indy car race scheduled for DIS in July would not be held and, pending further research and development, no roadster-type cars would race at Daytona. France substituted a 250-mile stock car race.[31] The race France substituted for the 300-mile Indy car event became Daytona's first Firecracker race.[32]

Evidently, blaming another driver for losing his life on France's speedway was not sitting well with the public. Pat Purcell, joined by USAC's Banks, parsed their words carefully, saying that the track could not be blamed for Teague's and Amick's deaths. Their reason for the deaths was that the "track was engineered far ahead of the automotive industry."[33] The rhetorical question was, who was responsible for engineering the track?

Louis Ossinsky, who fashioned the NASCAR incorporation documents, gave a rare interview connecting racing and safety two days before Teague's death. "Racing is the most hazardous operation about," Ossinsky said. "So, one of our greatest concerns has been with safety. In turn, this had led to better and safer automobiles for the American motorist." To make his point, Ossinsky used the illustration of how tire manufacturers improved their product after the first Southern 500 at Darlington.[34]

Ossinsky said he researched laws pertaining to speedways, which led to safety features in NASCAR regulations. When asked about his contributions to NASCAR, Ossinsky replied, "Oh, you know, I just listen to the boys talk and give them my advice. Sometimes they take it; sometimes they don't."[35]

Fans, however, always seemed to take their racing in whatever package it was presented. Sometimes not even a fire could force them away from a race.

The 8,000 spectators at the 100-mile Grand National race at the Wilson (North Carolina) Speedway were determined to see the March 28, 1959, event. An hour before the race, the wooden grandstand caught on fire and burned. The spectators, none of whom were hurt, simply moved to the catch fence area to watch Junior Johnson win the race in his Ford.[36]

Richard Petty said the weather was so cold in Wilson that spectators built fires under the grandstands to keep warm and burned them down. "They had to stop the race because the town's [only] fire truck was in the infield," he said.[37]

In May 1959, the Grand National cars were back at the Trenton (New Jersey) Speedway, but they were racing for a much smaller purse, $7,100. Sam Nunis was in charge of qualifying and said he would take all the 1957, 1958 and 1959 model cars that signed up. No mention was made of Pat Purcell being there to look over his shoulder. Tom Pistone, from Chicago, won the race.[38]

In another Grand National race in May, Junior Johnson was back in the winner's circle again at Hickory Speedway. Johnson turned his Ford over in practice, worked on it diligently and finished two laps ahead of Joe Weatherly.[39]

Lee Petty once again contested race results at the 150-mile Grand National event at Lakewood Speedway in June 1959. This time he protested against his own son. For about an hour, Richard Petty thought he had won the race. After fifty laps, the race was stopped because drivers were complaining that the dust was caking on their windshields, cutting their visibility. Petty presented his wife's scorecards as proof he won the race and NASCAR officials agreed.[40]

Elizabeth Petty was not a race competitor but she always came to the track prepared. Tom Higgins, a Charlotte sportswriter, recalled her involvement in a Greensboro, North Carolina, fracas. Higgins said that Lee Petty and DeWayne Louis "Tiny" Lund became fierce personal enemies. The Harlan, Iowa, native was anything but tiny, standing six foot six and weighing about 280 pounds. Lund drove for Petty for a while and their separation was acrimonious. When drivers were walking across the stage to be introduced, Petty and Lund passed each other and words were exchanged followed by blows. Petty was no match for

Lund even after his sons, Richard and Maurice, rushed in to help. Elizabeth Petty marched into the fight with her pocketbook and began banging Lund over the head with it. Lund, who had no problem with holding the three males in the Petty family at bay, was subdued by the wife and mother. Seems Elizabeth Petty always carried a pistol in her purse when she went to the races.[41]

Curtis Turner attested to that after a 1960 altercation he and Lee Petty engaged in before a race. "The purse didn't hurt so much when she hit me with it," he said. "But the revolver inside the purse sure as hell did."[42]

Lee Petty was the favorite for the first Firecracker 250 after having won the Daytona 500 five months earlier. Forty-two cars were entered for the $28,000 purse. France faced negative publicity, resulting more from Teague's death than Amick's, because the local driver was not only from Daytona but was exceedingly well liked. He fell back on his old habit of naming races and trophies after dead drivers. France announced the winner of the Firecracker 250 would receive the Marshall Teague Memorial Trophy and Patricia Teague would make the presentation.[43] The *Daytona Beach Morning Journal* ran a front page photograph of Patricia and Mitizi Teague holding the trophy.[44]

Fireball Roberts won the first Firecracker 250, on July 4, with an average speed of 140.58 mph, just barely topping Lee Petty's 139.42 mph in winning the first Daytona 500. Roberts drove a Chevrolet prepared by Smokey Yunick and owned by Jim Stephens, from Daytona Beach, and his share of the $28,000 purse was $4,100. France, in an unusual move, made public his probable gate from the race. He said he grossed in excess of $62,000 from admissions and the time trials. The Firecracker 250 drew only 12,019 in attendance compared to the 42,191 who attended the Daytona 500 the previous February.[45]

Once again huge crowds converged on the small South Carolina town for the Southern 500 at Darlington Raceway and all the events connected with it over the Labor Day weekend. Darlington, a small town of about 6,500, had learned to cope with crowds of 70,000 and 80,000.

NASCAR required all drivers to average at least 135 mph in qualifying for the 1959 Southern 500. The purse was $67,915. Cale Yarborough, from nearby Timmonsville, won the pole with a speed of 151.985 mph. Winner of the Southern 500 was Jim Reed, from Peekskill, New York, who had also won five NASCAR short track championships in the 1950s. Reed's Chevrolet averaged 111.836 mph on an asphalt track where the temperature was 104 degrees. More than 78,000 spectators braved the heat. His Chevrolet won on Goodyear tires, for the first time in a Grand National race, over forty-nine other entrants.[46]

Lee Petty repeated as the 1959 Grand National champion for the third time with winnings of $49,220. France paid out $289,175 to the top fifty Grand National drivers for the forty-four race schedule, an average race purse of $6,572.[47]

For many in stock car racing, the death of Marshall Teague cast shadows on NASCAR's concerns about safety, or the lack thereof, at super speedways. But, more were being built.

15

Charlotte, Atlanta Join the Super Speedways

∙∙∙∙∙∙∙

When Curtis Turner and Bruton Smith, from Charlotte, and Garland Bagley, from Atlanta, saw Bill France's potential profits from the building of his Daytona speedway, they decided to emulate him by constructing two new 1.5 mile tracks in their cities and attempted to build the $2 million facilities in less than a year.

A short track, located in the east Tennessee mountains and built in an entirely different manner, was also in the planning stages.

The combination of Turner and Smith, given their personalities, was an unlikely one from the beginning. Turner, the former whiskey transporter, was the suave, party-loving timber baron who associated with millionaires, corporate executives and movie stars such as James Garner and delighted in engaging in aeronautical high jinks.

His favorite partner, on the track and in the air, was Joe Weatherly. The two would fly side-by-side attempting to knock the flashing lights off each other's wing tips or see how close they could fly above and below each other. Weatherly never learned to navigate; he simply followed highways. They were scheduled to meet each other at the Charlotte airport. Turner arrived first and became anxious when Weatherly was thirty minutes late. When he landed, Turner rushed over, grabbed Weatherly by the collar and demanded, "Where in the hell have you been?" Weatherly replied, "I got lost. Yeah, they were doing construction on the roads so I had to follow the detour."[1]

Smith, something of Turner's opposite, sold cars but had little racing experience. The strengths he brought to the partnership were in promotion. He had been mentored in the business by Sam Nunis and knew the ins and outs of race promoting. Like Turner, it was questionable how much he knew about building a super speedway.

Neither group evidently paid much attention to France's problems in finding money for the construction of Daytona. Smith and Turner had contemplated building separate speedways in the Charlotte area but combined their money and egos into one operation. Their second biggest mistake was allowing only ten months for construction of the 1.5-mile paved track.

When France held the first Daytona 500 in 1959, he still had a construction deficit of

$159,138, which should have indicated how difficult such a project could be.[2] Turner, Smith and Bagley had a changing array of partners but apparently none of the deep-pocketed variety that France found.

Curtis Turner's initial speedway partners were Harold Brasington, who built Darlington Raceway, Enoch Staley, who build North Wilkesboro Speedway, and Alvin Hawkins, France's partner in the Bowman Gray Stadium lease. Their combined experience would have been a great asset to Turner. Chances were that Brasington, an experienced earthmover, would have found the mountain of granite underneath the track that caused so much trouble. Staley, and partners Lawson Curry and Jack and Charlie Combs, started out to build an oval track at North Wilkesboro with $1,500. When the money ran out, Staley adapted and ended up with a quirky five-eighths-mile dirt track with a sloping downhill front stretch and a backstretch that ran uphill. Hawkins, the NASCAR flagman and France's partner in Bowman Gray, was savvy about the ins and outs of racing staging. In order to get the Bowman Gray lease from the city of Winston-Salem, he and France had to promise to pay for the previous paving job on the track. Seems a midget car promoter convinced them to pave the track saying he would pay for it. The promoter failed to pay for the paving.[3]

When Turner decided to join forces with Smith to build the Charlotte facility, Brasington, Staley and Hawkins withdrew.[4]

Bagley and fellow real estate developers Walker Jackson, Lloyd Smith, Ralph Sceniano and Ike Supporter began to plan the Atlanta International Raceway in 1958. The group ran out of money and all dropped out except Bagley, who recruited Atlanta businessmen Warren Grennel, Bill Boyd, Jack Blunt and Art Lester as his new partners. They selected a site twenty-five miles south of Atlanta, in Hampton, Georgia, where land was less expensive.[5]

Racing columnist Ed Hinton, who was living in Atlanta at the time, had a problem with the Hampton site. "They should have built it up North," he wrote, "nearer to the mountains that spawned the 'shine runners that spawned the sport, nearer the passion, nearer the history and then Atlanta's race track for these fifty years would have been nearer the very heart of NASCAR."[6]

Turner and Smith selected farmland just inside neighboring Cabarrus County as the site for their speedway, and ground was broken July 29, 1959. They filed their incorporation documents with the North Carolina secretary of state on August 19, 1959. Turner, Smith and J. Richard Phillips, also from Charlotte, made up the board of directors who initially issued a million shares of common stock at one dollar each. Turner was president and Smith was vice-president. Phillips was one of Turner's partners in his National Timber Sales Corporation.[7]

By November, Turner and Smith were out of money and filed an amendment to their incorporation to restructure their shares. They divided their stock into preferred and common. The 100,000 shares of preferred stock had a value of five dollars each and the 2,000,000 shares of common stock were for one dollar each.[8]

While the two speedways owners labored to build their facilities, life in NASCAR's Grand National Division continued. Apparently, there was a dust up over the invitations Pat Purcell sent out for the Victory Dinner, where the 1959 awards were presented. Purcell had the invitations mailed only to the drivers. He was later forced to announce that drivers' wives could attend the two cocktail parties, at the Ellinor Village Country Club and the Daytona Plaza, but they could not accompany their husbands to the Victory Dinner at the Princess Issena Hotel. That was stag only.[9]

Champion Spark Plug, sponsor of the Buddy Shuman Award, gave the honor to Bill France that year. Speed Week 1960 was more or less like the previous year. There were the speed trials on the beach, eight days of National Hot Rod Association (NHRA) at the Flagler-Bunnell Airport's half-mile track, Midget races at the Memorial Stadium and Go Kart events at the Jai Alai Fronton.[10]

Things did not go well in the undercard's qualifying race. Bill France's new speedway looked like a demolition derby at the beginning of the 250-mile Modified-Sportsman race. Twenty-five of the 100 laps were run under the yellow flag due to rain and winds of twenty-four to thirty miles per hour. Gale strength winds began at thirty-two miles per hour. Of the sixty-eight cars entered in the race, thirty-seven vehicles were involved in a wreck that occurred in front of the grandstand on the first lap, sending eight drivers to the hospital.[11]

Fireball Roberts and newcomer, Marion "Bubba" Farr, from Augusta, Georgia, traded paint as they battled for the race lead. Roberts was slowly increasing his margin over Farr when his car sputtered to a stop and had to be pushed off the track on lap eighty-three. Farr, a former motorcycle racer who was a restaurant operator and movie projectionist, won the race in his 1956 Ford with a 1958 Lincoln engine.[12]

So many cars had been knocked out of the race that France held a consolation race in order to get as many cars as possible in the Daytona 500. During the race, the car driven by Tommy Irwin, from Spartanburg, plunged off the track and into Lake Lloyd. Horrified spectators watched as the car slowly submerged under the water and silently they waited for the driver to appear. Irwin finally exited the car, rose to the surface and swam to land.[13]

Curtis Turner won the consolation race followed by Ned Jarrett, from Newton, North Carolina, and Elmo Langley, from Wheaton, Maryland.[14]

The second Daytona 500 was the focal point of Speed Week and spectators were not disappointed. Junior Johnson made a discovery that forever changed how stock car drivers raced on high-banked tracks. Most of the media expected one of the Pettys, Fireball Roberts, Buck Baker or a number of other drivers to win. Johnson was not given much of a chance. More than 50,000 spectators saw something new other than the twelve wrecks where two drivers were injured. Tom Herbert crashed his Thunderbird coming out of the west turn and smashed the guardrail; the engine separated from the chassis, and the car's body disintegrated when it landed upside down. Herbert, when he reached the hospital, stood to lose the sight in one eye and possibly one hand. Tom Pistone lost control of his Chevrolet and suffered a concussion, fractured collarbone and internal injuries.[15]

George Green, from Johnson City, Tennessee, was in a car that caught fire in front of the grandstand. The car laid a carpet of fire as Green, a sergeant on leave from the U.S. Army in Frankfurt, Germany, steered the vehicle to the grass and bailed out.[16]

Daytona Beach sports editor Kahn wrote about what happened next. "At 190 laps, (Bobby) Johns looked as if he had licked the starting field of 68 cars, eight late entries were admitted. Then an ill wind blew out his back window and Junior Johnson won the race." Kahn explained that after losing his back window, the wind inside Johns' car lifted all four wheels off the track; he spun on the backstretch straightaway, barreled sideways through the turn and skidded within three feet of Lake Lloyd before he could get his car back on the track.[17]

Smokey Yunick, who built Johns' car, had a better explanation. He said Johnson qualified twenty miles an hour slower than Johns but, with his crew chief Ray Fox, kept improving his power during practice. Yunick said Johnson invented the drafting maneuver there at Daytona. "We were leading all day," he said. "At the end he sucked our rear glass out from the drafting. He won the race."[18]

According to Johnson's version, "I could see Cotton Owens coming off turn four in one of the Pontiacs. I got up to speed, just wide open. Here he came, up on me and went around me. When he did I ducked in behind him and dern, going down the backstretch, going into the third turn, I was running all over him." After another pit stop, Johnson went back out and was running just as slow as he had earlier. "I waited on Jack Smith. He had the fastest car. He was a little bit faster than Cotton but I could stay with him the same way I could with Cotton."[19]

Johnson described what happened as the race continued, "When I was sitting behind one of the Pontiacs, shucks, I wasn't running but about two-thirds throttle. But, I was turning a thousand RPM more." All the Pontiacs failed except for Johns'. "The Pontiac teams figured it out," Johnson recalled. "Jack Smith had burned out a wheel bearing and they fixed it and sent him out. They sent Jack out to pull Bobby up to beat me. When they went by me, it [the force of the draft] took Bobby's back glass out and he spun down the backstretch and when I came [around] he was sitting there. After I won the race, I told Ray Fox, 'We hitched a ride to the winner's circle.'"[20]

"And the whole damn race car was built in about three weeks by three or four men, including Junior," Yunick said. "Well, now that just about took the rag off the bush. Watching him with his success with Ray Fox and the Holman-Moody teams, I knew a new he-coon was in our woods." Yunick credited Johnson's success as a driver with his understanding of the physics of the automobile acquired when he was transporting illegal whiskey. He said Johnson developed theories regarding engines that had Detroit and universities listening and copying.[21]

That was not quite correct, Johnson later said. When asked if he went to General Motors engineers for help, Johnson replied, "Naw, but sometimes they come to me."[22]

Johnson was involved in another racing situation, in March 1960, at the 100-mile Grand National race at North Wilkesboro, but that time he was the victim. With fourteen laps to go, Lee Petty bumped Johnson out of his way to win his forty-ninth career race, one more than Herb Thomas. North Wilkesboro was considered Johnson's home track and spectators, angered by Petty's actions, responded by hurling rocks, bottles and any other objects that were handy at him in the winner's circle.[23]

Three years earlier, Petty had been warned by NASCAR about his rough driving and apparently ignored Pat Purcell's letter. Purcell, NASCAR's executive director, prefaced his letter by saying that Petty had always been his ideal of a true sportsman and he hoped he would take his note in the spirit it had been written. "We have recently received a great many complaints this season about rough driving on your part," Purcell wrote. "And, now things are piling in so fast and from so many different directions that it is going to be necessary for someone to put the 'eye' on you for the next several race meets."[24]

Purcell's note was exceedingly gentle for the man Bill France depended on to enforce his every rule and regulation. Apparently, it made little difference to Petty. Purcell went from soft soap to the hard line as he announced in April 1960 that NASCAR would no longer tolerate bumping like that between Petty and Junior Johnson. But, it took NASCAR three years to make and implement the rule.[25]

It did not take three years for what was about to happen at the new Charlotte speedway. It was a Murphy's Law project—if something could go wrong it did. Turner and Smith contracted with W. Owen Flowe to construct their race track. Flowe agreed, in the contract, to remove boulders for eighteen cents per cubic yard. There were no boulders, just 500,000 yards of solid granite. Flowe upped his removal price to one dollar per cubic yard.[26]

An exceedingly cold Carolina winter, with three winter storms containing sleet, ice and snow, hampered construction and caused labor costs to soar. When spring came work progressed on a twenty-four hour basis. Then the speedway was hit with another phenomenon of nature; hordes of hornets stung workmen as they went about moving three million cubic yards of dirt. By mid–April, there was no grandstand and paving had not begun. Turner and Smith asked France for a three-week postponement of the World 600 and he agreed, setting the new race date for June 19.[27]

Time trials for the World 600, the first 600 mile race in NASCAR, were set for June 16, with practice to begin on June 12. Drivers were anxious to compete for the $106,775 purse but the track paving was not complete. Flowe, claiming Turner and Smith owed him $75,000, parked bulldozers on the track to prevent the paving of the last section. Turner and Smith claimed they had overpaid Flowe and released the following statement, "To date we have paid W. Owen Flowe and Sons $541,500. This, according to our calculations, is an over payment based on the estimated cubic yards the firm has moved."[28]

Turner approached the local sheriff about the matter and was told that since it was private property, there was nothing he could do. Turner and Smith lacked the funds and the time to take Flowe to court. The two men gathered up Turner's brother, Darrell, a friend, Acey Janay, and driver Bob Wellborn. They piled into Turner's car and drove to the track where Flowe had parked the bulldozers. After exchanging angry words with Flowe, who refused to move his machinery until he was paid, Turner told Flowe and his employees to put up their hands as he and his associates brought out their firearms.[29]

Darrell Turner and Acey Janay hot wired the bulldozers and moved them off the track so paving could be completed. When practice began on June 12, chunks of asphalt came up, leaving big holes.[30]

Even at that late date, some of the pavement was taken up. Two days before the race the *Herald-Journal* reported, "More than 800 tons of asphalt and loose base will be torn from the 24 degree banked turns. It will be replaced with new asphalt, then treated with a special solution of liquid rubber. Huge trucks will then roll over the new pavement virtually until race time on Sunday."[31]

Practice by day, pavement patching by night, the Charlotte Motor Speedway was a mess. Joe Weatherly, in the pits during practice, described the track as "Rough, just as rough as Curtis Turner and that's plenty rough."[32]

Weatherly was not the only driver complaining about the track. Fireball Roberts called it a bad paving job. Richard Petty said, "The asphalt is chunking out in the second turn. You've got to be mighty careful out there." Bruton Smith, on Thursday, put the best possible face on their troubles. "We're just glad that it wasn't as bad as we thought it would be," he said. "We feel we gave the drivers a real test today. Any damages that would occur would happen today and we would have plenty of time to repair it before Sunday." Just as soon as practice was finished, paving equipment was brought in to patch the holes.[33]

Track surface was not their only problem. Just days before the race, Turner and Smith were short $75,000 for the purse. France told them that unless the money was in escrow the day before the competition, there would be no race. A few months earlier Turner had bought a small financial institution, the Bank of the Big Island, in Virginia. He flew to Lynchburg and had the bank president loan him $75,000 on a three-day note, although the bank had a $12,000 loan limit. France took Turner's cashier check to the Bank of Charlotte and asked Vice President Dewey Godfrey if it was good. "To me," Godfrey replied, "this is cash."[34]

Fireball Roberts won the World 600 pole with a speed of 133.904 mph, despite the track conditions, and picked up $500 in pole money.[35]

After seventy-nine laps, Turner led his own race, then Tom Pistone and then Junior Johnson. Halfway through the race, Turner's engine failed. Only twenty-four cars finished the race in which the yellow flag came out five times. After the first 100 miles, large chunks of asphalt began to come up to make driving even more difficult in the 90-degree weather. Jack Smith led for 198 laps before a chunk of asphalt split his fuel tank. Johnny Allen, Cotton Owens and John Wolford were involved in an accident that took out all three cars.[36]

An unknown driver, Joe Lee Johnson, from Chattanooga, won the race with an average speed of 107.752 mph and $25,650, from the $106,775 purse. Johnson, the 1959 Convertible Series champion, covered the 600 miles in five hours and thirty-four minutes. Johnny Beauchamp was second with $9,100; Bobby Johns, third, $6,200; Richard Petty, fourth, $3,675, and Lee Petty, fifth, $2,900.[37]

That was not exactly how the race went into the record book. Richard and Lee Petty, who were first and second in the Grand National standings, were disqualified along with Bob Wellborn, Paul Lewis, Al White and Junior Johnson for allegedly entering the pits improperly. Both Pettys had tires that blew out, spinning them off the track into the grassy area where pit lane was. So, instead of steering their limping cars back on the track, possibly causing other accidents, they drove into the pits. Pat Purcell and Johnny Bruner, NASCAR field manager, told drivers in the pre-race meeting they could only enter the pits through the entrance to pit row. Purcell said the violations were reported by technical inspectors in the pits and that he saw each one from his position in the control tower.[38]

When asked for his opinion, Bill France said, "I'm not certain whether such a ruling is in the books. But, it's possible it could have been part of the instructions issued at the drivers' meeting before the race." He added, even if the ruling was not in the book, race officials' decisions had to be followed by the drivers, who also had the right of appeal.[39]

Jim Foster, then a *Herald-Journal* sports reporter who later went to work for NASCAR, wrote, "We have been informed that the drivers were told in the pits to park their cars because of the infractions."[40]

Foster was wrong. If the two drivers had been disqualified in the pits, Pat Purcell would have made sure they parked their cars. Petty said he and his father did not know they had been disqualified until they went to the pay window, after the race, to collect their second and third place money only to be informed they had been disqualified and had no money. Richard Petty said he tried, without success, to explain that they did not drive into the pits; they spun into them.[41]

"You see, the NASCAR guys knew they were going to disqualify us at the time the spins happened," Petty wrote. "But, they let us stay out there and risk our lives and spend a lot of money on tires and gas, just to make their race look better. We had a pretty good following by then, so I guess they wanted to keep our fans at the race so they could buy hot dogs, pop or whatever."[42]

He said he heard Rex White, whom he called NASCAR's fair-haired boy, was the one who complained about their pit stop. "They disqualified Junior Johnson too for doing about the same deal," he continued. "It made us feel even more like those guys were playing favorites because Junior was in our boat. He wasn't very high on their hit parade either."[43]

The word disqualified, in most dictionaries, means out, banned, barred, prohibited and ineligible. However, in NASCAR's language it meant that Lee and Richard Petty, who were allowed to continue racing, would lose two positions in the points standings and then discover they had won no money in the World 600.[44]

After all the confusion and conflict in the World 600, the July 4 Firecracker 250 appeared to run smoothly at Daytona. Jack Smith breezed around the super speedway, making only one stop for fuel for an average of 146.832 mph. Lee and Richard Petty started in the front row but ended up finishing fourth and tenth respectively.[45]

Atlanta International Raceway (AIR) suffered much of the same problems that Turner and Smith experienced at Charlotte when weather delayed construction. The city not only had the famous Lakewood Speedway but an earlier one was built in 1907. Atlanta Coca-Cola magnate Asa G. Candler lent the Atlanta Automobile Association $130,000 at seven percent interest to build a two-mile track at Hapeville, south of the city. The association was to repay Candler after their first big race in 1909. The loan was not repaid and Candler lent them another $5,000 that year and $31,000 more in 1913. By 1914, the Atlanta Automobile Association asked Candler to take the property and forgive the loans. He closed the track, salvaged what he could of the materials, demolished the remainder and created Candler Field, which later became Hartsfield International Airport.[46]

AIR builders had an advantage over Charlotte—a later race date, July 31, providing more time for completion. However, Bagley and partners did not begin to lay down the 1,500 tons of asphalt, six inches thick, on the track until the last of June. They promised the track would be ready with permanent restrooms and grass in the infield.[47]

Truman Bisher, *Atlanta Journal* sports editor, said the track was not ready to be used when the July 31 race was run. "Some of the lower seats were so low that fans couldn't see over the retaining wall," he wrote. "The only bathroom facility in the infield was a three-hole outhouse."[48]

If spectators in the infield were miserable in the July Atlanta heat, driver Lee Petty was determined to be comfortable. Petty, forty-six years old, was one of the older Grand National drivers. He installed air conditioning in the 1960 Plymouth he was driving in the Dixie 300. "With the windows up to increase the aerodynamics and the motor revving high and the sun bearing down, racing a stock car made us hotter than a country stove at dinner time," he said. "What little power air conditioning takes is more than made up for by comfort and efficiency."[49]

Media reports of the attendance for the Dixie 300 ranged from 20,000 to 25,000. Track owners had expected 45,000 but would not have known what to do with them, as the facility's seating and fencing was not complete. Fireball Roberts scoffed at reports that the track surface was not very good; it had more time to cure than the Charlotte track. His average speed of 112.743 mph told another story. Richard Petty said the Atlanta track was harder on tires than the one at Charlotte. "It had long sweeping turns and it ground the tires down in no time at all," he said.[50]

Roberts collected $9,700 for first place; Cotton Owens, $4,850 for second and Jack Smith $2,850 for third from the $43,425 purse. Art Lester, AIT president, told the spectators that, when they returned for the 500-mile race on October 30, conditions at the track would be different. "This raceway will be what we wanted for you today," he promised, "everything designed for the comfort of the public."[51]

There was little comfort anywhere at the Southern 500 at Darlington in 1960. The fifty drivers had to contend with temperature on the pavement reaching a record 145 degrees, and the 80,000 spectators made a lot of noise, for a while. Smokey Yunick's prediction that something terrible would happen, if NASCAR failed to regulate bumping on the track, came true. About a third of the way into the race, Bobby Johns, from Miami, and Roy Tyner, from Red Springs, North Carolina, locked bumpers and began a tragic whirlwind dance. The two cars twisted and tumbled into the pit of Joe Lee Johnson at about 100 mph. Johnson, who had made a pit stop, saw them coming and gunned his motor to get back on the track. That move probably saved his life.[52]

NASCAR official Joe Taylor, from Charlotte, and mechanics Charles Sweatland and Paul McDuffie, from Atlanta, were all killed. Mechanics John Blaylock, Ralph Byers and R. M. Vermillion, Jr., all of Atlanta, were injured and hospitalized. Johns suffered a concussion but Tyner was only shaken up. The race, although three fatalities occurred, was not red flagged but fifty laps were run under caution, extending the time drivers were on the track to almost six miserable hours.[53]

Two laps from the finish, race leader Buck Baker blew a tire and finished the race on three tires and a rim. Rex White passed him, creating yet another scoring situation. Race officials directed both Baker and White to take their cars to the winners' circle. NASCAR officials checked lap charts and, initially, said it would be twenty-four hours before they announced a winner. That idea was trashed and three hours later they decided Baker was the winner with $22,000 out of the $90,000 purse. White got $9,600 for second place, and the points he accumulated propelled him toward the Grand National championship.[54]

In August, Purcell had problems with drivers entering races but failing to show up. Bennie Goodman, general manager of the Fairgrounds Speedway in Nashville, complained to Purcell that twenty-three of the forty cars entered failed to show up for his 200-mile Grand National race. "This poses a real problem for us," he wrote. "Needless to say we are in a very precarious position with the news outlets because of NASCAR's apparent laxity in dealing with drivers and car owners that enter and fail to appear."[55]

Four of the drivers withdrew from the race under NASCAR regulations. Purcell docked three drivers, names not mentioned, 500 points. Others—Jack Smith, Marvin Panch, Charlie Griffith, Joe Weatherly, Curtis Turner, David Pearson, Jimmy Thompson, Possum Jones and Joe Eubanks—simply failed to show. Part of the problem was the larger purses offered at the bigger tracks. The purse for the Nashville race was only $16,000.[56]

Daytona Beach Morning Journal sports editor Kahn offered advice to Bill France. Kahn proposed NASCAR needed a final deciding voice, a high commissioner, that would lend stability to stock car racing much like Kenesaw Mountain Landis did for Major League Baseball and Bert Bell did for the National Football League. He pointed out that the NASCAR by-laws called for it to render judgment on issues and that commission members included France, Ed Otto, vice-president; Pat Purcell, executive manager; Bob Sall, eastern division manager, and Bob Barkheimer, the California promoter who served as a western representative for NASCAR. Since "Cannonball" Baker's death, a new commissioner had not been appointed.[57]

Kahn pointed out lingering problems like the Darlington rain re-start and the premature openings of the Charlotte and Atlanta speedways. He suggested that a high commissioner should be given final authority to decide on appeals from the commission.[58]

There were two more October races to run—second races at both Charlotte and Atlanta of 400 and 500 miles respectively—before a champion would be determined.

Rex White, who was leading in the Grand National points, apparently had an intense dislike for Curtis Turner, Bruton Smith or both. Despite the fact that the Charlotte Speedway had a new coat of asphalt, he announced to the media that the track was "bumpy, rough and dangerous." White went even further by violating NASCAR rules when he took *Herald-Journal* sports reporter Jim Foster for a drive around the Charlotte Motor Speedway at speeds of eighty to 100 mph. Foster swallowed the bait and denounced the track as being dangerous and excoriated Turner, Smith and France for holding the race. Foster neglected to mention in his article that White had driven in the first World 600 at the track, when the surface was in much worse shape, and came in eighth winning $1,350.[59]

Edward G. "Fireball" Roberts, from Daytona Beach, is in his 22 Pontiac with some of his racing trophies in a 1958 photograph. Frank Strickland, standing, owned the Chevrolet team Roberts raced for at that time. The name "Fireball" came not from his racing but from Roberts' pitching style developed at the University of Florida and later with a semi-pro baseball team. Roberts won the 1962 Daytona 500 and died two years later from injuries received in the Charlotte World 600 (State Archives of Florida).

15. Charlotte, Atlanta Join the Super Speedways

Turner responded saying, "I have been around the track at better than 129 mph. I've been driving fourteen years and I've been lucky enough to win my share of them. The track is not like he [White] pictured it to the fans through his statements to the press." He added if White thought the track was unsafe he should not drive in the race. France pointed out that the track had been reworked since the June race, was safe and it was not as bumpy as it was for the first World 600.[60]

Foster jumped on France's statement about the track bumps and wrote, "What France didn't say was that he was not at the World 600 and he didn't know how bumpy it was." Foster was either terribly naïve, lacked the facts or was on a crusade for White but he was wrong. Bill France was certainly in Charlotte for the track's first race. After all, France went to a Charlotte bank to verify Turner's check.[61]

Whatever his motives in his media vendetta against the track owners, White was successful. Only 30,000 spectators showed up for the National 400 to see Speedy Thompson win $11,500 of the $65,000 purse. Once again, NASCAR officials Joe Epton and Johnny Bruner had problems with the lap scoring. They gave Junior Johnson two laps more than he completed and failed to credit Bobby Johns with one lap. The revised order was Thompson; Richard Petty, second, $4,725; Ned Jarrett, third, $3,125; Johns, fourth, $1,950; and Junior Johnson, fifth, $1,625. In the re-shuffle, Rex White was moved from fifth to sixth.[62]

The race ran for thirty-two laps under caution, bringing Thompson's average speed down to 112.905 mph. Lenny Page, from Buffalo, New York, was seriously injured when his car spun out in the fourth turn and was hit by a car driven by Don Odell, from Phoenix.[63] Having only 30,000 paid admissions certainly hurt Turner and Smith in their efforts to keep the Charlotte Motor Speedway afloat.

Speeds were also down at the Atlanta 500 on October 30. Fireball Roberts qualified at 138.975 mph while Bobby Johns' winning speed was 106.642 mph in a 1960 Pontiac. The difference was the rainy weather: more than 100 laps of the race ran under caution. When the rain began, Johns, from Miami, Florida, had a four-lap lead, and he narrowly beat Johnny Allen, from Greenville, South Carolina. There were so many wrecks and mechanical failures that only nineteen of the forty-six cars in the race were running at the finish.[64]

While owners of the Charlotte and Atlanta tracks planned their next moves, a new track was being contemplated in the east Tennessee mountains. Carl Moore and Larry Carrier, partners in a Bristol bowling alley, attended Turner and Smith's initial race at Charlotte, saw spectators paying from ten to twenty dollars a ticket and decided they could make some money building a smaller, paved race track. Their first site was in Piney Flats but the community's ministers protested having a track in their midst.[65]

The two men purchased a 100-acre dairy farm. Moore and Carrier went to Daytona Beach and met with France and Purcell about their venture. Moore said Purcell seemed to like them and awarded their yet to be built track two race dates on the spot. When they returned to Bristol, none of the area banks would lend them money to build the track.[66]

The Federal Reserve had clamped down on banks for not keeping the proper amounts in their reserve funds. Consequently, many financial institutions were carefully screening their loans.[67]

Moore and Carrier made another trip to Daytona Beach to ask for France's assistance in securing finances. France put them in touch with a New Jersey vending firm that lent money at twice the going interest rate. On January 1, 1960, the prime interest rate was five percent on commercial loans. Moore and Carrier worked out an agreement to borrow money from the vending company, which included the firm operating the concessions at the new track.[68]

Moore, Carrier and their new partner, paving contractor R. G. Opoe, built the track, a half-mile entity shaped like a paper clip, in a year from sketches and drawings they made on envelopes and brown paper bags, somewhat like Jack Prince did with his board tracks. The straightaways were sixty-feet wide and the turns, banked at twenty-two degrees, were seventy-feet wide. Forty-two cars started the first Volunteer 500 on June 29, 1961, but only nineteen finished.[69]

Media reported a standing room only crowd of 25,000. The race purse was $16,625, with $3,340 in lap money going to the winner. Jack Smith, from Sand Springs, Georgia, started the race in a Pontiac and Johnny Allen, from Greenville, North Carolina, was driving a Chevrolet. Allen's car caught fire and he dropped out of the race. Smith, during a pit stop, decided the heat inside the car was too intense. "I couldn't stand it," he said. "Heat was coming up through the floor board, my ankle felt like it was going to burn off." Allen got in the Chevrolet and drove it to victory. Smith was awarded the win and he and Allen split the first place money.[70]

France's DIS operated from January 1, 1960, to October 1, 1960, at a deficit. During that period, the speedway generated $38,124 in net income. Broken down, the figures indicated the sources of the money: $475,000 came from admissions after taxes; $79,234 from industrial tests; $18,169 from program advertisements; $8,064 from inside speedway advertising; $41,301 from radio and television; $15,492 from programs, and $30,293 from miscellaneous sources.[71]

The $635,524 in expenses included $189,009 for staging various races; $75,425 for administration; $55,737 for interest; $116,788 in depreciation for a new facility; $3,596 in hospital costs; $21,876 for insurance; $13,095 toward an annual premium for a $1,000,000 life insurance policy on Bill France; $59,365 for maintenance, and $8,450 in taxes and licenses. France purchased the life insurance policy from Lamar Life Insurance Company, which loaned him $600,000 enabling the completion of DIS.[72] Missing from the speedway's expenses were property taxes.

In November 1960, the City of Daytona Beach agreed to be a plaintiff in a lawsuit contesting Volusia County's right to put France's speedway on the on the tax rolls. The Daytona International Speedway had cost $2 million to build but the assessed evaluation was only $250,000. The county tax assessor put the speedway property on the tax rolls but collecting the taxes was another matter.[73]

Rex White handily won the Grand National championship in 1960. Richard Petty finished second followed by Bobby Johns, Buck Baker and Ned Jarrett. With big purses at Charlotte, Daytona and Darlington, the average earnings of the top fifty Grand National drivers reached $11,516, almost double the previous year's amount.[74]

As Turner and Smith struggled with their speedway's finances, France had additional problems not only dealing with discontented drivers and track owners but with safety issues, racing personnel and simple record keeping.

16

Caution Flags Everywhere

∙ ∙ ∙ ∙ ∙ ∙ ∙

While there were no fatalities in the last beach-road race, NASCAR suffered its fifteenth driver fatality of the year at the Richmond Speedway on March 25, 1958, when Gwyn Staley was killed during the Convertible race. Staley, the younger brother of track co-owner Enoch Staley, had won Convertible races at Langhorne and Norfolk in late 1957. He died from injuries sustained when he was pinned under his car during an accident on the first lap of the race when another car fishtailed into his vehicle. Staley's car rolled over three times before hitting a fence.[1]

Staley, thirty years old, left a wife and four children. He was third in the Convertible division standings when he died.[2] France named a race for him.

An earlier March race highlighted NASCAR's problems with race record keeping. Joe Epton was the traveling scorekeeper but it was impossible for him to keep tabs on every car running in a race. Wives, girlfriends or a designated person kept individual scorecards on laps their drivers completed. At the March 2 Concord, North Carolina, Grand National, Curtis Turner appeared to lead every lap. He was visibly upset when race officials gave the race to Lee Petty. He stormed the judge's stand demanding to see the scorecards.[3]

Turner was leading and had pitted after an accident brought out the caution flag and the pace car driver, Barney Wallace, was instructed to pick up the race leader. Wallace, for some reason, was unable to find Turner and waved all the cars by. Wallace finally found Turner as he came out of the pits. Thinking Petty was still a lap down and not knowing Wallace had waved him by, Turner let him pass. NASCAR refused to admit that Wallace's incompetence was a factor and gave the win to Petty.[4]

Before things were sorted out, the 12,000 spectators had left the track thinking Turner had won the race with Speedy Thompson second and Petty third. Petty protested and sent his scorecard, kept by his wife Elizabeth, to NASCAR headquarters in Daytona Beach. Officials gave the race to Petty, causing Turner to remark, "That Mama Elizabeth has the fastest pencil in NASCAR."[5]

Had Lee Petty been a better baseball player, Smokey Yunick said, there probably would not have been a Petty family in stock car racing. "Lee damn near made it in the St. Louis baseball organization as a pitcher," Yunick said when he wrote about inducting the driver and car owner in a hall of fame. "He and about eight or nine other guys got NASCAR going and never got the credit or pay for it either," he added.[6]

Another of those racers Yunick was describing was Buck Baker, who also had a problem with the NASCAR scoring system. Baker was leading by one lap at Hillsborough when the caution flag came out and he pitted. Race officials waved him to the rear of a pack of three cars. "I had to win the race again and I didn't have much time to do it in," Baker said. He passed the three cars in the remaining nine laps in the race and won.[7]

Questions abounded when the caution flag came out at Darlington's Southern 500 in September 1957, and that involved a racing fatality, drivers hurt and seventeen spectators injured. Twenty-seven laps into the race, Fonty Flock spun into the wall. Bobby Myers, from Winston-Salem, North Carolina, crashed into Flock's car and collected the cars of Tom Pistone and Paul Goldsmith. Myers' car hurtled over a four-foot retaining wall, striking spectators in an area off limits to them. Eight-year-old Alvin Helsabeck, from Germanton, North Carolina, was stuck by Myers' car and critically injured.[8]

Robert Edelstein, in his biography of Curtis Turner, described the carnage Flock saw from inside his car as he was waiting for traffic to pass so he could get out. "He looks up through his windshield to see Bobby Myers rounding toward him, boxed in, startled and going over 100 miles per hour. The instant before the impact, Flock can see Myers' eyes grow wide. The crash sends Myers' Pontiac flipping mercilessly, with metal flying everywhere and the engine wrenched from under the hood," hitting the car of Paul Goldsmith.[9]

The accident occurred directly in front of Myers' pit as his crew watched in stunned disbelief. When they saw no movement inside the car after the vehicle came to rest on its side, they suspected the worst.[10]

Myers, Flock, Goldsmith and Pistone were taken to a Florence, South Carolina, hospital. Billy Myers dropped out of the race to accompany his brother, who died an hour and a half later without ever regaining consciousness. The public address system made no mention of Myers' death but everybody on pit row knew he was gone. After the ambulances left and the crumbled metal mass that had been his car was towed off the track, Myers' crew covered his car with a tarp and walked away as though they could not bear to look at what had once been a sleek, gleaming vehicle that their boss thought could take him to victory lane.[11]

Flock charged that race officials were slow to throw the caution flag after he hit the wall. He accused France of using amateur drivers to fill out the field of fifty-one cars as he, other promoters and Darlington officials were more concerned about making money than drivers' safety. Flock was affronted that neither Darlington nor NASCAR officials visited the drivers in the hospital.[12]

Darlington Raceway President Bob Colvin responded that his track was one of the safest in the nation, that drivers were tested before their entries were accepted and that Bill and Annie France did visit the hospitalized drivers.[13]

Daytona Beach sports editor Bernard Kahn interviewed Smokey Yunick about what happened at Darlington. Yunick, who had two cars in the race, told Kahn he would tell him what he saw as well as what he thought. Colvin and Flock were mad at each other, he said, because the driver asked for $500 in appearance money and the raceway president refused. Yunick said Flock probably blew a tire as he was driving a "rattle-trap" that Herb Thomas bailed out of just before the race. He confirmed the yellow flag came when Flock hit the wall but said the caution could not be seen by all drivers.[14]

Yunick was critical not only of the track surface but the manner in which Darlington and NASCAR conducted the race. "There were rocks on the course which flew up, dirt and asphalt also blasted the windshields," he said. "They tried to correct it but only made it worse. I thought NASCAR official Norris Friel would get tossed right out of the track by Raceway officials because he criticized some condition on the track." Yunick agreed with Flock's assessment of the drivers in the Southern 500, "There aren't fifty drivers in NASCAR or USAC who can handle the speeds at Darlington.[15]

"The Southern 500 is a big national event, and it'll continue to be one long after I'm gone, but they operate it like a county fair," Yunick charged. "Some bad conditions exist there and there'll be a lot worse accidents unless they're corrected." He pointed out that officials failed to police the bad blood that existed between some of the drivers and that failure resulted in wrecks. One example, he said, was Lee Petty bumping one of his drivers, Curtis Turner, until he wrecked. "They've cut it [bumping] out at Indy and they've got to cut it out in stock car racing too, before it's too late," he added.[16]

Yunick's comparing the Southern 500 and its pre-race activities to a county fair resulted from a week long festival of concerts, cotillions, parades and beauty contests. The Miss Southern 500 beauty contest, that drew more than 12,000 spectators, was said to be second in size only to the Miss America contest. The big crowd draw that year was the appearance of actor James Arness, star of the television series *Gunsmoke*, as the parade's grand marshal.[17]

Flock recanted part of his accusations regarding the wreck and aftermath. He told *Winston-Salem Journal and Sentinel* reporter Hank Schoolfield, "I said some things I wished later that I hadn't said and I said some things I would still say." His remarks about greedy promoters, he said, were directed to Darlington officials. Flock was again adamant that neither raceway nor NASCAR officials came to the hospital.[18]

Flock said he was misquoted concerning amateur drivers. "There'll always be amateurs or there couldn't be any professionals," he said. "I was an amateur once myself." The reporter, Flock maintained, made it sound like he was mad at the amateur drivers. "I didn't say that at all."[19]

Speedy Thompson won the Southern 500 and $13,450 out of the race purse of $53,000. An estimated 75,000 spectators witnessed the death of one driver, career-ending injuries to another and seriously injured spectators. There was something obviously wrong with a paved race track where only twenty-one of the fifty-one cars finished the race.[20]

France scheduled fifty-one Grand National races in 1957, and his other divisions were more prolific. In one night's racing at Bowman Gray Stadium, France had 148 cars competing in Sportsman, Amateur and Hobby division races.[21] Despite the problems with his race management and the tragic deaths and injuries that ensued, France maintained, "The main thing I never want to lose sight of is the fellows NASCAR started out to take care of, the little independent fellows, they're the backbone of stock car racing."[22] His words rang hollow to some.

France made a diligent and successful effort at the 1961 Daytona 500 to carefully record the laps drivers led and eliminate indecision about who won the races. Joe Epton, NASCAR's traveling scorer since 1948, had 120 assistants at Daytona, three clocks and electronic timing devices for the 500-mile race. Epton had relays to the public address system, telesign operators and the massive scoreboard. There were two scorers for each car and two more placed at each end of pit row to check cars as they entered and left.[23]

The high banked track again claimed a life. During one of the practice runs, Harold F. Habering, from Phoenix, Arizona, was killed when his car rolled over, veered down the thirty-one degree banking, went back up the track before sliding down and overturning at the edge of the grass. France said Habering lost control of the car.[24]

Lee Petty and Johnny Beauchamp, the two drivers who drove to the spectacular finish in the first Daytona 500, again grabbed headlines but not in the same fashion.

Richard Petty crashed in the first of the qualifying races. He explained why such events were held. "It makes a whole lot more money for the speedway," he explained. "The fact that it gives every driver one more chance to crash up his machinery never enters anybody's mind." A collision with Junior Johnson sent Petty's car along the guardrails until it dropped four stories into the parking lot.[25]

Petty said he climbed out where the windshield had been twisting his ankle as he fell to the pavement. He lay there collecting himself. When the paramedics arrived they speculated about taking the unmoving driver to the hospital. Petty told them they would have to because his car was destroyed. "They both jumped about a foot," he recalled.[26]

When he returned to their pit, Lee Petty asked him if he wanted to qualify their other car. He declined and the older Petty went out on the track. Richard Petty described what happened when Banjo Matthews' car turned sideways in front of his father. "When Daddy backed off a little, Johnny [Beauchamp] must have froze or something because people who saw it happen said he hit Daddy full throttle, right in the driver's door—right on the number 42. Johnny's throttle was wide open, they said, when the two of them went right over the wall."[27]

Lee Petty's injuries kept him in the hospital for four months and, from all indications, the Pettys paid most of the bills. "At the end of the year [1961], after we paid all the bills—both race cars and hospital—we had cleared $4,000," Richard Petty said.[28] For all practical purposes, Lee Petty's driving career was also over.

The two Daytona qualifying races were won by the popular Fireball Roberts and Joe Weatherly. Weatherly, who came to Grand National racing from the Modified Division after winning five American Motorcycle Association championships, and was known around the tracks as a practical jokester with a dry sense of humor. He was one of the more outspoken drivers who criticized France's management of the sport.[29]

Roberts, who qualified at 155.709, had a commanding lead in the big race until he blew the engine in his Smokey Yunick Pontiac. "I was scared to death out there," Fireball said. Marvin Panch, in another Yunick Pontiac, won the third Daytona 500 and $21,050. Weatherly was second, $9,150, in another Pontiac; Paul Goldsmith was third, $5,900, also in a Pontiac; Fred Lorenzen, from Elmhurst, Illinois, was fourth, $3,825 in a Ford, and Cotton Owens, driving his own Pontiac, was fifth, $2,975.[30]

Smokey Yunick had instructed Panch to finish as high as he could but behind Fireball Roberts. "Everyone knew he [Fireball] had the fastest car," Panch said. "No one was going to outrun him if he didn't have trouble. I was content with second place. Bad luck for Fireball; good luck for me."[31] Panch set the track record of 149.601 mph. "The last lap in any race is the toughest," he said. "I was even talking to my car telling it to hold together until I got back to the finish line."[32]

After the disastrous qualifying, not a single caution flag was thrown during the 500-mile race much to the delight of the 51,000 spectators.[33] Only thirty of the fifty-seven cars finished. "With us running at this kind of speed, it's about time they did something in the way of making these guys take drivers' tests," Weatherly said. "They don't know enough to pull down when they're being overtaken. They're endangering other drivers." Roberts said rookies should carry stripes on their cars like the requirement at the Indianapolis 500. During the race, there were three major crashes and six minor ones.[34]

In March 1961, Bruton Smith proposed a 100-mile race at the half-mile Concord, North Carolina, speedway, with a purse of around $9,000. He pointed out there was no race on the Grand National schedule that weekend, April 2, and thought it would be a good opportunity for both NASCAR and USAC drivers to provide a show for the fans. He indicated that Buck Baker and Curtis Turner would drive in the race.[35]

Purcell, who was also NASCAR's director of competition, told drivers they had to ask for permission to race in an event not sanctioned by NASCAR. "When and if the [NASCAR] drivers ask this time permission will be refused," he stated. France said simply that Smith's Concord race was closed to NASCAR drivers.[36]

France had another reason to keep NASCAR drivers tethered to his plantation. He scheduled a ninety-nine-mile Grand National race for April 2 at the Hillsborough (North Carolina) Speedway that was won by Cotton Owens. France told the media, "Every real successful race ever run in the South has been sanctioned by NASCAR."[37]

France probably just forgot about the hundreds of thousands who descended on Savannah for the Grand Prize races, successful beach events staged on Ormond and Daytona beaches by William J. Morgan, the vast number of spectators Nunis drew at the Lakewood Speedway, or the contests staged by Joe Littlejohn, Ralph Hankerson and other promoters.

Most importantly, France did not want Smith meddling with a deal he was working on to bring in new drivers. France signed an agreement the previous February, in New York, with Tom Binford, USAC chairman, and Charles Moran, Jr., United States chairman of FIA, to make thirty-six Grand Prix drivers from eleven nations eligible for the 1961 Daytona 500. The agreement made NASCAR drivers eligible for the Indianapolis 500. "This is a great step forward in American motor sports," France said, leaving the impression the deal was long lasting.[38]

Eleven days later, Banks made his own announcement, saying the agreement that USAC drivers could participate in the Daytona 500 was a one shot deal. Banks told the Associated Press that he made the unusual concession in order to place two USAC representatives on the FIA's U.S. Committee. NASCAR was already represented on the committee by France and his new high commissioner, Harley Earle.[39]

If France still entertained hopes of luring USAC drivers into NASCAR on a regular basis, he certainly was not going to let Smith steal any of his thunder. None of France's plans to bring in new drivers was lost on his regulars.

The Rebel 300 at Darlington created another testy situation between France and his drivers and drew raceway president Bob Colvin into the mix. After seventy-five laps, the race was called because of rain. An earlier race, the Virginia 500, was also called because of rain after 171 laps at Martinsville, a track owned by France and Clay Earles. France rescheduled the Martinsville race for April 30, just six days before the planned resumption of the Rebel 300 at Darlington on May 6. France had other races rained out at Asheville-Weaverville and Hickory, North Carolina, and he was losing revenue.[40]

He prorated purse money based on 100 laps of the 500-lap Martinsville race and paid drivers for seventy-nine laps at the April 9 event. The *Herald-Journal* reported that, according to NASCAR rules, France did not have to pay them until the race was complete.[41]

Charlotte Observer sports reporter George Cunningham wrote that Colvin "was so furious that the color red was visible in his deeply tanned face." Colvin maintained that France scheduling the Martinsville race just six days before Darlington's Rebel 300 violated his contract. "I have a legal contract with France which says there will be no race scheduled or rain date scheduled one week prior to the Rebel 300," he stated.[42]

A testy meeting between France and Colvin changed nothing. "The way I understand the contract," France said, "no race could be booked [in the seven day time frame]. But this did not take into consideration rain dates." Every NASCAR sanctioning contract with the tracks had a line that required inserting a rain date.[43]

"I told them to hire some lawyers for I will go to court," Colvin said. "I've been a member of NASCAR too long to get a hosing like this. I'll guarantee you one thing if this [Martinsville] wasn't France's race track there wouldn't be any disagreement at all."[44]

Apparently, Colvin took his hosing because the Martinsville race, won by Junior Johnson in a Pontiac, was run on April 30 and then NASCAR trooped to Darlington on May 6. Drivers were angry that France decreed the race would be restarted with five laps of caution instead of under a green flag. Weatherly maintained the start was in violation of NASCAR's printed rules. "I want the race started according to the rule book and not one created by a drum headed ruling no one ever heard of before."[45]

France replied, "I don't think Weatherly understands the fairness of this particular ruling or our thoughts on it. It is an unparalleled situation and we are going to do the fairest thing for all drivers." In reference to earlier cancelled race, France pointed out that no red flag, which stopped a race and parked the cars, was displayed. "As far as we are concerned the cars are still sitting up there [on the Darlington Raceway] and it could still be raining."[46]

Weatherly would not let the subject rest. He urged spectators to bring green flags to the track and wave them in defiance of France's ruling. Weatherly, who won the Rebel 300 the previous year, finished fifteenth. Fred Lorenzen won the race after a bruising battle with Curtis Turner, a close friend of Weatherly's, before a crowd of 32,000. Lorenzen took $8,860 out of the $50,000 purse.[47]

The CMS's World 600, in May, had its highs and lows. The estimated 65,000 spectators were treated to an enormous display of driving talent by David Pearson, from Spartanburg, South Carolina, the 1960 rookie of the year. Pearson, in his Ray Fox Pontiac, had lapped the field twice. With less than two laps to go, Pearson's right rear tire blew and he limped across the finish line with flames spouting from his car as the tire rim scraped the asphalt. He collected $29,450 from the $115,000 purse with an average speed of 116.633 mph.[48]

Tragically, the low point of the race occurred when a car driven by Red Kagle, from Green Belt, Maryland, smashed into the third turn guardrail. Kagle's leg was impaled with a piece of the metal guardrail. His leg was later amputated just below the knee at a Charlotte hospital. His wreck brought out the caution flag for twenty-six laps.[49]

In July, France had a grudge to settle with USAC's Henry Banks. Banks had scheduled a 250-mile race at Atlanta that month. Since there was unfinished track construction, companies were unable to test their tires, and engineers considered track temperatures, which were just under 140 degrees, as being too dangerous. Banks, out of concern for his drivers' safety, cancelled the race.[50]

Nelson Weaver, AIR president, appealed to France for assistance due to the track's wobbly financial situation. Drivers, car owners and mechanics were in Daytona for the Firecracker

250, and France called them together. "Atlanta needs help," he told them. "The USAC cancellation left Atlanta in a bad position and they need a race. The economy of the Atlanta track is based on NASCAR competition anyway. It's up to you fellows."[51]

Twenty-four drivers signed up for the 250-mile Atlanta race. France heaped blame on USAC for the race cancellation. He had to do some juggling with the Grand National schedule. David Blunt, who ran the South Boston Speedway in Virginia, had a July 9 race scheduled and he agreed to move it to August.[52]

Drivers' comments indicated they sympathized with AIR's problem. Fireball Roberts said such a raw deal should eliminate USAC from racing in the South forever. "It was a terrible position to put a promoter in," he added. "They should have run those tire tests a month or so ago," Weatherly said. "We're just doing what we would do for anybody in trouble—going to their aid. Those Atlantans should have known better than to do business with USAC."[53]

There were five days between the Firecracker 250, won by David Pearson, and the new date for the Atlanta race, which turned out to be something entirely different from what drivers expected.

The track conditions at Atlanta chewed up tires indiscriminately. On lap seventy-one, Fireball's right rear tire blew and he hit the guardrail, knocking his car out of alignment. He was out ten laps while Smokey Yunick, the car's builder, realigned the vehicle. Ralph Earnhardt, from Kannapolis, North Carolina, was running second when he blew a tire on lap 101. Junior Johnson broke an axle. Pearson, Roscoe Thompson, Nelson Story, Johns and Matthews went out in the first half of the race. A wrecker towing one of the wrecked cars turned over on the track apron.[54] Bob Wellborn was running second to race winner Lorenzen when he also blew a tire.[55]

France almost lost one of his most popular drivers during the October 1961 National 400 at Charlotte. Fireball Roberts lost a tire, crashed into the guardrail and his Pontiac burst into flames. As he attempted to guide the car toward the pit entrance, his steering malfunctioned. Bob Morgan, from Annadale, Virginia, attempted to pass between Roberts and the wall but there was no room. Morgan's Ford smashed into Roberts' vehicle sending parts everywhere, but Fireball walked away.[56]

The Atlanta 500, originally set for March 20, 1962, was postponed twice due to rain. Before the first postponement, France vacillated for ten hours before canceling. The forty-six car field was impounded but it took hours for wreckers to pull spectators' cars out of the red clay quagmire in the parking lots. When darkness fell, dozens of vehicles were still in the lots.[57]

When the race was actually run in June 1962, it was shortened to 330 miles, again due to rain, after running sixty laps under yellow. The scoreboard listed Pearson as the winner but scoring cards favored Lorenzen. For the last 200 miles, Lorenzen and Matthews battled for the lead until they pitted. Pearson was leading, with Lorenzen and Matthews second and third, when he saw the red flag on lap 218 and stopped.[58]

Lorenzen and Matthews continued on around the track apparently completing lap 219. Race officials had no idea what happened and could not say with certainty when the red flag was thrown. "On the last lap, they were sliding off the wet turns," Pearson's crew chief Ray Fox said. "Somebody ran into Matthews and skinned his car up. None of the drivers could see, it was impossible to hold positions after that. Nobody knows what was going on after lap 218."[59]

AIR officials said the confusion stemmed from NASCAR's dithering over rules on races halted by red flags on short tracks and the longer venues. They said the short track rule called for cars to line up in the order in which they were running at the completion of the last lap before the race was stopped. NASCAR officials claimed they thought Pearson stopped because he ran out of gas. Scorer Joe Epton figured the finish, Lorenzen, Pearson and Matthews, on short track rules and the basis of 218 laps. Chief steward Johnny Bruner disagreed and said Grand National races were decided on the number of miles actually run.[60] Nobody seemed to know exactly when the red flag came out or what set of rules they were using.

After meeting with Epton and Purcell, France announced that Pearson failed to finish lap 218. Fox was apoplectic: "I saw the official scorecards, including Lorenzen's, right after the race and it had only 218 laps on it." Nevertheless, the results were: Lorenzen in a Ford, first, with $15,550; Matthews in a Pontiac, second, $9,494; Johns, also in a Pontiac, $5,200. They were followed by Roberts, Troy Ruttman and Goldsmith. Pearson found himself shuffled back to seventh and, instead of first place money, he won $1,420.[61]

Even with seventh place, Pearson fared better than Johnny Allen, from Greenville, South Carolina, did after winning a 200-lap race at Bowman Gray in June. Allen, in his first and only Grand National win, nipped Rex White by about six inches at the finish line. However, Allen kept going and crashed over the wall at the stadium. His portion of the purse, $580, fell far short of repairing the damage to his car.[62]

Fred Lorenzen, called by the media "The Golden Boy," appeared to believe the coverage. His attitude was never more apparent than in the Old Dominion 500 in September 1962, when he engaged in a battle of the bumpers with Roberts. Finally, tired of seeing Lorenzen crawling up his tailpipe, Roberts saw him approaching flat out and jammed on his brakes. A busted radiator took the Illinois driver out of the race, and he was livid, accusing Roberts of deliberately causing him to wreck. The race was won by Nelson Stacy. Roberts finished seventh.[63]

The 1963 Firecracker 400, won by Fireball Roberts, had a protest filed by the usually taciturn Glen Wood, builder of Marvin Panch's Ford that placed third behind Lorenzen. Wood's protest, alleging that Lorenzen passed Roberts under a caution, went to the NASCAR Racing Commission. The commission, composed of France, Purcell and other members of their choosing, took four days to reach a decision that was puzzling to say the least. "This verdict was arrived at because of the complete divergence of opinions express by those called into conference," they explained. "The official scorecards showed that Roberts and Lorenzen passed the starter's stand on the same second of the lap in which the violation was alleged to have occurred."[64]

The commission's verdict found that the yellow light might have flashed at that moment but stated the race was controlled by the starter's flag. The wreck that brought out the caution occurred when Tiny Lund blew a tire as he passed the starter's stand, crashed into the wall and spun into the infield.[65]

Wrecks often occurred during practice sessions. There were so many crashes on the new twisting, rugged three mile road course at the Augusta (Georgia) International Speedway that hours were required to repair the damage before practice could continue prior to the November 1963 race. Lorenzen, among others, spun out but his Ford was not damaged.[66]

The most spectacular crash occurred when Joe Weatherly's Mercury, traveling at 110 mph, left the course in one of the S turns. The car overturned ten times, slid down a seventy-five-foot embankment and landed in the woods right side up. Weatherly, the 1962 and 1963 Grand National champion, walked away from the crash, in an area he called "alligator hollow," with bruises and abrasions. Buck Baker won the race in a Petty Plymouth.[67]

After January 19, 1964, Weatherly never walked away from another wreck, pulled another prank, made any more humorous remarks nor confronted France over some of his cranky rules. He died during lap 101 of the Grand National race at Riverside's (California) twisting road race course partly due to his not wearing a shoulder harness. At the time they were not mandatory, nor were window nets to keep the driver's upper body inside the car. Weatherly died when his car skidded and his head was crushed between his car and the retaining wall.[68]

There was speculation that his engine may have blown or the accelerator stuck. Dan Gurney, who won the race, said he saw Weatherly fighting the steering wheel. "A bit of the stock car racing sport died with him," columnist Gene Granger wrote. Bud Moore, Weatherly's car owner, called his death a terrible tragedy.

Weatherly's death resulted in NASCAR mandating window nets in the driver's side door.[69] It is hard to determine how many lives would have been saved or injuries averted if that simple safety requirement had been in place decades earlier.

Smokey Yunick, who prepared cars for Curtis Turner among other drivers, described the close relationship between Weatherly and Turner, both on and off the track. "Joe and Curtis Turner had a very, very rare relationship," he said. "Each liked the other and enjoyed each other on and off the racetrack. In racing, for whatever reason, seldom do racers associate with each other socially."[70]

Yunick recalled the 1957 Southern 500 where Turner was leading the race when Lee Petty ran him into the wall, sending him to the hospital. Weatherly, after his wrecked car was repaired, went back on the track and ran Petty into the wall, returned to the pits, got into Turner's car, which Yunick had patched back together, and finished fifth. "He drove that son-of-a-bitch like it was brand new and there would be no tomorrow," Yunick said. "And he taught Lee not to f_ _ _ with his buddy."[71]

Turner left Weatherly's funeral, tears flowing down his face, saying, "There's four hundred ways that little bastard could have made a living but I don't guess he'd been happy doin' anything else."[72] Bob Colvin opened the Joe Weatherly Museum at Darlington a year later. Bud Moore restored the last car Weatherly drove and placed it in the enormous collection.[73]

Weatherly's death cast a shadow over the 1964 Daytona 500 and brought into question a number of track safety problems including wind and France's proclivity for urging drivers to use the high banked track in the rain.

Before the big race, France held the American Challenge Cup, a 250-mile race over the Daytona International Speedway track and road course, for prototype sports cars, Grand Turismo vehicles and anything else on wheels he could collect. Another tragic accident occurred when Emory University research chemist Ross McCain's Ford Lister went airborne in the east turn. The open cockpit car flipped over, skidded 200 feet and continued spinning, destroying the cockpit, windshield and roll bar.[74]

Jack Anderson, a spectator, and three others raced to the wreck and turned McCain's car back on its wheels. "He came into the turn and something just seemed to pick the car up," Anderson said. His description echoed the wind problems other drivers experienced on Daytona and other super speedways. Driver Johnny Rutherford, who also helped right what was left of the car, said, "I saw it go. It was like a fish out of water. It wobbled, then flipped on its back and kept spinning. He was crushed."[75] McCain, who had driven in similar races since 1961, suffered a mangled right arm, internal injuries and pavement burns on his back. Surgeons managed to save his right arm and he only lost two fingers.[76]

These deaths, injuries and a lack of track safety issues, unfortunately, continued. France, however, also had another problem.

17

Those Dreaded Teamsters

· · · · · · ·

Bill France used every maneuver he knew and certainly did not stint on spending money when NASCAR drivers began forming a union in 1961. He successfully convinced many that their interests were already in the best hands.[1] In addition, France attempted to convince the drivers and the public that he was fighting to protect the United States, which, according to him, was in danger of being taken over by Jimmy Hoffa and his Teamsters union. He had Purcell bring the acting president of the drivers' union into compliance by employing the same tactics he accused the Teamsters of using. France also had other fires to put out.

Small speedway owners and promoters, such as Joe Littlejohn from Piedmont Interstate Speedway, were concerned about drivers leaving their races and running in the larger venues for more money and more championship points. In March 1961, France instituted a new points system based on race purses. Winning drivers in races with purses from $4,000 to $6,000 would get 400 points, previously 200, plus an additional fifty points for each $1,000 in the purse. Those taking races with purses of $7,000 to $10,000 would get 500 points plus an additional fifty points for each $1,000 in purse money.[2] France stated, "The smaller tracks are responsible for the development of stock car racing so that super speedways such as Darlington, Daytona Beach, Charlotte and Atlanta could be constructed and if interest drops at the smaller tracks there will be limited development of new drivers, car owners and fans."[3]

Few drivers passed up a race with a $50,000 purse to run in a race with a $5,000 purse and 450 points. Consequently, the more popular drivers, whom crowds wanted to see, raced in events with larger purses. The points rule change favored France and those who owned the larger tracks.

Ned Jarrett started in 46 races and won the 1961 Grand National Championship with $41,056 in earnings. David Pearson started in only nineteen races and won $51,911. Fireball Roberts won $50,267 in twenty-two starts and Joe Weatherly garnered $47,079, in twenty-five races.[4]

France, not wanting to post another deficit from his super speedway, created a circus atmosphere around Speed Week in 1961. He mixed motorcycle races with the automobile time trials. His former NASCAR partner, William Tuthill, chairman of the newly formed United States Motorcycle Association, joined France, and they held the first international motorcycle championship race in three decades. France imported Blanche, a five and one-half ton Indian elephant, as a ride attraction. The nine and a half foot tall animal was owned by the Kelly-Morris Circus in Oak Hill, Florida.[5]

France was not the only track owner with financial problems. Turner and Smith knew their days at the Charlotte Motor Speedway (CMS) were numbered but continued laboring to save their speedway. Turner drove in the Convertible Division and hoped to win the Rebel 300 to help with their debts. The two men held a Modified race, prior to the March World 600, in an effort to bring in more money. Smith staged drag races at the track. In all, they held eight days of speed events.[6]

In April, C. D. "Duke" Ellington, a Louisiana lawyer and reputed financial expert, was named by the CMS board, in a testy four and one-half hour meeting, as the track's general manager. Ellington was brought in by James L. McIlvaine, a Charlotte banker and developer. Jerry Ball, also of Charlotte, had resigned from the board. Curtis Turner issued a terse statement saying, "Mr. Ellington has assumed responsibility for the financial and administrative control of the Charlotte Motor Speedway, Inc."[7] Turning over financial and administrative control of the corporation left Turner, as president, and Smith, as vice-president, on the outside.

The World 600 races gave the speedway a profit of $370,000.[8] Without a doubt, the Charlotte track was going to be profitable and eventually pay dividends. Ellington, claiming the $370,000 profit was not enough to save the track, led the charge for Turner's resignation. Of the seven-man board of directors, Turner thought he could count on Bruton Smith, G. B. Nalley and G. D. Smith to vote with him for a majority of four to three. Allen Nance, J. Lewis Patterson and Ellington he knew would vote against him.[9]

By Turner's estimate, the speedway debts had been reduced from $1.5 million to $875,000. He secured a New York bank's promise to loan the speedway $750,000. James L. McIlvaine, along with his partner Henry Morgan, smelled a money making operation at the track, and threatened to foreclose on the second mortgage they held.[10]

When Turner told McIlvaine he had a $750,000 loan in the works, the developer replied he and his partner were not interested. "Yeah," Turner replied, "I know what you're interested in." A board of directors' meeting was held but Turner was absent. Another board meeting was held on June 8 and Turner was there. He indicated he was not notified of the earlier session. When the votes were counted, the tally was four to three for Turner's resignation, which he tendered.[11]

Turner later told Max Muhleman, from the *Charlotte News,* that he was caught in the middle of a bad situation. "On one hand there were creditors determined to auction the speedway unless I resigned," he explained; "on the other there was my old partner Burton Smith, who was ready to help vote me out if I refused." Robert Edelstein, Turner's biographer, wrote that Smith denied he voted against Turner. However, when Smith resigned as vice-president of the speedway, he was rehired as general manger. The former whiskey runner, daredevil racer, party hound and timber broker went into seclusion and came up with a plan that shook NASCAR to its very roots.[12]

In July, Turner announced the formation of Turner Investors, which he planned to incorporate in Florida. Turner Investors would deal in real estate, timberland, mineral rights and acquiring stock of existing corporations. His partners were Seymour I. Somberg, from Durham, North Carolina, David Bullard, from Charlotte, and George H. Mason, from Roanoke. Turner planned to sell 300,000 shares of stock to fund the venture whose obvious purpose was to reclaim the speedway. In addition, the company would organize a pari-mutuel wagering plan.[13] Pari-mutuel wagering was legal in the southern states of Florida, Kentucky and Louisiana, but was tied to horse racing, not automobile racing.

Turner was still smarting over the loss of his speedway. William R. Rabin, a Charlotte accountant, put Turner in touch with Nick Torzeski, a representative of the Brotherhood of Teamsters, Chauffeurs, Warehousemen and Helpers of America headed by James Hoffa. Turner and Fireball Roberts went to Chicago the first week in August to talk with the Teamsters about including NASCAR drivers in the Federation of Professional Athletes (FPA) the union was working to establish. A few days later, they met with Torzeski in Washington to work out the details. Roberts agreed to be acting president of the group of drivers with Turner as secretary-treasurer. There was speculation that the $800,000 loan Turner so desperately needed for CMS hinged on his ability to sign up his fellow drivers for the FPA. According to Edelstein, Turner saw France and told him about the possible loan and his idea for organizing the drivers. He quoted Turner as later commenting that France did not say much other than he would give it some thought.[14]

Turner, who ran his speedway business as though he was conducting timber deals at 20,000 feet or looping his airplane between utility poles, surely knew about the Taft-Hartley Act, which became law in 1947, or at least his attorneys did. The act prevented a union from spending money for the express purpose of expanding its membership, which a loan from the Teamsters to Turner would have done.[15] Consequently, it was doubtful that Turner ever pursued a loan from the Teamsters or that they offered one.

Edelstein said France, after Turner told him about his plan, immediately headed for Washington to confer with Congressmen and government officials on what to do about the situation. At that time, Attorney General Robert Kennedy was using the federal government's vast resources to haul Hoffa into court on any charges he could find. Kennedy was also structuring the 1961 Federal Wire Act, which would make it illegal to use a wire communication transmission for bets, wagers and information assisting betting on any sports event or contest.[16]

Turner and Roberts found twenty-five NASCAR drivers who agreed to join the FPA. They emphasized a subject that had long been a sore problem between France and the drivers, the size of race purses. Turner, Roberts and Buck Baker pointed out when NASCAR began in 1948, France was paying $4,000 purses for 100-mile races and, thirteen years later, he was paying the same amount for some of the races, while the cost of fielding a race team had more than doubled. In addition to asking for more prize money, Turner said the FPA would help them achieve a pension plan, better health and death benefits, safety advancements and scholarships for dead drivers' children. According to a NASCAR form submitted to hospitals and physicians, France had a $3,000 hospital and medical limit on his drivers' insurance policies.[17]

The $3,000 medical insurance limit did not last long when a driver suffered injuries like Lee Petty. Petty, who almost lost his leg in the 1961 Daytona 500 wreck with Johnny Beauchamp, was hospitalized for four months and his family had to pay for the remainder of his medical treatment.[18]

Turner also wanted to institute a system of pari-mutuel wagering, similar to Thoroughbred racing, on stock car races. Pari-mutuel wagering was going to be difficult to achieve since many of the Grand National races were at North Carolina and South Carolina tracks and neither state allowed pari-mutuel gaming. If the populace criticized Harold Brasington for working on building Darlington on Sundays and Bill France for selling racing tickets on the Sabbath, they certainly were not going to welcome pari-mutuel operations in their states.

Fireball Roberts acknowledged that he stuck his neck out in joining Turner and being named acting FPA president, but he made a logical argument for their position. "We know our careers in auto racing are at stake and we're not backing down. We've made no demands, made no moves other than to try to sign up drivers for the union," he said. "We must have grabbed Mr. France where it hurts though from all the things he said in the papers."[19] Roberts later had to swallow his statement about "not backing down."

"Personally, I have violated no rules of NASCAR. I guess Mr. France can ban me from running in NASCAR because he has absolute power but I don't see how he can do it," he added. "If some of the other drivers would stop and think that because I've done something France doesn't like, he can ruin my career overnight, they would realize he could do the same to them." Roberts went on to lament that drivers had absolutely no representation in NASCAR and the FPA would give them some bargaining power. "We have no aim to put France or any other promoter out of business," he stated.[20]

"There are many things wrong with the way racing is operating now," Roberts continued, "and I don't think any drivers will deny that. Some of them, however, are afraid of the Teamsters. Actually, the Teamsters have no voice in our operation unless we call them in."[21]

Athletes seeking representation in the management of their sports was nothing new. The National Football League owners vetoed a players' association in 1956. George P. Marshall, owner of the Washington Redskins, not only opposed players' organizational efforts but called the idea ridiculous. However, NFL commissioner Bert Bell recognized the National Football League Players Association in 1957 without input from the team owners. Roberts indicated there was an earlier effort to organize drivers that began in 1956. "The drivers have tried in the past to organize for better representation," he said, "but each time we've tried the fellows who backed us up gradually melt away under pressure from France. This has been going on since 1956."[22] Roberts explained further, "We are affiliated with the Teamsters only in the sense that if we need backing in a time of duress, they will come to our aid. NASCAR is supposed to be our agents. The promoters, not NASCAR, are the drivers' employees. So, if France really had our best interests at heart, he ought to back us up."[23]

Torzeski lobbed a hand grenade into the situation that sent France into orbit. He told the *Charlotte Observer* that a majority of Grand National drivers had signed with the union. The Teamsters, he bragged, had control of the NASCAR drivers.[24] To say France was livid was a vast understatement.

The evening of the August 9 Bowman Gray race, France called a meeting of selected drivers, owners and mechanics that did not include Turner, Roberts, Buck Baker and Tim Flock. Turner, in Winston-Salem for the race, found out about the meeting and he and Flock watched and listened through an open window in the room. France reminded drivers of everything he had done for them in the past thirteen years—guaranteed purses, some insurance, taking the sport from dirt tracks to super speedways—and painted a rosy future. A union, he assured them, would destroy all he had accomplished. "Gentlemen make no mistake, before I have this union stuffed down my throat, I will plow up my 2.5 mile track at Daytona Beach—plant corn there—and other tracks that I am a part owner of. I will not be dictated to by the union."[25]

Turner mused that France's creditors would prevent his plowing up Daytona. France was just getting started. He promised those in attendance that all support from the automobile industry would dry up; that car owners would have to pay mechanics overtime to work on the weekends; that he had been in contact with U.S. senators and the Department of Justice about doing something about the Teamsters.[26]

After France had insulted the automobile manufacturers left and right about taking over his sport, he had no markers left with them. In addition, the automotive industry had been unionized since the United Auto Workers organized in 1933.[27] He also knew he was vulnerable on drivers' benefits, or the lack thereof.

France claimed he had tried to get drivers a pension plan the previous year but was unsuccessful because the drivers were independent contractors. "All retirement plans are based on weekly earnings," France said. "This does not exist in NASCAR, where every driver, every one of you in this room, is an independent contractor and does not get a weekly paycheck."[28] According to the October 26, 2001, issue of the *Chicago Tribune*, France, in the beginning, made sure drivers were classified as independent contractors so there would be no pensions to pay.

"For decades, drivers dared not challenge the relationship NASCAR established for them by its founder, 'Big Bill' France," racing columnist Ed Hinton wrote. "They were 'independent contractors.' They entered contests of their own free will. That meant that if they got hurt or killed, it was their own tough luck—this among myriad other responsibilities disclaimed by NASCAR in the lopsided bargain."[29]

France decreed, after the Bowman Gray race, no known union driver could compete in a NASCAR race. "And, if this isn't enough," he emphasized, "I'll use a pistol to enforce it. I have a pistol and I know how to use it. I've used it before." France suddenly found race track safety to be a pivotal issue. He said that barring union members from races was a safety measure. He used Turner as an example, saying he had been known to knock a driver out of a race on a whim. Apparently, he forgot that Turner and Junior Johnson had been knocked out of races by Lee Petty, on a whim. Then he launched into a tirade against pari-mutuel betting, saying it would not work with racing, which was a clean sport. "We've never had a scandal and I will fight any pari-mutuel attempt to the *last*," he roared.[30] NASCAR's very origins were scandalous and France had embraced and used that reputation in promoting his early races.

France was in a position where he had to appear to make some concessions, but he was not going to give drivers and owners any more money. He appointed a committee composed of NASCAR members and officials to hear grievances and work on a pension plan. This, of course, was the pension plan he told drivers it was impossible to create. The committee was carefully composed of drivers Lee Petty; Rex White; Ned Jarrett, if he resigned his union membership; a car owner few had ever heard of, Fred Lovett; Purcell and France.[31]

After surveying the room, France said, "If this union you have was really such a great thing then I'd join it." Turner leaned through the open window, threw down an FPA membership card and said, "Here's your application." France charged toward the opening, glared at Turner with wordless venom and slammed the window shut. After a moment, he produced his own prepared cards and suggested drivers who had joined the union sign his cards to renounce their ill-advised actions and promise to be good boys. After signing the cards, France told them they would be welcomed back into NASCAR.[32]

After the meeting, reporters asked France if he was going to allow Turner, Roberts and

Flock to drive in the race that evening. "They will have to make an affidavit and swear on the Bible," he bellowed. All but Turner and Flock eventually agreed to France's terms.[33]

France and Purcell used divide and conquer tactics in an effort to separate Turner and Roberts. Obviously, they decided Turner would be the more difficult of the two to approach since his association with France went back decades and it was possible he knew things France preferred to keep quiet. They decided Roberts was the weak link and went to work. Two days later Fireball Roberts had an abrupt change of mind. He released a statement saying he was pulling out of FPA because he feared his association with the Teamsters would hurt rather than help drivers.[34]

There were two different theories on how Roberts' FPA resignation came about. *Charlotte Observer* sports writer George Cunningham wrote that Roberts notarized and dispatched a letter of resignation on Friday to FPA, then was welcomed back into NASCAR in a telephone conversation with Bill France. Cunningham said Roberts made this statement to the Associated Press (AP) in Asheville on Friday: "Neither Bill France, the Teamsters, nor anyone else connected with FPA is aware of what I am doing. I drove slowly from Charlotte this morning and took the long way by Lake Lure and I thought this thing over from all angles. I'm withdrawing my support from the union and resigned as temporary president of FPA. It's as simple as that. I feel if I do anything to hurt the least man in racing, I will be doing a disservice to my fellow drivers who have been my friends for fifteen years and I'll have no part of it."[35]

Racing columnist Ed Hinton knew part of what happened to change the mind of Roberts, whom he called the brightest star in stock car racing with his charismatic personality, his name recognition and his driving style that was so like that of Junior Johnson. "On August 11," Hinton wrote, "France's right-hand wheeler-dealer and pressure man, Pat Purcell got Fireball Roberts to take a little ride with him. They drove almost a third of the way across North Carolina from Winston-Salem [where the race was held at Bowman Gray Stadium] to Asheville [where the next Grand National race was scheduled], talking. Pat Purcell had come out of the circus and carnival industry. He was the first man in NASCAR to carry a brief case. What he carried in there all the time was three bottles of Scotch for powwow purposes," Hinton recalled an old timer telling him.[36]

"In 1948, Purcell had gone to Virginia to a meeting of dirt track owners and invited them very cordially to join NASCAR. Casually he mentioned if any of them chose not to join, 'we'll put you out of business.'" Hinton's source was Martinsville Speedway founder H. Clay Earles.[37]

Roberts' public explanation was that he resigned for the most unselfish of reasons. "The Teamsters people have implied that to force the issue might disrupt all racing in the South," he said.[38] "Personally, I could live five years without getting behind another wheel but there are several on the racing circuit who are not that fortunate," Roberts added.[39]

France said, "As far as I am concerned he is welcome to race for NASCAR as long as he pleases and I know he'll be welcomed back by his fellow drivers. I think in future years, Fireball will regard this move as the best thing he ever did for sports in America."[40]

France's attitude about Roberts' return to NASCAR did not last. On August 13, he was quoted as saying, "Fireball's resignation won't have any effect. They'll always find somebody who'll do something for money."[41] France wanted to fan the proposed FPA flames for publicity purposes, but it was a decision that later came back to bite him.

France was unable to resist taking another shot at Turner. "We'll have nothing to do with Curtis Turner or anyone else promoting FPA or who is trying to bring gambling to auto racing," France opined. He said banning Turner from racing should put a halt to union activities.[42]

That, of course, contradicted his previous statement saying the union would find somebody else to head the FPA. Evidently, France forgot about his association with Smokey Purser, who was deep into the numbers racket while promoting automobile races with him in Daytona Beach.

France, then, went on another tirade against James Hoffa and the Teamsters Union. "The ultimate aim of the Teamsters and the man who heads it is to run the country," he predicted.[43]

On the day of the Western Carolina 500, at Weaverville, France held a news conference and emphasized that the FPA was just Hoffa's first stop in his effort to take over the entire nation. "As long as I live, I promise to do everything I can to keep them from taking over the country," he stated. He asked Charlie Smith, from the *Asheville Citizen,* and George Cunningham, from the *Charlotte Observer,* for their assistance. "I will need the help of you fellows and more like you from all over the country to keep Hoffa in check."[44]

France failed to elaborate on just how Hoffa was attempting to take over a representative republic government. Nor did he explain why he thought he was the person who could bring down the union president. France was unable to contain himself and continued to use Hoffa as a battering ram.

In an extended interview with Cunningham, France emphasized, "I don't think people realize the seriousness of this Teamster move." Then, he repeated Hoffa's plan to take over the country. France continued saying he had talked to "People in the football business. They certainly look at this [attempt to unionize drivers] with a dim view. If it happened, they said they would be out of business." He refused to tell Cunningham whom in professional football he had talked with and for good reason.[45]

The National Football Players Association was recognized by its commissioner in 1956. The National Basketball Association established its union in 1954. Baseball formed its first union, the Brotherhood of Professional Base Ball Players, in 1885, and the American Baseball Guild began in 1946. Major League Baseball's first collective bargaining agreement was structured in 1968 by Marvin Miller, who had been associated with the United Steel Workers of America.[46]

France continued his tirade promising to bring the labor union beast out in the open so the public would see their evil intent. "That's what the Teamsters don't want to happen," he said, "they know it will generate opposition." He added that he was not sure that banning Turner from NASCAR would stop the FPA.[47]

France charged that the Teamsters owned seven or eight pari-mutuel race tracks. Teamster representative Torzeski told Cunningham that not only had the Teamsters never owned any race tracks, but Turner had never tried to negotiate a loan from them.[48] The NASCAR owner did a masterful job in dancing around the pari-mutuel wagering issue since he sanctioned races in Canada, where betting was legal.

Now that France had his drivers or at least those he wanted, back on his plantation, he knew he needed to do some public relations work with the labor unions. First, he moved to shore up his base.

He gathered up support from track owners and promoters. France knew his track partners from Martinsville and North Wilkesboro, Clay Earls and Enoch Staley, stood with him in opposition to the Teamsters' FPA. Gene Sluder, owner of the Asheville-Weaverville Speedway, said, "I think it would be the devil for that outfit [the Teamsters] to get in. I believe all the promoters are going to stick with Bill." Nelson Weaver, AIR president, told reporters, "Racing would be much less attractive and not on as sound a basis. The efforts of the Teamsters Union to organize racing is [sic] destined to flop completely." Bob Colvin, Darlington Raceway president, chimed in, "This union business is one of the worst things we could have in auto racing. Everything I've seen the Teamsters touch, they had a tendency to tear down."[49]

Clay Earles, who built the Martinsville track, went a step further. Earles told Peter Golenbock in an interview for his book *NASCAR Confidential* that he also suspended Turner for his union activities. "I knew at the time that we couldn't run racetracks under a union," Earles recalled. "I'll tell you why we couldn't. Say we had sold a bunch of our tickets, maybe all of them, before the race and then on race day the union comes up with something they don't like and says, 'We're going to strike.' The people who bought the tickets would be there. They wouldn't stand for that. They'd stop going to the races if that happened and I knew that."[50]

Earles said he went to every race while Turner and Roberts were persuading drivers to sign with the FPA. "The Frances were afraid to go to the races," he said. "Back in that day the Teamsters Union had a bad name. They had some rough people. And so I went to every race fully dressed." Earles never considered himself fully dressed unless he was carrying two pistols.[51]

"One night I went over to the Starkey Speedway in Roanoke, a little weekly track," Earles continued. "I knew Curtis was going to be there and that night Curtis was talking to the other drivers about his union stuff. I suspended him. I sure did. I wrote his suspension in longhand. I wrote, 'Curtis Turner is suspended indefinitely for conduct unbecoming to racing.' That's the way I worded it."[52] Earles' suspension was not worth the paper it was written on.

France, however, had played with labor unions and their money before. The Central Labor Union (CLU) in Daytona Beach sponsored France's beach-road races for several years. The CLU also picked up the sponsorship of the American Motorcycle Association beach races when France promoted them from 1954 to 1957.[53]

Figuring he had better remember who befriended him when he needed them, France apologized to union officials for his remarks about the labor movement as a whole. While he was in Asheville, France asked to meet with local CLU president John Jarvis; T. M. Burrell, business manager of the Electricians Local, and Ray Stepp, business manager for the Plumbers and Fitters Local 487.[54]

Meanwhile, Purcell, reluctant to use the same tactics with Turner as he did with Roberts, jabbed him verbally. Purcell told the media, "If Turner was so deeply interested in the welfare of the drivers why didn't he institute or even suggest some of the reforms while he headed the Charlotte organization?" Purcell charged he was only interested in getting a loan to regain control of Charlotte Motor Speedway.[55]

Purcell was shadow boxing. Turner was part owner of a race track. He never held any position with the sanctioning body that would have enabled him to institute reforms. Turner was a member of NASCAR like all drivers, owners and mechanics. His ownership of a track, which signed sanctioning agreement with NASCAR, was the same as that of Clay Earles at Martinsville or Enoch Staley at North Wilkesboro.

Turner fired back saying drivers should have insisted on having such representation when NASCAR was formed thirteen years earlier. "I'm thirty-seven years old and about to quit driving. How I wish they had had something like this all during my career," he pointed out. "Race drivers don't think much about retiring or the future. And, a lot of them are caught short."[56]

In a last ditch effort, Tim Flock, whose dealing with France had not always been pleasant, went to talk with him. After France disqualified Flock's car at a beach race because it used wood, which France gave him, instead of metal, Flock left so angry that he shattered the glass in his front door. France listened to Flock and said, "I don't want you; I'm after Turner."[57] He suspended Flock anyway.

The laconic car builder Bud Moore said if, in the beginning, Turner and France had sat down and talked, even screamed at each other, the matter might have been settled. "But soon it took on a whole different level," Moore said. "And, when your friend basically tells you to disappear, and 'I never want to see you again,' that hurts. What happened between Curtis and Bruton, Curtis wasn't happy about it but I don't think it was completely unexpected. But for France to say that, the idea never crossed Curtis' mind."[58]

The rhetoric over drivers' unionization subsided somewhat as the Grand National schedule move from Winston-Salem to the Western Carolina 500, which was a total disaster at the Asheville-Weaverville Speedway on August 13. Two cars caught fire in the pits, and another crashed into the pit area, bounced off the fence and hit a pickup truck before careening into spectators. Two other cars collided, hit the wall and one landed on top of the other. Three big holes appeared in the track and officials stopped the race after 129 miles. Junior Johnson was declared the winner.[59]

About 4,000 of the 10,000 race spectators were incensed over the race being stopped. They stormed the flag stand demanding a ticket refund. Instead of immediately offering rain checks, race officials dithered, trying to figure out what to do. Fist fights broke out and some spectators locked and barricaded the only gate allowing drivers and mechanics to leave the infield. Police were unable to disperse the crowd and gave up. Finally, after four hours, dwindling daylight and drivers' pleas, the crowd permitted them to leave the track. Then, race officials announced that rain checks would be issued for another race at the speedway.[60]

The Teamsters, like the spectators at Weaverville, were not intimidated by NASCAR officials. The union provided an attorney, Jack Wiley, from St. Louis, to represent Turner and Flock. Wiley said banning the two drivers from NASCAR racing was an illegal black-balling. He also indicated that other track owners could be named in the lawsuit he planned to file. Turner and Flock claimed they lost testing contracts, worth $150 per day plus expenses, due to France's ban. France's claim they were not employees of NASCAR but independent contractors begged the question.[61] The legal battles between Turner and France had just begun.

Before the end of August, France finally achieved his speed record at Daytona. Art Malone, from Lutz, Florida, gave France the enclosed circuit speed record of 181.561 mph at the Daytona International Speedway. Driving the Mad Dog IV, built and owned by Bob Oslecki, from Charlotte, Malone pocketed $2,500 of the $10,000 France forked out; the remainder went to the car's owner. Mad Dog IV looked like an Indy racer with a large stabilizer on the rear and short wings on each side.[62]

The Labor Day race at Darlington saw about a 25,000 drop in attendance. The reason could have been the intense summer heat of 99 degrees, but most likely it was the absence of Turner, who was always a favorite in both the Convertible and Grand National races there. The raceway's failure to make the needed track additions and repairs had nothing to do with the crowd. The carnival atmosphere, however, may have reached the point where the Southern 500 was only a feature. The focus that year was on the fiftieth anniversary of U.S. Navy's flight program. On display was Astronaut Alan Shepard's space capsule, and daily air shows were staged by the Blue Angels with precision Navy parachuting demonstrations.[63]

The South Carolina heat was so intense that Fireball Roberts, fearing a heat stroke, relinquished his Pontiac to Marvin Panch. A newcomer, Nelson Stacy, from Cincinnati, won the race in a 1961 Ford and $20,225 from the $96,000 purse. Panch finished second, twelve laps behind Stacy.[64]

France's committee of drivers, owners and NASCAR officials met in September to consider drivers' demands arising from the union question. "We talked about all these things, maybe to get better insurance, more money for drivers at the back of the field and, to my knowledge, we never had another meeting after that," Rex White said. White added that France did not change the purses or do anything more at that time.[65]

Judy Judge, Fireball Roberts' fiancée and Yunick's sister-in-law, said she did not remember hearing much about the meeting other than the purses would get bigger and they would take care of their own. "But I didn't see much of their taking care of their own," she added.[66]

Things were heating up on the legal front as well. On September 11, 1961, Tampa lawyer Frank E. Hamilton, Jr., filed a nineteen-page complaint on behalf of Turner and Flock in Volusia County Circuit Court, in Daytona Beach, against Bill France and NASCAR. The complaint contended that by banning the two drivers France had interfered with their right to work and that the contract, which each NASCAR member-driver signed before each race, did not bar drivers who were union members. The Teamsters put up $100,000 for Turner's legal expenses.[67]

Not only was France represented by the ever faithful Ossinsky, but Charlotte lawyers Bob Sanders and J. W. Alexander, who had worked with Attorney General Kennedy, were added to the mix when the trial began September 21. Edelstein, in his biography of Turner, wrote that France's attorneys made sure the court knew of the bad blood between Hoffa and the Kennedys.[68]

Ossinsky's description of Turner and Flock's complaint was reminiscent of his lengthy, precise wording in NASCAR's incorporation documents. The drivers' claims, Ossinsky said, were "vague, indefinite, uncertain, irrelevant, redundant, repugnant, immaterial and contain scandalous matters." He pointed out that Turner and Flock were not employees of NASCAR but independent contractors. "But," he continued, "these drivers are nonetheless subject to the ruling body's rules and regulations, along with any other rules that might be added at any time during the season. And, Item 16, Section 4, clearly stated that NASCAR members agree to abide by official decisions."[69]

All sort of events unraveled in Judge Robert B. Wingfield's court as the trial began. Ossinsky had to contend with the fact that every newspaper in North Carolina that covered stock car racing, and most of them carried stories written by their own reporters or those from AP or UPI, reported Bill France's ravings and rantings at the Bowman Gray meeting and later at Asheville. However, first he addressed Turner and Flock's claim they had long been members of NASCAR in good standing. He had a point in that Flock had been banned and then reinstalled at least once. Ossinsky identified them only as being members from time to time.[70]

Ossinsky had a problem with handling all of the media coverage surrounding remarks that France spewed out for several days concerning Turner, Flock, Roberts and the FPA. To combat the plaintiffs' testimony about what was said at Bowman Gray, the attorney came up with a twist. Since neither Turner nor Flock was at the Bowman Gray meeting, he said, none of France's statements were material to the case. Turner and Flock's listening at the open window apparently did not count. Then Ossinsky made a declaration that came back to bite him, "Furthermore, Mr. France denies making any of these statements whatsoever."[71]

Not only did France deny his rantings and ravings at Bowman Gray and later at Asheville, but he set out to find drivers, mechanics and car owners who might be willing to verify his denial. France even went to see Yunick to ask for his assistance. Yunick told him that he and Turner were close as brothers. "I'd lie for Curtis and I'd lie against you," he told France. Yunick was not asked to testify for the defense.[72]

On November 28, the final day of the trial, judge Wingfield told attorneys, "However you wish to spend the time, I'll leave up to you." Ned Jarrett, a late witness, had been brought in by Ossinsky to confirm France's old bromide that NASCAR drivers did not use racing as their sole means of support. Jarrett said that he had a lumber business in addition to racing. Hamilton, however, outsmarted Ossinsky. Since Jarrett had been at the Bowman Gray meeting, Hamilton asked him about France's performance that evening. Jarrett confirmed that France had blown his cool, threatened to plow up his tracks and promised to use his pistol to enforce his rules.[73]

Turner's friend, Dr. D.N. Morris, from Charlotte, was in the courtroom that morning and wrote, "Jarrett had not heard France's testimony and testified to the truth which made France look like a prevaricator. Both the faces of Bill France and his wife were studies in contempt of Curtis."[74]

Wingfield's decision was no surprise. He refused to grant the injunction Turner and Flock requested. Their lifetime ban from NASCAR stood. He did not dismiss their case at that time, covering himself by saying it might come before a National Labor Relations Board hearing.[75]

Meanwhile, Turner lost all hope of reclaiming the Charlotte Motor Speedway and he would pay dearly for breaking the first commandment of NASCAR, which according to Edgar Otto was, "Thou Shall Not Disobey Big Bill France."[76]

In November 1961, creditors forced the Charlotte Motor Speedway into bankruptcy. U.S. District Judge J. B. Cravens, for the Western District of North Carolina, intervened and decided the speedway could and should be saved. He ordered CMS into Chapter 10 bankruptcy, cleared out the warring factions and appointed a committee headed by A. C. Goins and Richard Howard to raise $400,000, under the supervision of the court, and designated Robert N. Robinson as a trustee to oversee the operation. They were able to raise $350,000 to get the track in operation again.[77]

Control of CMS was returned to the stockholders, which included Turner and Smith, in 1962 with the provision for a five-year delay before the final decree was issued.[78] Two months later Turner's attorneys asked Wingfield to set aside the permanent injunction against them to race in NASCAR. The judge not only refused but dismissed their suit with prejudice.[79]

France, after spending a considerable amount of money, won the legal battle with Turner and Flock, but he was losing still more of his star drivers and battling dwindling track attendance.

Fireball Roberts, although he held more stock car records than any other driver, began reducing the number of Grand National races he competed in when he switched from driving Banjo Matthews' Pontiac to a Holman-Moody Ford in March 1963. Roberts' contract with Ford also called for him to do public relations work for the automobile manufacturer's performance division. He was a member of the original 1955 Ford factory team that included Turner, Panch and Weatherly.[80]

In the July Bristol race, Roberts' Ford caught fire after he skidded in one of the turns, as it rolled over three times. Roberts had a cut under one eye. The next month, his engine blew during practice at Darlington and the car's rear end rode along the top guardrail. "Boy, what a ride," he said. "If the old rail had been there I would have gone into orbit." He came back to win the Southern 500, after starting ninth.[81]

Nine months later, Fireball's luck ran out. On May 24, 1964, 68,000 spectators at the Charlotte Motor Speedway's World 600 watched in horror as cars driven by Roberts, Ned Jarrett and Junior Johnson collided and burst into flames on lap seven. "I lost it and tangled with Ned," Johnson said, "but I don't know whether Fireball hit Ned or not because when I saw him his car was flipping over." Neither Johnson nor Jarrett was sure which vehicle hit Roberts. Jarrett said he thought Johnson's car careened off the wall in front of Roberts. Johnson speculated his gas tank might have exploded, engulfing his and Roberts' cars in flames.[82]

Jarrett, the first to reach Roberts, suffered minor burns after he and Johnson jumped out of their cars and rushed to help Fireball. Roberts was hanging halfway out of his car that was enveloped in a billowing cloud of black smoke. "Oh, my God," he cried, "I'm on fire; help me, Ned."[83]

Marvin Panch also slammed into the retaining wall and caught fire after blowing a tire but was not hurt. Jim Pascal won the race. Roberts, 35, was burned over seventy percent of his body, including twenty-five percent with third degree burns. He was taken to Charlotte Memorial Hospital, where a representative said the skin was burned off more than half of his face and body and his survival depended on how well his kidneys functioned.[84]

Four days after the accident, the hospital took Roberts off the critical list but he remained in serious condition. He was able to move his arms and legs and talk with his family. The Charlotte Red Cross announced they no longer needed blood donors, as 119 people had already given blood for the driver. By the end of June, Roberts lapsed into a coma after a tracheotomy was performed to aid his breathing. On July 1, he was stricken with pneumonia and a blood infection and died the next day. Roberts, 35, was divorced but left a thirteen-year-old daughter and a fiancée, Judy Judge.[85]

They were to have been married on June 6 in Daytona Beach, where they had bought a house. Judge, an elementary school teacher, said Roberts planned to leave racing after the Southern 500. After his death, Judge moved to Atlanta where she taught for thirty-four years, but never married and never went to another stock car race. She blamed the lack of safety requirements for Roberts' death.[86]

John Holman, Roberts' car owner, said a fire safety device, such as those the U.S. Army used in their tanks, might have prevented Fireball from being critically burned. "We're going to install a carbon dioxide extinguisher in all our cars where, when triggered either automatically or manually, it will submerge the entire inside of the car with foam," Holman said. He said the device would be in his cars before the next race, the Atlanta 400, on June 7.[87]

In June 1964, the Daytona International Speedway held events for off duty firemen, from surrounding fire departments, to practice extinguishing a car blaze with a dry chemical spray. William C. France, France's son and DIS general manager, said NASCAR was working on improvements such as the check valve, which was supposed to prevent gas leakage when a car was upside down. "Right now, we're working on a better gas tank," he said.[88]

Yunick, whose cars Roberts raced for nearly four years, said, "If Fireball would have had a tire that could have stood up to the punishment he put on them, his record would be something that would have never been equaled." Yunick, who later insisted on rubber fuel cells in his cars, said, "Steel gas tanks got him, no guard in the filler cap area."[89]

More than 300 cars followed Roberts' hearse from the First Baptist Church in Daytona Beach to his burial in the Belleview Memorial Cemetery, the day after the Firecracker 400.[90] "I thought he was going to recover," said Bill France, who provided a plane to fly Roberts' parents to the Charlotte hospital to visit their son.[91]

Fred Lorenzen, the top money winner among Grand National drivers with $122,588 in 1963, said in July he was considering retirement but did not leave. Lorenzen stated his concerns were not only the cars' increasing speeds but the effect of high winds on super speedways such as Charlotte and Daytona. "The high wind in close traffic, coming off the second turn at Charlotte, triggered the accident in which Roberts was fatally burned," he said. "We're going too fast."[92]

Another driver, Marvin Panch, was also considering retiring over the high speeds.[93]

In September 1964, tragedy struck again. Jimmy Pardue, from North Wilkesboro, North Carolina, who sat on the pole for the World 600 in which Roberts was fatally injured, was killed while testing tires at the Charlotte Motor Speedway for the October 18 National 400. He either blew a tire or dropped a sway bar on the fourth turn and went through the guard rail. His 1964 Plymouth, estimated to be traveling at 140 mph, landed on a steel wire fence, tumbled down a seventy-five foot embankment and came to rest upside down in a drainage ditch. Pardue, who finished fifth in the Grand National points standing, died a few hours later at the Cabarrus Memorial Hospital of massive head and internal injuries.[94]

The carnage continued. More than 61,474 turned out for the Riverside (California) 500, the 2.7-mile road course race on January 17, 1965. It was the third running of the Riverside 500 and the third time it was won by Dan Gurney, from Costa Mesa, California. Two incidents eclipsed Gurney's win. A spectator, Ronald Pickle, from San Diego, was killed and four others were injured when the brakes on a truck used as a viewing platform failed and the vehicle rolled down an incline, spilling its passengers as it rolled over rows of those seated. Pickle was killed when he was crushed between the truck and a chain link fence.[95]

On lap 170, A. J. Foyt's Ford slid off the course, rolled down an embankment, flipped over several times and came to rest on its top with the driver hanging upside down. A doctor looked into the car and decided there was no hurry, that Foyt was dead. Parnelli Jones, a racing friend of Foyt's who had rushed to the wreck, heard a sound. Racing columnist Ed Hinton wrote that Jones crawled into the car and began digging the mud and sand out of Foyt's throat so he could breathe again. "Broken back, crushed sternum, bad concussion but all the toughest sonofabitch ever to drive a race car needed was that one gift of breath from Parnelli and here he would come again, kicking ass, raising hell and winning races."[96]

Hinton explained Foyt's attraction to NASCAR racing although he was a seven time USAC champion. He said Foyt was notorious for bullying other drivers but he loved being around the Grand National drivers because they were his kind of people. He said Richard Petty explained that Foyt never tried bullying NASCAR drivers because he knew he would get his butt kicked.[97]

During the Riverside race, Ned Jarrett's car caught fire in the pits and it must have brought back the horrible memories of Fireball Roberts' wreck. Jarrett escaped but three pit crew members were slightly burned while assisting him.[98]

18

Turner's Back

• • • • • • •

We could have won that case, Turner told Flock sometime after their trial ended. "Funny thing is," he said, "I bet if we had a union, we would have." Turner's decision not to pursue further legal action against France had a third party influence.[1]

For years, Turner had a successful business arrangement, in addition to driving their cars, with the Ford Motor Company, which owned vast amounts of timberland in several states. At issue, after the FPA flap, were 76,000 acres of prime timber in the Upper Peninsula of Michigan on Lake Superior.[2]

Turner's legal problems with NASCAR were creating problems for Ford, according to Edelstein, the driver's biographer. "Along with being the first-ever Ford factory driver, Turner had also become invaluable to the company for his timber brokering skills," he wrote. "The deal has long worked out well but Turner's legal troubles with NASCAR are creating a nightmare for the car maker. They offered an ultimatum: drop the lawsuit if he wants to continue these off-track dealings with them."[3] There was little doubt where the pressure on Ford came from to drop the legal proceedings. Although France was successful in defending NASCAR in Turner and Flock's lawsuit against the organization, he did not exactly emerge unscathed.

Turner, after agreeing not to pursue the lawsuit further, expected an immediate reinstatement. After all, Ford agreed to put in a good word with France for Turner's reinstatement. When nothing happened, he began calling France at the NASCAR headquarters. His calls were not returned. The only correspondence he received was an envelope with an official decree stating he had been banned from NASCAR racing for life.[4]

France failed to take into consideration, or did not care about, the effect his banning of Turner from the sport would have on the spectators who paid to see him race or, in turn, on track owners who would lose revenue when crowds failed to appear. France was further surprised that sports columnists such as the *Charlotte Observer*'s George Cunningham fanned the flames of fan disapproval and were quite vocal in their support of Turner.

The NASCAR ban failed to keep Turner from racing. He turned to USAC and the 14,110-foot Pike's Peak Climb. In July 1962, Turner's spectacular feat of negotiating the twisting, 156 switchback turns in less than fifteen minutes, 14:55.5 to be exact, drew raves from his fellow competitors. "That was the most spectacular damn driver I've ever seen go up that mountain," Parnelli Jones remarked. Dan Gurney said the race was right up Turner's alley. "It's dirt and is something you can't really learn down pat, like something you go over and over again," Gurney said. "It's a place where Curtis' natural gifts would show up." Turner said his time would have been better if he had not encountered a snowstorm in the middle of the climb.[5]

Cunningham used Turner's Pike's Peak win to suggest that if France was angry about the amount of money he spent to fight the FPA, he could recoup it by reinstating Turner to bring the crowds back to his tracks at Daytona, Martinsville and North Wilkesboro. Four days after Turner's win at Pike's Peak, Cunningham wrote in an open letter to France in his newspaper column, "I have been bombarded by readers who are also dyed-in-the-wool stock car fans. By an overwhelming margin, they say you should reinstate Curtis Turner [and Tim Flock] to your organization which is rightfully billed as auto racing's largest and finest."[6]

"I say by an overwhelming margin," he continued. "That may be the understatement of the year, for the actual tally according to the mail I have received is more than 800 for Turner and just five against him. I need not remind you of this, however, for I suspect your mail on the subject has been even larger and more one-sided than mine. I can't ignore my letters. Can you?"[7] There was no reply from France

In September 1962, when his buddy, Joe Weatherly, was the pole sitter for Darlington's Southern 500, a Charleston, South Carolina, newspaper ran an article about Turner, saying he was still "box office" in stock car racing.[8] To illustrate the point, the article recalled Turner's first stock car race at Mount Airy, North Carolina, in 1946 before a crowd of 1,800, who became fascinated with his go-for-broke style of racing. "Curtis Turner didn't win that race," the article continued. "In fact, he failed to last to the midway point but he did have 1,800 wild, raving race fans solidly in his corner when he loaded his race car for the trip home to Roanoke."[9]

Leonard Wood, who prepared the Fords that Turner drove, explained why USAC crowds loved to watch Turner race and matched the enthusiasm of their NASCAR counterparts. "He went into a turn behind three cars, and wove his way through all three in one turn," Wood said about one of his races. When the race was restarted, Wood said, Paul Goldsmith and Norman Nelson were on the inside and outside poles with Turner third. "Nelson backed off to let his teammate, Goldsmith, take the lead so Curtis wouldn't get him," he continued. "And, Curtis just goes down on the infield over the asphalt bumps and everything else and comes out side by side with Goldsmith! I mean you can't explain how good he was working traffic. He could be slower than the guy [in front] run up on him in traffic and then just pass him."[10]

The newspaper article recalled that Turner once won a race and turned around and gave his share of the purse to a driver hurt in that same race. The newspaper also questioned his lifetime ban from NASCAR, citing another sports columnist who polled his readers. He received 3,500 replies, ninety-nine percent of which favored Turner's return to NASCAR.[11]

Turner was grateful to Richard Howard for not only saving his race track but bringing him back to drive a Holman-Moody Ford at the Charlotte Motor Speedway in an ARCA race, a week after staging NASCAR's National 400 there.[12]

Howard had been badgering Turner for weeks to enter an ARCA race at the track he helped build. Turner made one excuse after the other: he had not raced in five months and had not driven on a super speedway in four years. Finally, he agreed. Howard and Holman-Moody had a car ready for him.[13]

Around 11,000 spectators, far more than the usual few thousand to attend an ARCA event, came to the track to see Turner race again. When he won the race, out-dueling an old rival, Tom Pistone, the crowd's cheers seem to go on and on. About a month after that race, Edelstein wrote, Turner went to Daytona on business with his Carolina Atlantic Timber Corporation partner, John Griffin, and he decided to take one last drive on the old beach-road course, slamming the car sideways as he roared over the sand. When they came onto the paved road section, a police cruiser stopped them and the officer shined his flashlight into the car and angrily demanded, "Who the hell do you think you are, Curtis Turner?"[14]

USAC did not have the numbers of races that NASCAR had. Turner ran in fourteen USAC races in 1963, winning twice and finishing fourth in points. In addition to his timber business, Turner began promoting stock car races in the South. France retaliated by scheduling NASCAR races at tracks in the same area.[15]

The influence of Turner's expulsion from NASCAR and the absence of the other drivers hit France in the pocketbook when the crowd for his 1965 Daytona 500 was down more than 11,000 from the previous year. When France attempted to introduce the drivers before the race, he was booed by the crowd.[16]

That impact of Turner's absence from Grand National racing, when he only made eight starts in 1961—the qualifier and Daytona 500, Atlanta, North Wilkesboro, Hickory, Darlington and the two Charlotte races—was a testament to his following created over two decades of racing.[17] Only 10,000 showed up for the Martinsville race in April 1965, as compared to the 23,000 who attended the previous year.[18]

Raceway president Bob Colvin was unhappy with the $35,000 Darlington lost on their spring race, the Rebel 300, and decided to force France to bring Turner back.[19] Colvin and other track owners wanted Turner back in racing because people would pay to see him race. Turner had been burning up the USAC, ARCA and Grand American racing circuits and drawing enormous crowds. Atlanta International Raceway President Nelson Weaver was so concerned about the attendance drop at his April Grand National race that he was considering switching sanctioning bodies from NASCAR to USAC after seeing the enormous crowd Turner drew at his track.[20]

Only one thing stood between the track owners having Turner bringing in huge crowds at their stock car races and that was France. Colvin led a group, including Charlotte Motor Speedway president A. C. Goins and general manager Richard Howard, to meet with France in his Atlanta hotel room on July 31. Accompanying France were his son, William C. France, Daytona International Speedway general manager, and Pat Purcell. Howard urged France to reinstate Turner immediately. He described the crowd that turned out for an ARCA race at Charlotte the previous October. "The place went crazy," he said.[21]

Turner was not the only driver creating problems for France and NASCAR spectators. France decided to ban the Chrysler Hemi engine, which had helped Richard Petty obliterate the competition and win the Grand National championship in 1964. Chrysler pulled out of NASCAR in protest. In addition to not having Turner, France's Chrysler decision also cost him the loss of another popular driver, Petty. The *Charlotte Observer*'s George Cunningham predicted the 1964 season would come down to Ford versus nobody. Cunningham was right. Before the end of July, Fords had won every Grand National race. France folded on the Chrysler issue and Petty won the Nashville race on July 31.[22]

"People love the man," Colvin told France in his efforts to get Turner reinstated. "Either that or they hate him but everybody wants to see him race." Colvin told France they could not afford to ignore the newly organized Grand American Racing Association (GARA) and the possibility that Turner would sign an extended contract with them and draw even more spectators away from NASCAR-sanctioned races.[23]

Clint Hyatt, from Sumter, South Carolina, the head of Mid-Carolinas Auto Racing Association, had organized GARA to attract top independent car owners and drivers. Factory teams were barred from GARA races. Former NASCAR drivers Speedy Thompson and Roscoe Thompson had joined Turner in some GARA races. Hyatt and Turner were scheduled to sign an agreement the first week in August that would give the Virginia timber tycoon an assured racing schedule and increased profits for tracks across the south.[24]

The pressure of Turner signing with GARA necessitated France make an immediate decision. There was much shouting and hurling of accusations back and forth in the Atlanta hotel room, much of it due to France's inability to cede even a little bit of control. Howard told him that something had to be done and done immediately. France, backed into a corner of his own making, finally agreed.[25]

Colvin dialed Turner on his car telephone that Saturday night and handed it to Purcell, who gave him the good news. France did not speak with Turner. NASCAR issued a news release under France's name saying, "Curtis Turner will, effectively immediately, be eligible for NASCAR membership again after serving a four-year suspension if Turner wants to rejoin the association."[26] A lifetime ban from NASCAR had just been reduced to a four-year suspension.

When Turner was banned from NASCAR in 1961, the Virginia driver was supposed to pay a $30,000 fine before he could ever be considered for reinstatement.[27] "There can hardly be any doubt about it," Hyatt said. "He was reinstated because he was supposed to come into this new association with us. I expected this kind of opposition. They've [NASCAR] controlled racing in this area for quite some time." Hyatt said he organized GARA for independent car owners and drivers because no independent had won a Grand National race in 1965—all the winners were in cars receiving factory support.[28]

Turner had yearned for four years to return to NASCAR racing and, with the end of his career in sight, he certainly was not going to turn it down.

Just when Turner and France met after the driver's reinstatement was not clear. Turner, elated over returning to NASCAR, immediately flew from Concord, North Carolina, where a GARA race had been rained out, to the NASCAR office at Winston-Salem. Bowman Gray Stadium racing officials Alvin Hawkins and Hank Schoolfield met him at the airport to sign the necessary documents. Hawkins told Turner that he had been pushing for his return to NASCAR for a long time. Bowman Gray was where France four years earlier banned Turner from racing for life for "actions detrimental to the sport of auto racing."[29]

Turner's first race back in NASCAR was a 250-mile modified sportsman event at Bowman Gray Stadium. Sports columnist Steve Hoar wrote that Turner's race appearance had restrictions. "NASCAR officials had said the suspension would hold until Turner paid a $30,000 fine," Hoar said. He quoted Bill France as saying only, "Turner's been punished long enough."[30]

France, during Speed Week in February 1965, reinstated Tim Flock, who did not return to racing. Flock was then working for Holman-Moody and doing public relations for the Charlotte Motor Speedway.[31]

Turner received much ribbing about having to place rookie stripes on his bumper for the Southern 500 at Darlington. According to NASCAR rules, any driver out of competition for more than three years had to have the stripes on his bumper when he returned to racing. Colvin was unable to exempt him from the rule but he created a photograph opportunity for Turner as the driver removed the word "BANNED" that had been placed beside his Darlington trophy.[32]

Colvin placed the convertible in which Turner won 22 races in that division in 1956 in the Joe Weatherly Stock Car Museum at Darlington. Turner, before the race, was inducted into the National Motorsports Press Association Hall of Fame at Darlington.[33]

The testy Colvin could have gone out of his way to create all that publicity for Turner to sell tickets or because they were close friends. Turner was a Darlington Raceway stockholder.[34] Without Colvin's aggressive campaigning, along with that of Howard, it was questionable if France would have relented and allowed Turner to return to NASCAR.

John Cowley, head of Ford racing, turned down Turner's request for a car to drive at Darlington, saying their efforts were concentrated on Fred Lorenzen, who Turner suspected was behind the refusal. Edelstein wrote that Turner told Cowley, "Maybe Freddie is worried that I might be planning to give him one more lick, like I owe him something. Tell you the truth, I do and I just might."[35]

Colvin was determined that Turner was going to be in his Southern 500 and helped him find a Plymouth, owned by Sam Fletcher, from Fort Wayne, Indiana, that had seen better days. To help shed the rust, Turner spent days on the Darlington track testing tires for Firestone. He managed to qualify eighth.[36]

Two laps into the race, the car of Reb Wickersham, from Longboat Key, Florida, broadsided the Ford of Buren Skeen, from Denton, North Carolina, so hard that it knocked Skeen's seat to the right side of the car. The impact sent Skeen's car into the concrete wall in turn three and he spun back across the track. Safety crews had to cut him out of the mangled vehicle. Nine days later, without regaining consciousness, Skeen died from, among other injuries, a basal skull fracture. A similar injury killed Dale Earnhardt three decades later.[37]

After making some progress when the race resumed, the Plymouth's wheel bearings gave out on lap fifty-one and Turner finished thirty-fifth. After he came in, Cowley appeared with Ford racing's liaison, Jacques Passino, who recalled the beauty of seeing Turner race on dirt. The two men told him he should talk to Glen Wood, who would be building him a new Ford to drive in the season's final four races. When Turner expressed his appreciation to Wood, the car owner replied, "Curtis, we wouldn't even be in this business if it weren't for you." His brother, Leonard Wood, reaffirmed, "We'll make you the car. All you have to do is go out there and do what you do."[38] Ned Jarrett won the Southern 500.[39]

Turner's appearance in his Wood Brothers Ford at the October 31, 1965, race at the new North Carolina Motor Speedway at Rockingham was a fitting end to the season. The result was worthy of a movie script.

Harold Brasington, now out of Darlington, was unable to stay away from the sport he loved. With former peach farmer and trucking executive Lindsay Dewitt, he built the $1.5 million, high banked one-mile North Carolina Motor Speedway in the southern part of the state, about 100 miles north of Darlington, at Rockingham. The grandstand capacity was 30,000 and the infield could handily hold 15,000.[40]

"I wanted a race track where the local grocer, mechanic or baker could drive their cars off the street and compete with their neighbors," Brasington said.[41]

What Brasington got was another Darlington without all the bands, parades, beauty queens and infield antics. The crowd of 50,000 paid from $8 to $14 a ticket to see not only Turner drive his Wood Brothers Ford but the return of Chrysler and Richard Petty to Grand National racing. In his Wood Brothers Ford, Turner qualified fourth behind Petty, Johnson and Pearson. His time was 116.273 mph compared to Petty's 116.260 mph.[42]

The rust was gone but Turner found it difficult to drive in practice with a broken rib. He flew to Charlotte to have his chest wrapped with copious amounts of tape. Leonard Wood fitted a special brace to his car seat to help. Everything proceeded as usual in the pre-race period for Turner. "He partied the whole night before," Glen Wood said, "the morning [of the race] he's at the track lying on the hood of his car, sleeping it off."[43]

Some of the reporters in the press box were openly cheering for Turner; others were doubtful. One yelled, "The old man's gonna run out of steam." Bob Moore said, "Maybe, but it's one hell of a story if he doesn't." Turner was tiring from five hours of being buffeted around in the car with a broken rib. Twice he brushed the wall in the second turn but recovered.[44]

After a hard fought battle with Yarborough, in another Ford, Turner won the American 500 purse of $13,090 by nine seconds. During the last laps, as Turner appeared to falter, the crowd rose to its feet each time he passed the grandstand cheering him to finish. Temperatures in the race car exceeded 100 degrees. Edelstein wrote, "When Turner crosses the finish line in front, the roar envelopes the brand new track and Turner closes his eyes as if admiring the sounds of a storm." The cheering was like an earthquake, he added. "I knew no car was better than the one Glen Wood prepared for me," Turner said, "and I knew better than anyone else that I wasn't over the hill."[45]

Yarborough, who mopped his beet-red face after the race, agreed, "He's still a great driver; I don't think there's much doubt about that."[46]

The Rockingham crowd wanted to not only share but also to savor Turner's victory with him. For the first time in anyone's memory, spectators remained at the track through the entire post-race trophy presentation. "We're gonna go home after this," Turner said, "and we're gonna start a brand new party every fifteen minutes. I think Little Joe would like that."[47]

During that party, reporter Bob Moore questioned Turner about running out of energy. Turner replied by taking another sip of his Canadian Club and soda. Moore persisted, saying he wanted to know if Turner brushed the wall twice accidentally or on purpose. "It's like you got too far ahead and wanted to make it exciting for people. You hit the wall and it woke everybody up. So?"

Turner's responded saying, "Listen, let's all go and wash our faces, comb our hair and come right on back. Another party's startin' in five more minutes." Moore did not buy it. "It's almost like he hits the wall and then all of a sudden, by doing that, he's back in the groove again, as if hitting the wall is what did it. It's like at that moment, he's back to being Curtis Turner again."[48]

That groove, Wendell Scott, unlike Turner, was unable to find.

19

The Man NASCAR Kept Overlooking

•••••••

Nineteen years before black race driver Wendell Scott was born in Danville, Virginia, the Southern Railroad's "Old 97" ran off a wooden trestle on September 28, 1903, and crashed into a ravine on property owned by Scott's family, killing nine and injuring seven. His grandfather, hired to help guard the contents of the mail cars from souvenir hunters, was given one of the car's doors and passed it on to his grandson.[1]

Some of the song lyrics, written about the wreck of "Old 97" and engineer J. A. Broady, being scalded by steam, mirrored Scott's racing NASCAR career to some degree.[2]

Wendell Scott's racing career was scalded, not by steam, but by the racism that existed in stock car racing. Scott came into Grand National racing at the worst possible time for a black driver, during the racial turmoil in the South during the 1950s and 1960s. Darlington Raceway turned down Scott's entries for years. Detroit automobile makers would not consider sponsoring him. Instead of championing what Scott could bring to the sport with his more than average talents, as Major League Baseball Commissioner A. B. "Happy" Chandler did with Jackie Robinson, NASCAR chose to ignore Scott whenever possible.

Scott's racing career began with winning a Charlotte bicycle race whose purse was five dollars. He credited the successful race to the fact that he was light-skinned for a black man. Always mechanically inclined, Scott began his love affair with the automobile while working with his father, a mechanic and driver for white families. He sharpened his talents while serving in the U.S. Army, in Colorado and Europe, as a mechanic. After his discharge, he opened a garage beside his house, near the scene of the wreck of Old 97. During the day, he repaired customers' vehicles and at night he transported moonshine whiskey.[3]

Scott, who said he did not drink the illegal whiskey, told author Sylvia Wilkinson that he knew every back road within fifty or sixty miles of Danville. He described some of the perils of whiskey transporting, in addition to being chased by the authorities. "I hauled liquor on this little road," he said. "It was dirt back then and just about wide enough for a car and a bicycle to pass each other. One night I left a whole load of liquor hid in the bushes right up here on this curve. Well, there was an old man who lived in a little log cabin right out there in the woods, who had got up early and seen me down there hiding it." When Scott returned, his whiskey was gone.[4]

Law enforcement, unable to catch Scott, began shooting out his tires, but he was always able to escape, leaving his vehicle behind. The only time Scott was caught was when he swerved to miss a bunch of drunks, hit a house and was unable to crawl out of his car. Since that was his first offense, Scott received probation but lost his car.[5]

Being a man who believed in keeping his word, as soon as his funeral director cousin bailed him out of jail he finished his deliveries. "I told him I needed to use his station wagon—they took my car—because I still had some whiskey to deliver that night," Scott recalled. "That station wagon wouldn't go over thirty-five. There I was with my foot on the floor, scared to death I'd get jumped again that same night. But, I had to make my money."[6]

In 1949, the Dixie Circuit was racing at the Danville Fairgrounds Speedway. Dixie promoter Martin Rogers wanted to boost his track attendance by using black drivers and asked the Danville police to recommend a good driver. They suggested Scott, whom they had been chasing unsuccessfully over the back roads through the city and county.[7]

Scott drove a borrowed 1935 Ford from his brother-in-law and, because of mechanical difficulties, left the race with two laps to go. Despite some boos from the grandstand, he was hooked. "Right from the first," he said, "I loved driving that car in that race. The racial issue didn't have anything to do with it. I'd been a fast driver all my life and I wanted to do it without paying any tickets."[8]

Being a fast learner, Scott described his experiences racing at the Fredericksburg Speedway. "I remember the first time I was there, I didn't run well at all," he recalled. "Back then, we would run tracks in one gear, either in second or high gear. And, I was geared wrong for that track. But, the next week they were having a 100-lap championship race and I went back and was geared right. During the first half of the race, I had lapped everyone in the field except Ray Hendricks and I was sitting on his tail and letting him set the pace. But, then I tore my rear end out and had to drop out of the race. I definitely would have won that night if that hadn't happened."[9]

Scott never forgot that Gayther "Runt" Harris, a white driver who grew up in Fredericksburg, once lent him enough money to travel from Richmond to Fredericksburg so he could enter a race there. Ned Jarrett attempted to get Scott a Detroit ride without success. Other drivers and racing teams also helped Scott. Richard Petty, Joe Weatherly and Fireball Roberts gave Scott parts, tools and tires. Franklin Scott, his son, recalled, "I remember Tiny Lund one time in Jacksonville came over and told me to come with him. He gave me four tires for us to qualify on."[10]

Scott was ever mindful of his race both on and off the track. He scored his first feature win at the Lynchburg track in July 1952, dominating the amateur field. Scott asked the promoter, Eddie Allgood, if he could run the sportsman race. Allgood asked the crowd to vote. More than half the 2,500 spectators stood up signaling their approval. During the race, he hit a bump that broke his rear axle. Parts flew into the inadequately protected crowd in the grandstands, injuring several spectators.[11]

Three spectators were rushed to the hospital and Scott followed, dusty and dirty from the race. Frances Dalton, who voted for him to race, was struck in the face by the wheel off Scott's car. "His tears were streaming down his face," she said. "He came up to me and the first thing he said was, 'Honey, are you all right?'" She assured him that she was and had only cut her tongue. Dalton said Scott stayed at the hospital for two hours talking to those who were hurt. "His tears were just flowing," she added, "The only clean place on his face was the streaks his tears made."[12]

Raymond Riley, who suffered fractured ribs and collarbone, had not regained consciousness when Scott left the hospital and he returned several times to visit him. On one visit, he took his son, Wendell, Jr., who was frightened about entering a white hospital. Riley and the nurses put the young boy at ease and told Scott the patient would probably heal even if he did not visit so often.[13]

There were a number of drivers who not only liked Wendell Scott but admired his work ethic. Richard Petty said that Scott would actually stop working on his car to help another driver and the favor was returned. Petty wrote, "Those cats helped Wendell and said they weren't worried about the color of his skin because he wasn't that competitive—they weren't threatened by him. But if Wendell had found, say, 50 more horsepower, the help would have come to a screeching halt."[14]

Ralph Moody, part of the famed car-building team of Holman-Moody, also helped Scott with parts. "Once, I called Wendell and told him to get his hands on all the money he could and come down to Charlotte with a truck and a trailer," Moody said. "Well, we loaded him down with engines, transmissions, rear ends, gears, brakes and even Fred Lorenzen's complete 1965 race car. I asked him how much money he had and he gave me a wadded up $60. I said, 'thanks,' and sent him on his way. He ran that equipment for years."[15]

Ellis Oldham, who raced against Scott in the 1950s, talked about him being a likable, easy-going fellow. "He was one of the hardest working guys in the pits," Oldham said. "Of course, all of us back then worked on our cars and drove too but I remember him coming in off the tracks and sliding under his car and working on it and then going on back out. He used to wear white coveralls and they would be filthy by the end of the night."[16]

Oldham said Scott was always a real competitor. "He didn't have much equipment to go with but he did the best he could with what he had," Oldham recalled. Scott said he was always conscious of saving his car for the next race and the one after that because he was unable to make expensive repairs if he had an accident by pushing too hard.[17]

Not everybody was kind to Wendell Scott. Some of the tracks, such as those in Winston-Salem, High Point and Eden, North Carolina, refused to let Scott race. "I've been to tracks where they refused to let me race," he said, "but, because I'm light skinned it sometimes would be until right before the race that they turned me down."[18]

Scott repaired the car Holman gave him and towed it to Winston-Salem hoping to enter one of the races France and Alvin Hawkins staged at Bowman Gray Stadium. In his biography of Scott, Brian Donovan wrote, "At first track officials didn't notice that the light skinned Scott was black. They told him he'd have to put a safety belt in the Ford and he bought one at the track store. As Scott was installing the belt, with his darker friends gathered around him, the officials realized that he too was black. They said he'd have to leave."[19]

Scott drove to another NASCAR sanctioned race at High Point after being told over the telephone that he could enter. When he got to the track, officials told him he could not race but a white driver could run his car. He was turned away from a Dixie Circuit race at Eden, North Carolina, without being given a reason.[20]

Not all promoters treated Scott in that manner. George Powell, driver-promoter at the Fredericksburg Speedway, said Scott brought paying customers into his track. Powell would pay him $25 or $30 just to show up and race.[21]

Scott, however, persevered. On June 1, he was third at a Dixie Circuit race in Camp Butner, North Carolina. Then, on June 4, he won his first big race at the half-mile track at Sharder Field, in Lynchburg, Virginia.[22]

During Scott's early racing days, some of the drivers knocked him around on the track. Eddie Allgood, Dixie Circuit president, gave them a warning. Donovan quoted Allgood as saying, "Listen, either Wendell races or you don't race."[23] "I remember every driver that drove dirty against me," Scott said. "There have been a lot of them."[24]

One of those drivers was Jack Smith, from Sandy Springs, Georgia. Smith was angry when Scott set a track record in time trials in Savannah. Scott's son, Franklin, who was sometimes his father's entire pit crew, recalled that Smith threatened to wreck his father. After the race, Franklin Scott said, it was Joe Weatherly, not Smith, who came to their pit to apologize. "Wendell," he remembered Weatherly saying, "I just came to apologize for the rest of these stupid sons of bitches."[25]

Smith, according to Franklin Scott, did wreck his father at a Winston-Salem race. At the next race, when Smith pulled alongside Scott and pointed his finger at him, the Virginia driver was prepared. Scott had placed a revolver in his car earlier. He pointed the weapon at Smith, and that was the end of his problems with the driver.[26]

In 1950, Scott had transformed a 1939 Ford into a stock car with money he made running moonshine. Two years later, Scott's second car had a DeSoto body, a Kaiser rear end and a Straight A Commander motor out of a Hudson Hornet. "That thing would really run, too," Scott said. He won 128 races, most of them in the Sportsman class.[27]

Donovan pointed out that Scott drove for other owners like Bob Neal, from Gretna, Virginia, and Howard Cook, also from Danville, who were both white. He began to accumulate fans such as Buck Drummond, who complimented Scott on his driving at a Waynesboro race and began showing up at other races.[28]

At a Zion Crossroads race, promoters told Scott his carburetor failed to meet track specs and he put in another one they approved. However, after Scott won the feature race, the promoter refused to pay him, claiming the carburetor was illegal. Drummond, a strapping six-footer, threatened to beat the hell out of the promoter and Scott collected his winnings. The Drummond and Scott families, although from different races, became close friends.[29]

As NASCAR began to sanction more races on the Dixie Circuit, Scott decided to apply for their races. His initial effort was at the quarter-mile Richmond (Virginia) Speedway, where Maurice Poston, NASCAR's chief steward for that region, gave him a license to race in the sport. Poston said that NASCAR officials in Daytona Beach raised hell with him for issuing Scott's license.[30]

Scott drove Bob Neal's 1938 Ford in the Sportsman beach-road race at Daytona in 1953, finishing thirty-third and receiving twenty-five dollars. According to Donovan, Scott thought he finished higher but did not question the score cards.[31]

After the April race at Raleigh was rained out, promoter Enoch Staley told drivers he would pay them tow money, usually around fifteen dollars, and he did, except for Scott. The next day, at a race at Lynchburg, Scott told France about Staley's refusal to pay him tow money at Raleigh. Staley and France were not only friends but had been business associates for more than a decade. He said France told him that his race had nothing to do with anything and that he would be treated just like other NASCAR members and gave him thirty dollars.[32]

At the beginning of Scott's NASCAR adventures, France appeared to make an effort to treat him like other drivers. At another race in Lynchburg, Scott won the race after swapping paint with Ward McDonald. After the race, McDonald not only rammed Scott's car but intended to fight him until some friends intervened. France sent out a memo saying that anyone who deliberately wrecked Scott would be suspended.[33] With those gestures, France won Scott's loyalty.

Scott raced in the Sportsman Division, and probably ran some Modified races during the 1950s. There were disagreements over the number of races he won. One account credited him with 180 wins in short track, minor league races. Another listed him as the winner of 128 races in the Sportsman Division. According to the *Star-News,* he held the record for half-mile dirt tracks through 1988.[34]

In 1959, Scott was racing in the Fifth Annual Tobacco Bowl, promoted by France and Alvin Hawkins, at Bowman Gray Stadium. On a good day, France could cram 19,500 spectators into the stadium. Initially slated for New Year's Day, the race was rained out and rescheduled for January 3. Scott was racing along with Curtis Turner, Ned Jarrett, Ralph Earnhardt, Glen Wood and other Grand National drivers. Carl Burris, from Leakesville, North Carolina, won the race, Curtis Turner was second and Whitey Norman, from Winston-Salem, was third. The purse was another of France's miserly amounts of $1,700, although his gate probably grossed over $100,000. Burris' amount for winning the race came to $250.[35]

In 1959, Scott won twenty-two races at the Richmond Speedway and was the track champion that year.[36] In 1961, Scott entered twenty-three Grand National races, finished five times in the top ten and won $3,240.[37] Not bad for a rookie season, but there was no way NASCAR was going to recognize Scott's efforts.

The manner in which France decided the Grand National Rookie of the Year raised a multitude of questions. Scott's application was yet to be accepted for any race at Darlington. Donovan quoted Spartanburg sports writer Gene Granger as saying, "If you want to talk about where Wendell really got screwed, he should have been Rookie of the Year. He really got screwed out of that. There's no doubt in my mind there was a conspiracy.... They did not want a black man to get it."[38]

Granger was a sports reporter who knew racing and had no hesitation about asking tough questions. "The first fifteen years of NASCAR would be totally lost without Gene's foresight," Smokey Yunick wrote about the Spartanburg scribe.[39]

France awarded the 1961 Grand National Rookie of the Year honors to Woodrow "Woodie" Wilson, from Mobile, Alabama. A comparison of the two drivers' records was quite revealing. Scott entered twenty-three races and Wilson only drove in five. Scott had five top ten finishes while Wilson had only one. Scott won $3,240, during the season and Wilson $2,625. Scott ranked thirty-second in the Grand National standings while Wilson was forty-first.[40]

Scott acknowledged that he picked the most difficult sport in which a black man could succeed. His timing could not have been worse. "I thought about giving up a lot of times," he said, "but I didn't. I didn't want to do what they wanted me to do."[41] The decision France made on the Rookie of the Year turned sports reporter Gene Granger into a Wendell Scott fan, and he wrote about his racing activities in articles whenever possible.

The next year, Scott competed in forty-one Grand National races winning $7,133. He won the pole at the July Savannah race.[42] At the same time, he continued running the Sportsman Division. Scott raced in forty-seven of fifty-five Grand National races France scheduled from California to New Jersey and from New York to Florida in 1963. He had one fifth place finish and was in the top ten in fourteen races. For his efforts, Scott won $10,966, with, for the most part, inferior equipment.[43]

Wendell Scott reached the apex of his career during the 1964 season when he raced in fifty-six of the sixty-two Grand National races and accumulated winnings of $16,495.[44] More importantly, he won a Grand National race.

Donovan, in his biography of Scott, wrote that Doris Roberts once asked her husband Fireball Roberts what would happen if Scott should win a race. "They won't let him do that," Fireball replied, "They'll find a way not to give it to him."[45] Roberts, speaking from his past NASCAR experiences, was almost correct.

The official Grand National season ended November 3, 1963, at Riverside, California. The 1964 season began a week later at Concord, where Ned Jarrett won a 125-mile race and Augusta with Fireball Roberts the winner of a 417-mile race. The third race of the 1964 season was a 100-mile race on the half-mile dirt Jacksonville Speedway, the last NASCAR race held there.[46]

Scott, after examining the bumps and ruts of the dirt track, decided to remove one of the two shock absorbers from each wheel of his Chevrolet, which allowed his car to run better on that track. He started fifteenth in the twenty-two car field. Jack Smith, his old nemesis, qualified first. After numerous wrecks and the top drivers experiencing mechanical difficulties, Scott found himself second to Richard Petty. After Petty went out with a damaged steering arm on lap 176, Scott took the lead. When he glanced at the scoreboard that gave each driver's position, expecting to see his car's number, 34, it was blank.[47]

Still in the lead, Scott ran what should have been the last lap but the official in the flag stand did not wave the checkered flag. He ran another lap just to be sure. When the official did bring out the checkered, he indicated Buck Baker had won the race with Jack Smith second and Scott third.

Ronnie Rohn, a track worker, said that Scott, who was usually a real gentleman, nearly exploded when Baker was declared the race winner. Rohn thought Scott had run two extra laps. Clayton Morton, a spectator at the track that day, said, "He actually raced 101 miles. I remember him running up and telling Buck, 'You know damn well I outraced your ass.'"[48]

Reporter Gene Granger was in the pits at Jacksonville that day and said the consensus was that Scott had won the race. Meanwhile, Baker and Smith were arguing about which of them won the race. Scott told NASCAR scorer Joe Epton that he was sure he won the race. Meanwhile, race officials took Baker to the winner's circle where he hugged Miss Florida and prepared to go home with the elaborate trophy.[49]

Granger said he kept asking, "What's going on folks, did he win it or not?" Four hours later, after Miss Florida and the 5,000 spectators left, NASCAR officials decided there had been a scoring error, someone neglected to credit him with two laps, and Scott had won the race and $1,000. Granger said he wondered what would have happened if no reporter had been at the race. Donovan wrote that Buck Baker maintained that he never received a trophy that day. Granger said, "Buck ran off with the trophy."[50]

"Somebody took off with my trophy," Scott said. "I wanted the trophy for winning that race." Scott finally got a trophy, of sorts, at the next Grand National race at Savannah on December 29. Donovan described the trophy, presented only after NASCAR officials detailed how many cars had broken down during the Jacksonville race and that attrition helped Scott to win. "It was a small block of wood, obviously inexpensive, the sort of trophy a child might get at a fourth grade field day, quite different from the trophies Scott had seen other Grand National winners receive."[51]

According to the *Charlotte Observer,* NASCAR awarded Scott's family a real trophy for the Jacksonville win in 2011, forty-eight years later, after Wendell's death.[52]

Scott took Curtis Turner's 1963 Ford that Ralph Moody sold him for a dollar, worked it over and took it to Daytona for the 1964 Firecracker 400, where he finished fourteenth. Scott recalled finding an old cam that Holman-Moody had thrown away thinking it was no good. "I polished that thing up and it was the runningest cam I ever had," Scott said. In 1987, at a Holman-Moody reunion, Scott and Moody recalled their racing days and all the assistance Moody had given him. It was an emotional time for both men in the autumn of their lives.[53]

During his racing career, Scott won $226,563. Some of his peers collected that amount in a single season.[54]

Wendell Scott was loyal to the core and, at the end of his career, refused to say anything personally damaging about Bill France, although his inspectors had given him problems with his cars that took so long to correct that he was unable to get in any practice laps before races. "That was just their [NASCAR's] way," Scott said. "Old man France was nice. He always treated me as a person, but his son was altogether different. He would pass right by you and wouldn't even look at you."[55]

Scott continued, "He [William C. France] won't realize that its people like me that put NASCAR where it is today. At the time I got into racing, NASCAR was just getting started good. And, guys like me went all over the country and helped promote races and put on a show for them and very little thanks we got for it. NASCAR won't care if you come down broke."[56]

20

Big Boys Return

• • • • • • •

NASCAR, suffering from the deaths of two star drivers, the banning of another and declining race attendance, badly needed resuscitating in the early 1960s. Despite France's opinion about automobile manufacturers' involvement in stock car racing, he needed Detroit. And Detroit needed stock car racing.

The Ford Motor Company announced in June 1962 it was abandoning the 1957 Automobile Manufacturers Association (AMA) pact and would return to racing. Henry Ford II claimed the AMA rules were so loosely interpreted by his company and other manufacturers that the ruling no longer served any purpose.[1]

The real reason was General Motors (GM) cars won the first thirty-one races of the 1962 Grand National season. France had a dancing partner again. "I think it's a good honest move," he said. "The industry resolution was and always has been one which restricted development of safer automobiles."[2]

Bringing Ford back into NASCAR racing again allowed France to play one automobile manufacturer against the others. More importantly, the move gave France a promotional tool to get spectators back to the tracks by promising competitive races.

The winning cars in 1962 Grand National fifty-three race season were GM, thirty-six; Chrysler, eleven; and Ford, six. Those numbers changed dramatically in 1963. GM won twelve races; Chrysler, nineteen; Ford, twenty-three; and Mercury, one. At the end of the 1964 season, Ford had won thirty-four races and Chrysler twenty-five. The only GM car in the winner's circle was Wendell Scott's home-built Chevrolet.[3]

France was back where he started three years earlier.

The crowd for the 1965 Daytona 500 was down 11,056 from the previous year. Bob Colvin, Darlington president, attempted to account for the drop by saying it was hurt by a massive rainstorm, which shortened the race to 332 miles. Lorenzen won in a Ford. Colvin had some advice for France. "Either have all the factories in or have them out," Colvin said. "I prefer to go back to the stock car class instead of these high speed engines today." He pointed out that the sport was built on stock car competition, not special racers. "I'd like to see the cars that race comparable to the passenger automobiles sold to the public with such safety features as roll bars and beefed-up frames and steering allowed. Keep the engines as close to stock as possible."[4]

According to United Press International, the power plants in use at the time were: Pontiac, 421 ci; Dodge 413 ci; Chevrolet, 409 ci; and Ford 406 ci.

France, however, was going to do things his way. He had banned the Chevrolet 427 ci engine, claiming it was not available for purchase by the public, and the Chrysler Hemi-head engines because, he charged, they were winning too many races.[5]

Richard Petty was out as a result of the Chrysler ban and turned to drag racing with disastrous results in February 1965. At the Southeastern International Dragway, about thirty-five miles northwest of Atlanta, Petty's Barracuda lost a wheel, swerved from one lane to another, slammed into an embankment, turned over, flew up into the air, cleared a wire fence and landed on its front end among spectators. Petty was thrown from the car. Eight-year-old Wayne Dye was killed when hit by the car's wheel and his father, Ronnie Dye, was among seven persons injured.[6]

Only 10,000 showed up for the Martinsville race in April as compared to the 23,000 who attended the year before. The biggest cheer from the Darlington fans at the Rebel 300 was for Richard Petty in street clothes. France's explanation for the drop in track attendance was the lack of personalities. "If we still had Little Joe [Weatherly] and Fireball [Roberts], it wouldn't matter if they were all driving Fords."[7]

Tracks were feeling a fiscal pinch. Along with his counterparts at the Bristol and Charlotte tracks, Colvin asked France to meet with them. The track officials urged France to reinstate Chrysler and their star drivers and told him if he refused they would all suffer. "We desperately need these cars and drivers," Colvin urged. Still, France rejected their appeals.[8]

Colvin's predictions came true. At the June 13, 1965, Dixie 400, won by Marvin Panch with A. J. Foyt as the relief driver, Atlanta experienced a 16,000 drop in attendance from the previous year. France knew he had to backtrack on his decision to ban Chrysler, its drivers and Hemi-head engines from competition. The Dixie 400 was the twenty-sixth straight Grand National race Ford had won.[9]

Two days later, France announced, along with USAC's Henry Banks, that Chrysler and its Hemi-head engines could return to competition but with certain provisions. The Hemi-head engines were approved only for the Plymouth Fury and Dodge Polara, using a 119-inch wheelbase, for tracks at Daytona, Atlanta, Charlotte and Darlington. For tracks with distances of one mile or less the engine could be used in Plymouth Belvederes and Dodge Coronets, with wheelbases less than 119 inches.[10] France continued, "I am happy to say for the first time in stock car racing history the major associations have adopted a uniformity for specifications. This is the most powerful step forward."[11]

There were more problems. Two more drivers were killed on the track. Buren Skeen, from Denton, North Carolina, was in a four car wreck on the second lap of the Southern 500 at Darlington on September 7. Skeen, who had to be cut out of his car with an acetylene torch, suffered multiple internal injuries, a skull fracture and a ruptured spleen. He died a week later without having regained consciousness. Harold Kite, from Augusta, Georgia, was killed when four cars collided on the first lap of the National 400 on October 17 at Charlotte Motor Speedway. The collision was so severe that Kite's roll bar was knocked loose from the frame. Jimmy Helms, injured in the crash that killed Kite, called for rigid driver testing before accepting race entries for super speedways. For the first time, Bob Colvin instituted such a procedure at Darlington.[12]

Cotton Owens had another solution to keep his driver, David Pearson, as safe as possible from injuries in a collision. NASCAR required the cars to have one roll bar but Owens used three heavy-duty roll bars around the driver's compartment to provide additional protection in case Pearson was hit on the driver's side. The seat in Pearson's car rested on metal runners, connected to the left side roll bar. A left side impact, carrying enough force to move the roll bars, would move the seat and driver with them. "I'd never take a car on the track unless I know every possible thing had been done to make it the safest there," Owens said. "I'd never put Dave in a car I wouldn't drive." Owens added he had been using the additional roll bars for two years.[13]

Chrysler was back in Grand National and the 1966 season looked promising for Bill France. On December 13, 1965, France said, "The historic agreement recently concluded on race car specifications between NASCAR and USAC will allow every American manufacturer to participate in racing in 1966. I can only emphasize what I have said earlier, that we are on the threshold of stock car racing's greatest years. In 1966, we will have some of the finest, most exciting and swiftest competition in our history."[14]

Four days later, Ford, heady with winning forty-nine of the fifty-five Grand National races in 1965, announced it would race the next year with the new single overhead cam engine. Car builder Smokey Yunick described the differences, "The Ford 427 ci high rise engine this year ranged from 500 horse power for an average one to 525 for a good one. With the single overhead cam, the average ones will have 600 horse power and the good ones 610 or 615." Yunick said the Chrysler Hemi-head engines and the Ford high rise engines were very much alike except for this single overhead cam addition.[15]

Ford public relations director Leo C. Beebe said the engines were consistent with their understanding of NASCAR rules. Bill France said, "The V-8 overhead cam engine introduced by Ford Motor Company is, at this time, strictly a racing engine and not one for stock autos. The engine will be looked on as experimental this year and will be reviewed next season."[16]

Bernard Kahn wrote that France and Beebe had reached an honest accord in Chicago on December 22. "Ford decided to swallow its muscle and race its 427 ci engine in 1967," Kahn wrote. "It was a grand Christmas present for Bill [France]."[17]

Of course, it was, but 1966 did not turn out to be the banner year France expected.

In January, the man known as France's enforcer, Pat Purcell, was hospitalized with a heart condition. After being in and out of the hospital for three months, Purcell died in April 1966.[18]

A month later, France hired Purcell's replacement but he lacked the power of intimidation and the knowledge of the man who had been there from the beginning. L. A. "Lin" Kuchler had been executive secretary of the American Motorcycle Association for thirty years when he became NASCAR's new executive director.[19]

The 1966 Daytona 500 was coming up and France wanted all the famous drivers, including six from USAC, in the race.

In particular, France was elated to have the USAC rookie of the year and previous Indy 500 winner Mario Andretti, from Nazareth, Pennsylvania, driving. The race was FIA approved, which opened it to USAC drivers. Andretti was in Chevrolet's Chevelle prototype which Semon "Bunkie" Knudsen, head of Chevy racing, insisted that Smokey Yunick prepare for the race. The Chevelle had a shorter wheelbase, 115 inches, and a GM 427 ci engine. Yunick was reluctant to race the car but Knudsen insisted.[20]

The Chevelle had a part that was not approved by NASCAR. Yunick blamed the steel fuel cell for contributing to Fireball Roberts' fatal accident. He had Firestone build him a

22-gallon rubber fuel cell using military helicopter specifications. When he took the Chevelle through inspection, NASCAR technical inspector Norris Friel told him to take out the rubber cell and put in the steel tank. Yunick refused and started to leave the track. France, after conversations with Friel and Knudsen, stopped Yunick and told him Knudsen wanted to speak with him. Yunick explained to Knudsen the problem with the fuel cell. Knudsen told the car builder he wanted to see the car run. Yunick assured Knudsen, "You will. France wants Mario in the race more than he wants to screw Miss Pure Oil."[21]

France followed Yunick and asked him what Knudsen had said. Yunick replied, "He said to put it in the barn, then run it in USAC." France asked to see the rubber fuel cell his inspector had kicked out. After examining it, he told Yunick he could use it just this one time and then he had to go back to the steel. "They'll need snow tires in hell before I take that rubber tank out," Yunick replied. France started to argue when Yunick interrupted and asked, "Have you seen Fireball lately?" France had no reply and told him to take the Chevelle back to the inspection station, where it was approved for the race.[22]

Others were pushing for the rubber fuel cell besides Yunick. Car builder-owner Bud Moore was also demanding that NASCAR not only use the rubber fuel cell but also mandate a strap connecting the driver's shoulder harness to the seat. At some point, France acquiesced. In December 1965, NASCAR was presented Firestone's Coated Fabrics Division's Industrial Award of Excellence for developing a rubber fuel cell to fit inside a steel gas tank.[23]

Not ready for prime time, the Chevelle's engine blew early in the race, which Richard Petty won in a Hemi-head Plymouth in dramatic fashion. Falling back to twentieth because of tire problems, Petty regrouped to beat Cale Yarborough, ending Ford's domination of Grand National racing. David Pearson was third in a Dodge; Fred Lorenzen was fourth in a Ford; and Sam McQuagg, from Columbus, Georgia, was fifth in another Dodge.[24]

Still sticking to his standard of paying ten percent of the gate into his race purse, France was now in the big time. Daytona tickets were averaging fifteen dollars each. Multiplying the average ticket price by the crowd attendance of 97,400, France from his gate alone (not counting fees, concessions, programs and parking) grossed around $1,460,100 while the race purse was $140,000.[25]

Three years earlier, France's entire Grand National season purses for fifty-five races amounted to only $884,858, an average of $16,088 per race. For six of those races, two each at Winston-Salem, Dog Track Speedway in Moyock and Tar Heel Speedway in Randleman, all in North Carolina, the purses were under $4,000.[26]

After Daytona's Speed Week, France announced at a meeting of track operators that Ford could race its single overhead cam engines but only if it built passenger cars with those engines. Track owners were angry.[27]

"Sure there were some disgruntled track owners," France admitted, "but they were in favor of banning the overhead cam in February. Their complaint is that now we have taken action, it's affecting their ticket sales." France alleged that Ford agreed to sell the overhead cam engine in passenger cars and then changed their minds. "Until they start selling these engines, they obviously don't want to race," he added.[28]

France was unable to let well enough alone. He then took Ford to task for paying their drivers while they were not racing in NASCAR. "We hope either the drivers will break with Ford or new ones will come along to take their place."[29] The days were long gone where France could ban drivers for infractions that might or might not be in the rulebook or determine what they were paid by car owners. The drivers' contracts with the automobile manufacturers did not need France's approval. Drivers were, after all, independent contractors.

France's complaint that Ford was paying their drivers a salary was nothing new. That practice was confirmed two years earlier by Smokey Yunick, in an interview with Bernard Kahn, in the *Daytona Beach Morning Journal*. Kahn said the manufacturers denied paying their stock car drivers. "But, they do," Yunick said. "You just can't sign a top driver otherwise. They may not pay him directly for driving but, some way, they arrange it so a driver gets from $8,000 to $15,000 a year so he'll be available to drive the car when they want it to race."[30]

Yunick continued, "The factory support is a key factor and NASCAR has tried to do something about it. An independent can't afford a pit crew that cost $1,000 a race." He added that it would cost an independent $100,000 to enter a car in only the major Grand National races. "There's just no way to make the independents competitive unless the factories get mad now and quit," Yunick added. Otherwise, he said, the rules would not help the independents.[31]

France wanted the independents back in racing. He could control them more easily than the automobile manufacturers.

In April 1966, Henry Ford II announced that the Ford Motor Company was pulling its factory-backed cars from Grand National racing but might return in 1967. Ford's decision came after NASCAR and USAC instituted rules requiring cars to carry an additional 427 pounds if they used the overhead cam engine. France promised to review the overhead cam engine in 1967 if Ford put the engine in mass production and cut the cost. He added, "We survived the 1957 Automobile Manufacturers Association resolution and we can survive this."[32]

France suggested if Ford wanted to stay in Grand National racing, it should race their overhead cam engine car, with the weight restrictions, against a Chrysler, with a Hemi-head engine, to prove the weight restrictions were too severe. Then, France said, the rules could be changed to make them more fair.[33]

It was obvious from France's statements that he had conducted no tests before changing the rules. Ford was not going to placate France by attempting to prove a negative. France only said the rules could be changed, not that they would be. He also did not say when such a change could occur.

"We race to create an image for our products," a Ford spokesman said. "We don't create a favorable image by losing, even if just to prove a point." France accused the Ford brass of acting like children. "I just don't understand it," he said. "The ruling is the fairest that racing has come up with in a long time." He insisted the additional weight of 427 pounds, which Ford complained about, was not that much of a problem.[34]

Ford's answer was to pull their factory-backed cars out of the Columbia and Greenville, South Carolina, races. A Ford representative pointed out that the additional weight was indeed a problem because France's edict mandated changing the entire structure of the car, the braking and the tires.[35]

Henry Ford II said he told France in a telephone conversation, "We couldn't possibly continue with the rules as they exist. I believe the racing officials have to develop some rules that are fairer to everyone. Up to now they don't seem very fair."[36]

At an April 21–22 meeting in Charlotte, Ford officials told their drivers all the company's equipment would be placed in storage. In addition, Ford drivers would not be able to operate cars as independents.[37]

France stuck to his guns and attendance at Grand National tracks took another nosedive. The crowd at the Virginia 500 at Martinsville was only half of capacity. NASCAR officials blamed the low attendance on the absence of the Ford factory-backed drivers. And they made another scoring mistake. Paul Goldsmith, from St. Clair Shores, Michigan, driving a Plymouth, was declared the winner of the Martinsville race until Jim Pascal, from High Point, North Carolina, filed a protest. Scorers neglected to note Goldsmith's pit stop on lap 268. Pascal, also driving a Plymouth, received first place money of $4,550; Goldsmith was second, $2,150; and Richard Petty, in another Plymouth, was third, $1,250.[38]

Grand National drivers who previously drove Fords scattered. The *Sarasota Herald-Tribune* reported that Ned Jarrett had left Ford's racing team and would drive his own Ford in the World 600 at Charlotte. Marvin Panch was in a Lee Petty Plymouth, Curtis Turner in a Yunick Chevrolet. Fred Lorenzen, Dick Hutcherson, Bobby Isaac and Cale Yarborough were still looking for rides.[39]

Yarborough decided to drive one of the dragsters Holman-Moody was building for Ford. "Cale wanted to drive a dragster, so we put him in one and he went through the catch fence at the end of the quarter-mile, so that was his last drag race," Ralph Moody said.[40]

Ford, meanwhile, had leased the Darlington Raceway to test its single overhead cam engine. There were rumors Ford could be back in Grand National racing sometime between the Firecracker 400 and the Southern 500 on Labor Day.[41]

Before a Ford-NASCAR settlement arrived, Chrysler announced on June 22, 1966, that it was withdrawing from stock car racing at the end of the 1967 season. Chrysler's director of racing, R. M. Rogers, said the withdrawal was to return stock car racing to a more independent status. Such a gesture had more to do with money than with concern about the independents in NASCAR. Chrysler had won twenty-one of the twenty-six Grand National races so far that season. Chrysler had poured more than $3 million into stock car racing that year. The automobile manufacturer, Rogers said, would fulfill its contracts with the Pettys, Paul Goldsmith, Norm Nelson, Jim Hurtubise, David Pearson and Sam McQuagg.[42]

The next month, July 1966, ACCUS ruled that Ford could race its single overhead cam engine in its Galaxie and Fairlane models without additional weight in 1967, if 550 of those vehicles were built, with the overhead cam engines, and sent out to dealers. Ford, however, was finishing out the season with the 427 ci wedge engine.[43]

Not only did France have warring automobile manufacturers, he had car builders taking advantage of the situation and making a mockery of his rules. Things came to a head at Atlanta International Raceway's Dixie 400 on August 7, 1966, when Junior Johnson's Ford and Smokey Yunick's Chevelle resembled nothing that ever came out of Detroit. Sports reporter Bob Moore said Johnson's crew had to lift driver Fred Lorenzen up through the window opening and slide him into the driver's seat. "There was no way he could climb in it normally because the roof was slanted," Moore said. "And, the front windshield was sloped down at an angle. The left side of the car was down about three inches lower than the right side of the car."[44]

Racing columnist Tom Higgins said that because the car carried sponsor Holly Farms' yellow paint scheme it was likened to a banana. Higgins added that the rear end of the car was raised higher than normal. "I built the car," Higgins quoted Johnson as saying, "because

John Holman was a friend of mine and asked me to help him out. He said, 'Build me something that will run' and I did. We had a heck of a time getting through inspection. We took the car to body shops all around Atlanta, making changes before we got it close enough for NASCAR to approve."[45]

Higgins continued, "It was the first—and only—time the car with a body so radically curved like a banana or a boomerang was allowed to race. NASCAR, sensitive to a barrage of criticism, quietly told Junior not to bring it back."[46] In his book *Cheating,* Tom Jensen described Yunick's black and gold Chevelle as being built to approximately seven-eighths the size of its stock counterpart and carrying an oversized engine. "Amazingly, both cars sailed through tech inspection much to the outrage of Cotton Owens, who owned the Dodge that point leader David Pearson was driving that weekend."[47]

"A ruckus raged over both cars," Higgins said, "but they were cleared to race by NASCAR, which rejected three other machines, including those of Ned Jarrett, Bernard Alvarez and Cotton Owens, fielding a Dodge for David Pearson. Owens' car was rigged with a device to lower it from the cockpit after the race started. Turning away Jarrett, Alvarez and Owens—while clearing the cars of Junior and Smokey—further fueled an already incendiary situation. The discord doubled, both among fans and competitors, when Turner won the pole at 148.331 mph. Lorenzen qualified third fastest."[48]

Higgins quoted Owens as saying, "I realize that Lorenzen and Turner are valuable drawing cards but that doesn't make what's happened right."[49]

Turner racked up fifty-eight laps in the Yunick-built car before going out with a distributor problem. A blown tire caused Lorenzen to crash after leading twenty-four laps. Richard Petty won the 1966 Dixie 400 and $13,525 with an average speed of 130.244 mph before an Atlanta crowd of 25,000.[50]

"One of France's most dramatic uses or misuses of power involved allowing two flagrantly illegal cars to compete to appease Detroit auto execs eager to get Ford and Chevrolet racing again, as well as Atlanta track owners who wanted all three automakers competing to revive attendance, which had sagged badly in 1965–1966," Jensen wrote. "The Atlanta race in 1966 would forever represent the high-water mark—or low-water mark, depending on your point of view—for cheating, innovating, creative engineering, whatever one cares to call it. When the teams arrived at Daytona in 1967, NASCAR was waiting with its first body template."[51]

The Southern 500 on Labor Day was the first time a Ford factory-backed team faced off against a Chrysler factory-backed team since the 1966 spring races. The contest was won by an independent, Darel Dieringer, driving Bud Moore's Mercury Comet in a duel with Richard Petty. "I raced my heart out," Dieringer said. David Pearson was third in a Dodge and Marvin Panch was fourth in another Plymouth. Fred Lorenzen was fifth in a Ford.[52]

After a season of bending and disregarding what rules NASCAR had, the Old Dominion 500 at Martinsville and the American 500 at Rockingham were no different.

Three Fords were in the first two rows of the starting grid at the Martinsville race. Fred Lorenzen and his Ford came in first in the Old Dominion race on September 25. NASCAR inspector Norris Friel found his gas tank held 1.1 gallons more fuel than the twenty-two gallons allowed. NASCAR field director John Bruner said Lorenzen's fuel tank rendered "the car automatically disqualified according to the rules." Bruner placed Lorenzen fourth and gave the race to Darel Dieringer in Bud Moore's Comet.[53]

Lin Kuchler, NASCAR's new executive director, claimed the car's fuel tank met specifications. Kuchler was concerned about a statement Lorenzen made in his post-race interview. The *Charlotte Observer* quoted Lorenzen as saying, "If they are going to check just my car and no others and take my money and give it to someone else, then you're seeing the last of me. I'm never going to return south to race again." Ralph Moody yanked Lorenzen out of the press box before he could do any more damage. Kuchler, in an effort to strengthen his decision, only made matters worse. He claimed Lorenzen's pit stops were comparable to those of other top finishers in the race.[54]

"That's a lie," Bud Moore protested. "We were Lorenzen's nearest competitor and were getting 130 laps and running out of gas. Lorenzen was getting 183 laps between pit stops." Cotton Owens agreed with Moore, saying his driver, David Pearson, was getting 120–125 laps in his Dodge between pit stops. Both men pointed out that Lorenzen's cars were noted for their oversized fuel tanks.[55]

NASCAR, unable to stop commenting on their decision, gave the race win back to Lorenzen. Kuchler repeated that Lorenzen's fuel cell met specifications and had an expansion factor of twelve to fourteen percent. Moore shot back, "The only way Lorenzen's tank could have been expanded was for someone to take an air hose and blow it out or for it to have had a larger pan than allowed."[56]

Because his other expansion explanations did not fly, Kuchler tried something else. "The container in Lorenzen's car had a slight dent from a wreck he was involved in Friday and this could account for the extra 1.1 gallons in his tank after the race," he added.[57]

An indentation in the fuel tank would have decreased, not increased, the capacity.

The fuel tank matter lingered for five days after the race. John Holman, builder of Lorenzen's Ford, had a private meeting with Bill France, who upheld the ruling that Lorenzen was the race winner.[58]

NASCAR officials attempted to avoid the Martinsville problem in the last race of the season at Rockingham, the American 500, in which Lorenzen also finished first after running fender to fender with Richard Petty for the first 320 miles before the Plymouth's engine blew.[59]

Ray Nichels, who prepared the second place Dodge Charger for USAC driver Don White, from Keokuk, Iowa, filed a protest after the race. Nichels pointed out that NASCAR officials did not perform routine pre-race weight checks and asked that Lorenzen's car weight, size and fuel tank be checked by officials. John Holman, who built Lorenzen's car, demanded that, if his car was examined, then the first five finishers' cars all be checked, including those of Dieringer, Ned Jarrett, Cale Yarborough and Tiny Lund in a Junior Johnson Ford.[60]

Lorenzen said, "This protesting is getting to be ridiculous. I guess there are too many hot dogs around now and when they get outdone they think something is wrong with the other fellow." NASCAR allowed Lorenzen's win to stand.[61]

Lorenzen, called the "Golden Boy" by the media, appeared to hold himself above the fray. When he came into stock car racing, he had little experience on dirt and had to spend considerable time practicing to be able to compete. Whenever possible, Lorenzen returned to his home in Elmhurst, Illinois, between races.[62]

Consequently, Lorenzen was often the butt of pranks from drivers like Turner and Weatherly. Before a Darlington race, most of the drivers were staying at the same motel and were tired of swimming in the shallow part of the pool because the police car they had driven into the pool's deep end had not been removed. There was poolside talk that Lorenzen was too chicken to come out of his first floor room and join the fun, which included tossing fully-dressed waitresses into the pool.[63]

Turner volunteered to get Lorenzen out of his room and Weatherly was more than happy to help. Everybody crowded around the pool fence with an idea of what was going to happen. The two drivers got in Turner's Ford, parked nearby. Turner turned to Weatherly and explained, "Now remember, Pops, it's all about getting the angle right." Turner gunned the car's engine and slammed into Lorenzen's motel room, taking out the door and its frame and evidently scaring the hell out of Lorenzen.[64]

"Freddie," Turner called out, "you in there? Some of the guys said you were too chicken to come out here but I wouldn't have none of that," Edelstein wrote. "Lorenzen slowly appears, his head going up and down, surveying the damage. At poolside, the cheers rang out."[65]

The American 500 at Rockingham was Ned Jarrett's last race and his distinguished driving career ended on a note that had to be disappointing, although the track had declared the event "Ned Jarrett Day." There was a moment of concern when Jarrett pulled what he thought was a lever to tighten his seat belt and instead triggered the car's fire extinguisher.[66]

Plymouth (16) and Dodge (18) gave Chrysler thirty-four wins in the forty-nine Grand National races in 1966. Ford had ten, Chevrolet, three, and Mercury, two. The top fifty drivers split $932,245, less than one of Bill France's Daytona gates. David Pearson was the Grand National champion with $78,194; James Hylton, from Inman, South Carolina, was second with $33,688; and Petty third at $23,052.[67]

Although they won nearly seventy percent of the 1966 Grand National races, Chrysler cut its stock car racing budget sixty percent due, it said, to decreased sales. The decision could also have been prompted by the increased costs in building stock cars and by France's ever-changing rules. In 1959, the cost to build a Grand National car was around $18,000. By 1966, the cost had climbed to $50,000. Car builder Bud Moore said no independents could successfully compete with Ford and very few corporations were going to do so.[68]

There were rumors of a merger between the Charlotte Motor Speedway (CMS) and the Daytona International Speedway (DIS). Why would Richard Howard and the CMS stockholders want to be in business with France and DIS? Emerging from bankruptcy, CMS showed a 1966 profit of $151,527, and paid a dividend of 7.5 cents per share. In addition, the speedway had $244,893 in the bank.[69] There were also rumors of another track that might change hands. Curtis Turner, who still had his CMS stock, was reportedly negotiating with the Atlanta International Raceway to purchase that facility for $2 million.[70]

The 500-mile race at Riverside on January 22, 1967, saw Billy Foster, from Victoria, British Columbia, die in a practice accident. Foster's car slammed against the retaining wall at about 140 mph, causing massive head injuries. The force of the accident sheared all the sheet metal off the vehicle's right side.[71] Track physician Dr. Irving Omphoy said the USAC driver's helmet probably struck the wall as his car hit the barrier. He said Foster died instantly but did not specify it was a basal skull injury. Media accounts of the accident detailed the extensive damage to the right side of the car without explaining how Foster sustained the fatal injury when he was driving on the left side. A memorial race was planned to start a fund to educate Foster's three children.[72]

Another death affected the stock car racing world. Bob Colvin, instrumental in bringing

Curtis Turner back into NASCAR, died of a heart attack at his desk at Darlington Raceway on January 24, 1967. He had been Darlington president since 1953. A Darlington native, Colvin became a peanut broker after graduation from Clemson and piloted a PT boat in World War II. Bill France, who often clashed with Colvin, said, "I know he loved the sport; for the last eight years it has been his whole life."[73]

France invited British Grand Prix driver Innes Ireland from London to drive in the 1967 Daytona 500. He announced that Ireland would drive a Ray Fox Dodge in the race. Not impressed with France's promotions surrounding the race, Ireland said, "Commercialism is going to ruin racing if it hasn't already done so. It's taking the sport out of motorsports."[74]

Fred Lorenzen and his gas tank picked up where they left off the previous year. He won one of the Daytona qualifying races, 100 miles, without stopping for fuel, in a Ford at 174.587 mph. LeeRoy Yarbrough won the other in a Dodge at 163.934 mph, and again called attention to Lorenzen's Ford. "I don't think anybody can run 100 miles [on this speedway] on twenty-two gallons of gas," he said. "It's funny nobody else could do it." Lorenzen claimed he ran out of gas just before he got to the finish line. The Chryslers could only go eighty laps without refueling. France appeared to have everything evenly divided between Ford and Chrysler going into the 1967 Daytona 500. Then, Smokey Yunick brought his new Chevrolet Chevelle to the track and Curtis Turner blew everybody away by setting a qualifying record of 180.831 mph.[75]

When the public address announcer gave Turner's record setting pole speed, near dead silence descended on the speedway. France had spent two years cajoling, pleading and dealing to get Ford and Chrysler to do what he wanted. Then, along came a has-been driver and a car builder who enjoyed poking holes in his rulebook but who was backed by Chevrolet, and they embarrassed him before Ford and Chrysler executives at his biggest racing spectacle, the Daytona 500.

Bob Collins, *Indianapolis Star* sports editor, wrote rather tepidly about Turner's record setting qualifying. "Turner is something of a problem to NASCAR public relations writers who, in this era of big purses, are trying to drum up an image of the clean-cut-golly-gee-whiz youngsters racing stock cars over the southern circuit. Curtis doesn't fit ... he believes that clean living went out with Jack Armstrong. He's been called, appropriately, 'the last of the good old boys.'"[76]

There was a possibility that Turner and Yunick might not only win the Daytona race but do so in Daytona's first televised event.

A decade after Sam Nunis first explored televising automobile races, France put together a pay-per-view television package for the Daytona 500 in 1967, when he signed a two-year contract with the TelePrompTer Corporation. Fourteen cameras, strategically placed around the high-banked track, caught all the action.[77]

Profits from all the events surrounding Daytona's Speed Week were going to be France's fund to build another super speedway. Daytona 500 tickets were selling from $6 to $20, and around 94,250 paid to see the race. His gate was somewhere around $2 million. The purse was $200,000, still in the ten to eleven percent range of his gate. In addition, there was admission revenue from the 35,000 who paid to see the qualifying races; the ARCA race and its qualifiers; the concessions, parking and program proceeds, and the pay-per-view television.[78]

An estimated 300,000 to 350,000 paid to see the race televised live in venues across the nation. Joe Littlejohn sold out the Spartanburg Municipal Arena at $8 per seat; Alvin and Joe Hawkins sold out the 5,000 seat Winston-Salem Auditorium at the same price. The Detroit telecast drew 7,000. At Reading, Pennsylvania, 1,800 watched the race at the Rajah Temple. Associated Press reporter Bloys Britt, who once wrote a book with France, theorized, "Thus, if even 300,000 paid the auditorium price that makes a TV gross of $2.4 million dollars."[79]

France possibly grossed around $5 million from all the Daytona events that year.

Once again, France was lucky and Turner and Yunick were not. Yunick described what happened on lap 143 of the Daytona 500: "Mario [Andretti] gets the lead in a Holman-Moody Ford. Curtis has brain fade, and mashed the gas hard. In a lap, he catches him but one of the connecting rods breaks. The million buck–Chevelle looks like the world's best mosquito sprayer. It blew all to shit. Oh yes, it had the rubber [fuel] cell."[80]

The young USAC driver Mario Andretti, from Nazareth, Pennsylvania, won the race in a Holman-Moody Ford seventeen seconds in front of his teammate, Fred Lorenzen. Andretti said Daytona's high banks represented the toughest kind of racing.[81]

Ralph Moody, who with John Holman built Andretti's car, said there was no way the USAC driver should have won the Daytona 500. "First of all, his car was loose as hell and he was crossed up and sideways all around the track like he was on dirt. Then he ran out of gas three times." Andretti had virtually no practice time in the car and he could not find his pit. "Mario would be out there running way up high, because that was the fastest line around the track," Moody said. "We'd signal him to come in for fuel and he'd drive right by us on pit lane. He couldn't find our pits. He did that three different times. He'd fall down a lap each time, then un-lap himself and lead again. It's a wonder he won the race."[82]

Nursing his less than average equipment, Wendell Scott finished fifteenth ahead of David Pearson (24), Turner (25), Gordon Johncock (30), Gary Bettenhausen (31), LeeRoy Yarbrough (34), Cale Yarborough (39) and A.J. Foyt (37). Scott took home $2,200.[83]

Chevrolet and Yunick, meanwhile, were building another Chevelle. They skipped the short track races at Weaverville, Bristol, Greenville and Winston-Salem and set their sights on entering Turner and the car in the Atlanta 500 on April 2.[84]

France, unable to savor his Daytona success, was busy trying to referee another fight between Chrysler and Ford. Chrysler threatened to boycott the Atlanta race, charging Ford was using intake manifolds and cylinder systems unavailable to the public as NASCAR rules required, since at least 500 of the systems had not been manufactured and made available through dealers and parts outlets. A boycott by Chrysler would have taken Richard Petty, LeeRoy Yarbrough and David Pearson out of the race. Ford denied everything and Lin Kuchler backed France and Ford, saying the parts were simply an improvement over those formerly used and were generally available.[85]

Kuchler informed Chrysler, "That is our interpretation and we plan to stick by that interpretation." France, falling back on the old axiom of catching more flies with honey than vinegar, promised, according to Chrysler vice-president R. M. Rogers, to reconsider NASCAR's position after the Atlanta race.[86]

Turner's bragging to the media that he could win the Atlanta race was giving France fits with Chrysler and Ford. A Georgia newspaper credited Turner with winning 355 NASCAR races, in all divisions. "And, that ain't includin' all them little ones back in the dirt track days," Turner added.[87]

Yunick described his Chevelle: "I've got a full house, 427 cubic inches with three, two barrels screwed in the Chevelle. It had 650 horsepower at 7,600 rpm, so when you mash the right pedal in this thing you need to have a good grip."[88]

During the March 20 practice for the 1967 Atlanta 500, Turner came out of the pits and tucked the Chevelle behind Cale Yarborough's Ford Fairlane. Coming out of turn four, Turner was ahead of Yarborough and the Chevelle abruptly turned right."[89]

Yunick said Turner and Yarborough, for reasons he never understood, just flat out did not like each other. "Turner was so proud of his car that he wanted to show Cale a thing or two," Yunick said. "Least that's the way he planned it.[90]

"Turner slides and hits the concrete retaining wall with the force of a roundhouse," Edelstein wrote, "and the car ricochets backwards into the air, sailing some twenty feet upward. Yarborough, without taking his foot off the gas, glides right below Turner's car, missing part of the fender by three inches. Yunick, glaring from the pits, sees the rear bumper of the Chevelle reach high above the last row of the grandstand seats and he starts running."[91]

Turner described the Atlanta wreck: "You wouldn't believe it but a wreck is pretty quiet to the man who's in it. When the car is in the air—and that's a lot of the time—it's so quiet you could hear a pin drop. I noticed that when I was flipping at Atlanta."[92]

Yunick and T. A. Tooms pulled an unconscious Turner out of the car. Turner was released from the hospital the next day. Yunick had what was left of the Chevelle squashed into a four foot square but Knudsen told him to build another one for 1968.[93]

Turner and Yunick argued for days about the mechanic building him another car. Finally, Yunick said, "Curtis, I'm sorry. You and I ain't gonna race no more because I think you're over the hill. I don't expect you to agree with me but you're gonna have to, about driving my car because I'm not gonna let you drive the damn thing anymore. I don't want to take the chance on killing you because I have too much fun at the parties."[94]

Around 80,000 turned out for the Atlanta 500 but there was no Curtis Turner among the forty-four drivers to thrill them with his flat out, sideways style of driving. But there was plenty of excitement. Yarborough won the race after Richard Petty and A. J. Foyt blew their engines, and Andretti hit the wall.[95]

After the Atlanta race, France met with Chrysler executives. He pointed out that he only agreed to discuss the rules concerning the changes Ford made on their engines, not change them. In addition, he said USAC also approved the change. "We have our interpretations and Chrysler has its interpretations," he repeated.[96]

Actually, Chrysler was not faring badly in competition with Ford in the Grand National races. After the first fifteen races, Chrysler had won eight, Ford, five, and Chevrolet, two. The next twelve Grand National races were all won by Chrysler, including Petty's win in the Rebel 400 and Paschal's taking the World 600.[97]

Fred Lorenzen, before the World 600 at Charlotte, decided to retire, citing his problem with ulcers. Ford gave him a new car and NASCAR honored Lorenzen, the only driver to win the Grand National's grand slam—Atlanta, Charlotte, Darlington, Daytona and Rockingham—at the race. Richard Howard, CMS general manager, asked him to drive the pace car. Lorenzen said he would remain with Ford but declared, "I'll never be back in a race car." Lorenzen's retirement set off a musical chairs routine of drivers. David Pearson left Cotton Owens to take Lorenzen's place with Ford. Owens signed Bobby Allison, from Hueytown, Alabama, to replace Pearson.[98]

In a two-month period, from the Bowman Gray short track race through the Southern

500 and the North Wilkesboro race, Richard Petty won ten consecutive races in his Plymouths. The Pettys followed Yunick's practice of building their cars with features not covered in France's rulebook.[99]

The Pettys surmised their car would handle better by placing as much weight on the driver's side of the car as possible, which made it easier to take the corners. Eventually, NASCAR figured out what they were doing and not only regulated but began inspecting weight distribution for each side of the car.[100]

Just before the North Wilkesboro race, France turned up at a Birmingham meeting of the Alabama League of Municipalities with the Daytona Beach mayor, Owen Eubank. France, trolling for investors, announced at the meeting the results of a feasibility study indicating that a $3.5 million race track near Talladega, Alabama, was economically justified. The grandstands, he said, could be expanded to hold 200,000 spectators. France pushed the idea of selling bonds to pay for the project, which he said would cost about $1.5 million annually to operate. Eubank chimed in about how many tourist dollars the Daytona speedway had brought to his town. The windfall was so great, Eubank boasted, "it had enabled residents to go from eating catfish and collards to steak."[101]

Not everyone in Daytona Beach was enthralled with France and his new speedway. The Birmingham announcement opened up old wounds that were the subject of a city commission meeting a week later. Former state Rep. Kermit Coble proposed special legislation to be introduced to repeal the property tax exemption the speedway had enjoyed since 1959. France vehemently claimed the commission was harassing him over the property tax issue. Accompanied to the meeting by his attorney, C. A. Vincent, Jr., France did most of the talking. Thomas T. Cobb, attorney for the Daytona Beach Recreation and Racing Facility District, explained the city leased to the district the land where the speedway was built, and the district in turn leased it to France's corporation.[102]

"I'm weary of this harassment," France informed the commission. "The speedway doesn't own the property it occupies, can't sell it or borrow money on it and its use of the property is limited and restricted. Now, if you want to tax it, turn over the deed to the speedway. This harassment is hurting Daytona Beach and it hurts the speedway."[103]

France had borrowed money, with the commission's approval, on the same facility twice during the construction of the speedway to meet critical financial obligations.

Bernard Kahn speculated that if the city commission put the speedway tax squeeze on France there might be dire consequences. France, he wrote, could be provoked to move NASCAR headquarters from Daytona Beach to the new track he planned to build in Alabama.[104]

The speedway's tax exemption was a battle France would fight for the next ten years with local authorities.

Part of his problem with the municipality and stockholders may have resulted from his failure to pay a dividend on Daytona International Speedway stock. There were three million shares of DIS stock, but only 450,000 of those were publicly held. On the other hand, there may have been lingering resentment that France allegedly sold some of the stock for one dollar a share while his family and corporate officers paid only ten cents a share.[105]

In a June 1967 letter to stockholders, France claimed DIS's six month financial statement indicated net profits were down sixteen percent from the previous period. Income, he said, was $1,427,569, and expenses were $1,062,303. "Our first closed circuit telecast of the Daytona 500 was received very well," he wrote. "The telecast didn't show a profit this year. However, the prospects for the future are promising." France declined to speculate about paying stockholders a dividend.[106]

The man the media referred to as the czar of stock car racing was raking in the money while short track owners were losing their shirts. Drivers and car owners were directing their resources to the bigger venues where the purse money was much better. Car builder Cotton Owens was an example. He said he withdrew from the 100-mile races at Columbia, South Carolina, and Hickory, North Carolina, because he did not have the money for the necessary parts. "I've always went with the best and tried to build competitive cars," Owens said. "If I don't have the equipment to go that way, then I won't race."[107]

Owens said he could run the 250 milers and the major races because he was getting help from Chrysler. He added he got nothing from the manufacturer for the shorter races and was unable to compete.[108]

Bud Moore, a Spartanburg car builder, suggested creating a division in Grand National for the smaller cars, that he called sedans. Moore said the salvation of small tracks, now approaching financial disaster, could be the racing sedan-type cars. The big name drivers, Moore said, passed up the short tracks to run for the bigger purses major tracks paid. He said some short track owners paid those drivers "deal money" just to show up at the track. Moore said he could build a Cougar, with a 289 ci engine averaging 120 mph, for about $9,000 as opposed to $30,000 or more for a Grand National car. Moore said he and Joe Littlejohn went to Mansfield, Ohio, for a sedan race and were surprised at the large crowd. Both men thought the sedan races might answer the problem of the short tracks.[109]

France had experimented with a Sports Car Club of America Trans-American race, called the Paul Revere, beginning at midnight prior to the 1967 Firecracker 400 race in July. The race was called a "Baby" Grand National.

Curtis Turner, who drove Joey Chitwood's Cougar in the race, predicted that he would do well in the Paul Revere because he liked the night air. "It's like a tonic to me, especially before a big race," he said. Turner speculated that he might have finished better in the 1966 Firecracker 400 the previous year if Smokey Yunick had not insisted that he get a lot of sleep. "Smokey kept a hawk-like eye on me," Turner said, "even ran a bed check on me just as if I was a freshman in college or a GI in basic training. I knew sleep was getting me down and I tried to slip out a couple of times but couldn't get by Smokey's watchdogs."[110]

The Paul Revere field included six Cougars along with Alfa Romeos, Porsches, Austin Mini Coopers, Alpines and Volvos. Parnelli Jones won the race that ended at 2:30 a.m., in a Cougar build by Bud Moore.[111]

By the Labor Day race, the Southern 500 at Darlington, Chrysler had won twenty-nine of the first thirty-nine Grand National races. Richard Petty, in his Plymouth, not only sat on the pole but also won the 500-mile race. Chrysler announced it would continue its stock car racing program in 1968, and indicated it would be interested in a rule change that would allow two four-barrel carburetors on its Hemi engines. Under the current rules, Chrysler could use only one four-barrel carburetor while Ford was allowed to use two with its wedge-type engine. In September, France promised ACCUS would examine the manifold and carburetor questions.[112]

France, apparently fearing that the loss of short track revenue would hurt his operation, announced in October there would be a Grand National sedan division with its own championship. The sedan season opened in March 1968 at Rockingham with a 250-mile race with a $15,000 purse. Other sedan races were scheduled for Atlanta, Darlington, Daytona Beach, Charlotte, North Wilkesboro, Asheville-Weaverville, Bristol and Richmond. France said cars eligible to run in the division included Cougars, Mustangs, Camaros, Firebirds, Darts, Javelins and Barracudas.[113]

France was still fighting South Carolina over its blue laws. Assistant Attorney General J. C. Coleman ruled that stock car racing was not a bona fide athletic event, as France's lawyers had contended; the drivers were not athletes and the race was not exempt from blue laws. As a result, 4,000 fans were turned away from a Sunday race at the Charleston Speedway.[114]

Two months after telling Chrysler there would be a discussion of the manifold-carburetor question, France made an announcement. "We are happy that ACCUS has decided there will be no major changes for 1968," he said. "This will allow stock car racing to continue to be highly competitive without additional expenditures for development of new parts on the part of participants." He added that Grand National cars would carry 3,650 pounds instead of 3,500.[115]

NASCAR sanctioned 1,027 events in 1967 and paid out $3,212,104 in prize money. Out of that prize money, $1,099,477 went to the top fifty Grand National drivers. Richard Petty won the championship and $150,197. He was followed by James Hylton, Dick Hutcherson, from Keokuk, Iowa, Bobby Allison, and John Sears, from Ellerbe, North Carolina. Finishing tenth in the standings was Wendell Scott. Chrysler took thirty-six of the forty-nine Grand National races, Fords won ten, and Chevrolet, three.[116]

21

Who Was Running NASCAR?

....

In the late 1960s, it was difficult to determine just who was running NASCAR. Was it Bill France, whose sometimes strange actions were beginning to bring into question his otherwise slick deal makings? Was it the automobile manufacturers? Was Detroit developer Lawrence LoPatin a concern?

In September 1967, Firestone announced the withdrawal of its support of racing. Goodyear was expected to follow suit. Both companies spent approximately $30 million to $35 million a year in direct support of motor racing.[1]

Since NASCAR was privately owned by the France family, their internal records were and are just that, private. Certainly, it was up to them whether to make any data available. In following the concept of keeping everything from the public, even the Rules of Racing, the Frances ran the risk of being defined by those who disagreed with them.

Before the 1968 Daytona 500, France, Ford, Chrysler and everybody else in Daytona were curious about the Chevelle Yunick was preparing for Gordon Johncock to drive in the race. Yunick was adamant that Turner would not drive the car because he was concerned his friend's best driving days were behind him and that he might be killed on the track.[2]

Would the car blow by everything like Turner's Chevelle did in Daytona qualifying the year before? If so, what could be done? Everybody knew that Yunick, with Knudsen's Chevrolet backing, had probably created a monster of a car. He had. NASCAR inspectors were gleefully waiting for the car in pre-race inspections.

"I pulled out the grill, cut the air entrance in half and drained the air from the front and back wheel wells by creating negative air pressure pockets just behind all of 'em," Yunick said. "I split [the] front bumper lengthwise and added two inches. This kept air out from under the car and, together with the wheel well modifications, really helped eliminate front lift from packing air in the engine compartment." He called NASCAR's rear roof spoiler ridiculous. "So, I still had a small rear roof spoiler, and slid the body back [a] couple of inches and moved the wheel wells to fit the new contours front and rear," he continued. "I think my plan on control in rear axle down force was [the] biggest deal of the bunch."[3]

He built a rotisserie in his garage where he could rotate a car a full 360 degrees. "There were no rules against it then, so I faired the bottom of the car in, including fuel cell, from front bumper to rear bumper. I decided to quit fooling around and use[d] the engine as a frame member to stiffen the chassis in twist.... I built a frame myself to eliminate twist. For weight and safety I installed a Lexan windshield and rear glass. Here's something that took a lot of work, I moved all the other glass damn near flush with [the outer] skin. To move more weight where it would do some good, I shoved the driver two inches to [the] left and three inches back. This car was light, so I was able to add 100 pounds to [the] left side. They didn't check the left to right weight bias back then."[4]

While he was working on the car, Yunick came down with pneumonia and was exhausted. He heard rumors that Ford and Chrysler had told France they did not want to be embarrassed again by having a Chevrolet on the Daytona 500 pole. Yunick went to see France and asked him if the rumors were true. France assured him he would never do anything like that. Yunick, while harboring suspicions to the contrary, went back to work on the Chevelle. He spent three months figuring out how to build the exhaust system. The Chevelle passed the initial NASCAR inspection but failed the last inspection before they filled the car with gas.[5]

Yunick said Bill Gazaway, NASCAR's chief inspector, was a big fan of Spiderman and Superman comic books. He had been so busy working on the car, he said, he had not bought the inspector any new comics recently. Gazaway just could not wait to get his hands on the Chevelle. An hour and a half before qualifying, he handed Yunick a list of eleven things that had to be corrected before the car could qualify. Gazaway's list, which would take weeks if not months to accomplish, called for replacing the frame Yunick built with a stock frame, removing all inner panels to let inspectors check for hidden fuel cells, replacing all "handmade beam joint suspension" with stock suspension and on and on. Yunick told Gazaway he would leave before he would make those changes and the inspector extended the invitation. "Do it," Gazaway invited.[6]

Union Oil refused to provide gas for Yunick to drive the car back to his garage and he decided he could drive it anyway because he built in a concealed fuel line that was one inch in diameter. However, due to inspection, the car had no gas. Yunick got some gas, came back to fill the car and an inspector attempted to prevent him from breaking the NASCAR seal on the filler cap. He knocked the inspector on his rear end, broke the seal, poured in some gas and drove away. Lin Kuchler ran after him screaming, "France wants to talk to you." Yunick replied he did not want to talk to France; he wanted to kill him.[7]

France followed him to his garage where Yunick said he threw a four-pound hammer at him. The hammer missed France by inches and put a big dent in the fender of his new Pontiac. France left rather quickly. The following week, Bob Bolles wrote in *Circle Track* magazine that France sent Smokey a check for $1,500 to cover his expenses building the car. "Smokey said he took the check into the bathroom, soiled it and sent it back," Bolles added. "This car [the Chevelle] was like the NASCAR cars of today and in some ways more advanced."[8]

"I think if NASCAR had allowed it to compete, it could have changed the face of stock car racing long before custom frames were allowed and innovation suppressed. Imagine for a moment if stock car racers were as free to design and build creatively, similar to the Smokey car, like they do in Formula 1, where the sport would be today," Bolles concluded.[9]

A year later, when Knudsen left Chevrolet for a job with the Ford Motor Company, Yunick went to work for him. He learned what he suspected about the collusion between Ford, Chrysler and France, regarding his Chevelle, was true. "The big company [Ford] joke was how they got the '68 Chevy kicked out [at Daytona]," Yunick wrote. Kudson said that Ford and Chrysler told France if the Chevelle ran at Daytona they would cancel all their ads in his race programs. The loss of Ford and Chrysler revenue from forty-nine Grand National race programs, plus those of NASCAR's other divisions, would have been a considerable amount. France was willing to do whatever necessary to remain in Ford and Chrysler's good graces. A few months later, Yunick wrote, Firestone hired him to test tires with the Chevelle at the Daytona speedway but France cancelled the test when he discovered the Chevelle was the car they planned to use. Yunick said, "The car was barred from ever competing on a NASCAR track by silent decree." That Chevelle, he contended, was the most famous race car in the world that never ran a lap in competition.[10]

The Daytona Beach newspaper danced around the conflict about the Chevelle. Sports columnist Lee Moore, on February 5, 1968, simply wrote that Ford was concerned about Yunick's Chevelle.[11]

Six days later another Daytona Beach newspaper article appeared saying the Chevelle's wheelbase was 112 inches when NASCAR rules required a minimum wheelbase of 115 inches.[12]

France covered all his bases in keeping the Chevelle out of the 1968 Daytona 500 while keeping Ford and Chrysler happy, spending money in his race programs and competing in his races. Yunick thought, with the right driver, the Chevelle could have hit 200 mph. Five drivers, Cale Yarborough (185.758 mph); Tiny Lund (185.754 mph); LeeRoy Yarbrough (184.354 mph); David Pearson (183.894), and Richard Petty (182.785 mph), broke Curtis Turner's 1967 record set in Yunick's previous Chevelle. Cale Yarborough took the race pole in a Mercury Cyclone at 189.222 mph.[13]

France, during the twin qualifying races, appeared to have some questionable moments. Gene Granger, sports editor of the *Spartanburg Herald-Journal,* wrote, "An all-day rain made it impossible to get off the first of the two races. When everyone considered all hope was gone, there was France driving a white Chevrolet around and around the track. It was still raining but France wouldn't consider it hopeless."[14]

During a break in the weather around 1:00 p.m. France had drivers for both preliminary races take their cars out and try to dry the track. Cale Yarborough said it was useless, "The water was picked up, thrown on the windshield and dropped back on the track." Rain began again around 3:15 p.m. France said not to worry, the shower would only last about fifteen minutes, and asked the drivers to go back out when the downpour stopped. Several drivers groused they would not go back out even if the weather did clear up. Stopping just short of telling the drivers they had to race, France offered them $10,000 if they would qualify on the wet track. Yarborough said he liked the money but his health was more important. Richard Petty said he would race. Bud Moore, owner of Tiny Lund's Mercury, said he was not going to blow everything in such weather. Bobby Allison had already wrecked his car while trying to dry off the track, but said it would be repaired in time for the Sunday race.[15]

The Daytona 500 belonged to two South Carolina drivers. Cale Yarborough, from Timmonsville, drove a Wood Brothers Mercury Cyclone that came in first, ten car lengths ahead of another Cyclone, driven by LeeRoy Yarbrough, from Columbia, and owned by Junior Johnson. There were so many cautions that over a quarter of the race was run under the yellow flag. The pace car drove so many laps it overheated and had to be replaced. Again there was a scoring problem. Al Unser was held at the end of pit row until the pace car passed and made a second lap. The mistake was corrected and Unser finished fourth with Bobby Allison third and David Pearson fifth. Wendell Scott finished fifteenth.[16]

Some speedway official, who probably had not received the memo on crowd estimates, announced that 101,821 spectators saw the 1968 Daytona 500. With an average ticket price of $16.50, France had a gate of approximately $1.7 million. France did not disappoint. The race purse was $155,550.[17]

Daytona Beach Morning Journal sports editor Bernard Kahn wrote, "Official paid attendance figures are not announced by the speedway." He estimated that 80,000 saw the race. France had a reason for keeping the lid on his attendance figures.[18]

Other promoters and track owners had watched France fatten his bank account while seldom paying more than ten percent of the gate to his drivers. Consequently, track owners and developers looked at building their own super speedways or merging. Owners of four of the five major tracks in the south—Charlotte, Darlington, Rockingham and Bristol—were talking about a merger in July 1969. Richard Howard, vice-president of the Charlotte track, said the merger would be an exchange of stock attractive enough that they were confident the stockholders of the four corporations would approve the move. The tracks were valued from $2 million to $3 million each, and, unless he was a stockholder, France had no interest in them at that time. They were all debt free and paid dividends, which the Daytona track had yet to do. Howard had paid the Charlotte mortgage in full including interest, $260,000, a year earlier and had another $50,000 saved for track repaving.[19]

Howard, who was pushing the proposed merger, said he told France about their plans. The track owners' other object was to protect their holdings from Detroit attorney and real estate developer Lawrence LoPatin, who had just finished building the Michigan International Speedway in Brooklyn. LoPatin was gobbling up racing venues as fast as possible.[20]

The merger never came about and LoPatin was on his way to acquiring controlling interest in the Atlanta International Raceway. He had agreed to buy forty-seven percent of the Riverside, California, track and had an option for eighteen percent of additional stock. LoPatin was also building another major speedway in Bryan Station, Texas.[21]

LoPatin had built the 2.5-mile Ontario, California, speedway with $25.6 million in revenue bonds. On his board of directors were USAC official Tom Binford; J. C. Agajanian, Ascot Speedway owner and promoter; and USAC driver Parnelli Jones. Ontario was only twenty-five miles east of populous Los Angeles.[22]

If Howard was correct that France was initially supportive of the merger of the four tracks, then Bill France appeared again to be playing both sides, much as he did with Ford, Chrysler and Chevrolet. France had been courted by LoPatin. In a newspaper article, LoPatin was lavish in his praise of France. "I can't over emphasize France's role in our program," he said. "He has a lot to do with our activities and aggressiveness; we would not have been able to accomplish what we have done."[23]

"I'm a johnny-come-lately to racing," LoPatin continued, "and France is Mr. Racing. I also want to say that while some other sanctioning bodies dragged their feet when we approached them, France and NASCAR recognized our needs and gave us the help we needed." France, who owned an interest in the North Wilkesboro as well as Martinsville and Asheville-Weaverville tracks in addition to Daytona and was building Talladega, signed a ten-year agreement with LoPatin for NASACR races at his tracks.[24] LoPatin was rushing to build and own as many tracks as possible and that led to his downfall.

France had big plans for the 1969 Daytona races, as usual, but with tragic results. Rain often plagued the February races and, along with winds gusting thirty to thirty-five mph, created dangerous racing conditions. Nine laps into the Permatex 300 Sportsman race, the Comet driven by Don MacTavish, from Dover, Massachusetts, hit the concrete wall in turn four and broke in half. MacTavish lost control from the wet pavement, oil on the track or some other reason that was never clear. Bunky Blackburn, from Daytona Beach, several cars behind MacTavish, said, "I've never see a car disintegrate like that. It went [off] like a bomb. Boy, did that son-of-a-gun come apart." MacTavish's radiator tore out the oil pan in Blackburn's car.[25]

MacTavish's car broke in half after hitting the wall, spun around and came to rest on the bottom of the track with nothing to protect him except part of the roll bar cage. The race course was covered with automobile parts and cars were attempting to miss both the debris and MacTavish. Sam Sommers, from Savannah, had no place to go and hit what was left of MacTavish's car head-on. It was not clear just when MacTavish, the 1966 Sportsman National Champion, died, whether from the impact with the concrete wall or the second crash with Sommers, which cut off both his legs.[26]

After MacTavish's wreck, the race continued but was red-flagged three times due to the rain. LeeRoy Yarbrough won the race with an average speed of 105.365 mph, which was 35.058 mph slower than James Blackburn's average of 140.423 mph the previous year. Despite similar weather conditions in the intervening years, the Daytona 500 was not cancelled due to rain until February 2012.[27]

NASCAR was not very diplomatic in its media comments regarding MacTavish's death. "He died the way he lived, with his foot on the floorboard," said Earl Merrell, a NASCAR steward. "He was a red-blooded American boy who enjoyed fast living on and off the track."[28]

Pete Hamilton, one of MacTavish's best friends, was philosophical about the accident. "Everything is fine when you win," he said. "Winning is the only thing that makes up for a lot of the bad times and you—everyone—lose more than you win. What happened to Don could happen to me. It really could. But, the risk is worth the taking. I mean, there's nothing more satisfying than winning a race."[29]

Hamilton admitted that most race drivers were gamblers. "We all enjoy gambling," he said. "We play poker a lot. Every top driver I know likes to play and is good at it. None of us play bridge, too sophisticated. The guys who drive are pretty much flat-out individuals."

One of those flat-out individuals was LeeRoy Yarbrough, originally from Jacksonville, Florida, who won the Daytona 500 that year in a Junior Johnson Ford. Yarbrough, along with the Daytona victory, won the Winston 500, the Coca-Cola 600 and the Southern 500 at Darlington—one of only three drivers to win those races in the same year. During the 1969 season of fifty-four races, Yarbrough started thirty times, won seven races and had twenty-one top ten finishes. His earnings of $193,211 were second only to Grand National Champion David Pearson's $229,760 from fifty-one starts and eleven wins.[30]

Yarbrough's passion was cars. Before he was old enough to drive, he began working on a 1934 Ford, dropping a Chrysler engine in it and later terrorizing police in the Westside area of Jacksonville. He won his first race at nineteen at the local track and neighborhood kids helped him work on his cars. One of them bragged he was going to be as famous as LeeRoy. His name was Ronnie Van Zant, founder of the band Lynyrd Skynyrd. In three years, LeeRoy won eighty-three races in NASCAR's Modified series before moving into Grand National in 1960.[31]

"LeeRoy had just one speed—wide open," Richard Petty said. "He didn't figure nothin', didn't plan nothin', just ran flat-out lap after lap. And if he could get by with it, he was up front. If he didn't, he was in the pits. He put everything into that one strategy—full speed ahead."[32]

Yarbrough took that same strategy to Trans-Am series when he drove a Mercury Cougar for Bud Moore's racing team and to the Indianapolis 500 when he drove for the former Grand Prix driver Dan Gurney. "LeeRoy came to race," Gurney said. He explained how, when drivers gathered in the same room, they attempted to intimidate each other. "You wanted to give the impression," he said, "that if you and I were going into the same corner, side by side, that you should probably be the one to back off. And LeeRoy was very good at that, very good."[33]

France had problems with one of his track owners. France had assisted Larry Carrier and Carl Moore in obtaining financing to build the Bristol Motor Speedway in 1961. Carrier and Moore wanted to advertise their facility as the fastest half-mile track in the country but they could never get past the speeds set at the Asheville-Weaverville Speedway, in Weaverville, North Carolina, owned by France and Enoch Staley. "NASCAR called both of them a half-mile," driver Johnny Allen recalled, "because back then anything close to a half-mile was a half-mile." Allen, a Greenville, South Carolina, native, said the speeds at Asheville-Weaverville were faster because that track was shorter than Bristol's. "Bobby Allison did 90.407 mph at Asheville-Weaverville but nobody could break 89 mph at Bristol," he added.[34]

NASCAR refused to make any distinctions between the distances or recalculate the track's mileages. Between the Southeastern 500, on March 23, 1969, at Bristol and the Volunteer 500 on July 20, Carrier and Moore dug up their track and re-shaped it. "We are going to bank the straightaways twenty degrees with banking becoming progressively higher as cars head into the turns," Carrier said. "The beginning part of the turn will be banked thirty-one degrees with gradual increases to thirty-five degrees at the steepest part of the turns."[35] France's Daytona speedway had banking of thirty-one degrees.

Carrier got what he wanted, and more. Bobby Isaac won the pole for the March race at Bristol with 88.669 mph. Cale Yarborough's pole winning speed for the July race was 103.432 mph. The reconfiguration of the track changed the distance from a half mile to .533 miles. Asheville-Weaverville Speedway closed in 1970.[36]

The July Bristol race coincided with NASA astronauts Neil Armstrong and Buzz Aldrin's televised moon walk. Racing columnist Tom Higgins wrote that the 32,000 spectators began leaving early to see the lunar landing and because David Pearson had a three-lap lead in a crash filled race. "Stunningly," Higgins wrote, "in the cockpit for the final 146 laps of 500, running in relief of Pearson, was his arch-rival, Richard Petty. Petty's car had blown an engine on lap sixty. Pearson was stricken with the flu. "A soaring thermometer that reached 104 degrees, with accompanying high humidity, had further weakened him." Petty said, "They've ruined a good race track."[37]

"The combination of wrecks and high heat, which caused engines to fail, left only ten of thirty-two starters running at the finish," Higgins wrote. He added that the tenth place driver, Roy Tyner, from Red Springs, North Carolina, was a whopping ninety-seven laps down at the checkered flag.[38]

Higgins and other reporters were worried they were going to miss the lunar landing but Richard Howard, general manager of the Charlotte Motor Speedway, announced he had rented a suite at the Holiday Inn in Boone, North Carolina, where they could stop on their way back to Charlotte and watch the televised moon landing. He instructed his associate,

Eddie Proctor, to have champagne waiting. "How this was going to be accomplished mystified me," Higgins wrote. "It was a Sunday and there strictly were no alcohol sales on the Sabbath in either Tennessee or North Carolina. But, when those of us invited by Howard arrived in Boone about 9 p.m. during a heavy rainstorm, we found Proctor waiting with the refreshments."[39]

Howard and his twenty guests watched the lunar landing and Armstrong's famous words, "That's one small step for man, one giant leap for mankind," amid much cheering, back thumping and even some tears of pride. A man in his underwear pounded on the door and demanded they hold the noise down since he and his family were trying to get some sleep before going to the Tweetsie Railroad theme park the next day. One of Howard's guests explained they were celebrating Americans landing on the moon. The man replied he did not care what they were watching, he wanted the noise to stop. "You unpatriotic S.O.B.," one of the guests yelled, "you're going to see Tweetsie though black eyes cause I'm going to give you the whipping of your life." The man took off in his skivvies, running through the parking lot with the offended journalist right behind him. The police were called but Howard explained their situation and the lawmen said no harm, no foul.[40]

Higgins said in 2003, he took his grandson, Jeffrey McCarter, to Kitty Hawk for the centennial celebration of the Wright Brothers' first flight. Among the honored guests were Armstrong and Aldrin, but Higgins and his grandson did not meet them. "If we had," Higgins wrote, "I'd have told Armstrong the tale about a guy I know chasing a stranger in his underwear through the rain around an inn in Boone. It would have been a first person story."[41]

Higgins' story had a satisfactory ending but the futures of some Grand National drivers were questionable for a while. Charlie Goltzbach was seriously injured when he was shot by a disgruntled employee at his heavy equipment business in Edwardsville, Indiana, on November 30. Surgeons dug two .22-caliber bullets out of his abdomen and he recovered.[42]

Cale Yarborough was seriously injured at the December 7, 1969, Texas 500, in Bryan Station, when his car blew a tire and crashed into a concrete wall at about 175 mph. Yarborough's shoulder was injured to such an extent it was initially thought his driving career might be over. However, he returned after doing some serious physical therapy.[43]

David Pearson won his third and last Grand National championship in 1969. He had eleven wins in fifty-one starts and won $229,760. Petty was second with ten wins in fifty starts for $129,906. They were followed by James Hylton, $114,416; Neil Castles, $54,367; Elmo Langley, $73,092; Bobby Isaac, $92,074; John Sears, $52,281; Jabe Thomas, $44,989; Wendell Scott, $47,451; and Cecil Gordon, $39,679. The average purse for the fifty-four race season for the top fifty drivers was $35,434, an increase of $10,597 from the preceding year.[44]

After a rather tumultuous year, one of France's former drivers, Fonty Flock, had plans for a new super speedway in Alabama that would honor his racing family. France, not happy with Flock's plans, had his own ideas and began work implementing them.

22

Eastaboga and the PDA

•••••••

Truman "Fonty" Flock's widow Marjorie and his son, Victor, recalled hearing about plans to build the Eastaboga track and their expected move to Alabama in the mid–1960s. Fonty Flock based his property acquisition on the model that Walt Disney set up for Disney World and the Epcot Center, Victor Flock said. "He planned to get the landowners together to sell the property needed for the track at a lower price and they would make it up on the lands purchased by hotels, restaurants, gas stations and other businesses the track would draw to the area."[1] Flock said his father planned to build the Alabama track similar to Darlington Raceway. "Dad said Darlington was his favorite track because it was a driver's track, not a car's."[2]

Smokey Yunick's accounts of three Daytona Beach visits, both exhilarating and heartrending, from Flock concerning his new track verified what Marjorie and Victor Flock said.

Flock, seriously injured in the 1957 Southern 500 wreck, in which Bobby Myers was killed, had been working for France as NASCAR membership director since 1964. Yunick had known Flock since his racing days and said he was a hell of a driver, second to none. What endeared him to Yunick was that he knew how to keep a car in contention without destroying the equipment. Yunick failed to mention the dates of Flock's two visits to his garage, but the first was probably in 1967. During that visit, Flock showed Yunick the blueprints for what he said would be the fastest race track in the world, a monument to the Flock family's racing legacy. Flock told Yunick he had the property purchased, the contractor was his partner and all he needed were two Grand National race dates from France for his new track at Eastaboga, Alabama.[3]

Yunick said around 4:00 p.m. the same day, Flock returned to his garage driving a new Dodge station wagon with a NASCAR Insurance logo on the door. He quoted Flock as saying, "France loved it, Smoke. He loved it! I got the two dates." Flock added that France wanted part of the track, somewhere in the neighborhood of five percent, and had made him director of NASCAR's insurance division. Yunick told Flock that he had better keep a jar of Vaseline handy.[4]

About a year later, Yunick said, Flock came back to his garage driving an old Oldsmobile and said he needed to talk to him. After they went into Yunick's office, Flock broke down crying. "Smoke, the insurance deal is over; I have no job, I'm sick, very sick," Flock said, "I don't own Eastaboga anymore. I don't even own one percent. That son-of-a-bitch has got together with my partners and Governor George Wallace and General [Curtis] LeMay and I'm not even the janitor there. Zero. Totally screwed out of the whole deal."[5]

Yunick acknowledged that he heard only half of the story but apparently did not doubt Flock's version. "He went back to Atlanta and died not too long after," Yunick wrote. "What's shocking is, now, thirty some years later nobody knows the real story of Eastaboga. Nobody really knows what a major part Fonty played in the foundation of NASCAR; 98 percent of NASCAR fans got no idea what a super driver Fonty was."[6]

France apparently teamed up with William Ward, a Talladega insurance executive, to cut Flock out of the deal. In France's world, there was no longer room for the Flocks, who actually helped establish stock car racing in Georgia.

In May 1994, George J. Tanber, a reporter for *The Anniston Star,* interviewed Ward, who said he worked with both Flock and France on locating the track. Flock, according to Ward, selected a 400-acre site on U.S. 77 West. Tanber had the idea Flock was moved out of the picture at that point. France told Ward he needed a site with at least 1,000 acres, but that he was also considering a site near Spartanburg, South Carolina.[7] Ward, for a time, enjoyed France's largesse until they parted ways, of course, over money.[8]

The Spartanburg newspaper reported the speedway, originally scheduled to be built there, was later constructed near Talladega. "The problems that would have resulted in trying to stage Sunday races in Spartanburg County were too much to overcome," the article stated.[9] France, who had been battling South Carolina's Blue Laws for two decades without success, used the rumored Spartanburg track as a straw man for his successful negotiations in Alabama.

Ward, Tanber wrote, finally found an old airfield, north of Talladega, with approximately 1,700 acres that the federal government had sold to the city for one dollar. The name of the site was Eastaboga Air Field. Ward, who had earlier raced midgets, called France, who liked the location. France brought Ward, Talladega Mayor James L. Hardwick and a local delegation to the Firecracker 500, and wined and dined them. Construction, according to Tanber, began in May 1968, and the first race was set for September of the following year. Ward and France were big buddies, for a while. France sent him a Mustang to drive in the Bama 200, a preliminary event for smaller cars, and he just happened to win the race.[10]

Ward stopped going to the Alabama International Motor Speedway races in 1975. "Ward no longer speaks to the [France] family, the result of a disagreement with the elder France over money. Ward calls it a misunderstanding and declined to discuss it further," Tanber wrote.[11] Ward's recollections failed to match those of Yunick.

Yunick, who saw Flock's blueprints and discussed details of the track with him, described the track's location. "Eastaboga," he said, "is actually what you call Talladega now. Same piece of ground but named for bigger town not too far away."[12]

Newspapers of the 1950s and 1960s had numerous references to the Eastaboga Air Field. The *Gadsden Times,* in its initial coverage of the first race at France's new speedway, carried an Eastaboga dateline. The newspaper's sports editor, Jimmy Smothers, wrote about the new speedway built at Eastaboga.[13] Once the speedway was in operation, the name Talladega, instead of Eastaboga, began appearing in newspaper datelines, as the track's site.

NASCAR, as late as 2006, was still practicing revisionist history regarding the speedway. According to the NASCAR version, which contained no mention of Fonty Flock, Ward met France in Daytona in the mid–1960s and, following a casual conversation, helped him find the land and set up meetings with track officials in an Anniston restaurant in 1966. "Several obstacles had to be overcome, including financing," the NASCAR article stated. "With France as the guiding force, however, construction began on the 2,000 acre site on May 23, 1968."[14]

Daniel S. Pierce, in his book *Real NASCAR, White Lightning, Red Clay and Big Bill France,* advanced the theory that France, alone, discovered the Eastaboga site. In an endnote Pierce wrote, "France always claimed that while these individuals had talked about a much smaller project in that section of Alabama, he found the site on his own." Pierce furnished no source for France's statement.[15]

In November 1968, Flock filed a $4 million lawsuit against France and NASCAR in U.S. District Court in Atlanta alleging France had violated the verbal agreement he had with Flock regarding the establishment of the Alabama International Motor Speedway at Eastaboga. Attorney Edward Brookings said Flock had obtained the Alabama site for France, and had been promised a partnership in the venture.[16] Records of the results of the lawsuit, if any, were not found.

While Bill France was engaged in taking down one of his former drivers who dared oppose him, the 1968 racing season continued. Yunick built a Camaro for Bobby Unser to drive in the Paul Revere 250-mile midnight race before the Firecracker 400. Unser went to the lead on the first lap; on the second lap his headlights began to blink. An electrical fire dashed their hopes and Lloyd Ruby, from Wichita Falls, Texas, won the race. However, Bunkie Knudsen had Yunick build an engine for Unser's Chevrolet in the Pike's Peak Climb. "I built him an engine you couldn't run at sea level where the air is heavier," Yunick said. "Bobby set a record that lasted about fifteen years."[17]

France, meanwhile, was hanging on the coattails of a governor who was a presidential hopeful, envisioning a possible high-level appointment and planning to get Alabama taxpayers' money to build his new track. France arranged for Alabama Governor George Wallace, a segregationist, to speak to more than 70,000 at the 1968 running of the Southern 500 at Darlington. In introducing Wallace, France told the crowd, "George Washington founded this country and George Wallace will save it."[18]

The Miami News political writer, Morris McLemore, referred to the Daytona speedway as "Bill France's mammoth money factory where George Wallace buttons were seen on every lapel."[19] France's money factory was more successful than Wallace's presidential campaign.

Before the Alabama track was finished, Wallace, unable to succeed himself as governor, arranged for his wife, Lurleen, to succeed him and she was elected. Wallace began setting his pegs for the 1972 presidential race. Mrs. Wallace continued the largesse to France's racetrack. In May 1967, Gov. Lurleen Wallace signed a bill calling for Talladega and Calhoun counties to use their road building equipment to clear sites on their common border near the track.[20]

Another bill Gov. Lurleen Wallace signed authorized the sale of bonds to finance the track under the state's industrial development act and allowed the city of Talladega to acquire land outside of its boundaries. At the same time Alabama state government was pouring money into Bill France's race track, Gov. Wallace proposed a 3.6 percent cut in funding for schools in the state.[21]

Using an Alabama industrial bond issue to build the speedway, Bill France wanted more. He wanted another bond issue to build the International Motorsports Hall of Fame next to the speedway. Despite the fact that France provided thirty-five acres of land next to the speedway for the building, that bond issue failed to materialize. An article in *The Encyclopedia of Alabama* about the hall of fame said state Senator Gerald Dial headed a commission that raised public and private funds for the project. Apparently, it took Dial and the commission some time to raise the funds for the hall of fame since the ground for the building was not broken until 1981. The 15,000-square-foot building was completed in 1983.[22]

Talladega leaders saw an opportunity to levy a tax on the speedway itself, tickets and facilities adjacent to the track; hence, the expansion of boundaries. "Some Talladegans must have wondered what they were getting, however, when France used strong arm tactics to oppose incorporation of the speedway into the city and quieted talk among county commissioners of a 50¢ per ticket tax," Daniel Pierce wrote. To get his point across, Pierce said, France told the local newspaper editor a parable about a dog bringing home a bone. Seemed the dog crossed a bridge, saw his reflection in the water and opened his mouth to get the bone he saw in the water and dropped the real one.[23] The moral of the story was that the locals were out of luck as France had no intention of sharing his cash bone with anyone. He was still battling that problem in Daytona Beach. Gov. Lurleen Wallace approved a tax exemption for his Eastaboga track.[24]

It was not by chance that sports editor Kahn wrote a column about France after the February 1969 Daytona 500 portraying him as being bigger than life, knowing where all the stepping stones were. The column probably arose from France's efforts at the Daytona twin qualifiers to push drivers to go out on the track in a rainstorm by offering them $10,000. When most drivers refused, he attempted to shame them by driving around the track himself. "He can be rough as the toughest," Kahn wrote, "I have seen France unblinkingly and unflinching stand up to a wild mechanic who threatened him with a knife. The assailant backed down. I have seen him arm himself with a gun when ruthless racketeers tried to muscle in and bust up NASCAR. The union faded away." He claimed France cried at Weatherly's funeral.[25]

Kahn continued, "Strong willed, independent and articulate racing men who say what they think—such as Smokey Yunick and the late Glenn Fireball Roberts—are not among his favorite people." He painted France as having an exceptional grasp of complex engineering and mechanical operations, as creative and imaginative, loyal to friends and formidable to adversaries, and a man who always thought of today and tomorrow, not yesterday. Kahn acknowledged that France changed NASCAR rules at a whim but claimed that was due to expediency. "But, the facts, when they are not particularly pleasant, still aggravate him," he concluded.[26]

One of France's biggest aggravations in years lay just ahead. In July 1968, work on the Alabama International Motor Speedway was slightly ahead of schedule. The 2.66-mile quad-oval's turns were banked at 33 degrees. Pat Turner, job supervisor for Moss-Thorton Construction, said he did not think an expected steel strike would have any effect on the job. France was also building a 6,000-foot runway adjacent to the track.[27]

A year later, construction had reached the point where France had tour buses bringing visitors in to see the track. Tickets for the Eastaboga track's first race were selling from $8 to $25. The 300-acre infield could hold 50,000 spectators at the $5 million facility. France's speedway stock, which had been selling for 65 cents to 75 cents a share in August 1968, had jumped to $8 a share a year later.[28]

France was getting ready to reap another $1.8 million or perhaps $2 million gate at his new speedway. None of this was lost on the NASCAR drivers, who knew they had been getting the short end of the cash stick for two decades and decided to take matters in their own hands. Nature, an entity France was unable to control, intervened.

Category Five Hurricane Camille roared up through the middle of Mississippi, turned and followed an eastward path through Kentucky, Tennessee, West Virginia and Virginia on August 17–18, 1969. Camille packed winds of fifty to sixty miles an hour more than 150 miles on each side of the main storm. Just how much damage France's Alabama race track sustained, although it was not in the storm's direct path, was at first difficult to ascertain. Drivers LeeRoy Yarbrough and Donnie Allison tested Goodyear tires at the track on August 8–9, and had nothing but good things to say about the track's smooth surface. Yarbrough ran 194.87 mph while Allison hit 192.5 mph in the morning hours. During the afternoons, when the track surface temperature reached 115 degrees, Goodyear suspended the tests with plans to return before the initial race.[29]

In the interim, the facility suffered massive damage. The track surface Allison and Yarbrough described from their tire tests three weeks earlier no longer existed. A September 12, 1969, Associated Press photograph, two days before the first Grand National race, showed machinery moving material from a huge pile of debris stacked on the track apron while a car was running practice laps in the background. The track surface was in deplorable condition, chewing up tires every few laps during practice for the 500-mile race.[30]

France claimed there was a foreign substance on the track and he would have it cleaned up. The Goodyear tire representative said there was no foreign substance on the track, that its surface was in such poor condition that tires could not stand up under the wear. France promised to have people, on foot, examine the track inch by inch.[31] Walking the turns on the thirty-three degree surface would have been a feat in itself, much less examining the track surface.

Most media reports concentrated on the tire wear without explaining what had happened to the track surface. A few alluded to the drastic change in track conditions from Allison and Yarbrough's tire tests a few weeks earlier without going into much detail.

France, from all indications, was overwhelmed with the damage to his pristine track that he saw as his racing legacy. He would never have allowed the general contractor to stint on the asphalt or leave such a huge pile of debris on the track apron just days before his first big race at the showcase track.

In addition to the deplorable condition of his new super speedway track, France had another festering dilemma, and the two were about to merge.

A month earlier, while in Michigan for a Grand National race at Larry LoPatin's new track in Brooklyn, a group of drivers met with attorney Lawrence Fleischer, counsel for the NBA Players Association. They organized the Professional Drivers' Association (PDA). Richard Petty was elected president; Cale Yarborough and Elmo Langley were vice-presidents. The board of directors was composed of LeeRoy Yarbrough, David Pearson (who won the Michigan race), Pete Hamilton, Charlie Gotzback, Donnie and Bobby Allison, Buddy Baker and James Hylton.[32]

Petty said their non-profit organization was formed in an attempt to obtain long-term benefits for drivers, improved working conditions and better financial returns.[33] Unlike Curtis Turner's FPA, the new organization had no association with organized labor and had no motives other than to bring about better conditions for the drivers and an equitable increase in their share of race purses.

"Some of these fellows have gotten to be big heroes," France said in an August 20 interview. "They have apparently forgotten how they got here." In his typical egotistical manner, France attempted to convince everyone that the PDA drivers had achieved success, not by their own talents and efforts, but only through his largesse. "NASCAR will post our prize money and if these boys want to run, okay. If not, there are no contracts between the drivers and NASCAR."[34] That statement, like many others he blustered while angry, came back to haunt France.

In another interview on the same date, France pointed to LeeRoy Yarbrough and said, "I can't see why LeeRoy Yarbrough, for instance, would want such a group. He's won $150,000 this year alone. That's not too bad."[35] France failed to note that Yarbrough probably retained less than half of his winnings; nor did France reveal that he paid only ten to twelve percent of his gates into the race purses Yarbrough won.

It was Bowman Gray all over again with France's mouth in overdrive. He said NASCAR drivers should not be compared with athletes such as football players who already had bargaining representatives.[36] Earlier, he claimed that his drivers were athletes. In his fight with South Carolina ministers over Sunday racing, France then argued vociferously that his drivers were athletes.

"They can't go without factory cars," France boasted. "I'm not worried about any strike. I am pretty certain that, if these fellows decide to sit out, the factories will find men to drive their cars. And, they'll look upon the drivers with disfavor."[37]

France, despite his posturing, surely knew his current relations with the automobile manufacturers were more of a liability than an asset. There was little chance Detroit would back him against the drivers. Regardless, he plowed forward. "NASCAR has been pretty good to this bunch," he continued. "I drove in a time where there was zero prize money posted and track operators were rinky dink guys who were not responsible people."[38]

It was doubtful if France ever drove in a race without prize money being posted. His painting of track owners and promoters as thieving scoundrels was a smoke screen that was wearing thin, but it drew public attention away from the real question of drivers asking for bigger purses, more benefits and input in scheduling.

The week before the Alabama International Motor Speedway's first race, Petty asked France to postpone the race for a month. "It's nobody's fault," Petty said attempting to be diplomatic. "There's nobody to blame. The track is just too new and there hasn't been enough time to test the tires." A Firestone representative backed Petty, saying, "We only went down there once a few weeks ago to test and it rained two of the days we were down there. That just did not leave us enough time to prepare." According to the *Gadsden Times,* Firestone withdrew their tires from the race.[39]

David Pearson said the surface was so rough that it was hard to stay in the only groove on the track. Bobby Allison said the track was rough as a cob. "The roughness bounces the car around so much it feels like it's tearing the wheels off in the corner," he said. "The only way they're going to fix it is to repave it."[40]

Knowing that many of the drivers flew their own planes, France, in an effort to persuade drivers to race, attempted to equate the track surface to storm conditions they might encounter while flying. It did not work. "Bill," LeeRoy Yarbrough said, "when the weather is as bad as this track, I don't even take off."[41]

France not only refused to postpone the race for repaving but suggested tire wear would improve if drivers just drove at lower speeds during the race. Drivers were concerned about cheating the public who paid to see them race. "That wouldn't be fair to the people who come to see us race at 200 mph," LeeRoy Yarbrough countered.[42]

"Don't you boys worry about the fans," France boasted. "I'll take care of the fans. But, there will be a race and money will be paid out."[43]

Donnie Allison, who had no problems with the track in August, before the hurricane, said he tore up tires on three different occasions during practice. Allison confronted France about his lack of concern for the drivers' safety, "You are our president and you should look out for the interests of all of us." Backed into a corner, France lamely replied, "I am looking out for your interests."[44] There was no doubt among the drivers about whose interest France was protecting.

"Speed is not the problem here," Petty said. "The track is real rough and breaking up. Tires are a problem and so is safety. We've never run here and don't know what to expect. The only other track where we've ever approached these kinds of speed was at Daytona and that is real smooth. Here we'll be lucky if the cars don't break. Because of the speed you have to tighten the car to be able to get around the corners and I'm afraid a tight car can't stand these bumps."[45]

James Hylton said he put three laps on his tires and they came apart. "They've created a monster here," he said, "and if something isn't done someone is going to get killed. There is no tire that will stay together [here] at speeds of 198 mph."[46]

Hylton also pointed out that France had already violated his own rules on tires. He said eight cars qualified on Goodyear tires but planned, with France's approval, to race on other tires, a violation of NASCAR rules. Hylton said three cars in the March Atlanta race qualified on one kind of tire, put on others to race with and the drivers were punished by starting in the rear of the field. France's defense, that he suspended the tire rules for safety reasons, supported the drivers' argument about track conditions.[47]

France was wrong about the automobile manufacturers supporting his decision to hold the race. AP reporter Bloys Britt wrote that most of the car owners backed the drivers' request for a postponement of the race. "Tire engineers agree that they have not been able to develop a tire that would stand such speeds [200 mph] for any length of time without coming apart."[48]

Track owners and promoters backing France included those at Charlotte, Rockingham, Darlington, North Wilkesboro, Martinsville and LoPatin's four tracks, according to an Associated Press report. However, the *Spartanburg Herald-Journal* article pointed out the possible pitfalls in France's position included not only injury to drivers, but the very real possibility of death.[49]

Independent driver Roy Mayne, a U.S. Air Force sergeant from Sumter, South Carolina, who withdrew from the race, gave a chilling description what happened to cars because of the track conditions. "Sheet metal on the Daytona [Dodge] Chargers cracked at high speeds. The upper control arm on the front end of the Daytonas was breaking due to the roughness of the track. This let the front end down. Charlie Glotzbach's car broke control arms twice in one day."[50]

Mayne, whose day job protected him from Bill France's wrath, felt free to comment where some drivers kept their mouths shut. Another driver, who did not wish to be identified, said, "The track is tearing up in the third turn," he told sports reporter Gene Granger. "We inspected it at lunchtime. You can move it [the asphalt] with your hand."[51]

The statement that the pavement could be moved by hand indicated there was damage from the hurricane's torrential rains that changed the properties of the asphalt. After examining the descriptions of the track's condition before and after the hurricane, noted asphalt chemist Edward Minter, from Frankfort, Kentucky, said the excessive amount of water probably penetrated the asphalt mix. But, there was another factor. Slag with tin filings was purchased from Birmingham steel mills to mix in the asphalt for better traction just as France had used at Daytona. "Slag was the guilty party, as it absorbs water like you wouldn't believe," said Minter, who retired from the Kentucky Department of Transportation. "The combination of an excessive amount of water absorbed by the slag in the asphalt, combined with the metal filings, supplied all the ingredients that not only ate up the tires but caused the asphalt to come apart."[52]

Steel slag filings, highly angular in shape, maintained that shape. Instead of eroding smoothly as the crushed stone aggregates did from water damage, the filings in the slag kept their sharp edges. "About the time the Talladega track was built, engineers were experimenting with slag in asphalt and didn't know exactly how it would handle the water," Minter added.[53]

An asphalt expert at the Western Research Institute in Laramie, Wyoming, Raymond E. Robertson, wrote, "Upon invasion into the asphalt, water will affect the mechanical properties, typically softening it. The action of water is somewhat like the dilution of asphalt with a low molecular weight solvent. This typically results in reduced strength further resulting in rutting or other deformation."[54]

Maynes said the tire manufacturers announced on Saturday morning, before the Sunday race, they did not have a tire that would hold up on the track surface. He said France was out of line in asking the drivers to reduce their speed. "What if professional football players had [such] restrictions put on them?" he asked. "It's like holding back a race horse at three quarters rein and trying to win a race."[55]

Driver Jabe Thomas, from Christianburg, Virginia, gave Granger his opinion of the track surface and France's refusal to cancel the race. Granger wrote that Thomas' statement about France and the track could not be repeated in his newspaper.[56]

The Sumter Daily Item sports editor Charles Paschal backed the drivers' refusal to race because of the track conditions and the lack of a safe tire and faulted France for his apparent inability to change with the times. "France has been the head and ruler of the sport so long," Paschal wrote, "that he knows no other way. In my opinion, he did not have the best interests of the drivers at heart."[57]

Petty called the drivers together for a final discussion. France tried to shove his way into the meeting. Cale Yarborough, a former Golden Gloves boxer, blocked his way and informed him the meeting was for drivers only. France, who towered over the stocky Yarborough, turned away.[58]

Thirty drivers, including Maynes, Richard Petty, Donnie and Bobby Allison, John Sears, James Hylton, Cale Yarborough, Cecil Gordon, Elmo Langley, Buddy Baker, LeeRoy Yarbrough, Ed Negre, Buddy Young, Jabe Thomas, E. J. Trivette, Bill Champion, Bobby Mansgrover, Bill Seifert, Bill Devies, Henley Gray, G. C. Spencer, Dave Marcus and J. M. McDuffie, loaded their cars and equipment into haulers and drove through the track gate to go home.[59]

France managed to turn up thirty-six drivers, many of them from the Grand Touring series or ARCA, and two physicians, Donald F. Tarr, from Miami, and Wilburn Pickett, from Daytona Beach, who he knew were amateurs.[60]

The France version of the organization of the PDA and their boycott of Talladega's inaugural race was quite different from media reports. William P. Lazarus, in his book *The Sands of Time: A Century of Racing at Daytona Beach*, blamed the drivers for organizing themselves and said their boycotting the race was because of LoPatin and the Ford Motor Company. The copyright on Lazarus's book was held by NASCAR and its sister company, International Speedway Corporation, where the author worked.[61]

Impetus for the PDA's organization came from LoPatin, Lazarus maintained, because the drivers were in Michigan for his Motor State race on August 17, 1969, when they organized, nearly a month before the Alabama race. Lazarus claimed that LoPatin had Ford's backing to either force France out and take over NASCAR or replace it with a new sanctioning body.[62]

At the Sunday morning drivers' meeting, Lin Kuchler thanked the drivers for their appearance and apologized that France and his son, William C. France, were not there. He told the drivers the Frances also expressed their appreciation. "Right now they are making amends to a lot of people in Alabama who were embarrassed by this situation," Kuchler said.[63]

Whatever the embarrassment, it was created by France, his dictatorial management style and his determination to hold the race regardless of the dangers to drivers' lives.

Bobby Isaac, who sat on the pole with a speed of 196.386 mph, finished fourth and had to change twenty-one tires. Richard Brickhouse, a farmer from Rocky Point, North Carolina, and former PDA member, won the race and the $24,550 first place money with an average speed of 153.778 mph, which was what Bill France suggested they run. France ordered caution flags thrown every twenty or twenty-five laps to slow down race speeds and give drivers an opportunity to change tires. Brickhouse said he had been trying for a long time to get a factory ride and he could not turn down the opportunity to drive Ray Nichels' Dodge. "I felt like one of them [PDA members] would have done the same thing in my position," Brickhouse said.[64] Although he started in thirty-eight other NASCAR races, the Alabama 500 was the only race Brickhouse ever won.[65]

Grand Touring driver Jim Vandiver, from Huntersville, North Carolina, came in second, collecting $12,400, and ARCA driver Ramo Scott, from Keokuk, Iowa, was third with $7,500. Buck Baker, whose son Buddy boycotted the race, finished eighteenth in a Firebird. Richard Childress, from Winston-Salem, North Carolina, was twenty-third in a Camaro. Out of the thirty-six cars entered in the Alabama 500, only sixteen finished. An estimated 65,000 spectators—100,000 had been expected—attended the race. France paid out the announced $120,600 purse.[66]

Speedway tickets sold for an average of $16.50, which gave France a gate of approximately $1,072,500. Consequently, his purse was an estimated eleven percent of the gate. Had the expected crowd attended, he would have had a gate in the range of $1.6 million to $2 million.

After the race, France gave a convoluted explanation of what had occurred. "Winners never quit and quitters never win," he said. "As far as I am concerned the boys quit. The boys who raced Sunday saved Talladega and the boys who quit owe their future to those who raced."[67]

Sports editor Charles Paschal continued to take France to task for his actions. Paschal quoted France as saying, "You boys do what you want to. You don't have to run. It will be perfectly okay if you don't run." Then, Paschal wrote, France turned around and began talking about requiring the drivers who boycotted the race to provide an appearance bond for the next race. France could get away with requiring an appearance bond in the old days, he added, but in 1969, NASCAR was a member of the Automobile Competition Committee for the United States (ACCUS) and such actions required that board's approval.[68]

Paschal supported France in saying that drivers signed no contracts to race for NASCAR; they simply filled out entry forms and paid their fees. Consequently, they were perfectly free to pull out of a race whenever they chose for whatever reason.[69]

Herald-Journal sports editor Gene Granger interviewed a car owner who said France was out of line about drivers being compelled to drive in his races. "The rules are as such now I can go home anytime I feel like it and there's nothing they can do," the car owner, speaking anonymously, told Granger.[70]

The day after the Alabama 500, Petty said the PDA members planned to drive in the 100-mile race at Columbia the next Thursday night and the 250-mile event at North Wilkesboro on Sunday. France and NASCAR officials flew into action postponing the North Wilkesboro race a week while they created a new entry form for drivers and car owners. The Alabama 500, where drivers' lives hung in the balance, could not possibly be postponed until track corrections were done, but the North Wilkesboro race could easily be re-shuffled in the schedule for a change to the drivers' entry form.[71]

The new entry form stated that once a car had earned a starting position in a race, the vehicle would be impounded at the track until the race was over. The driver and owner could leave but the car remained at the track. NASCAR's explanation for the new entry form was to "Protect the public and the promoter/speedway from anything like what happened last weekend at Talladega."[72]

The new entry form protected France's bank account and prevented the massive drain of rain checks, estimated to be worth $600,000, that he offered the Talladega spectators for another race at the Alabama track or at Daytona.[73] NASCAR officials explained, "In signing this blank, both driver/drivers and car owners recognize their obligations to the public and race promoter or speedway corporation posting the prize money and conducting the event. Therefore, we agree to compete in the event if humanly possible unless the event is cancelled or if the car fails to qualify for the starting field."[74]

After the Alabama debacle, Petty held a day-long meeting at a Charlotte motel on Thursday, September 24, with PDA members, Ford and Chrysler representatives, car and track owners and accessories firms. France held a meeting on Wednesday night in High Point, North Carolina, with track owners and told them not to attend the PDA meeting.[75]

In an effort to counteract whatever came out of the Charlotte meeting, France threw the drivers a bone by announcing a $150,000 addition to the points fund bonus divided among drivers at the end of the season. That was $33,000 more than was awarded from the previous year's points fund.[76]

According to newspaper reports, H. Clay Earles, from the Martinsville track and a France partner, and Richard Howard, from the Charlotte track, were at Petty's meeting. J. Elsie Webb, from Rockingham, and Larry Carrier, from Bristol, planned to attend the meeting. France was a no-show at the Charlotte meeting but sent Lin Kuchler and NASCAR attorney John Cassidy, who had no comment.[77]

Petty said he wanted to get everybody together to discuss what the sport needed. "I think we eased some of the fears that the promoters had before they came here," he said after the meeting. Petty said PDA drivers would run the 1969 and 1970 Grand National schedules but wanted to be involved in planning future schedules. PDA attorney Larry Fleischer said he was disappointed that Bill France refused to meet with them.[78]

France's new Alabama International Motor Speedway track was quickly and quietly repaved after that first race.[79]

23

Not as Easy as It Once Was

•••••••

NASCAR's Grand National series, from 1950 through 1969, averaged forty-seven races a year. In 1964, Bill France scheduled sixty-two events, all but six of them in the South. Grand National races, which became Winston Cup events in 1971, declined to an average of only thirty-three a year despite construction of a number of new speedways.[1]

After the debacle he created at Talladega's first Alabama 500, France again tinkered with the rules of racing, claiming it was all in the name of parity. If Ford and Chrysler cancelled their support of factory teams, France could regain better control over the stock car drivers. As long as the car manufacturers were paying their drivers a salary, they were, for the most part, off France's plantation.

The PDA was still a thorn in his side. That problem lessened when the automobile manufacturers eventually accepted the new entry form. France's ability to force drivers into submission emerged once again. In January 1970, Richard Petty, James Hylton and E. J. Trivette, from Deep Gap, North Carolina, scratched out the "good faith" clause in their entry forms for the Motor Trend 500 race at Riverside. "This man still wants to keep control 110 percent and it can't be done," Petty said. "The sport has outgrown a one-man operation."[2] Petty was partly right. NASCAR was no longer a one-man operation. It was a one-family operation and remains so today.

Lin Kuchler, NASCAR's vice-president, said that Petty's entry form was returned to him because it had been altered. Petty could race, he said, if he signed the new official NASCAR entry form and returned it intact.[3]

Chrysler agreed to the new entry form but Ford initially held out. Although they had misgivings, a Ford spokesman said they would accept the form which required car owners to provide a substitute driver in case the scheduled driver did not show up for the race. France said NASCAR designed the new entry form to prevent another driver boycott.[4] If a race was scheduled at a track with a dangerous surface, drivers were required to race regardless of possible injuries and fatalities because it was a France rule.

The 1970 Grand National season did not have an auspicious beginning. In the 500-mile road race at Riverside, won by A. J. Foyt by three seconds over Parnelli Jones, attrition was costly. Of the forty-four cars starting, only twenty-one finished the race, which lasted more than five hours. Buddy Young, from Fairfax, Virginia, had a spectacular crash. His car hit an oil slick, rammed head-on into the wall, went end over end, and rolled fifteen times before stopping in the infield. Young walked away with only a mild concussion.[5] Jim Cook, from Norwalk, California, hit the wall head-on on lap 103 and the car literally doubled up. Cook was in critical condition with head trauma and other injuries after the race and never raced again in Grand National competition.[6]

Problems followed the circuit to Daytona. During the second 125-mile qualifying race for the Daytona 500, Dublin, Georgia, automobile dealer Talmadge Price died. Price blew an engine and slid up the track, where Bill Seifert, from Skyland, North Carolina, hit him in the driver's side door. The two cars were then involved in another collision when Johnny Hartford, from Spartanburg, ran into them. All three cars came to rest on the track apron. Price, who had driven Sprint and Sportsman cars for ten years, was killed instantly. Seifert, hospitalized with a concussion, later returned to racing.[7]

Before the running of the Daytona 500, there were rumors the automobile manufacturers might withdraw their factory-backed teams from stock car racing. Money was tight and new car sales were down. Interest rates were at eight percent and climbing. The nation was immersed in the Vietnam conflict, which spawned protests and riots.[8]

A new driver went into the Daytona 500 winner's circle. Pete Hamilton, from Dedham, Massachusetts, driving a blue Plymouth Superbird for the Pettys, won the race over David Pearson. On their last pit stops, Hamilton took four tires and Pearson went with two. Hamilton collected $46,400 while Pearson had to settle for $20,105. Hamilton credited Richard Petty with teaching him how to drive around the high-banked track. France had a crowd estimated at 103,800. With an average ticket price of $16.50, his gate probably reached $1,712,700. The purse, $204,185, was nearly twelve percent of the gate.[9]

Hamilton, whose father was a Northwestern University professor, was among the first of a new breed of hip NASCAR drivers from outside the South. He had been a drummer in a band he organized. At nineteen, he was a mechanical engineering student at Northwestern but dropped out of college. "I kinda got this feeling in my gut that I wanted to race," he said.[10]

There was a glitch in the ABC-TV coverage of the Daytona 500. Rain delayed the start of the race thirty-eight minutes. The network had blocked the race into a 5:00 to 6:30 p.m. time frame. In order to give their viewers a chance to see the finished race, the network extended the telecast thirteen minutes but, even then, the results were uncertain. Announcer Bill Fleming, apparently provided with faulty information, first said Bobby Isaac won the race. Then told viewers it appeared that Pete Hamilton had won the event.[11]

After the debacle at Talladega the previous year, track surfaces became a focus for drivers, track owners and the media. J. Elsie Webb, at Rockingham's North Carolina Motor Speedway, was lauded for repaving that track for the Carolina 500 in March. The project was a "correctional" repaving, as the track surface claimed twenty-three of the forty starting cars in the American 500 the previous fall. "They finally made a race track out of it," Dodge driver Charlie Goltzbach said. "The new asphalt is smooth as velvet." Richard Petty, who won the race, said there were some dips coming out of the turns but it was a good job on the repaving.[12] Webb was so proud of the track paving he offered $1,000 to the driver who posted the fastest speed over 140 mph in addition to the $90,000 purse.[13]

Petty won the race by three laps before a crowd of 38,000 after surviving two spinouts and collected $18,215. Cale Yarborough was second; Dick Brooks, in another Petty Plymouth Superbird, was third; Bobby Allison was fourth; Pete Hamilton, another Petty driver, was fifth, and Wendell Scott finished eighth.[14]

The Carolina 500 marked the beginning of the end for Ford's factory backed teams. David Pearson and Donnie Allison did not drive in the race. When some of the Ford crew chiefs asked Webb for deal money to drive in the Rockingham race, he refused. Pearson said his team would have a sponsor after the Atlanta 500 in late March.[15]

If the Atlanta 500 was scheduled, it usually rained. Twelve times the race was postponed due to rain. Apparently, it never occurred to NASCAR to rearrange the schedule to get the big 500-mile race out of the rainy season. The 1970 race was no different; it was postponed a week due to the rain. One fan was quoted as saying, "This is the fourth time I've come to Atlanta; it's the fourth time the race has been postponed. I won't be here for number five." In addition, Atlanta was another track whose surface was questionable. Cale Yarborough said the track was full of bumps and needed resurfacing but he almost won the race anyway. During the last pit stops, Yarborough took only fuel and Bobby Allison took fuel and new tires. Allison's winged Dodge beat Yarborough's Mercury by five seconds.[16]

Regardless of the asphalt surface, Allison set a track record of 139.554 mph in the Dixie 500. His fifty-yard win over Cale Yarborough paid $22,825. Yarborough received $11,875; Pete Hamilton, third, was awarded $6,800. Lee Roy Yarbrough was fourth with $4,400; Richard Petty's fifth place was worth $3,475.[17]

Surface was no longer a problem at the Alabama International Motor Speedway for the Alabama 500 in April. The 2.6-mile track had been repaved. In late March, Buddy Baker set a timed closed circuit record of 200.447 mph. Bobby Isaac set a blistering pole speed of 199.658 mph. Baker, in a last laps duel with Pete Hamilton for the win, provided ABC's television cameras with excitement for their hour and a half telecast. Baker's Dodge caught fire and skidded for about 1,500 feet as the driver attempted to free himself. Finally, Baker dived out the window, suffering second-degree burns on his legs and back. He refused to go to the hospital.[18]

Hamilton won the race in a Petty Plymouth with Isaac second, one lap down. Pearson, Benny Parsons and Cale Yarborough finished in the top five. Attendance was estimated at 53,000. France paid a race purse of $138,100.[19]

NASCAR's decision to remove the side glass windows from the cars was still creating problems. The decision could have been made by Vice-President Lin Kuchler or chief technical inspector Bill Gazaway, but it was not implemented without France's approval. Drivers and owners were concerned that removal of the side windows would affect the handling of their cars. In addition, there was a safety factor. If a car's engine caught fire, the windowless vehicle, drivers said, would act as a conduit for the flames.[20]

Fred Lorenzen, who said he would never drive another race car three years earlier, came out of retirement to drive a Dodge in the World 600 at Charlotte in May. Perhaps Lorenzen was tired of doing nothing, as he put it, or the track's general manager and vice-president Richard Howard may have sweetened the pot to lure Lorenzen back to increase attendance. Howard said having Lorenzen in the race conservatively added $100,000 to $150,000 to the track's gross. The Dodge Lorenzen drove in the race was owned by Howard.[21]

Lorenzen's return to Grand National racing ended on lap 252, when his engine blew and he hit the wall. The day appeared to belong to Pearson, who was leading by two miles when he pitted. He was unable to move due to a broken clutch in his Ford. "God, I thought I had it won," Pearson said, "had it in my hands." But, the glory that day was shared by his Ford teammates, Donnie Allison and LeeRoy Yarbrough.[22]

Yarbrough's car went out with a bad clutch on lap 177. As he was walking toward a helicopter, someone yelled that Allison needed help. The insulation had burned, or melted, away in Allison's car leaving only a thin piece of sheet metal between the driver's feet and the red-hot exhaust pipes.[23]

Yarbrough, always a hard charger, changed back into his driving suit, replaced Allison, who suffered burns on his feet, drove the remaining forty-five laps and won the race over Cale Yarborough.[24]

LeeRoy Yarbrough drove for another hard charger, his car owner Junior Johnson. Racing columnist Ed Hinton wrote Yarbrough was the only driver who had the balls to run Johnson's cars as fast as they would go. "Never again would Junior be so completely satisfied with a driver," Hinton wrote. "He would win six Winston Cup Championships, three with Cale Yarborough and three with Darrell Waltrip in the 1970s and 1980s. But all the while, Junior would mutter about this gnawing urge, 'I want me a driver I can slap on the helmet and say, lissen boy, you go out there and you hold that thing wide open until you crash or I tell you to quit. You understand me.'" Hinton said he never found another LeeRoy Yarbrough.[25]

Obviously, Bill France had a lucrative contract with ABC television for the Grand National races and it was understandable why the Alabama 500 would be televised. The selection of the 250-mile Gwyn Staley race, at North Wilkesboro, for television instead of a longer race at a larger track was probably because France owned an interest in the facility. NASCAR learned a few things from the earlier telecasts. There were no yellow flags thrown at the North Wilkesboro race, which Richard Petty won coming from sixteenth starting place.[26]

Bobby Isaac was second; LeeRoy Yarbrough was third; James Hylton and Dick Brooks came in fourth and fifth.[27]

Petty again claimed the show before 43,000 spectators at the Rebel 400 at Darlington in May, but not in the expected manner. Coming off the fourth turn, Petty's Plymouth ran into the concrete retaining wall, skidded down the front straightaway, hit another concrete barrier, flipped over in the air several times, came down in front of the main grandstand upside down and spun around like a top. Petty suffered a dislocated shoulder, cuts and bruises.[28] This incident, along with the entire race, was televised by ABC. After hitting the wall four times in practice, Pearson won the Rebel 400 in a Ford, one of only six races Ford won that year.[29]

France's multi-year contract with Larry LoPatin's American Raceways, Inc., did not assure the Detroit promoter would follow the rules. Deciding the winner was Cale Yarborough took nearly three hours after the 400-mile race, at his Brooklyn, Michigan, track was over and, even then, officials sent the scoring charts to Daytona Beach for further review. Sports reporter Gene Granger wrote that Yarborough was two laps down on the two-mile track. "How he made up the two laps was a mystery to everybody on pit row," Granger wrote.[30]

Richard Petty said he was two laps ahead of Yarborough when he pitted and there was no way he could have made up the two laps on the leader, Pete Hamilton, Petty's teammate. Yarborough said Pearson outran him all day. "Later, I looked up and saw that I was leading the race," Yarborough said, "I had to laugh."[31] Yarborough's win went into the record books.[32] LoPatin, to assure their presence, had agreed to pay Cale Yarborough and LeeRoy Yarbrough $2,000 each in deal money, against the purse, to enter the race.[33]

Richard Petty, from Randleman, North Carolina, is surrounded by a bevy of beauty queens after winning the 1971 Daytona 500. In the background is the race trophy sitting on Petty's famous blue 43 Plymouth. Petty, whose career in stock car racing included Grand National and Cups events, is the only NASCAR driver to win 200 races (State Archives of Florida).

Charlie Goltzbach strongly protested the absence of side windows in his race car, at the Michigan race, saying if chief technical inspector Bill Gazaway did not bring them back, somebody was going to burn to death. Goltzbach blew an engine and his car caught on fire. Without the side windows, he said, the flames were sucked into the driver's compartment. "If I had not been wearing a full face helmet, my face would have been burned," he said.[34]

The rains were no problem for the August 1970 Dixie 500 at Atlanta but Atlanta International Raceway's cash flow was. Initially, France told drivers not to report to the speedway because there was no money in escrow for the purse. LoPatin was in Detroit attempting to solve his financial problems with Diversified Financial Services. Although he had initial success with American Racing, Inc., LoPatin had expanded his race track empire too rapidly and his money ran out. Unlike France, who did whatever was necessary to keep long-time associates like Joe Epton, Bill Gazaway, Pat Purcell, Lin Kuchler and Houston Lawing, LoPatin fired his associates at will. Because of a disagreement over the PDA, he forced out Les Richter, one of his managers and stockholders. Richter, an eight-time Pro Bowler with the Los Angeles Rams, eventually took over the corporation after LoPatin's racing empire collapsed and later spent a decade as a NASCAR executive.[35]

On the matter of the escrow account for the purse, France dealt with Charles Black, president of the Atlanta track. Black came up with the $106,000 in certified checks for the race purse. LoPatin was threatening to sue France and NASCAR.[36] Whatever his management faults were, France adhered like glue to the requirement that purse money had to be in an escrow account before race activities began.

The Dixie 500 purse money was secured but some drivers had difficulty surviving on the track where the pre-race track temperature was 144 degrees. Richard Petty, who led all but forty-nine miles, won the race setting a new track record of 142.712 mph.[37]

For those not involved in the Petty show, there were some close calls. LeeRoy Yarbrough, who was as tough as they came, reached his pit, got out of the car and collapsed from heat exhaustion before he could reach the pit wall. Yarbrough was driving with a broken rib. Charlie Goltzbach got into his car and finished third behind Cale Yarborough, who said the track surface was like driving 500 miles on dirt. Pearson said he began to feel groggy before a leak in his car's exhaust system was discovered. By the time he pitted, Pearson said he had inhaled so many fumes he did not know where he was.[38]

Lorenzen, Pearson and Yarbrough were taken to the infield care unit. The others were released but Yarbrough was taken by helicopter to an Atlanta hospital due to concerns about his blood pressure and his broken rib. He was treated and released.[39]

Before the August 1970 Yankee 500 at LoPatin's Michigan International Speedway, NASCAR decided to require the use of restrictor plates to lessen the numbers of blown engines. Restrictor plates were aluminum plates with holes—the various sizes determined by NASCAR—drilled into them. The plates were placed between the carburetor and the intake manifold to reduce the flow of air and fuel into the engine and decrease the car's speed.[40]

Kuchler and Gazaway met with drivers and mechanics two weeks before the race to discuss restrictor plates along with tire use. Kuchler said use of the restrictor plates would provide better competition. "It stands to reason that competition will be better if there are more cars running at the end," he insisted. Goltzbach was happy that Gazaway reinstituted the use of side windows.[41]

Regardless of the side windows, Goltzbach not only won the race but also sat on the pole. Goltzbach and Cale Yarborough were in a fight for the lead until Yarborough's engine blew. Goltzbach was challenged by Bobby Allison, but the race ended under the yellow flag. In all, Goltzbach led 116 of the 197 laps. When the public announcer called Goltzbach the winner, many of the 34,500 fans booed because they wanted Allison to win. Dick Brooks, from Porterville, California, who came in second, said he learned a lot about driving from Allison during the race. "I watched Bobby run the track," he said. "He was zigzagging to break the draft. I have never tried that before but I did today. I had a problem early in the race in trying to get away from some of them guys. Then I saw him [Allison] and did the same thing. I would drop low and under them and cut them off. It worked."[42] Not everybody was happy with their cars. Buddy Baker said, "My car wouldn't have outrun a slow milk cow today."[43]

Media estimates reported the Yankee 400 cars ran about forty-five miles slower with restrictor plates than they did at the same track in June and noted only two of the forty cars in the race had engine failure.[44]

David Pearson, who was driving for Holman-Moody when NASCAR initiated use of restrictor plates, talked about how crew chief Jake Elder circumvented the rules by keeping a different restrictor plate taped under the fan cover. "Back then," Pearson said, "NASCAR would hand you the plate and you would turn around and put it on. Old Jake just turned right around and stuck the one NASCAR gave him up under the fan cover and pulled out the other one and put it on the car."[45]

The Grand National cars went to France's Alabama track for the Talladega 500. France boasted that the restrictor plates would increase the cars' speed by fifteen miles per hour and predicted a speed of 190–193 mph would take the pole. Pete Hamilton, in a Petty Plymouth, won the spring race at 152.321 mph. He also won the August race only slightly faster at 158.517 mph.[46]

Both the Alabama track surface and the restrictor plate racing were complimented by drivers. James Hylton said the new track surface was like driving on the interstate. Isaac said the new surface made the track easier to drive but there were still some rough spots in turns one and two. Petty said restrictor plates made it easier on the cars. "You have ten competitive cars; five of them used to drop out," he stated. "Now, I believe you will see only one or two drop out. There will be more running at the end."[47]

Buddy Baker left his slow milk cow car behind and won the 1970 Southern 500 at Darlington on Labor Day, as his father did in 1964. LeeRoy Yarbrough deserted Junior Johnson's Ford for the USAC championship chase in California. Fred Lorenzen was Yarbrough's substitute driver. That did not work out too well, as Lorenzen hit the wall four times. Cale Yarborough challenged Baker in the last half of the race until he wrecked passing a slower car and slid off the track. Isaac was second; Hamilton, third; Pearson, fourth; Petty, fifth.[48]

Curtis Turner had not driven in a Grand National race since 1968, but he had not left racing. In 1970, he was planning a new venture: a 1.58-mile race track with partners John Griffin, Bob Baughman and Ray Austin near Norwood, North Carolina, about midway between Charlotte and Rockingham. Financing was in place and core drill samples revealed there were no hidden mounds of granite on the property. Turner envisioned grandstand seats on pivots, a horse racing track in the infield and a 7,200-foot runway adjoining the track. Running horse races would have meant he had to get state approval of pari-mutuel wagering.[49]

Turner flew from his home in Roanoke to Charlotte on October 3, rented a car and drove to the speedway he and Bruton Smith built. He drove the rental car around the track a couple of times. Track Vice-President Richard Howard met him on pit row and tried to get him to drive in the National 500 race the next week. Howard told him that he never received a fitting send-off from the sport that idolized him and that he had a Dodge that Turner could drive to thrill the fans one more time and announce his retirement.[50]

Turner, age forty-six, was probably tempted, but he had more timber deals in the works. Turner and Smokey Yunick, who was waiting for him in Miami, were flying to Ecuador to complete a big timber purchase. First, he had to fly Baughman to DuBois, Pennsylvania. Turner and a friend, golf professional Clarence King, dropped Baughman at the DuBois Airport, ate lunch and headed back home. They were in the air for only a few minutes when the Aero Commander's left engine failed and the plane went into a death spiral. King had a heart attack and Turner, thrown forty-feet by the impact, was killed instantly. Baughman identified their bodies and had to inform Turner's family and legion of friends of his death.[51]

Yunick, meanwhile, was waiting for Turner at the Miami airport to go to Ecuador. He had to go to Ecuador alone and explain to their contacts that there would be no timber deal. He was unable to go to the funeral. "What really pissed me off," Yunick said, "was France was a pall bearer. With the suspension and all he put on Turner, suddenly he loves Curtis. What a phony deal."[52]

Yunick said Turner was the real racer. "He lived and drove like there was no tomorrow," he recalled. "For you race fans, who never saw him drive, I doubt you can envision the circus he put on. I called it Southern style, belly to the ground, ears and tail straight back. He'd ask me, 'If I can get the front end through, the rear end will follow, won't it?'" Yunick was resentful there was never a NASCAR race named for Turner.[53]

Following Turner's death, it was most fitting that another racing rebel, Bobby Isaac, won the Grand National championship and that 1970 was the last year the Grand National cars raced on dirt tracks, where Turner reigned supreme during his early driving career.

24

Money Infusion and Restrictor Plates

· · · · · · ·

In November 1970, Ford and Chrysler announced they were pulling the plug on their factory-supported teams. The exceptions were the Pettys' Chrysler teams. Ford's pullout involved car owners Junior Johnson, Banjo Matthews, the Wood Brothers and Holman-Moody and drivers LeeRoy Yarbrough, Donnie Allison, Cale Yarborough and David Pearson.[1]

According to Bernard Kahn, sports editor of the *Daytona Beach Morning Journal,* Ford Motor Company was paying the owners $2,000 per race for their crews; drivers were on a public relations contract for around $15,000 per year and purses were usually split evenly between drivers and car owners.[2]

France appeared to have lost his grip on the sport and his game of playing car manufacturers against each other was wearing thin. NASCAR-sanctioned races faced the possibility of even fewer spectators at the tracks. Stock car racing badly needed an infusion of new money and Junior Johnson found it. For all practical purposes, Johnson saved stock car racing for future generations.

Ford Motor Company said it was leaving racing to divert more money to ecology, which even then was more politically correct, and the safety programs mandated by the federal government. Matthew S. McLaughlin, Ford's vice-president for sales, said, "Effective immediately we are withdrawing from all forms of motor sports competition except for limited divisional and dealer support of drag and off-road racing." The fact that Ford had won only ten Grand National races to thirty-eight for Chrysler in 1970 was undoubtedly a factor in its decision.[3]

For all the millions and millions of dollars the automobile manufacturers had poured into NASCAR racing and its promotion over the previous decades, France could have displayed some degree of graciousness. Instead, he chose to say, "Detroit car builders have been in and out, in and out for the past fifty years. We live with them; we live without them. It matters very little."[4] Fifty years earlier, France was not involved with promoting. "Auto racing will grow. Manufacturers such as Ford and Chrysler cannot make or break it. I recall times when they tried to put pressure on racing's sanctioning bodies by hiring name drivers to sit on their duffs and protest some rule. It never really worked."[5]

It still stuck in France's craw that the automobile manufacturers, by paying their drivers a salary, broke his stranglehold on them. It was unhealthy, he asserted, for top drivers to have contracts with car manufacturers and be on their payrolls.[6] By being on salaries, the factory drivers could compete in races sanctioned by other organizations, something that once led France to ban drivers from NASCAR. He had lost that control.

France went so far as to say races would be more competitive without Ford and Chrysler since more independent owners and drivers would have an opportunity to compete at a reduced cost. "It should also open the door for more sponsorship by companies outside the automotive field," he said. France added that he expected General Motors to get back into stock car racing and boasted that all the big name drivers would be in Daytona in February.[7]

With the car manufacturers leaving NASCAR, France found one bright spot. One of his acolytes turned adversary, Larry LoPatin, finally bit the dust when he was pushed out of American Racing, Inc., by a group headed by his former employee Les Richter. A two time All-American at the University of California, Berkeley, Richter left the corporation a year earlier but retained his stock. After World War II, the Los Angeles Rams traded eleven players to the Dallas Texans for Richter, a linebacker and middle guard.[8] The other reason for France's elation was the entry of R. J. Reynolds Tobacco Company (RJR) into NASCAR. France knew that NASCAR desperately needed an infusion of cash after the manufacturers left.

In 1970, Junior Johnson knew that R. J. Reynolds and other tobacco companies would be unable to advertise their products on television after that year due to federal government regulations. Since Ford left racing, Johnson needed $100,000 backing for his race team and went to see Ralph Seagraves, whom he had known for years. Seagraves, RJR's lobbyist in Washington for the past decade, was looking for an outlet for the vast amount of advertising dollars the company had been spending on television. Johnson suggested that RJR take over the sponsorship of Grand National racing and the Winston Cup was born. Johnson put Seagraves in touch with France.[9]

Whatever racing differences Johnson had with France earlier, he knew the sport badly needed an infusion of money. Johnson saw the bigger picture and saving stock car racing was more important to him.

Reynolds was ideally suited to pour millions of dollars into NASCAR for a number of reasons. The company was located in North Carolina, as were a growing number of drivers, owners and car builders. Many RJR executives such as Seagraves had close connections with drivers and car owners. Bowman Gray, Jr., who ran the company from 1937 to 1967, was the son of the man for whom Bowman Gray Stadium in Winston-Salem was named and whose facilities France leased. Under the younger Gray's leadership, RJR routinely increased its profits seven percent a quarter.[10]

RJR was not the only tobacco company sponsoring automobile races. Philip Morris began sponsoring the USAC series in 1971. Liggett and Myers were underwriting the Sports Car Club of America Continental series.[11]

RJR executives met with France and, over the next several months, worked out a complicated arrangement. France recognized that to save the sport he would have to relinquish a great deal of control to RJR. On December 15, 1970, marketing services manager A. G. Weber and France made the big announcement. RJR would use the name of one of its cigarette brands, Winston, for the 500-mile race at Talladega and put up the $165,000 purse; RJR would add $100,000 to the points championship that would be awarded drivers three times a year instead of at the end of the season. Holding the points money until the end of the season allowed NASCAR to draw interest on the funds. The RJR decision put the money in the hands of the drivers more often. The series would be known as the Winston Grand National, which was later shortened to Winston Cup.[12]

RJR required NASCAR to make a number of changes, which created a new, shorter schedule. Grand National races were reduced from forty-eight to thirty-two, all over 250 miles. More races were scheduled at larger tracks and fewer at the short tracks. No other cigarette manufacturer could sponsor a race, but other brands could sponsor a team. Drivers' points to determine the champion would be awarded based on their finishing position in each race.[13]

In addition, the tobacco company would spend at least $500,000 annually on national advertising and promotion campaigns for NASCAR. "We've been looking very carefully for over a year for a venture we could promote that would be of interest to consumers and also help us sell cigarettes," Weber said. "We discovered race fans are the most loyal fans of any sport."[14]

France said that during the past year RJR made a complete investigation of NASCAR and asked him a hundred thousand questions.[15] While the RJR deal was being implemented, the racing season continued.

Associated Press reporter Hubert Mizell poked fun at France and his racing empire when he wrote, "Next St. Valentine's Day, some 110,000 persons will pay $2 million for the three hour privilege of witnessing grown men drive at lunatic speeds on a highway to nowhere."[16]

France, however, did not yet own all of his racing empire. Attorney Louis Ossinsky, who drew up NASCAR's incorporation documents and represented France in the lawsuit Curtis Turner and Tim Flock filed against him in 1961, still owned his original ten percent of NASCAR. Whether Ossinsky ever received a dividend from NASCAR during the more than two decades he was a stockholder was not known.[17]

After Ossinsky successfully defended France against the drivers' charges that he and NASCAR violated their right to work in the 1961 case in Volusia (Florida) Circuit Court, the attorney faded from the picture. According to newspaper accounts, another attorney, Vincent Arnold, represented France dealing with local taxation of the Daytona track. After Ossinsky's death in January 1971, France purchased his NASCAR stock from Ossinsky's estate.[18] After that, NASCAR was truly entirely owned by his family and still is today.

Before the 1971 Daytona 500, France decided to tinker with NASCAR rules again, all in the name of safety and parity. Mandating the use of restrictor plates to reduce speeds for the 1971 season, he said, was to insure more cars would be around at the end of races. Actually, his move had more to do with Chrysler winning thirty Grand National races in 1970, to only fifteen for Ford and three for Chevrolet. France played around with the size of the restrictor plates for different makes of automobiles until he had things in such a mess he was forced to throw out restrictor plate requirements in the middle of the season.[19]

For the Daytona 500, the Mercury Cyclones of A.J. Foyt, David Pearson and LeeRoy Yarbrough had Boss 429 ci engines. Richard Petty, Pete Hamilton, Cale Yarborough and Fred Lorenzen were in Plymouth Roadrunners with 426 ci Hemi engines. The Dodge Chargers of Bobby Isaac, Buddy Baker and Bobby Allison also had 426 ci Hemi engines. They were all running with restrictor plates. The Dodge Daytona of Dick Brooks, the only winged entry in the race, had a 305 ci engine without a restrictor plate.[20]

"Everyone knows that the speeds have to come down," Cale Yarborough said, "but this isn't the way. Here are these master mechanics who have spent a lifetime learning the tricks of a mess of steel and then Bill France slaps a 75-cent piece of metal on them. He should have just reduced the engine size from 427 to 300-cubic inches and then let the wrenches see what they could do with it."[21]

While France used restrictor places to reduce speeds at Daytona, he had a Porsche 916 as the race's pace car.[22]

The only factory-backed cars in the race were Petty's Plymouth and Baker's Dodge. "I don't feel the least bit sorry because we're the only ones in factory-backed cars," Richard Petty said. "Show me any of these cats out there today who have been running in NASCAR's Grand National stock car racing since 1949. We deserve everything we get."[23]

Glen Wood, from Stuart, Virginia, who built Foyt's car, had reservations about the restrictor plates. "In a way," he said, "it's a shame to put shackles on a good race car and a good driver. But, in the long run I think it will help the sport."[24] Wood later changed his mind about restrictor plates.

On a track known for wind problems, France was not about to cancel one of the preliminary races just because the wind gusts reached more than fifty miles an hour at Daytona. Red Farmer, part of the Allisons' "Alabama Gang," said he won the race only by driving very carefully. Just seventeen of the forty starting cars finished.[25]

Perhaps one reason for not canceling the race due to the high winds was that France was still complaining about the $600,000 he paid out to honor the ticket exchange agreement he made with fans at the first Talladega race that drivers boycotted in 1969. He said if not for that expense, he could have expanded the grandstand seating at Daytona.[26] It was France, after all, who made the offer to the crowd if they would remain at Talladega for the race.

Rookie Troyer Maynard, from Spencerport, New York, blew his engine in the 500-mile race and flipped over four times on lap twenty-five. Maynard suffered a skull fracture but recovered to drive in future races. There were seven cautions in the race for forty-five miles. Media estimates of the Daytona crowd ranged from 95,000 to 103,000.[27]

Richard Petty won the race after competition from his teammate, Buddy Baker. A. J. Foyt was in the mix until he ran out of gas and finished third. Petty's average speed, with the restrictor plates, was 144.744 mph, far below his last Daytona win in 1966 of 160.627 mph.[28] Foyt described how smooth Petty was in handling the draft at Daytona. "When Richard comes up behind you, you can hardly feel it."[29]

Wood and Foyt made sure the driver did not run out of gas two weeks later in the first Grand National at the Ontario (California) Speedway, forty miles east of Los Angeles. Over 100 drivers entered the Miller High Life 500, which had only fifty-one starting positions. The race purse, for the 2.5-mile, nine degree banked oval, was a record $207,675. The fifty-one cars started in rows of three instead of the customary two. Track president David B. Locton said using rows of three was NASCAR's idea. Petty and Baker tested tires on the track before the race.[30] "When we drove into that infield, it was the most beautiful track we had ever seen," Baker recalled. "It was fast, we could pass, the garage and facilities were second to none and we'd have guys like Steve McQueen and Muhammad Ali walking up and down pit row."[31]

Larry LoPatin's track should have been beautiful. The facility cost $25.5 million, based on an over-inflated feasibility study. There were unrealistic revenue projections from tele-

24. Money Infusion and Restrictor Plates

vision revenue although the track was financed with an attractive bond package. Included in its operational budget was a $1 annual million payment to bond holders.[32]

Foyt won the race by nineteen seconds. Petty was leading by half a lap when he had to pit. He missed his pit stall and had to drive around another lap. His engine blew up as he crossed the finish line behind Baker, who was second. Fred Lorenzen's bad luck continued when his car caught fire in front of the main grandstand and he had to drive it into the wall to stop. He was not hurt.[33]

Only three cars, those of Petty, Baker and Isaac, covered the entire distance of the Carolina 500 at Rockingham in March in what the media called a dull race despite some spectacular wrecks. Bobby Wawak, from Villa Park, Illinois, blew a tire, colliding with Elmo Langley, from Landover, Maryland, and Cale Yarborough. Wendell Scott ran into Langley and Lorenzen collected Wawak. Scott finished fourteenth. Only sixteen of the forty cars were still running at the end. The crowd was estimated at 32,000.[34]

When April came, the Atlanta track had more worries than the weather. Atlanta International Speedway's finances were a mess. In February, a court-appointed trustee gave the track one last chance. Trustee Neal Batson, an Atlanta attorney, said the April 4 race had to be profitable to save the track. Richard Howard and the Charlotte Motor Speedway rapidly backed away from the merger they had pursued earlier. In addition to LoPatin's meddling, the track also had problems with Henry County's tax structure. Wealthy Spartanburg businessman Walt Nix, an avid racing enthusiast, raised $200,000 to enable the track to run the Atlanta 500. The purse was $106,000.[35]

"Poor management had to be the cause of the financial troubles," Nix said. "There's no reason why the Atlanta International Raceway hasn't made money. I've got some of my dough in there now and you can be sure I'll keep a close eye on it." Not only did Nix keep a close eye on the track but he and L. G. DeWitt, a major stockholder in the North Carolina Motor Speedway at Rockingham, eventually accumulated ninety percent of the stock in the process of keeping the track profitable. Nix became chairman of the AIR board.[36]

An anonymous stock car driver suggested the name of the race be changed from the Atlanta 500 to the Bootlegger 500 since the factories were still supplying drivers and car owners with assistance and parts under the table. In a conversation with an AIR official, the driver stated, "The factories will never get out of racin'. That'd be like trying to stop the grass from growing 'round that track out there, now wouldn't it?" He added that drivers were bootlegging parts like crazy. "It's just a moonlight operation."[37]

The driver was not the only one complaining. Bobby Allison said the restrictor plates had rendered every car in stock car racing in 1971 as light as skimmed milk. Fred Lorenzen said he did not care whether they used restrictor plates or not as long as everybody was running about the same thing. Buddy Baker said, "It's put some sizzle back into the sauce. I've never seen tougher and tighter racing." Richard Petty's attitude was, "Long as the plates serve up some fine racing and the fans like it, who cares?"[38]

The weather was sunny, 52,000 showed up for the Atlanta 500 and hundreds of thousands watched the race on television. Everybody got their money's worth and the track survived. A. J. Foyt edged out Richard Petty by 1.8 seconds for the win. "If I had had just a fruit jar of gasoline, I wouldn't have had to make that last pit stop," Petty said. He was followed across the finish line by Pete Hamilton, David Pearson and Bobby Isaac.[39]

On Saturday night, before the race, Foyt asked to speak with the drivers. He apologized to them for a quote attributed to him in a *Sports Illustrated* article about the Ontario race. Foyt was quoted as saying, "Now that I've taken care of these hillbillies, I'm looking forward to beating those long-haired European fags." Foyt fell all over himself apologizing to the drivers. "It's a damn rotten lie," he said about the quote. "I don't even know what a hillbilly is and if I thought a guy was a hillbilly I would tell him to his face."[40]

Foyt sued *Sports Illustrated* and its parent company, Time, for libel and asked for $1,000,000. A federal court jury in Texas awarded him $75,000. Seems the reporter quoted Jackie Stewart, a Scottish Formula 1 driver who won three World Championships and twenty-seven Grand Prix races, as the source for Foyt's alleged statement. Stewart, however, testified that he heard the remark from another driver, not Foyt.[41]

The question at the Rebel 400 at Darlington in May 1971 was not if the track would survive, but would the drivers? The race could have been called the Junkyard 400. *The Sumter Daily Item* news editor DeVere Williams wrote that the race suffered from fallout but the fallout was not radioactive. "The fallout was composed of engine failure, differential problems, faulty lug nuts, bad brake drums, steering malfunctions, a few minor wrecks and other sundry ingredients."[42]

Those sundry ingredients included what happened to pole sitter Donnie Allison. After leading 244 laps, his engine failed. "I worked my fannie off out there today," he said, "and then it ends like this. I felt I was faster than Richard and Buddy most of the day, but, at the end Buddy was gaining on me." Petty's car caught on fire on lap 185 and he used an in-car fire extinguisher to put out the flames. He finished twentieth. Baker said when he took the lead with five laps to go, he could hear every rattle in the car. "That was the hardest part of the race," he said.[43]

The Rebel 400, seen by a crowd of 46,500, was run on a Sunday. That meant France had finally won his decades-long battle with South Carolina's Baptist ministers.[44]

The first Winston 500 was run at Talladega in late May. Sports reporter Tommy Tucker wrote, "A bunch of R. J. Reynolds front office brass saw their cigarette chase turn into a stock car classic." Some of the drivers—David Pearson, Bobby Isaac, Bobby Allison and Dick Brooks—initially said they would not drive in the race without deal money. "John Holman couldn't afford to pay me any of the deal money he got from Talladega so I definitely will not be racing there," Pearson said. "I've always gotten half of everything, including deal money." According to sports reporter Gene Granger, deal money for the race was being paid by NASCAR to the Wood Brothers, Ray Nichels, Fred Lorenzen and John Holman.[45]

Deals were worked out since Pearson drove in the race. He went out with distributor problems. Isaac ended up in the hospital with kidney stones and Dave Marcis, from Wausau, Wisconsin, drove his car.[46]

A blanket could have covered the top three cars as they crossed the finish line. Donnie Allison, who was scheduled to drive A.J. Foyt's Coyote Ford at Indianapolis, won the race by a car length over his brother, Bobby. Both the Allisons were in 1969 Mercurys and, during the last laps of the race, as they passed in front of the grandstands, the crowd cheered for the "Alabama Gang." Buddy Baker, driving a 1971 Petty Dodge, was only three feet behind Bobby Allison. Finishing out the top five were Pete Hamilton and Fred Lorenzen in 1971 Plymouths. Donnie Allison got $30,600 out of the $165,000 purse.[47]

According to the Daytona Beach newspaper, a crowd of around 63,500 saw the race. If the average ticket price was $18, which was charged at Daytona and other large tracks,

France grossed around $1,142,000. The $165,000 purse for the Winston 500 was paid by RJR.[48]

France got what he wanted from the restrictor plates in the World 600 race at Charlotte. Thirty-six cars qualified within a range of eight miles. Charlie Goltzbach took the pole in Junior Johnson's Chevrolet at 157.788 mph. "The restrictor plate is the key," Pearson said. "NASCAR watches us like a hawk while some cars aren't inspected too often. From what I hear, some fellows run without the plates at times and that can add an extra fifty to 100 horse power."[49]

The World 600, however, was all about the Allison brothers, Bobby and Donnie. Bobby Allison won the race by more than a mile over his brother and collected $29,400. Donnie Allison picked up $15,250 for second place but came out of the weekend with the most money, including his sixth place winnings of $30,000 in the Indianapolis 500 the day before. However, the Allisons' winnings paled in comparison to the $275,000 Al Unser received from the $1 million purse for winning the Indy 500 in 1971.[50]

Pete Hamilton finished third in the World 600, one lap down, followed by Richard Petty and Buddy Baker. Pearson left the race early because an oil leak was again creating toxic fumes in his car. "It was time to eat, anyway," he said.[51]

In June 1971, before the Motor State 400, at Brooklyn, Michigan, Plymouth and Dodge drivers alleged they were losing up to seventy miles per hour to Ford and were no longer competitive due to the different size of the restrictor plates NASCAR issued. "Our management had mixed emotions about our even being here," Ron Householder, Chrysler's stock car manager, said. "It all hinges on being competitive. We could pull out at any time. The new ruling stinks. It's ridiculous. It has no engineering basis. It's one of those things that came out of the sky."[52]

"Every time we get close they just speed up a little," complained Richard Petty. "You pull up along side those cats and they just look over at you, grin and drive off. I don't know what the answer is but there is going to have to be something done, somewhere down the line, to square things up." Neil "Soapy" Castles, an independent Chrysler driver from Charlotte, said, "It has damn near put us out of business. They just decided to slow all the cars down and when we all had the same size plates it wasn't too bad. Now, we know who is going to win the race before we leave home." Castles added, "The only way Petty is winning is because he is out-handling them."[53]

Toledo Blade sports columnist Dave Woolford wrote, "The injustice had better stop or NASCAR will have to find a way to justify a much smaller field on race days." He added that Bill France initially issued restrictor plates with 1.25-inch opening and later decided to let the wedge engines use plates with a 1.50-inch opening.[54]

Restrictor plates and other issues dogged France during the Firecracker 400 at Daytona. Grand National champion Bobby Isaac arrived in Daytona Beach for the race but his car was not there, although NASCAR had advertised that both car and driver were entered in the race. Car builder Henry Hyde, in Daytona Beach with Isaac, said he expected the car to arrive by Thursday's time trials. Nord Krauskopf, Fort Wayne, Indiana, insurance executive and owner of the 1971 Dodge, said the car was in Charlotte and it would stay there.[55]

Krauskopf strongly complained to Bill France about the variation of the restrictor plate sizes allowed for different makes of automobiles and threatened to park his cars until rules were made that were fair to all. From all indications, concessions were made for the Dodge and its wedge-type engine. "I wouldn't say I'm overjoyed," Krauskopf said, "although we took them off the hook by hurrying up installation of our only wedge engine and getting the car here." He continued, "I did it for Bobby, Henry Hyde and the race fans who come to see Bobby run. But, the speedway (Daytona) did something almost unforgivable when they announced two days ago the car was entered. It wasn't entered until 11:35 a.m., Friday."[56]

According to the Daytona newspaper, Isaac's Dodge had a larger restrictor plate opening. Even with that advantage, Isaac, who started twenty-first because he missed qualifying, almost lost the race to Richard Petty. Five laps from the race finish, the front portion of Isaac's hood flipped up and he was faced with the decision to pit and lose the race to Petty or continue racing. He stayed on the track, keeping one eye on the charging Petty and trying to keep the other on the track in front of him.[57]

Not only did Isaac win the race, but three of his Chrysler teammates, Petty, Buddy Baker and Pete Hamilton, followed him across the finish line. Donnie Allison was fifth in his Wood Brothers Mercury.[58]

France, although he was most fortunate in having the RJR millions to revive his sport, made a decision in August 1971 which defied reason. France simply could not stand to lose one of the NASCAR divisions and, of course, the money it generated. He threw out his own rule book. After working with RJR on the realignment of the sport, which included the elimination of most of the short tracks, France decided to combine Winston Grand National and Grand American entries for races of less than a mile at short tracks.[59]

Drivers, especially those with the PDA, Richard Petty, Elmo Langley and James Hylton, threatened to boycott the next two short track races at Winston-Salem and Ona, West Virginia. The Grand American Division, composed of smaller cars such as Mustangs, Javelins and Camaros, was dying on the vine and France was trying to keep it alive. NASCAR had planned to run forty Grand American races in 1971. By August 1, only ten races had been held. The Grand American cars were 600 pounds lighter than the Grand National cars and more maneuverable on the short tracks.[60]

While the drivers were in Atlanta for the Dixie 500, France, in Daytona Beach, and Lin Kuchler, in Atlanta, initiated a conference call with Petty, Langley and Hylton that lasted an hour. The drivers outlined their opposition to France's latest idea. Petty said the combination would downgrade the Grand National Division. "If I'm embarrassed at Ona, what is the fan going to say should I win the Michigan pole?" Petty asked. They finally worked out a compromise that covered the next two races at Winston-Salem, where France had the track leased, and at Ona, West Virginia. The starting field at the quarter mile Winston-Salem track would be enlarged from twenty-two to thirty cars. If five Grand American cars were added, five Grand National cars would be added. "It was a compromise," Langley said. "We did the giving again. They always want us to give. They [NASCAR] never give. I can't afford any more of these experiments."[61]

"I can understand what they are trying to do," Hylton said. "They are trying to save the Grand American Division." Langley added, "If we aren't satisfied after two races, we aren't going to run any more of the short tracks. Although I'm going along with it for two races, I think it is one of the most unfair things they've done in all my years of racing."[62]

Petty was embarrassed but it was in the August 1971 Winston-Salem race, not Ona, where Bobby Allison beat his high powered Plymouth with a Holman-Moody Mustang.

"What they ought to do is send them [Grand American cars] home and leave them there," Petty said. "If we're going to run Grand American races, let's run Grand American cars."⁶³

Only 25,000 saw Petty win the Dixie 500 at Atlanta International Raceway over Bobby Allison by two car lengths. Lost wheels, blown engines and other mishaps accounted for fifty-eight laps of the race run under caution. Petty's portion of the purse, $20,560, boosted his lifetime winnings to $1,018,203 over fourteen years. "Ten or twelve years ago I didn't know there was $1 million," Petty said. "I always thought $1 million is what you read that other people had."⁶⁴

During the August 500 mile race at Talladega, Petty and Bobby Allison again banged fenders for the last fifty miles of the race. Allison held him off for the win. Buddy Baker's car caught fire as it spun onto the grass, and he suffered burns on his left arm and hand.⁶⁵

It was also in August that Bill France and car builder Glenn Wood came to a meeting of the minds. Wood had threatened that the 1971 Daytona 500 would be his last race if France did not authorize same size restrictor plates or make Chrysler get rid of its exotic manifold. Wood said his Fords and Mercurys simply could not compete. By August, France agreed that Ford could use its 1969 medium high riser heads on its wedge-type engines with 1⅜–inch restrictor plates, the same as the Chrysler cars. Fords, with similar engines, previously had been required to use 1½–inch restrictor plates.⁶⁶

From all indications, driver unrest continued. Before the end of August, France agreed to take the carburetor issue before the ACCUS board.⁶⁷

Although France said restrictor plates was one of the greatest things NASCAR had ever done, he announced that, after September 15, 1971, restrictor plates would no longer be used in Winston Grand National racing. Instead, he said the carburetor base openings would be limited by sleeves in each of the bores and the rule would be effective with the National 500 at Charlotte on October 10. "The junked carburetor plate requirement created a lot of division," France said, "and the new NASCAR move is seen as erasing some of this friction without lifting the limitations on the horse power control and speed of the special racing stock cars." He added that he did not expect to see any real difference in the top speeds of the Grand National stock cars.⁶⁸

France's new plan for control speeds called for the following carburetor base openings: Chrysler's Hemi and Ford's Boss engines, 1⅛–inch openings; for Ford's Tunnelport, 1¹³⁄₁₆–inch opening; for the non–Hemis, 1¾–inch openings; and for all 306–366 ci street type engines, 1¹¹⁄₁₆–inch openings. He said if the new carburetor base openings did not work out, "Here come the restrictor plates again." An Associated Press article suggested that France's initial restrictor plate rule was intended to gradually force the withdrawal of manufacturers' support.⁶⁹

The Southern 500 was the last 1971 Grand National race to use the restrictor plates. The most spectacular event at Darlington that Labor Day weekend came in practice when Fred Lorenzen crashed the Wood Brothers Mercury. Lorenzen lost control of the car coming out of the fourth turn. Sports reporter Gene Granger described what happened: "The racer's right wheels climbed the four foot wall protecting the grandstand, riding the unrelenting barrier with the front wheels on [the] top for more than 100 yards. The car then slipped back onto the track and skidded another 150 yards before slamming head-on into the inside concrete wall protecting the pit area. The impact blasted a gap twenty feet wide in the six-inch thick, three-foot high wall. Watermelon-sized chunks of concrete sprayed through the pit area at the pagoda."⁷⁰

Driver Joe Frasson, the first to reach Lorenzen, said the car was on fire and he thought it was going to blow up. "When I got to Freddy, he wasn't breathing," Frasson said. "I unfastened his harness and started to put him out. He gurgled and started breathing." Frasson was initially unable to get Lorenzen out of the car because his foot was caught in the twisted roll bar. Another driver, Bill Siefert, climbed in the car, freed Lorenzen's foot, and they carried him about thirty yards from the burning car. He did not regain consciousness until he was in the ambulance on the way to the hospital.[71]

Much as with earlier serious wrecks on NASCAR tracks, such as those that killed Fireball Roberts and George Amick, drivers and spectators, not emergency medical personnel, were usually the first to reach the cars and rescue the competitors, if they were still alive.

Charlie Goltzbach, whose car was hit by one of the chunks of flying concrete, was critical not only of the track but of the lack of maintenance. "This track was built twenty years ago and it's obsolete. It's just plain murder." Darlington personnel had spread an asphalt sealer, known as bear grease, on the track two weeks earlier. "It's slick as ice," Goltzbach continued. "These promoters are interested only in putting money in their pockets and not the safety of drivers. If not, they would repave this track and make it safe."[72]

Darlington Raceway president Barney Wallace said they put down bear grease to seal the track before every race. There were those who suspected the mixture was used to create more exciting racing. Wallace, who was unable to locate Curtis Turner—the race leader—when he was a pace car driver, had a lame excuse for not keeping the track in good repair. He said major drivers who claimed to be track experts were asked to examine the track surface and make recommendations but the raceway received no suggestions.[73] Glen Wood said, "I don't know if we will come back here or go to any track. We will go home and think about the new rules."[74]

More than 70,000 watched as Bobby Allison left Richard Petty a mile and a half back in his mirror as he won the Southern 500. LeeRoy Yarbrough, who started only six races in 1971, was suffering from too many headaches and, many suspected, from abusing pain killers and possibly alcohol,[75] and did not have a ride in the race. ABC-TV paid him $500 to do interviews and assist in the taping of the Southern 500.[76]

Yarbrough interviewed Allison from the winner's circle. Yarbrough had suffered two bad crashes in as many years. While tire testing for Junior Johnson at Texas in April 1970, Yarbrough crashed into a concrete wall and his head hit the roll bar, knocking him unconscious for an hour. He was treated and released from a College Station hospital, where it was determined he had a slight concussion. Yarbrough had another bad crash at Indianapolis the next year.[77]

It was not a crash that put Petty behind but a dangling gas cap. He had pitted for water and a crew member, thinking he needed gas, unfastened the gas cap as Petty roared out of the pits. NASCAR called him back to the pits to fasten the gas cap. Regardless, he finished second. His teammate, Buddy Baker, finished third. Baker was still suffering from the burns he received during the Winston 500. "My hands were hurting so bad after about the halfway point that I could hardly drive the car. I was lucky to finish, much less finish third."[78]

Dangling gas caps, Lorenzen's wreck, and Yarbrough's interviews were all very exciting but were eclipsed by the biggest story of the race that few heard about. Independent driver Wendell Scott started last and blew his radiator halfway through the race. He went to his pit, took the radiator out of a Sportsman car he raced two days earlier at Myrtle Beach, installed it in his Grand National car and finished thirteenth in the Southern 500.[79]

Luck had nothing to do with Bobby Isaac's persistence in winning the Old Dominion 500 from the pole at Martinsville in September 1971. It was helpful that the race was relatively free of mechanical difficulties, as twenty-two of the thirty entries finished. The remarkable fact was that Isaac had just returned from setting twenty-eight land speed records for stock cars at Bonneville Salt Flats in Utah.[80]

The National 500, at Charlotte Motor Speedway, was beset with problems. Sports reporter Gene Granger wrote that some of the cars in the race were using the carburetor sleeves while others were using restrictor plates. Lin Kuchler, the NASCAR official in charge of the race, was unhappy that rain delayed the start for two hours. Kuchler was determined to give the 52,000 spectators a race. The first ten laps were run under caution. Finally, after 357 miles, Kuchler called the race. Bobby Allison, who won the race, talked about how slick the track was by the time Kuchler made his decision. "I figured they would either have to slow the race under cautions or stop it," he said. "Not only that but it was getting dark. If it had gone on much longer we would have needed headlights."[81]

Normally drivers did not resort to legal actions over wrecks on the race track. That was not the case in the September race at Richmond, Virginia. Tommy Ellis spun Sonny Huchins out on the track. Both drivers were from Richmond. Huchins swore out a warrant for Ellis charging him with assault with a deadly weapon intending to maim, injure, kill or cause disability. NASCAR suspended Ellis for thirty days.[82]

Attrition again reared its ugly head at the American 500, at Rockingham, in late October; only twenty-three of the forty-one cars finished. There was the usual outcome—Richard Petty won the race. His teammate Buddy Baker, who finished second, raised a question about Petty passing him during a caution. Petty said he did not see the caution when he passed Baker. Apparently, race officials did not want to touch the issue. "I have no hard feelings," Baker said. "Anyway, it happened way back in the race and he probably would have passed me anyway." Petty's share of the $106,000 purse was $17,620, Baker's $9,745, and Bobby Allison's $6,320 for third place.[83] The Rockingham win virtually assured Petty of his third national championship.[84]

In November, NASCAR announced the new format, with sixteen fewer events per the RJR agreement, for the 1972 Winston Grand National racing season. There would be thirty-two races (only thirty-one were held) at the longer tracks for purses of about $2 million, with a minimum purse of $30,000. RJR would contribute $100,000 to the points fund. The short track divisions, for the Camaros, Mustangs, etc., were divided into the Grand National East and Grand National West races of no more than 150 miles. RJR would contribute $15,000 to each of the two lower divisions. The schedule restructuring required ACCUS approving the change at its December meeting in New York.[85]

Two Grand National races were scheduled for Charlotte, Daytona, Talladega, Darlington, Atlanta, Michigan, Texas, Riverside, Ontario, Dover and Rockingham. The short track schedule included Martinsville, Richmond, Nashville, Bristol, North Wilkesboro and Byron, Georgia. Missing from the schedule were some of stock car racing historic venues: Hickory, Asheville-Weaverville and Winston-Salem, North Carolina; Maryville and Kingsport, Tennessee; Malta and Islip, New York; Columbia and Greenville, South Carolina; South Boston, Virginia; Ona, West Virginia; Macon, Georgia; and Houston, Texas.[86]

Regardless of the championship race, Richard Petty and Bobby Allison battled each other in December 1971 at speeds up to 185 mph at the Texas 500 at College Station. France actually postponed the race for a week due to rain. It was fender-to-fender racing until Allison's rear tires began to smoke. Only about 18,000 spectators turned out for the race whose purse was $80,000. Allison, despite a broken valve that occurred on lap 240, finished third behind Buddy Baker. Once again, attrition took its toll, with only twenty-three of the forty-nine cars finishing the race. After the race, Petty left for a tour of military installations in Vietnam.[87]

Petty won his third Grand National Championship and $351,071. James Hylton and Cecil Gordon, from Horse Shoe, North Carolina, were second and third in the points standings. Bobby Allison, who ran four fewer races than Petty, was fourth and Elmo Langley was fifth.[88]

After more than two decades of contributing the most advance aerodynamics and engineering concepts to stock car racing while aggravating Bill France, Smokey Yunick left NASCAR for USAC racing. France told him he would be back. "If you don't think I'm gone, count the days til I come back," Yunick told him. France had repeatedly refused to include some of Smokey's practical suggestions such as an air jack for pit stops. For years, Yunick pushed the idea of softer, movable crash walls for race tracks made from used tires, but that idea was also rejected. He wrote, "In my world, the Bill France benefit is over—in my world, I'd have died before I'd have come back."[89]

25

A New Boss Takes Over

· · · · · · ·

On January 12, 1972, Bill France stepped aside from the day-to-day operations of NASCAR and installed his thirty-nine-year-old son, William Clifton France, as the president. The elder France retained his position as the head of the International Speedway Corporation, which owned the Daytona and Alabama speedways and shares in Martinsville and North Wilkesboro.[1]

It was possible that once he had secured full and complete ownership of NASCAR, France felt comfortable in making his oldest son the titular head of the organization. His other son, James, was always listed as a lower officer in the family companies.

Before France stepped aside, he made an agreement with four car owners and their drivers to insure their appearance at all thirty-two Winston Grand National races. In return for that guarantee each of the teams would receive $2,000 for each super speedway race over 400 miles and $1,500 for short tracks less than 400 miles. France explained that appearance money had previously been paid before each race and the new arrangement would make it easier for the teams to make their plans if they had the money up front. NASCAR handled all the appearance money contracts.[2] Sports reporter Bill Brodack stated that appearance money had been paid teams for years. "The deals have all been on an individual basis and finding out what one owner got compared to another was like trying to pick the lock at Fort Knox."[3]

The four teams who agreed to race the entire thirty-two race Grand National schedule were Bud Moore and David Pearson in Fords; Henry Hyde and Bobby Isaac in Fort Wayne insurance executive Nord Krauskopf's Dodges; Lee and Richard Petty in Plymouths; and Junior Johnson and Bobby Allison in a Chevrolet owned by Richard Howard, general manager of the Charlotte Motor Speedway. Tracks were expected to ante up part of the appearance money since Howard told sports reporter Gene Granger that the Atlanta and Macon speedways would not pay into the appearance money program.[4] Granger wrote that in 1971, Goodyear had charged drivers $68 each for their tires. Beginning in 1972, Goodyear agreed to furnish free tires to the top ten qualifiers at all races.[5] Regarding appearance money for the four teams, the new NASCAR president, William C. France, said the deal could go over into 1973.[6]

The first race of the season, at the Riverside road course in California, was a mess. The race start was delayed by two hours due to the weather and was halted after 387 miles due to fog and darkness. Richard Petty told an interviewer, "If you think it is scary trying to drive through dense fog, how would you like to drive nearly 400 miles around a country road going 100 mph?"[7]

The Western 500 had three leaders, Petty, A. J. Foyt and Bobby Allison. Foyt played bumper tag with the other two until his transmission failed on lap 108. Allison lost a cylinder and Petty beat him by sixty-one seconds. "This isn't my kind of course; you need an extra hand and foot to drive it," Bobby Isaac, who was third, remarked.[8]

The Riverside win was the first win of the decades-long association between the Pettys and STP millionaire Andy Granatelli. The Associated Press reported that Granatelli had paid the Pettys an estimated $1 million for their racing operation.[9]

In his first Daytona Speed Week as NASCAR president, France may have wished he and his father had paid more attention to Smokey Yunick's idea of softer race track walls instead of the hard concrete ones. During the second of the two 125-mile qualifying races for the Daytona 500, a massive thirteen car wreck claimed the life of Chattanooga driver Raymond "Friday" Hassler. The melee started when the Ford of David Boggs, from Morrisville, North Carolina, blew a tire and spun. Attempting to avoid Boggs, the Dodge of Verlin Eaker, from Cedar Rapids, Iowa, hit the concrete wall and ground against it down the backstretch. Hassler's Chevrolet hit the concrete wall and went into a spin that collected other cars. Jimmy Crawford, from East Point, Georgia, hit Hassler's crumpled car, knocking it back into the wall. Hassler was killed instantly from massive head and neck injuries. G. C. Spencer, from Jonesboro, Tennessee, jumped out of his Plymouth to render aid to Hassler. "I just looked at him and turned away," Spencer said, "and began directing traffic."[10]

Raymond Williams, from Chapel Hill, North Carolina, said the wreck was like a bomb exploding and the smoke was so thick drivers could hardly see. Richard Petty said there were car parts flying everywhere. Jimmy Crawford suffered a fractured jaw and lacerations. Joe Frasson, from Minneapolis, had neck injuries.[11]

NASCAR threw the caution and then finally red-flagged the race, a first at the speedway. Qualifying was changed, as officials took the first fifteen cars from each of the qualifying races and the other ten were made up from those fastest in time trials. A.J. Foyt, in a Wood Brothers Dodge, won the race rather handily by almost two laps over Charlie Goltzbach in Cotton Owens's 1971 Dodge. He collected $45,400 from the $178,000 purse. Foyt, winner of three Indianapolis 500s, five USAC championships and the 24 Hours of Le Mans, broke LeeRoy Yarbrough's 1969 track record of 157.950 mph by averaging 161.550 mph. Goltzback's second place netted $16,250. James Vandiver, from Huntersville, North Carolina, was third with $10,475 in O. L. Nixon's 1970 Dodge. Benny Parsons was fourth, $7,150 in a 1970 Mercury owned by L. G. DeWitt. Fifth place went to an independent driver, James Hylton, $5,925, in his own 1971 Ford.[12]

If one ignored the toll Daytona Speedway's concrete walls collected, then the younger France's first Speed Week was a successful operation that drew 250,000 for ten races that paid over $300,000 in purses. The crowd for the Daytona 500 was estimated to be between 98,000 and 100,000.[13]

None of Hassler's friends from the Alabama Gang, Bobby and Donnie Allison, Red Farmer and others, attended his funeral on Sunday since they were driving in the Daytona 500. *Gadsden Times* sports editor Jimmy Smothers speculated that Joanne Hassler and her four young sons perhaps preferred a quiet funeral without any fanfare. According to Smothers, NASCAR paid for Hassler's funeral and his driver's insurance paid his widow $10,000.[14]

The Carolina 500, at Rockingham, drew a record 42,500 to the mill country on a windy March day. The race was televised by ABC. It was fitting that Bobby Isaac, who used to work in the nearby mills, won the race. "He really needed this one," Patsy Isaac said as she held onto their twins, Robin and Rhonda. "He's been so down in the dumps lately that he's been hard to get along with." Richard Petty was second, followed by James Vandiver, LeeRoy Yarbrough, from Jacksonville, Florida, and Dave Marcis, from Wausau, Wisconsin.[15]

Nobody disputed that Bobby Allison probably had the best car in the race. Allison's car owner, Junior Johnson, decided to switch the tires on the car just before the race. Apparently, that was in violation of NASCAR rules and race officials sent Allison to the fortieth position. His car was so good that, in the first two laps of the race, he picked off nineteen cars. Isaac took the lead when Allison's engine blew. "There was no way I could keep up with Allison while he was running," Isaac said. "He could pull away from anyone anytime he wanted to."[16]

His fourth place finish in the Carolina 500 was one of LeeRoy Yarbrough's best finishes in his last year of Grand National racing. Yarbrough drove a Bill Seifert built Ford. The independent car builder, a former jet plane mechanic, said he built his cars from scratch. "We don't buy parts; we make them," Seifert said. He said he was lucky that Yarbrough was available to drive his car.[17]

Luck was not LeeRoy Yarbrough's companion in the early 1970s. Suffering from head injuries, like the one he received at Indianapolis that split his helmet open when he crashed into the wall, Yarbrough seldom knew where he was or what he was doing. His fellow drivers and car owner tried to help him. Cale Yarborough flew him to a race at Rockingham because he did not want him piloting his own plane. The next week he had no memory of Cale flying them home to South Carolina. Junior Johnson, his car owner, said he there was a point in a race at North Wilkesboro when he had to stop the car and get Yarbrough out. "He didn't know what he was doing," Johnson said. "It was something to see someone so talented to be so destroyed by something. I only got one good year out of him but I never stopped trying to help."[18]

It was Junior Johnson, not NASCAR or USAC at whose sanctioned events he received concussions, who spent $250,000 taking Yarbrough to doctors and four hospitals seeking a diagnosis. "I took him to an institution in Asheville and they wound up calling me to come and pick him up because he was fighting with everyone. I really tried to get him back on his feet but he couldn't remember anything." Johnson said initially Yarbrough could remember everything from 1970 back but nothing after that. "You'd go to dinner with him and they'd put a plate of food in front of him and he'd just sit and look at it until you said, 'LeeRoy eat.' Then, he'd pick up his knife and fork.[19]

"I think he could have been one of the best drivers of all time," Johnson said. "He had one thing I've never seen out of any other race car driver. He had no fear. It was hard to believe. He was as good a driver as I've ever seen come across."[20]

Media coverage of Yarbrough's problems generally avoided using the word "concussion," in connection with his mental health problems. There were rumors he caught Rocky Mountain spotted fever from a tick bite on a 1971 hunting trip, but that was a year after Johnson said his memory stopped. He degenerated to picking up tin cans in Jacksonville ditches for money. He was charged with attempting to strangle his mother, Minnie Yarbrough, but his siblings questioned if that actually happened.[21]

Yarbrough kept going back to what he remembered, racing. On one of his last trips to Daytona, Jim Hunter, NASCAR public relations director, volunteered to pick him up at the airport. Hunter said he circled the terminal three times before he recognized Yarbrough. His curly black hair was gray and his trim physique had disappeared. He failed to recognize Hunter, whom he had known for years. "He didn't know where he was," Hunter said. "I felt so sorry for him."[22] For the most part, LeeRoy Yarbrough was forgotten as the Grand National season proceeded amid William C. France's efforts to get a handle on the family business.

Newspaper headlines screamed, "Chevy is back," at the Atlanta 500 in late March, and there was no rain. Bobby Allison responded with the appropriate action in Junior Johnson's 1971 Chevrolet. Allison thrilled the crowd of 70,000 as he passed Bobby Isaac with five laps to go and then flew by A. J. Foyt on the backstretch. "I didn't let off at all and Allison just flew by me," Foyt said. The Associated Press reported it was Chevrolet's first major NASCAR win since Junior Johnson won the Dixie 500 at Atlanta and the National 500 at Charlotte in 1963.[23]

Then it was April, the spring sap was rising, dogwoods were blooming and it was time for the Rebel 400 at Darlington. David Pearson, who had not won a race in two years, owned Darlington for that race. Associated Press racing reporter Bloys Britt did his research on the driver. "Pearson won the pole position for this spring's classic, capturing it on the 13th day of the month exactly 13 years since he first sat in a Grand National car. Not only that but his pit pass was no. 13 and he once crashed a car that bore the number 13," Britt wrote. Pearson said his crash in the number thirteen car was his fault and had nothing to do with bad luck omen. "When I qualified on the pole," Pearson said, "I told the Wood Brothers, my car owners, we'd do well in the race."[24] He did.

So did Richard Petty in the Gwyn Staley 400 at North Wilkesboro later in April. "For most of the race, I just sat back and watched the dog fight between [Bobby] Allison and Bobby Isaac," Petty said. "They really had themselves a whing-doddle. It was one of the best two-car fights I have ever seen and I had a ring-side seat 200 yards back." He remained back, he said, because he was afraid they would wreck each other and he would get caught up in it. Petty, in a Plymouth, made his move on Isaac, in a Dodge, on lap 309. He finished the race two seconds over Allison, in a Chevrolet, and five seconds over Isaac. Only those three finished all 400 laps. Independent James Hylton was fourth in a Ford and Benny Parsons, a former Detroit taxi driver, was fifth in his L.G. DeWitt Mercury.[25]

Meanwhile, Bill France was once again in the headlines. He was vacationing on his yacht in the Bahamas when former Alabama Gov. George Wallace, while campaigning for president, was shot in Laurel, Maryland, by Arthur H. Bremer, from Milwaukee. "I'm saddened and shocked," France said. "This horrible act is an insult against our system and our government." France soon switched his allegiance to Republican Richard Nixon and was named vice-chairman of Florida Democrats for Nixon by former Texas governor John Connolly.[26]

France attempted to run the Florida Democrat Party the way he operated NASCAR and it failed to work. State Democrat Chairman Jon Mayle, from Palm Beach, wanted to subject France to disciplinary action for his switch since he was a delegate to the Democrat National Convention, which nominated Sen. George McGovern as the party's presidential candidate. France claimed he represented only Wallace's supporters at the convention. France brushed off Mayle by saying the state chairman was just upset, but he would get over it.[27]

At France's Alabama International Motor Speedway in Talladega in early May, Bobby Isaac set a blistering qualifying speed of 198.428 mph for the Winston 500 pole. His speed on the backstretch was clocked at 215 mph. David Pearson was in the other front row position in the Dodge that Foyt won with at Daytona. Foyt was driving in a USAC race that weekend. Pearson and Isaac had driven to the race together. Richard Petty and Bobby Allison were in the second row. The race was red flagged twice due to rain for thirty-one minutes. Isaac pitted for gas five miles from the end of the race when he was leading, allowing Pearson to win. Either his pit crew failed to secure his gas cap or it came loose during the race. William C. France told reporters that crew chief Henry Hyde was asked to bring Isaac in to fasten the gas cap and Hyde refused. Isaac was black-flagged but he continued racing. "It took me a couple of laps to figure out that the black flag was for me," Isaac said. "By that time, I'd been driving too hard and too long to quit."[28]

France let Isaac's second place finish stand, did not dock him any points but fined him $1,500. Isaac said he thought the fine was pretty steep. Had he pitted, Isaac would have finished no better than fourth, which paid $6,095. By continuing the race, he finished second which paid $13,985 and, after paying the fine, still made more money. Pearson said he probably would have also ignored the black flag.[29]

"I don't think I could stand that long ride [home] with Isaac telling me how he blew me off," Pearson said. "I'll probably have to listen to Pearson telling me how he won the race," Isaac said, "but it's better than walking home." Buddy Baker, whose father, Buck Baker, finished forty-first, was third.[30]

Lorenzen was fourth and Petty was fifth. There were some other interesting drivers in the race. Darrell Waltrip, from Owensboro, Kentucky, later a three-time Cup champion, was thirty-ninth. Ron Keselowski, from Troy, Michigan, an uncle of 2012 Cup Champion Brad Keselowski, was nineteenth. Country music singer Marty Robbins, who finished eighteenth, confessed to race officials the inserts that fell out of the sleeves in his carburetor were illegal. "I just wanted to run with the big boys," the singer lamented. Robbins was then placed last.[31]

A news conference William C. France held at the track before the Winston 500 indicated the change in NASCAR leadership was minute when it came to their public utterances. "Auto racing hasn't yet had to resort to gimmicks to draw people," France said. "It depends on its concept of thrills, on its relation to people who own cars and its integrity as a sport free of scandal for its growth." France boasted that all the Grand National races up to that date had sold out, had standing room only or spectators were turned away.[32] He probably just forgot the elephant rides his father used to attract spectators to Daytona's Speed Week activities.

In late May, the World 600 at Charlotte was all about the Bakers, Buddy and his father Buck. It all came about while William C. France was attempting to wean the sport from its colorful, rowdy and illegal distilling southern past. A former illegal whiskey transporter and World War II veteran, Buck Baker was Grand National champion in 1956 and 1957. He was still driving at age fifty-three and had come to Charlotte to race. When he arrived, Baker discovered he had no ride because he had been fined, suspended, put on probation or something over a messy incident the week before at a race at the Ona Speedway in West Virginia.[33]

No one from NASCAR had bothered to tell Baker there was no ride waiting for him at Charlotte.

Herald-Journal sports reporter Gene Granger heard about the incident and began an investigation. He was unable to find anyone in NASCAR to talk with him and finally located Baker, who was more than willing to tell his side of the story. Baker said he was running second in the Ona race when H. H. Bailey, from Houston, Texas, was four laps behind and tried to put him into the wall. The two drivers had apparently had run-ins before. Baker said, since both drove Pontiacs, Bailey had to get his parts from him and was unhappy with the situation. "He waited for me to come around," Baker told Granger, "and deliberately tried to put me in the wall. Then he dropped his car in third gear and tried to put me in the grandstand. The race was stopped because of another accident. I talked to NASCAR officials but got no action. After the race, I signed autographs and waited to talk with him. I saw to it that he didn't leave the speedway."[34]

Granger said that Baker initially went to look for Bailey with a gun but another driver took the weapon away from him. Baker continued, "After a while I went after him with a blackjack. I could have messed him up or killed him. I didn't do more than hit him three or four times. There were two cops standing nearby." Baker acknowledged that what he did was wrong. "But, who committed the greater offense?" he asked. "I've seen guys get killed on a short track. What he had in mind wasn't racing."[35]

Baker told Granger that, after the incident, he called William C. France and told him what happened. Baker said France told him they would talk on Friday at the Charlotte Motor Speedway and there would be a ruling. Upon his arrival at the speedway on Wednesday, Baker said he learned he had been fined $500 and suspended for the season, which took away his ride. Baker said on Thursday NASCAR vice-president Lin Kuchler told him he was eligible to drive but, by then, he had no ride. Baker again tried to contact France but was told he was out of his office for the rest of the week.[36]

The World 600 was the series' longest race and it would have been unusual if France, in his first year as NASCAR president, had not been there. Baker was a brawler and had been all his life. It was possible that France, a younger but smaller man, was afraid to face the former moonshine transporter who towered over him.

Granger finally found what he considered a reliable source, but not one from NASCAR, who told him that Baker was fined $500 and put on probation for two years. Buck Baker must have enjoyed watching his son win the World 600 before 81,500 at the Charlotte Motor Speedway. Buddy Baker and Bobby Allison banged fenders until Allison had a flat tire fifty miles from the finish of the race. "I know how Allison feels," Buddy Baker said. "I was leading the 600 two years ago when I ran out of gas."[37]

The Buck Baker incident came only a few weeks after William C. France had his public relations staff crank out news releases bragging about NASCAR's success. The organization had 22,000 members; sanctioned races at eighty tracks in the United States and Canada; was seen by approximately eight million people; had drivers in its six divisions competing for more than $6 million in purses, and was shedding its former image. "The organization," the release said, "has come a long way from the hominy grits and cornpone image it once had because of its roots in the deep south."[38]

The younger France, in July 1972, told Bernard Kahn that he seldom talked to his father about NASCAR. "In the six months I've been in charge, I haven't talked to my father more than a total of one hour about NASCAR business," he said. That was probably true, as he retained the same staff his father used—Lin Kuchler, Bill Gazaway, Joe Epton, Houston Lawing, Russ Moyer and others.[39]

Bill France, however, had his hands full fighting the Daytona Beach Racing and Recreational Facilities District Board. In December 1971, some of the members wanted to roll back his speedway's tax exempt status, according to newspaper reports. The articles on the proceedings were written, not by sports editor Bernard Kahn, but by Ray Ruester, the newspaper's political editor. The fact that France was grossing $2 million gates on the Daytona 500 races, plus proceeds from twelve or fifteen other such events during the year, and collecting revenue from concessions, parking, programs, speed and tire testing, did not escape the notice of Daytona Beach voters who asked that the speedway be placed on the tax rolls. At that time, France was paying the district $6,000 a year rent on the fifty-year lease. The district, in turn, paid the city of Daytona Beach $4,750 a year.[40]

Through his attorney, Aubrey Vincent, France offered to pay more rent but to do that he required certain concessions from the district. If there was a tax levy, France wanted the taxes deducted from his rent, he wanted unrestricted use of the property, or if the tax was levied, and it was in excess of the lease amount he paid, the district would deed him the 374 acres owned by Volusia County. The original lease, which they were operating under, gave the district the right to use the property during certain times of the year but they had never exercised that option, as they had no money.[41] The city of Daytona Beach owned the other seventy-three acres of the land where the speedway was located.[42]

France was unable to sway public opinion but he wanted the matter settled. In the 1960s, previous unsuccessful efforts were made to put the speedway on the tax rolls. It was a subject that would not go away. In 1965, the Florida Supreme Court upheld the tax exemption on the speedway, saying the matter would stand until the legislature acted to repeal the current law. France, in an unusual proactive move, proposed a new rental schedule for the remaining thirty-six years on the lease as follows: $35,000 the first five years; $45,000 the second five years; $55,000 the third five years, and $60,000 for the next twenty-one years.[43]

The district board, before they would agree to modify the lease for unrestricted use of the speedway property, requested a commitment from Daytona International Speedway to continue racing there. There was some question of whether the lease could even be modified. The Florida constitution, Article VII, §10:202.2, was revised in 1968, eleven years after the lease was signed, to restrict cities, counties or special districts from giving, lending or using their taxing powers or credit to aid any corporation, association, partnership or person.[44]

Should the Daytona International Speedway be included on the county tax rolls, France wanted the taxes paid by the district out of increased rental fees. Ruester wrote, "If the lease was terminated by the District, a sum equal to ten times the corporation's gross income on all activities for the preceding fiscal year would be paid. At the present time, the District would have to pay the corporation in excess of $10 million to terminate the lease."[45] Ruester concluded his article, "It would seem to this writer that if the property is to be used strictly or predominately for commercial purposes, the public should recover the lease at that time and make the property available to the highest bidder."[46]

Aubrey Vincent, France's attorney, said his client did not want any restrictions due to difficulties in financing construction and improvements. Vincent complained that France could not go to a bank and borrow money on the lease the way it was. During construction of the speedway, under the lease, France used the same leasehold on the 347 acres as security for a loan not to exceed $250,000. He even used the grandstands for collateral for another loan before the speedway was finished. Under the conditions of that transaction, the mortgagee could possess all the 347 acres and improvements if the speedway defaulted.[47]

There were no quick solutions and France would fight to keep the speedway off the tax rolls for the rest of the decade. Residents of Daytona Beach and Volusia County expected the France family to pay their share of taxes just like ordinary citizens.

In July, before the Firecracker 400, William C. France, following his father's line, told Bernard Kahn that the sport was better off without the factory teams. He acknowledged that some teams would suffer. "But the overall result from the standpoint of the sport is that we're healthier now," France said. "Factories have a tendency to escalate the cost of racing. They try to out run each other. In the event factories were to want to come back with racing teams, I think we have resolved how to handle it. NASCAR suffered a lot of bad publicity."[48]

France said if somebody wanted to build a bigger engine, NASCAR would simply slap a plate on it. He did not see that as retarding progress. France also announced the expansion of the Daytona International Speedway grandstands by 5,300 more seats. The addition to the existing 50,000 seats would be achieved by putting twenty rows of seats at the top of the grandstand.[49]

While Bobby Allison and Richard Petty were banging each other around, David Pearson took the lead in the Firecracker 400 with fifteen miles to go and effectively blocked the two other drivers to win the race. "Richard was running a little bit stronger than I was up the straightaway," said Pearson, who won the race in 1961. "I was kind of tickled when he didn't pass me from the fourth turn to the finish line." Petty said Pearson was two car lengths faster down the straights but he could stay with him in the corners. Allison said he planned to draft Petty around Pearson but it never happened. Clifton "Coo Coo" Marlin, from Columbia, Tennessee, was fourth, James Hylton was fifth and LeeRoy Yarbrough was sixth.[50]

Independent driver James Hylton, one of the PDA founders, often referred to by the media as a perennial also-ran, surprised everybody and won the Talladega 500 in August 1972, and the $24,885 that came with the win. "Now I can walk a bit more proudly through the garage area," Hylton said. "I can hold my head up because I proved that I can build a car and drive a car as good as anyone." Hylton started twenty-second and took the lead when a wreck on lap 103 took out Bobby Isaac, David Pearson, Buck Baker and Richard Petty. Ramo Scott was second followed by Bobby Allison, Red Farmer and Buddy Arrington, from Martinsville, Virginia.[51]

Although competitive, Winston Grand National drivers were normally an easy going lot not prone to seriously criticizing each other in public. That was not the case in the Southern 500 at Darlington on September 4, 1972. Drivers were ready to drum Fred Lorenzen out of the brotherhood. Donnie Allison said Lorenzen was not only hogging the groove but driving too slowly, causing the field to jam up. "If you can't drive the car fast enough to ride the high speed groove properly, you ought to move over and let the others go ahead and race," Allison said.[52]

LeeRoy Yarbrough was involved in a seven car pile-up he said was caused by Lorenzen going too slow. Bobby Allison, who won the race after he slipped by David Pearson seven miles from the finish, said Lorenzen acted like he did not want to run and was holding everybody back.

Benny Parsons, from Ellerbee, North Carolina, defended Lorenzen, saying he was just protecting his advantage and may have thought his car would work better later in the race. Dick Brooks, reaching for his water tube, drifted down into Buddy Baker. "After I tagged him," Baker said, "I cocked the wheels so he wouldn't start flipping and then stood on it until both of us got out of the groove. If we had stopped in the groove, it would have been history for both of us."[53]

The next week at the Capital City 500 at the Richmond Fairgrounds Speedway, Bobby Allison and Richard Petty began banging on each other again. One clash between them claimed Buddy Baker. According to an Associated Press report, "Coming into the No. 4 [turn] Allison was on the inside with the nose of his Chevy up beside Petty. Petty came down and metal hit metal. As Petty's Plymouth went sideways, Allison got on the brakes but Baker was in the middle and his 1972 Dodge had nowhere to go. He rammed into the side of Petty's car carrying him into the rail. Petty's car went up on the rail, bounced back down on the track and somehow managed to keep the lead."[54]

"I just knew that I was out of the race," Petty said. Allison and Petty pitted under one of the seven cautions that took up seventy laps of the race. Somehow or other Petty's car suffered less damage than Allison's and he won the race by almost a lap. Baker finished seventeenth. David Pearson was twenty-fourth and behind him was a young driver named Richard Childress.[55]

Perhaps no other race was more indicative of the Winston Grand National points battle between Bobby Allison and Richard Petty than the October 1, 1972, Wilkes 400 run at the five-eighths-mile North Wilkesboro Speedway. During the first 200 miles, they took turns trading paint. On lap 362, Max Borman, from Wallburg, North Carolina, spun and took out James Hylton and the yellow flag came out.[56]

On the restart, Allison was in the lead but Petty caught him. From that point on, they raced side by side continually battering each other. With eight laps to go Petty went around Allison and almost hit the outside barrier. With three laps to go, they clashed again and both bounced off the retaining wall that time. Allison drove high on the track to avoid debris from Petty's car and he dived under him to take the lead. Petty's battered car crossed the finish line first at about half speed with Allison behind him, his tires smoking from rubbing against the car's crumpled sheet metal fenders.[57]

After the race, both drivers had their say. "There's not going to be any trouble until he hurts me; he's playing with my life out there," Petty said. He threatened to sue Allison for assault. "He hit me so hard he bent my fender in," Allison said. "When he did that, I just ran back into him." NASCAR officials advised both drivers to clean up their acts.[58]

The next race was the October 8 National 500 at Charlotte, which came down to a rather calm duel between Bobby Allison and Buddy Baker. Richard Petty would probably have been in the mix but he wrecked and finished eleventh. Trailing Allison and Baker across the finish line were Pearson, Foyt and Butch Hartman, from Zanesville, Ohio. There was no crunching of sheet metal in the American 500 at Rockingham on October 22 as Allison had an easy win with Petty two miles back. Before the race, Allison and Petty were observed sitting beside each other at the track church service.[59]

The Pittsburgh Press reported that Buddy Baker drove the best race of his career as he defeated A. J. Foyt by a fender length in the Texas 500 at the Texas Speedway, in Bryan Station, on November 13. Foyt won the pole with 170.273 mph and received an Angus bull and

$500. Baker protested that NASCAR did not count his second and fastest qualifying run. Lin Kuchler told Baker he was down in the low groove and the light beam was unable to catch him as he crossed the finish line. Kuchler said he had warned drivers that they had to qualify in the middle groove where the light beam could catch them and Baker was out of luck. "That bull should have been mine," Baker said. "If they hadn't missed my best lap I'd be taking him back to North Carolina."[60]

Richard Petty, who won eight races to Bobby Allison's ten wins, came out 128 points ahead to win his fourth championship and collected $40,000 of the $100,000 points fund RJR put up. Allison, however, accumulated $346,939.99 in winnings to Petty's $339,405. With seventeen fewer races, the Grand National average purse jumped from $42,385 in 1971 to $74,478 in 1972.[61]

All told, William C. France's first year at the NASCAR helm called for no major decisions, but the next year was quite different.

26

Total Control

• • • • • • •

Bill France's backing of Richard Nixon in the 1972 presidential election garnered invitations to the January 1973 inaugural celebration for himself and his wife, Anne, and William C. France and his wife, Betty Jane. *Daytona Beach Morning Journal* sports editor Bernard Kahn bragged that Bill France was almost as much at home those days in Nixon's Washington as he was in Daytona Beach.[1]

While the Democrat Frances were whooping it up in Washington with the Republicans, the Winston Grand National season opened with the Western 500 at Riverside, California, on January 21. Much to everybody's surprise, a box-like American Motors car, the Matador, built by Roger Penske, from Philadelphia, and driven by Mark Donohue, from Newtown Square, Pennsylvania, won the race. The Matador, whose lineage went back to the Hudson Hornet, was the product of a merger between Hudson and Nash-Kelvinator. The car had disc brakes, which Donohue said were an advantage on a road course over the drum brakes used in the other cars.[2]

Bobby Allison was second; Ray Elder, from Carruthers, California, third; Bobby Unser, from Albuquerque, New Mexico, finished fourth, and Jimmy Insole, from Mission Hills, California, fifth. Both David Pearson and Richard Petty went out with mechanical problems. After the race, Allison looked at the younger Donohue, grinned and asked, "Who gave you permission to run here, anyway?"[3]

To celebrate the 1973 Speed Week events, Kahn wrote an eight-chapter history of Bill France, NASCAR and the beginning reign of William C. France for the Daytona Beach newspaper. He quoted Bill France as saying, "There's no connection between NASCAR, Inc., and the International Speedway Corporation (ISC). The association is that the speedways at Daytona and Talladega run races sanctioned by NASCAR, that's all." Kahn reiterated there was no connection between the two entities and then proceeded to list the officers of both corporations. William C. France was the president of NASCAR, James Carl France was vice-president, Anne France was secretary treasurer and Bill France was a consultant. The officers for ISC were: Bill France, president; William C. France, vice-president; Anne France, secretary treasurer, and James C. France, assistant secretary treasurer.[4] That was the party line and nobody seriously questioned it until the Kentucky Speedway filed an antitrust lawsuit against NASCAR, ISC and the Frances in 2007.[5]

Buddy Baker put his Henry Hyde Dodge on the Daytona 500 pole at 185.622 mph for the February 18, 1973, race. Hyde, from Brownsville, Kentucky, was a legendary, crusty car builder known for his encounters with NASCAR officials. Some said Hyde took over that adversarial position when Smokey Yunick left. He built cars for Nord Krauskopf that Bobby Isaac and then Baker drove. Baker said he followed his father's advice, "You hit the wall as hard at 179 as you do at 184, so you might as well go wide open and take your chances." Baker said, "We came here to race. When there are cars running on the track, my skin crawls up my back and I want to be out there with them." He was the pre-race favorite.[6]

Baker did run wide open, leading the 157 of the first 194 laps. He was challenged by Cale Yarborough, who had returned to Grand National racing after a stint in USAC, and Petty. Yarborough blew an engine and, after the race, was critical of NASCAR officials for running the first thirteen laps of the race under caution in order to dry the track. "It rained out there one or two times hard enough so that the race should have been stopped. It was mighty dangerous out there," he said. With five laps to go, Baker's engine gave out on the backstretch. Petty won the Daytona 500 for the fourth time and claimed $34,100 of the $236,325 purse.[7]

France actually postponed a NASCAR race in progress at Bristol in March. Cale Yarborough, in his Junior Johnson Chevrolet, set a qualifying record of 107.607 mph to win the pole on the five-eighths mile track redesigned in 1966 with thirty-six degree banked turns. Yarborough led fifty-two laps when a massive downpour forced NASCAR to postpone the race two weeks.[8]

When the race restarted on March 25, drivers took the same positions they had when the race was stopped. Yarborough led the entire race. Petty was second, two laps down, followed by Bobby Allison, Dave Marcis and Benny Parsons. Yarborough was the first driver, since Darel Dieringer at North Wilkesboro in 1967, to lead an entire race.[9]

Pearson almost did the same thing at the Carolina 500 in Rockingham on March 18, leading 491 of the 492 laps. When he pitted, Bobby Allison led the other lap. Pearson's share of the $100,000 purse was $14,975. "That old goat needs to win once in a while to keep from going hungry," Bobby Isaac joked. "He's always complaining about the high cost of food."[10]

Cale Yarborough was second followed by Buddy Baker, Bobby Allison and Dick Brooks. Finishing in the top ten were Darrell Waltrip, sixth, and Richard Childress, ninth. Childress, who crashed in the 1972 race, said Richard Petty helped him. "Petty told me how to drive through the turns at Rockingham," he said, "and you wouldn't believe how much better the car handled when I did what he told me to do." Childress' Chevrolet Laguna had a body built by James Hylton, a chassis by Bobby Allison and a motor from Chuck Wright, Akron, Ohio. The car was owned by Tom Garnes, Seaford, Delaware, president of L. C. Newton Trucking Company, the team's sponsor.[11]

When drivers continued to grumble about the Grand National race purses, William C. France did exactly what his father had done. He brought in other drivers. Scheduling moved the spring Darlington race from May back to April and another 100 miles was added to the race distance. The Rebel 500 was designated a FIA race, opening it to USAC drivers. However, it was Darlington and the Bob Colvin rule on rookie drivers was still in force. All USAC drivers who had not previously driven at Darlington had to take their rookie driving test on the track.[12]

Pearson won the Rebel 500 in a disaster of a race that Smokey Yunick predicted a decade earlier would occur if the raceway was not properly maintained. Only thirteen out of the forty cars finished. Pearson spent most of his time dodging wrecks strewn over a track built twenty-three years earlier for cars whose speeds only reached 75 mph. A massive pileup thirty-three laps from the finish took out contenders Richard Petty and Dick Brooks.[13]

Pearson's part of the $95,100 purse was $15,000. He said it was not much money for wrestling a bear all afternoon. "They [Darlington owners] are cheap," said Cale Yarborough, who went out of the race in a five-car wreck. He pointed out the spectators paid an average of $10 each for tickets, making the gate $482,000.[14]

Roy Mayne, a driver from Sumter, South Carolina, said he did not blame Darlington Raceway president Barney Wallace. "He's only running a business and if he can get cars for $95,000, then why pay $150,000?" Mayne asked. "I do blame NASCAR," he continued, "for not putting the punch on promoters. They have a minimum amount for a 500 mile race but it looks like it should be higher." He added that unless NASCAR failed to do something soon there would be no cars left to run.[15]

The minimum purse amount, Mayne mentioned, was instituted by RJR when it took over the Winston Grand National sponsorship, and agreed to by France and NASCAR.

Pearson complained that drivers were going too slow at Darlington. "They would motion you by and then slide up into the high groove," he said. Racing Columnist Ed Hinton wrote that Pearson, at any given millisecond, could put himself in the optimal position. "You could stand inside treacherous old Turn 4 at Darlington," Hinton wrote, "and watch practice for five minutes and see the difference in Pearson and all the rest. The others would exit the turn flailing at their steering wheels, fighting for control. Pearson would come out of the turn with his steering wheel barely moving at all, so precisely did he position himself through one of the toughest corners in NASCAR."[16]

Pearson repeated his win at Darlington with the short track race at Martinsville and the Winston 500 at the Alabama International Motor Speedway on May 6, before 77,000 spectators. The Big One occurred at Talladega on lap ten and collected twenty-one cars traveling at more than 190 mph. Ramo Scott hit the concrete outer barrier and his car scattered oil and parts over the four lane track. Pearson was trailing Buddy Baker, Bobby Allison and Cale Yarborough in a draft with Richard Petty when the wreck happened. "Just as quick as I went into the second turn, I saw doors flying and I started stopping," Pearson said. "I don't know how I got through; I just wiggled through it."[17]

That wreck ended Wendell Scott's racing career. He suffered broken ribs, a fractured pelvis and numerous lacerations and was hospitalized in Talladega for a week. Earl Brooks had a fractured skull. Ambulances and wreckers spent an hour clearing the injured drivers and mangled vehicles off the track. Taken out in the wreck were Buddy Baker, Cale Yarborough, Bobby Allison, James Hylton, Joe Frasson, from Golden Valley, Minnesota, and Slick Gardner, from Buellton, California. Bad as the wreck was, Yarborough said, "It was the greatest miracle in auto racing that nobody was killed." Buddy Baker said, "It was the worst thing I have ever seen. There was simply no way to avoid it. I consider myself extremely lucky."[18]

For some reason, the field for the Winston 500 was increased from fifty to sixty cars. Prior to the race, William C. France held a news conference that left reporters not only puzzled about his answers but wondering why he even bothered to stage the event. Sports reporter Gene Granger wrote that France gave evasive answers and would spend five or ten minutes on meaningless examples. In 1972, Granger quoted France as saying the NASCAR purses would double in a couple of years. Granger said the biggest issue facing NASCAR was the grumbling by car owners and drivers over the size of the purses. When asked about his previous statement on increasing the size of the purses, France said, before race purses could grow, ticket prices would have to increase or facilities would have to add more seats.[19]

When asked if NASCAR set the size of the race purse, France replied, "We usually have a pretty good understanding." NASCAR, in its sanctioning agreement, set the amount of every purse at tracks where it sanctioned races. France predicted NASCAR would probably go to a smaller block engine in two or three years. He was not sure about any rule changes for 1974, and denied that he had paid any additional deal money to get enough cars to fill out the sixty-vehicle field for the Winston 500.[20]

The Music City 420, at the Nashville Fairgrounds Speedway on May 12, had one of the smallest purses on the circuit, $43,000. By NASCAR rules, the purse was perfectly legal, as the race was less than 500 miles. Cale Yarborough's win was worth $5,255. Benny Parsons, however, needed to finish only one lap in the race to win the first part of the Winston Cup Points and $10,000.[21] Parson finished the required lap, led two laps of the race and came in second. Buddy Baker was third.[22]

Buddy Baker again owned the World 600 at Charlotte, on May 27, where he sat on the pole in his K&K Insurance Dodge. However, his third victory at NASCAR's longest race was a close win, only two seconds over Pearson. Fifteen laps of the race were run under caution because of rain. After lap 265, the race was halted for thirty minutes due to a heavy downpour. Baker's share of the $170,000 purse was $25,200. The crowd was estimated to be between 75,000 and 82,000. Cale Yarborough, Bobby Isaacs and Benny Parsons finished out the top five. Rookie James Vandiver, who was sixth, won the Curtis Turner Outstanding Achievement Award, which was given to Wendell Scott in 1972. Darrell Waltrip was seventh and Richard Childress was eleventh.[23]

There were changes and ramifications in and from the July Daytona race. What had once been the Firecracker 500 reverted back to a 400-mile race. William C. France changed the carburetor rules from the use of the sleeve devices back to restrictor plates. Engine builders had figured how to bring speeds back with the sleeve devices. NASCAR officials told the Associated Press the re-issuing of restrictor plates was not intended to reduce speeds but to provide longer engine life. Neither Pearson nor Buddy Baker accepted this explanation. They said the plates would reduce their speeds by at least five miles per hour.[24]

Driver Dave Marcis charged that NASCAR was up to its old trick of parity in making Chevrolet more competitive with the new rule. The new restrictor plate rule provided more than ample evidence that Marcis was correct. The rule called for a 1 7/16 inch plate for the Chevrolet 427 engine; 1 3/16 for the Chrysler 426 Hemi-engine; 1 3/16 for the 429 Ford Boss; 1 3/8 for the 427 Ford wedge, and 1 1/2 for the 427 Chevrolet wedge. "If NASCAR wanted to make sure the Chevys would be competitive, they need not worry," Marcis said. "They've taken care of that." He suggested that NASCAR should have made the plates all the same size. "How do you explain the fairness of the rule when the Chevys, after the change, run faster than before the change and the rest of us run slower?" he asked.[25]

William C. France denied the parity argument and finally agreed to meet with Henry Hyde, who had been harassing NASCAR technical inspectors all week over the new restrictor plates rule. After his meeting with Hyde and his car owner, Nord Krauskopf, France said it was a congenial meeting. "I wish all my meetings went as smoothly," he said. The meeting apparently did not help Hyde and Krauskopf's position, as they wanted to skip the Firecracker 400. Baker said he asked them to let him race. They did and he finished third.[26]

Pearson, in winning the Firecracker 400, became the first NASCAR driver to win twenty super speedway races. "I didn't like them [restrictor plates] because they slowed me down and helped the Chevrolets," he said. Glen Wood, Pearson's car owner, said, "I'm not satisfied with them but sometimes you have to live with things you don't like."[27]

Pearson was kidded about whether his nickname was the "Gray Fox" or the "Silver Fox." Pearson took off his Purolator cap, ran his hand through his pewter-colored hair, grinned and remarked, "I prefer the Slick Fox." Richard Petty was probably calling Pearson some other names. "I didn't like the way Pearson raced me," Petty said. "I don't mind getting outrun but I hate like hell to be played with. Pearson played with me until the last eight or ten laps and then he picked up half a second a lap."[28]

Dave Marcis and other drivers, who criticized NASCAR for mandating various sizes of restrictor plates at Daytona in order to favor Chevrolet, proved their point at the conclusion of the Volunteer 500 at Bristol on July 8. The first five cars to cross the finish line were Chevrolets. Benny Parsons won his second race but had a relief driver, John A. Utsman, from Bluff City, Tennessee. The temperature in the cars reached 140 degrees. L.T. Ottinger, from Newport, Tennessee, was second. Cecil Gordon, from Horse Shoe, North Carolina, was third but was relieved by Richard Petty, whose car was forced out by mechanical problems. Lennie Pond, from Petersburg, Virginia, was fourth and J. D. McDuffie, from Bridal Veil, Oregon, was fifth, twenty-seven laps behind the leader. Bobby Isaac also went out with mechanical problems. Cale Yarborough and Bobby Allison collided after Allison hit the wall on lap 343.[29]

The Allison-Yarborough collision was nothing compared to the blow Larry Smith suffered in the Talladega 500, on August 12, when he hit the concrete wall in turn one after a tire went down. Smith, from Lenoir, North Carolina, had been involved in the massive twenty-one car wreck at the spring race at the Alabama International Motor Speedway. "I've got a score to settle at Talladega," Smith said before the race. "I got sucked into that multi-wreck here in May and I want to make up for that."[30]

The score was not in Smith's favor. His Mercury hit the concrete wall on lap fourteen with such force that his headrest was broken. The vehicle, after riding the six-foot barrier for more than 100 yards, rolled down to the infield and stopped. Smith was dead on arrival at the infield care center. Wendell Scott, still recovering from injuries suffered in the spring race wreck, was a press box guest for the race. Scott said Smith was the first person to reach him and render assistance when he was injured in the May race.[31]

Smith's death occurred several years after Smokey Yunick advanced the idea of building flexible race track walls, utilizing discarded tires, to relieve the severity of head on crashes into the concrete walls. It would be almost three decades, and numerous other racing deaths, before NASCAR finally instituted Yunick's idea of flexible race track walls.

On lap ninety of the Talladega 500, Bobby Isaac, who knew nothing about Smith's death at the time, heard a voice telling him to quit racing. Isaac did not wait until the next caution or after the race. He drove to his pit, got out of his Bud Moore car and said he was through with stock car racing. Moore put Clifton "Coo Coo" Marlin, from Columbia, Tennessee, in the car as a relief driver and he finished thirteenth in the Ford.[32]

Dick Brooks won the Talladega 500 with Buddy Baker second and Pearson third. Pearson was racing for the win in order to become NASCAR's second millionaire driver. James Hylton and David Sisco, from Nashville, were fourth and fifth. Darrell Waltrip and Richard Childress finished seventh and thirty-seventh respectively. Baker's crew chief, Henry Hyde, argued with race officials over a yellow flag they threw when Baker's car started smoking. Apparently, officials thought Baker had blown an engine. There was no engine problem and the order of finish was not changed.[33]

"I didn't have anything to prove to myself or anyone else," Isaac said. "I know how it feels to drive and I know how it feels to win and lose. I know how it feels to be a champion. And, now I know how it feels to quit." A month later, Isaac had no regrets about leaving Winston Cup racing. He competed in some Sportsman races in Virginia and South Carolina but had no plans to race on a regular basis. "Sportsmans are fun to drive," he said. "You can go to a race and get home by midnight on the same day."[34]

Sport columnist Gene Granger wrote that Isaac had invested his winnings wisely, did not have to race for a living and could often be found on a golf course. At that time, Isaac was in New York with his friend David Pearson. Paul A. Cameron, president of Purolator, Pearson's sponsor, had sent his private jet to Spartanburg to pick up the two men for the company's fiftieth anniversary celebration. Pearson, said, "I'll tell you something about Bobby, when he decides to do something, he does it on the spot." Bud Moore picked Darrell Waltrip to take Isaac's ride.[35] Actually, Isaac later returned to Winston Cup racing and made nineteen starts from 1974 to 1976.[36]

Events at the 1973 National 500 at the Charlotte Motor Speedway, on October 7, reflected badly on France, NASCAR and what integrity the sport had. Tim Higgins and Steve Waid, in their biography of Junior Johnson, wrote of the sport in the early 1970s, "There were so many controversial changes that it seemed the sanctioning body had no real sense of direction."[37]

Their assessment was an understatement. NASCAR's problems at Charlotte began with the pole qualifying. Charlie Glotzbach, in his Charles E. "Hoss" Ellington Chevrolet, won the pole and the $1,000 that track President Richard Howard put up. Three days later, technical inspectors found the Glotzbach had an illegal restrictor plate on his car, took away his pole position and the money, fined him $500 and made him re-qualify. Racing writer Benny Phillips wrote, "The penalty of disqualifying Glotzbach is like putting someone in jail on Saturday for being drunk on Wednesday."[38]

Things got even worse. Insurance executive Nord Krauskopf, owner of the car Buddy Baker drove, had been protesting the various sizes of the restrictor plates since France enacted the newest rule in July. Krauskopt allowed Baker to start the National 500. Baker was in fourth place and 159 miles from the end of the race when Krauskopf, for some unknown reason, ordered him to come in off the track. Krauskopf refused to let NASCAR inspect his car and Baker was disqualified.[39]

Krauskopf threatened to take his Baker-Hyde team to USAC. "Ever since NASCAR changed the rules on carburetor plate(s) on July 4, we've been at a disadvantage," he said.[40]

Cale Yarborough, in his Junior Johnson Chevrolet, won the National 500 by 1.4 seconds over Richard Petty in a Dodge. Bobby Allison was third in his Chevrolet sponsored by Coca-Cola. Allison, who had driven for Johnson the previous season, was suspicious of Yarborough's and Petty's engines because they put six or eight car lengths on him down the straightaways. After the race, Allison sought out chief inspector Bill Gazaway, posted $200 to protest the finish and accused Yarborough and Petty of having oversized engines. NASCAR returned Allison's money. Racing columnist Bob Hoffman wrote that if the sanctioning organization had accepted Allison's money, he would have had a right to inspect all the goodies in the two engines he had questioned.[41]

Although NASCAR inspectors returned Allison's protest money, they did a post-race inspection of the cars of Johnson, Petty and Allison. Inspectors finished with Allison's engine in about fifteen minutes and declared it was legal. Hours passed and there was no word on Yarborough's and Petty's engines. Finally, after ten o'clock Sunday night, Gazaway said the measurement of the engines would be sent to NASCAR headquarters in Daytona Beach and that a final decision would be made on Monday. William C. France, at five o'clock Monday afternoon, announced that the National 500 results were official—Yarborough first, Petty second and Allison third. France said, although the pre-race inspection procedures were inadequate, NASCAR determined the cars conformed to the rules.[42]

France could not have chosen worse words or phrasing for his explanation. NASCAR and France, caught between drivers and promoters, were in a no-win situation of their own making and it had been going on for a long time. The problems Smokey Yunick had with the comic book reading inspector, Bill Gazaway, at Daytona several years earlier paled in comparison.

Allison was furious but stated his case with clarity. "The cars were caught and they were illegal; the penalty is disqualification," Allison fumed. "Why are they changing the inspection system if the two cars were legal? I was told Sunday night by a member of the technical inspection crew that both cars were illegal. The guy said one [engine] was a whopper and the other was close but still too big." Allison said such things as the National 500 debacle was what kept NASCAR from becoming a major sport. "NASCAR hasn't helped us become a major league sport," he said. "If a good clean organization had been running stock car racing for the last twenty years, it would be ahead of professional football now."[43]

"I hate for Bobby Allison to get the racing world upset because he can't outrun a Junior Johnson Chevrolet," Cale Yarborough taunted. "If I was going to get caught for cheating," Richard Petty said, "it wouldn't be penny-ante stuff. It would be something super. With all my years in racing, do you think I would be stupid enough to cheat seven inches? That's not enough to mess with."[44]

Jackie Rogers, from Charlie Glotzbach's crew, told AP writer Dick Waters that he saw one of Petty's crew disconnect the carburetor breather to give the car more air and horsepower.[45]

Richard Howard was furious with the Frances and NASCAR. Howard railed that he had been paying the NASCAR technical inspectors all week to insure the cars were legal at his track and, after the race, NASCAR decided they were not inspected properly. "What have I been spending my money for?" he asked. "If they rule against the order of finish that the fans saw on Sunday, I'm going to court. By letting the cars start, NASCAR inspectors said they were OK. Now, they are reneging. I'm not bluffing about this. I'm sick and tired of seeing stuff like this be allowed to happen, possibly leading to the ruin of a great sport."[46]

Four days later, Allison said he was entertaining the idea of suing NASCAR and pulled his entry from the Rockingham race. He said he had been getting calls from people offering to put up the money for him to sue. He called what NASCAR had done at Charlotte grand larceny and compared the $6,815 he received for third place to the $43,425 Yarborough got for first and the $15,272 Petty received for second. Allison's threats to quit NASCAR attracted national attention to the debacle, none of which was favorable to stock car racing. Yet, William C. France allowed the situation to fester for a week before he had a meeting with Allison in Atlanta on October 15.[47]

Only those two people knew what happened in that meeting but there was immense speculation aroused by Allison's actions. Allison came out of the meeting saying the situation was resolved, he would race at Rockingham and had confidence that NASCAR would avoid such misunderstandings in the future. Tom Jensen, in his book *Cheating,* wrote that Allison said, "I have received satisfactory restitution and you can read that any way you want." Jensen said there were rumors that France wrote Allison a $50,000 check to make the issue go away.[48]

Herald-Journal columnist Gene Granger printed the news release sent out by NASCAR to the media saying it was a joint statement from both Allison and France. The news release quoted Allison as saying, "I am confident that NASCAR will take positive steps in the future to avoid any misunderstandings about rules and penalties. The meeting was most constructive and for the good of stock car racing." Granger was unsuccessful in attempting to reach Allison for a comment. He said another reporter contacted Allison's business manager and was told the driver would have no further comment on the subject.[49]

Tim Higgins and Steve Waid, in their biography of Junior Johnson, wrote that Allison later denied receiving any money from France. The authors also said that NASCAR promised to institute a post-race inspection at Rockingham to check carburetor plates, air cleaners and engines. Johnson, they wrote, swore his engine was not oversized and, if he was going to cheat, he would run an engine sized no less than 500 cubic inches.[50]

Lin Kuchler chimed in saying the restrictor plate device in Johnson's car was illegal since one of the plate holes that carried fuel and air to the engine was larger than the rules allowed. "What somebody's got and what NASCAR says he's got always creates some kind of conflict," Johnson said. "NASCAR just didn't have the right kind of measuring equipment you really needed to pinpoint if an engine was legal or if it wasn't legal." He explained that NASCAR procedure was to arrive at the total engine displacement by measuring one cylinder and multiplying that number by eight instead of measuring all of the cylinders individually.[51]

Ten days after the Charlotte race, France was still undecided if all cars would undergo post-race inspections. "We haven't determined the exact number yet," he said. "We haven't had a chance to discuss how many or how far back."

Bob Hoffman, racing columnist for *The Tuscaloosa News,* wrote, "Most people close to the inside of Grand National racing feel that NASCAR made a giant boo-boo in the way it handled the protests following the recent National 500 in Charlotte, North Carolina." Hoffman had some advice for France, "Perhaps what NASCAR needs to do is hire someone like Junior Johnson or Banjo Matthews as a chief technical inspector. Then, if the [engine] builders are smart enough to get something by those birds, call it legal and let it go!"[52]

What happened at the next race at Rockingham, on October 21, was no surprise. Yarborough's car was disqualified during time trials for having an oversized restrictor plate. "Everybody is playing it close to the vest," Richard Petty said. Chief technical inspector Bill Gazaway and NASCAR must have listened to Junior Johnson because, during the pre-race inspection of engines, they measured all cylinders, not just one as had been customary. Bobby Allison said, "There are just some people who are just not confident enough without cheating." Petty, who won the Rockingham pole at 135.748 mph, said, "The Charlotte thing is over with. This is a new controversy. I think somebody somewhere has a better way of checking engine sizes."[53]

An event occurred during the Rockingham race that could have given NASCAR much needed positive publicity if their public relations people had been on the ball. Benny Parsons only needed a good finish in the American 500 to win the Winston Grand National championship. On lap thirteen, Parsons was in the middle of a multi-vehicle collision and his car was so badly damaged a wrecker had to pull it to the garage area. Parsons sat on a bench in the garage and wept as he saw the championship slipping away from him.[54]

Parsons was held in such esteem by the racing fraternity that other teams sent all the men they could spare to help Parsons' crew repair his car. After an hour and a half, they had rebuilt the rear end, stripped all the sheet metal off the right side of his car and sent him back on the track. Although the car was handling badly, Parsons finished twenty-eighth and won the 1973 Winston Grand National Championship by sixty-seven points over Cale Yarborough. David Pearson won the American 500, boosting his winnings to $228,408, although he drove in ten fewer races than Parsons, who raced in all twenty-eight events. Yarborough won the most money, $268,513, followed by Richard Petty with $234,389.[55] Richard Childress and Darrell Waltrip finished fifteenth and twenty-eighth respectively in the points with winnings of $37,880 and $42,466.[56]

William C. France told reporters he was unsure how the shortage of gasoline would affect stock car racing in 1974. "We don't use that much gasoline in our stock car program," he said. Automobile racing was the seventh highest consumer of gasoline.[57]

France installed a new points formula for what had become Winston Cup racing. "The physical size of the track will not be a determining factor on a driver's entry but the amount of the promoter's posted awards will be," France said. He explained it this way: if a driver won $50,000 in track purses at twenty races, his total points would be $50,000 times twenty races times .001 to equal 1,000 points.[58]

Bill France, chairman of the National Motorsports Commission, said automobile racing had pledged to reduce their gas usage by twenty-five percent during the fuel shortage. "We will do that and as much more as we can reasonably do," France promised. He claimed nine million gallons of fuel was used annually on race tracks. Actually, the sport consumed 93.6 million gallons of gas a year. Riverside and Indianapolis tracks planned to reduce practice time. William C. France, after meeting with track owners and promoters, said NASCAR would reduce race distances by ten percent and, to make up the other fifteen percent cut, would use smaller fields and limit practice time.[59]

27

Ever Evolving NASCAR Rules

• • • • • • •

NASCAR had a few surprises before the 1974 Daytona 500. William C. France sent his executive vice-president, Lin Kuchler, out to make an announcement about the controversial restrictor plates. Kuchler said restrictor plates would be replaced by a small four barrel carburetor before the Atlanta 500 in March. He claimed final tests had been completed only two days earlier and said that was the reason for the late announcement. He asked the media to downplay the decision as it did not apply to the Daytona 500.[1]

Then, Kuchler made a statement that guaranteed every reporter, wire service and publication writing about automobile racing would carry the story. "With all running the same size carburetor," he said, "we hope to eliminate the discussion of who has the largest holes."[2]

Car owners and builders had to purchase the Holley carburetors from NASCAR for between $75 and $85.[3] Those carburetor sales were perfectly legal under NASCAR's by-laws, drafted by the late Louis Ossinsky in early 1949.

Car owner W. C. "Junie" Donlavey, from Richmond, Virginia, said he thought the move to similar carburetors would even things out. "All the mechanics I've talked to seem to like it. I've not heard one complaint," he said. Donlavey added that he still thought it would be hard to beat his chief rival, the Wood Brothers.[4]

Henry Hyde, chief mechanic for Nord Krauskopf's Dodge, said he would not be in any worse shape. "The rules give me an option," Hyde said. "I can stay with the Hemi engine or go to a smaller one. I like the idea." Krauskopf, who had already pulled his car from the Daytona 500 and the Carolina 500, said he would enter his car only when it was competitive.[5]

In the days leading up to the Daytona 500, the Frances' favorite sports editor, Kahn of the *Daytona Beach Morning Journal,* devoted columns to extolling the virtues of Bill France and his son. Kahn reached back to Charlotte's National 500 mess in an effort to paint NASCAR in the best possible light. He wrote that illegal skullduggery in racing garages was a very complex business that NASCAR tried very hard to curb. "But," he wrote, "detecting cheating by ingenious mechanics is a slippery game and the National Association for Stock Car Automobile Racing, Inc., leaders have had to tighten their inspection procedures to be a little more sure they are not being tricked by the tricksters."[6]

Kahn sang the praises of chief technical inspector Bill Gazaway. "Gazaway is an extremely competent automotive expert," Kahn wrote. "In the NASCAR hierarchy, Gazaway must take his final orders from the higher ups."[7]

Bobby Allison, Kahn wrote, was a hero for blowing the whistle on the engine situation at Charlotte. He quoted Allison as saying, "I think the way they're doing it now, there is less chance of a big illegal engine getting by inspection." Allison continued to maintain that Yarborough's and Petty's engines at Charlotte were illegal.[8]

Three days later, Kahn wrote another article about Bill France, then chairman of ACCUS. He went into great detail about how France had survived all his attackers over the years: Curtis Turner, the Teamsters, Larry LoPatin, the automobile manufacturers and the PDA boycott of the initial Talladega race. Kahn, as was his style, neglected to provide any details unflattering to his subject. Bill France, he concluded, was an absolute genius.[9]

Bill France, however, was not running NASCAR. William C. France was and, due to the constantly changing carburetor rules, nearly brought the sport to its knees in 1974. Gene Granger, racing columnist for the Spartanburg *Herald-Journal,* wrote that NASCAR rule changes were usually implemented at the France-owned Daytona speedway. However, there was a problem. Somebody at NASCAR had fouled up again. There were not enough of the small carburetors for all the cars in Winston Cup racing. The rule implementation was postponed until the Atlanta race.[10]

An early promoter foe of Bill France's resurfaced in stock car racing in 1974. Bruton Smith, whose nation-wide operation of automobile dealerships made him a multi-millionaire, had been quietly buying up shares of Charlotte Motor Speedway stock. Smith was determined to reclaim the track he and Curtis Turner built. In a bitter proxy fight, Smith defeated Richard Howard to reclaim the board chairman's position. There was irony everywhere in the battle. Smith was, of course one of the original builders, but Howard was the man credited with saving the track when it went into bankruptcy. The owner of furniture stores and restaurants, Howard said the Charlotte Motor Speedway grossed $1.7 million in 1973, and had a net profit of $170,000 after spending $270,000 for improvements.[11]

Another familiar face showed up for the Daytona 500. "I didn't realize how much Grand National [Winston Cup] racing meant to me until I quit," Bobby Isaac said. "Racing has been my life, has given me everything I have and it's hard to stay away from it." Isaac said he would probably drive a Banjo Matthews Chevrolet. He had lost none of his talent and finished sixth.[12]

Donnie Allison had a thirty-six second lead over Richard Petty when Bob Burchman, from Chattanooga, blew an engine. Allison ran over some of the wreck debris, which flattened one of his tires. He had to pit, finished sixth and Petty won the race. While Allison was pondering his bad luck, a woman asked if he would pose with her for a photograph. Allison kindly said he would. As the woman settled herself beside him for the photograph, she gushed, "You know, next to Richard [Petty], I think you and Bobby [Allison] are the greatest ever."[13]

"Coo Coo" Marlin charged that NASCAR stole the race from him when he was black flagged. "They said I was called back [to the pits] because I was missing a lug nut on a rear wheel," Marlin explained. "When I came in there was nothing wrong and they sent me back out. I think it was NASCAR's way of letting me know that was no way they are going to let me win a race."[14] Marlin raced in Grand National and Winston Cup competition from 1966 to 1980 and never won a race.[15] However, it was possible that his skill levels and equipment were not equal to those of the more successful drivers.

The first seven cars behind Petty's Dodge were the Chevrolets of Cale Yarborough, Ramo Stott, Coo Coo Marlin, A J. Foyt, Donnie Allison, Darrell Waltrip and Bobby Isaac.[16]

Since the Daytona speedway lacked turnstile counters, crowd counts were estimates. Sports columnist Kahn placed those attending the 500-mile race at 95,000. Apparently, the gas shortage was not a factor for travelers, as more than 225,000 crowded into Daytona Beach for 1974 Speed Week activities although the twenty-four-hour endurance race was cancelled. Bill France said all his grandstand tickets were sold for the race.[17] Multiplying the average ticket price of $18 and Kahn's estimated crowd suggests that the gate for the 500 mile race was in the neighborhood of $1,805,000. The race purse of $275,000 was just over fifteen percent of the gate.

William C. France asked the city commission to grant an ordinance to permit infield camping at the Daytona International Speedway for ten to twelve days before the 500-mile race and at least two days afterwards. Other campground owners fought the decision and asked for an injunction against Daytona International Speedway. The Frances received the usual legal home cooking in Daytona Beach when Judge J. T. Nelson denied the injunction. Campground owners threatened a continued legal fight.[18]

The 1974 Winston Cup racing season was one of extreme weather variations. The first race of the season, the Western 500, at Riverside, was postponed for a week due to rain. When the race was stopped at 164 miles, Bobby Allison had a three second lead on Petty. On the last lap of the resumed race, Petty sliced Cale Yarborough's thirty second lead down to five by the time they crossed the start-finish line. "I played a 'Cool Luke' hand there at the finish," Yarborough quipped. Pearson was third, Benny Parsons fourth and Bobby Allison fifth.[19]

The Southeastern 500, in March at Bristol, was run in a partial snow shower but 18,000 hardy souls turned out to see Yarborough win the race over Bobby Isaac. Yarborough credited the cold weather for making the race an enjoyable driving experience. "I didn't get tired," he said.[20]

Racing at Atlanta in the spring usually meant rain. The 1974 Atlanta 500 was different only in that a violent storm struck the track four days before the race. There was more than $250,000 in damage to the facility that was attempting to climb out of the bankruptcy of Larry LoPatin's American Racing, Inc., empire.[21]

The Atlanta race was no help for NASCAR's new carburetor program. Pearson, in his Wood Brothers Mercury, with a small 351 ci engine, blew everybody out with his pole qualifying speed of 159.242 mph. "Taking everything into consideration," Pearson said, "this has to be the best qualifying run I ever made in racing." Petty, who qualified tenth with a 426 ci Hemi engine in his Dodge, said Pearson blew NASCAR's whole case for the new carburetor. "David proved today that the small block engine was already competitive under the old rules," he added.[22]

"They [NASCAR] have really messed up things now," Cale Yarborough said. "We knew the big engine would last. That's the reason we came with it rather than the small engine." Petty scoffed at the longevity theory of the big engines. "I was the first one here to blow an engine in practice," he said. Cotton Owens, who maintained A. J. Foyt's Chevrolet that failed to qualify, said, "The new carburetor rule has killed the big engine. A lot of guys didn't have a chance to switch to the smaller engine but I'll bet all of them have one for the Rebel 500 on April 7."[23]

Races were won as much by circumstances as by equipment and drivers. Pearson had a lengthy pit stop of 30.6 seconds, went a lap down to Yarborough and was never able to catch him. "Had I been forced to pit under the green, I'd still be chasing him," Yarborough said after the race. Petty, who finished sixth in Atlanta, agreed with Yarborough. "Except for his unlucky element in his pit stop, Pearson would have had this won and nobody could have stopped him."[24]

Pearson had no pit problems in the Rebel 500 at Darlington in April, which was actually only 450 miles due to the gas situation, and he nosed out Bobby Allison for the win. Buddy Baker, Donnie Allison and Cale Yarborough followed them across the finish line. That was about as far as Pearson was able to drive his Mercury. His pit crew had to push him into the winner's circle. Richard Petty finished twentieth.[25]

Petty was determined such a finish would not occur a second time. He showed up at North Wilkesboro for the Gwyn Staley Memorial 400 in April with a hand built, $50,000 engine that was mid-range and fit NASCAR's new carburetor rules. Petty so dominated the short track race that he led all but thirty-six of the 360 laps. "We didn't know whether it would even run or not," Petty proffered, "but we figured North Wilkesboro was the place to try it." Petty said he always ran well at the track and if the engine held together they might have something for Talladega the next month.[26]

Petty's margin of victory over Yarborough, in a Chevrolet, was just under a mile. Bobby Allison, Benny Parsons and Lennie Pond followed in Chevrolets.[27]

Complaints over the carburetor rules had not lessened. Finally, Junior Johnson's car owner, Richard Howard, ferreted out the reason in early May. William C. France admitted that he was disappointed in his own rules and said NASCAR would keep trying until they got them right. That was only half the story. The president of NASCAR apparently had no idea about how to find the solution to the problem he created. Howard must have blown a gasket when he discovered that France and NASCAR had not run any carburetor tests before imposing the new rules. "They just picked a number," the outraged car owner said. "They didn't run any tests!" Howard said Cale Yarborough and Buddy Baker would test the carburetors at Talladega and Atlanta. "We wanted to include Darlington Raceway in the tests but the track reportedly has a big hole in it."[28]

Holley supplied the carburetors, Goodyear furnished the tires, France provided the inspectors and, apparently, Howard and Baker's team owner, Nord Krauskopf, risked their drivers and equipment to do the carburetor tests NASCAR neglected to do before imposing the new rule.[29]

The amiable Buddy Baker had finally had enough of Krauskopf entering his car and then withdrawing from races and the two parted ways. Krauskopf withdrew his Dodge from the World 600 because he said the carburetor rules rendered his car less competitive. Baker moved to the Bud Moore team to drive a Ford.[30]

NASCAR and France changed the carburetors rules again, ten days before the World 600 at Charlotte, because of complaints that the big engines' carburetors were not competitive with those on the smaller engines. The new regulations called for the big engine cars to use a carburetor with a 390 cubic foot per minute fuel flow on tracks less than 1.75 miles. On the larger tracks, the cars could use a carburetor with a 411 cubic foot per minute fuel flow.[31]

Junior Johnson said, after Yarborough and Baker's carburetor testing at Atlanta and Talladega, cars needed a carburetor in the 600 cubic foot per minute fuel flow range. Coo Coo Marlin said, "Every time they make a change, it takes about six months to find out what's going on. We [independents] have to test our engines on the track. The hotdogs can test theirs on a dynamo in their shops."[32]

Petty said the larger engines, even with the new rules, were still over 100 horsepower short of what the cars with smaller engines produced. He and Yarborough, the leading drivers in the Winston Cup points standing at that time, said that fact would not keep them from possibly boycotting NASCAR briefly to protest the current rules.[33]

Petty and Yarborough echoed what sports writers were saying about Winston Cup racing and NASCAR. In late April, Gary Logan, with the Wilmington, North Carolina, *News-Star,* wrote of the long list of problems that were plaguing NASCAR. "The major problems (in NASCAR) today range from charges of preferential treatment for certain drivers to seemingly endless rule changes to battles that keep popping up between the sanctioning body and its super stars."[34]

Logan said there were sometimes daily rule changes and car builders and drivers were complaining about that, as well as the costs and time involved in adjusting to one change before another came along. In addressing long-standing complaints about the biased interpretation of the rules, Logan suggested that NASCAR review its 136-page rulebook. "It is simply an ineffective document openly ridiculed and joked about by the most respected people in the sport."[35]

It was not just southern sports writers taking NASCAR to task. *Toledo Blade* sports writer Dave Woolford pointed out on June 14 that NASCAR had changed carburetor rules three times since March and planned another change after the Motor State 500 in Michigan on June 16. "Over the last four years," he wrote, "NASCAR had changed rules governing carburetor setups eight times."[36]

The May 26 World 600, reduced to 540 miles, was won by Pearson in his small engine Mercury by 1.6 seconds over Petty's Dodge that was involved in a spin with Cale Yarborough's Chevrolet. "We didn't see the oil and when I started sliding, I hit Cale. I got sideways but when I hit Cale he helped me get straight," Petty said of their close encounter. "Pearson pulled out coming off the second turn, passed me and pulled away before we got to the third turn. That was nothing but pure power anytime you can do that in a quarter of a mile."[37]

Behind the Pearson-Petty duel, Bobby Allison and Darrell Waltrip were fender to fender in their Chevrolets five laps behind the leaders. Allison won the battle by a few feet. Canadian driver Earl Ross, in a Chevrolet, was fifth. Yarborough came in eleventh.[38]

Tragedy struck again at the Winston 500 at Talladega in May. Donald Miller, the gas catch can man for the Matador crew of Gary Bettenhausen, was hit by a car driven by Grant Adcox, from Chattanooga, when it slammed into Bettenhausen's car in the pits. Dr. James L. Hardwick, the speedway's chief physician, said Miller would lose his leg below the knee.[39]

"While most did not want to be quoted," sports columnist Patrick Zier wrote, "there is a feeling among many crew chiefs that the NASCAR rule requiring crews to position a man behind the car to catch the overflow is primarily for show."[40]

On June 22, Bobby Allison announced he was cutting the work force at his Hueytown, Alabama, shop due to a lack of good racing parts. "Our Chevrolet is not competitive and we can't cope with the latest rule changes," he said. "I've got five engines of the small block design and now they are all illegal." Allison, who became NASCAR's third driver to win a million dollars, said he would concentrate on Sportsman races in Alabama and might not run in the Firecracker 400.[41]

It was possible the engine problems were part of the debacle at the June Motor State 400, in Brooklyn, Michigan. Only fourteen of the thirty-six cars were running at the finish.

Caution flags came out for some of the oil spills and debris on the track but not for others. Cars were dropping drive shafts, blowing engines and wrecking from the oil spills.[42]

Petty, who won the race, said J. D. McDuffie's car blew an engine and began dropping oil in front of him, but he managed to miss the slick. NASCAR's chief inspector Bill Gazaway denied McDuffie's car spilled any oil and refused to call a caution.[43]

While running third, Joe Frasson ran over debris left after Dean Dalton, from Asheville, North Carolina, dropped his drive shaft on the track. Frasson hit the wall and afterwards had a heated discussion with chief steward Johnny Bruner, Sr., about his failure to call a caution.[44]

Travis Tiller, from Triangle, Virginia, broke his oil pan due to debris on the track when Bruner failed to call a caution. "There was junk all over the track," Tiller said. "They [NASCAR] can see a piece of cloth on the track but they can't see a drive shaft? You've got to be kidding."[45]

Before the Firecracker 400, Glen Wood, Junior Johnson and Richard Petty asked NASCAR to set a maximum engine displacement, draw up a set of rules and stick to them. Wood said he was committed to the 351 Ford engine they had had been running since March. "Besides, that seems to be the direction they are pushing everybody toward," he added.[46]

Johnson said nobody could run with the Wood Brothers Mercury and the lax inspection procedures by NASCAR were partially responsible. "There's things getting by that just shouldn't be and as long as NASCAR is doing that, I'm not going to run a small engine," Johnson stated. Petty said the latest carburetor rule change restricted his Dodge. "A Hemi can't breathe right with it," he said. "All the rule changes are becoming too expensive." Petty suggested that NASCAR revert back to 1970 rules that limited engine size for everybody.[47]

The Daytona Speedway's Firecracker 400, run on the tenth anniversary of Glenn "Fireball" Roberts' death, was the first 1974 race to run its full distance after gasoline restrictions were lifted. Pearson and Petty again banged fenders while being critical of each other's driving after the race. Pearson said it was all about driving; Petty said it was all about dirty driving. Passing the grandstand and the crowd of 65,000 on the final lap, Pearson cut his Mercury's throttle with Petty's Dodge glued to his back bumper. "I never thought he'd let off that quickly with somebody so close behind," Petty fumed. "I had to let off otherwise I couldn't have turned the steering wheel enough to miss him." Pearson said Petty tried to run him into the pits. "I'd have wrecked him before I'd have gone on the grass," he added. Petty said he gave him a lane but neglected to mention that it was the track apron.[48]

With a slingshot move, Pearson, who sat on the pole, crossed the finish line by half a car length ahead of Petty. Their winnings were $18,000 and $10,925 respectively. Third place was even closer and more unusual. Buddy Baker in his Bud Moore Ford and Cale Yarborough in a Junior Johnson Chevrolet came across the finish line in a dead heat. Baker got more money, $6,087, to Yarborough's $5,912, because of equipment and qualifying money. Bobby Allison was fifth, $4,650, in Roger Penske's Matador.[49]

The Dixie 500 was held in Atlanta on July 28, and the usual happened. It rained on Friday and Saturday before the race. The media had a field day with driver interviews, when they could find them. Buck Baker hung out at his motel with his family. Cale Yarborough said he was just staying out of the rain. Bobby Allison was complaining about something and Petty put a piece of tape over his mouth. Pearson said he was trying to figure out something else he could do to beat Bobby Isaac. Charlie Glotzbach quipped he was spending his time listening to all the lies.[50]

Petty, Pearson and Baker were the top finishers in the Dixie 500 followed by Darrell Waltrip and Lennie Pond.[51]

The August 4 Pocono race, the Purolator 500, was unusual but for a different reason. Before the race, Petty was the best man at the track wedding of the president of his fan club, David Carter, from Raleigh. The race was halted four times by wrecks and rain but Petty won the contest in front of Baker, Yarborough, Pearson and Parsons. A. J. Foyt passed on the race and went to Talladega where, in an Indy car, he set the world's closed course speed record with 217.315 mph.[52]

Wendell Scott had his cars sabotaged during the 1960s but NASCAR never experienced anything like what happened before the August 11 Talladega 500. Eleven cars suffered damage from foreign substances in their gas tanks, tires slashed, belts sliced and handling mechanisms altered. The culprits, according to investigators, were racing insiders. Talladega County sheriff Gene Mitchell said, "Our security was based on keeping someone out rather than catching someone who was in there. We didn't suspect something like this—drivers or their crew members sabotaging each other." The garage was guarded by two security officers, outside the building. Mitchell said he needed to talk to every member of every crew but they had scattered across the country.[53]

According to the sheriff, there had been previous incidents of sabotage at other tracks. Mitchell said there appeared to be no link between the alleged sabotage to Lenny Pond's car at Atlanta and at Talladega. However, Mitchell surmised there was a link between the damage to Bobby Allison's car—wheat in the gas tank—at a recent race and at Talladega. He said it was unusual to put wheat in a gas tank.[54]

"The person who did it knew the top cars and went after them," Mitchell said. "It looks like he got the top qualifiers." The sheriff suspected the culprit hid in a van inside the garage, got out and did his work and got back in between the guards' rounds. Bobby Allison, suspicious since the earlier incident, inspected his car early Sunday morning, found the wheat and alerted the other teams.[55]

Petty, whose car had alignment damage, oil lines cut, tires slashed and sand in the gas tank, said the vandal did too much damage to his car. "If they really wanted to hurt somebody, they would have done only a little and then let the guys worry about it during the race. The toe-in adjustment on my car was so far out it was hard for the crew to push the car." The cars of Pearson, Yarborough, and Donnie Allison were also damaged. NASCAR allowed drivers to run the first thirty-nine laps of the race under the yellow flag to make sure their cars were functioning properly. It was another Pearson-Petty race to the finish line.[56]

"I used a cross draft and cut down real quick and was beside him before he knew it," Petty said. "He moved down a little and our cars hit each other and he let up a second. That's when I got ahead of him." Petty emphasized there was no revenge resulting from Pearson's sling shot move in the Firecracker 400. Rounding out the top five were Bobby Allison, Yarborough and Parsons.[57]

Don Naman, track manager, promised similar sabotage incidents would not happen again. Before the next race, he said, the garage would be surrounded by a ten-foot fence with barbed wire, high powered lights would flood the interior and three or four sentry dogs would prowl the garage at night.[58]

At the last race of the season, the Los Angeles Times 500 at Riverside, Bobby Allison was caught with an illegal tappet valve in his Matador. While Allison won the race, he was not required by NASCAR to forfeit the win. William C. France defended his decision to allow Allison to keep the win by pointing out the driver's fine of $9,100 was the largest ever levied against a winning car. Lin Kuchler, France's vice-president, said Allison's fine would be added to the points funds.[59]

In November 1974, both Frances were busy. Bill France's attorney, LaRue Williams, asked federal District Judge George Young not to take up the legal question of Volusia County's right to tax the Daytona International Speedway until the state courts reached a decision. William C. France was attempting to clean up the mess NASCAR had made with their ever-changing engine rules.[60]

According to driver Cecil Gordon, NASCAR sent out a bulletin saying that all Winston Cup cars would be required to use the small block engine and the rule would be applicable during the entire 1975 season. Gordon said by setting the rule in advance that a year would help car builders. "In the past," he said, "when you bought a piece of equipment it might be extinct overnight because of NASCAR's policy of experimenting with various rules changes."[61]

To nobody's surprise, Richard Petty won his fifth Winston Cup championship, with ten wins out of thirty races, for $432,020. Cale Yarborough was second, $363,782; David Pearson, third, $252,819; Bobby Allison, fourth, $178,437, and Benny Parsons, fifth, $185,080. Two young drivers, Richard Childress and Darrell Waltrip, won $50,249 and $67,775, and finished sixteenth and nineteenth respectively in the points standings. The average race purse increased from $88,097 in 1973 to $98,544.03 in 1974.[62]

Would the average stock car race purse have exceeded the $100,000 mark by 1974 had Willie K. Vanderbilt, or his successors, continued supervision of the sport? Willie K. paid forty percent of the gate into the race purse instead of the ten to twelve percent France was designated for that purpose. By 1974, which marked the twenty-fifth anniversary of NASCAR, Willie K. had been gone for three decades. The sport he established in 1908 followed a meandering route through measured mile events, beach-road racing, wooden tracks, dusty fairground venues and, finally, super speedways. along the way, illegal whiskey transporters forever stamped their southern imprint on stock car racing. Those transporters, or trippers, were the famous or infamous drivers who drew spectators to the tracks and provided the initial fiscal bedrock and sport needed.

Bill France built stock car racing from the base Willie K. established. The resemblance ended there. France was interested in making money; Vanderbilt had money.

France saw his chance to make money after the NASCAR organizational meeting in December 1947 in Daytona Beach. Those attending left thinking they had a nationally structured organization for their sport with a governing body made up of drivers, car owners, promoters and track owners. Two months later, they discovered that Bill France privately owned NASCAR, they had no part of it and the incorporation documents made it legal. Those legal documents only established NASCAR's base which began with a capital of $500. France cut corners whenever possible to save money. Race purses were minuscule. NASCAR races were sanctioned at tracks with little or no safety protection for either drivers or spectators. The resulting carnage over the years exceeded anything that Vanderbilt experienced with the stock car road races he organized and sanctioned in New York.

Vanderbilt's races were governed by ACA and AAA rules. France's rules of racing were as fluid as the oil in the cars' engines. Safety measures usually came after a famous driver was killed; after Joe Weatherly was killed at Riverside, France mandated window nets for the driver's side of the car, and after Fireball died from burns sustained in his fiery crash at Charlotte, France resisted a change from a metal to a rubber fuel cell but finally conceded. He refused to mandate the installation of impact-absorbing walls inside tracks, a change that might have saved scores of drivers from death or serious injury on the track.

France made the fortune he sought, ruled his drivers with an iron fist for years, built his mammoth tracks at Daytona and Talladega, and created the International Speedway Incorporation to own other tracks where NASCAR races were held but something unexpected happened to him in his later years. France developed Alzheimer's disease, which slowly robbed him of his memory and finally claimed his life in 1992.

William C. France struggled in his first few years running NASCAR but he did not deviate from the lessons learned from his father and his mother. He savored total control of the sport and was tight-fisted with money. As president until 2000, he took NASCAR to levels his father only dreamed about, overcoming various legal threats along the way. In all that time he refused to require the installation of softer walls inside the race tracks. Only when the sport's star driver, Dale Earnhardt, smacked the hard concrete wall of the Daytona International Speedway and was killed did William C. France require partial installation of softer race track walls. Despite or because of its danger, the sport privately owned by the France family had grown to become the second most popular spectator sport in America.

Chapter Notes

Introduction

1. Dan Pierce, *Real NASCAR: White Lightning, Red Clay and Big Bill France* (Chapel Hill: University of North Carolina Press, 2010), 213–214.

Chapter 1

1. Raymond Flowers, Michael Wynn Jones, *One Hundred Years of Motoring* (London: McGraw-Hill, 1981), 10.
2. Allen E. Brown, *History of America's Speedways Past and Present* (Comstock Park, Michigan: America's Speedways, 1984), xi.
3. *New York Times*, 23 March 1910. William R. Tuthill, *Speed on Sand* (Ormond Beach, Florida: Ormond Beach Historical Trust, 1978), 89, 95.
4. Sylvia Adcock, "Driving in the Fast Lane," lihistory.com/specpio/road.
5. flaglermuseum.us.org. volusia.org/history/speed. *Pittsburgh Press*, 1 October 1911.
6. vanderbiltcupraces.com.
7. *New York Times*, 25 April 1908.
8. *The Automobile*, Vol. 20, 25 March 1909, 493–494.
9. vanderbiltcupraces.com.
10. Douglas Nye, *The United States Grand Prix and Grand Prize Races* (Garden City, New York: Doubleday, 1978), 10. Julian Pettiffer and Nigel Turner, *Automania, Man and the Motor Car* (London: Guild, 1984), 39–40. Frank Coffey and Joseph Layden, *America on Wheels: The First 100 Years* (Los Angeles: General Publishing Group, 1996), 29.
11. Julian K. Quattlebaum, *The Great Savannah Races* (Athens: University of Georgia Press, 1957), 16.
12. Quattlebaum, xiv, xv, xvi.
13. Quattlebaum, xi, xii, xii.
14. Ibid.
15. Ibid. *New York Times*, 18 October 1911. americangrandprizeraces.com.
16. *New York Times*, 16 November 1908.
17. Ibid.
18. Quattlebaum, 44.
19. Nye, 13–15.
20. americangrandprizeraces.com.
21. *New York Times*, 20 March 1908
22. Quattlebaum, 44–45. Nye, 15.
23. Nye, 25.
24. Ibid. Quattlebaum, 44–45.
25. americangrandprizeraces.com. Nye, 16, 20, 26.
26. "Indy Speedway History," indymotorspedway.com. *New York Times*, 20 August 1909.
27. brooklands.org. brooklandsmuseum.com. "Indy Speedway History," indymotorspeedway.com.
28. Ed Hinton, "The First Indy Races Were Stockers," ESPN, 25 July 2009. indianapolismotorspeedway.com/history.
29. *New York Times*, 15 August 1909.
30. *New York Times*, 15, 20 August 1909. measuringworth.com.
31. *New York Times*, 20 August 1909.
32. *Indianapolis Star*, 20 August 1909.
33. *Indianapolis Star*, 20 August 1909.
34. Hinton, "The First Indy Races Were Stockers."
35. Ibid.
36. Ibid.
37. *Indianapolis Star*, 20 August 1909. vanderbiltcupraces.com.
38. *New York Times*, 20 August 1909.
39. indianapolismotorspeedway.com.
40. Hinton, "The First Indy Races Were Stockers."
41. *American Motorist*, Vol. 1, No. 6, July 1910, 264. *American Motorist* was published by the AAA.
42. Ibid.
43. indianapolismotorspeedway.com.; hemmings.com.; marmon.com.
44. *New York Times*, 2 January 1910.
45. Randal L. Hall, "Before NASCAR: The Corporate and Civic Promotion of American Automobile Racing in the American South, 1903–1927," *The Journal of Southern History*, Vol. 68, No. 3, August 2002, 629–668. Brown, xi.
46. *Motor World Wholesale*, Vol. 24–25, 4 August 1920.
47. *New York Times*, 26 March 1910.
48. *Reading Eagle*, 17 February 1919.
49. "Tommy Milton," Motorsports Hall of Fame and Museum. *Daytona Beach News-Journal*, 12 February 2003. "Sig Haugdahl," National Sprint Car Hall of Fame and Museum. William P. Lazarus, *The Sands of Time: A Century of Racing in Daytona Beach* (Champaign, Illinois: Sports Publishing, 2004), 49, 53. "Henry Segrave," booklandsracing.co.uk, National Motor Museum, Brockenhurst, England.
50. "Malcolm Campbell," bluebirdelectric.net/Campbell. racingcampbells.com. J.A. Martin and Thomas F. Saal, *American Automobile Racing: The Milestones and Personalities of a Century of Speed* (Jefferson, North Carolina: McFarland, 2004), 38. *Los Angeles Times*, 28 November 1924. Lazarus, 58–63. themanwhosuperchargedbond.com. theselvedgeyard.worldpress.com
51. *Daytona Beach Morning Journal*, 2 February 1959.
52. Ibid.

53. *St. Petersburg Times*, 22 February 1928. the selvedgeyard.worldpress.com. Martin and Saar, 38.
54. "Malcolm Campbell," racingcampbells.com. Tuthill, 127.
55. *Miami News*, 16 April 1936.

Chapter 2

1. Florida Department of State, Division of Corporations. Larry Gilson, reference/genealogical librarian, Volusia Public Library, City Island, Daytona Beach.
2. *Daytona Beach Sunday News-Journal*, 16 July 1974.
3. Ibid.
4. Sylvia Wilkinson, *Dirt Tracks to Glory: The Early Days of Stock Car Racing as Told by the Participants* (Chapel Hill, North Carolina: Algonquin Books, 1983), 20.
5. Ibid.
6. Ibid.
7. Ibid.
8. Sigmund O. Haugdahl biography, the National Sprint Car Hall of Fame and Museum. historicracing.com. *Dallas Morning News*, 18 February 1995. "Sig Haugdahl and the Wisconsin Special," floridamemory.com. Don Radbruch, *Dirt Track Auto Racing 1919–1941* (Jefferson, North Carolina: McFarland, 2004), 253. *The Popular Science Monthly* (New York: McClure, Phillips, 1922), July 1922, Vol. 101, No. 1, 63.
9. Bill Fleischman and Al Pearce, *Inside Sports NASCAR Racing* (Detroit: 1998), 4. buzmckim.com. *Miami News*, 20 February 1936. *Sarasota Herald-Tribune*, 2 March 1936.
10. *Sarasota Herald-Tribune*, 2 March 1936. *The Milwaukee Journal*, 9 March 1936.
11. *The Milwaukee Journal*, 9 March 1936.
12. Ibid.
13. Ibid. *Miami News*, 3 March 1936.
14. *Herald-Journal*, 17, 26 October 1924, 12 November 1925
15. Fleischman and Pearce, 12.
16. *News-Courier*, 14 April 1927.
17. Neal Thompson, *Driving With the Devil* (New York: Crown Publishers, 2006) 84–85. Fleischman and Pearce, 12. *Daytona Beach Morning Journal*, 12 March 1957, 28 January 1953. *St. Petersburg Times* 7 October 1944, 12 May 1951.
18. Dan Pierce, *Real NASCAR: White Lightning, Red Clay and Big Bill France* (Chapel Hill: University of North Carolina Press, 2010), 48.
19. Tuthill, 20.
20. *Daytona Beach Morning Journal*, 4 February 1950.
21. Fleischman and Pearce, 12.
22. *Reading Eagle*, 6 March 1955.
23. Ron Payle, *The Iowa State Fair in Vintage Postcards* (Charleston, South Carolina: Arcadia, 2006), 60 Papers of Gardner Willis "Sec" Taylor, State Historical Society of Iowa. "Ralph Hankinson," National Sprint Car Hall of Fame and Museum, 17 February 1990. *New York Times*, 5 August 1941. *Reading Eagle*, 13 April 1941.
24. *New York Times*, 5 August 1941. *Reading Eagle*, 13 April 1941. volusia.org/history.
25. Lazarus, *Sands of Time*, 87–90. Lazarus had written programs for International Speedway Corporation tracks.
26. "William 'Bill' France, Sr.," International Motorsports Hall of Fame. France's actual name was William Henry Getty France.
27. *Daytona Beach Morning Journal*, 13 February 2003. Neal Thompson, 210.
28. Neal Thompson, 86–88.
29. *Spartanburg Herald-Journal*, 17 July 1938.
30. *The Free Lance-Star* (Fredericksburg, VA), 21 June 1977. *The Wilmington Star-News*, 17 October 1976.
31. *Daytona Beach Morning Journal*, 24 June 1938.
32. *Lewiston Daily Sun*, 3 July 1981.
33. *Milwaukee Journal*, 4 June 1971.
34. *Daytona Beach Morning Journal*, 10 February 1938. *Daytona Beach News-Journal*, 1 February 1989.
35. *Daytona Beach Morning Journal*, 3 March 1939.
36. *Daytona Beach News-Journal*, 4 February 1989.
37. Neal Thompson, 109.
38. Neal Thompson, 109–110.
39. Steve Pappas, "Labor Rides a Motorcycle," *American Motorcyclist*, February 1956. *Daytona Beach Morning Journal*, 14 August 1940, 29 December 1954.
40. *Daytona Beach Morning Journal*, 12 March 1951, 28 January 1953, 22 February 1963. *St. Petersburg Times*, 7 October 1944, 12 May 1951.
41. *Daytona Beach Morning Journal*, 24 February 1940.
42. *Daytona Beach Morning Journal*, 20 June 1940.
43. Ibid.
44. *Daytona Beach Morning Journal*, 28 August 1940.
45. *Sarasota Herald-Tribune*, 2 September 1940. Lazarus, 100.
46. *St. Petersburg Times*, 31 March 1941.
47. *Daytona Beach Morning Journal*, 1 July 1941.
48. Ibid. Neal Thompson, 118–120.
49. *Evening Independent*, 25 August 1941. *Daytona Beach Morning Journal*, 1 July 1941.
50. *Miami News*, 10 April 1946. The number of spectators at a race was often questionable if the information came from those promoting the event.

Chapter 3

1. merriam-webster.com/dictionary/redneck.
2. Joe Menzer, *The Wildest Ride (Or How a Bunch of Good Ole Boys Built a Billion Dollar Industry Out of Wrecking Cars)* (New York: Simon & Schuster, 2001), 58–59.
3. Menzer, 59.
4. Betty Boles Ellison, *Illegal Odyssey: 200 Years of Kentucky Moonshine* (Bloomington, Indiana: 1st Books Library, 2003), 2.
5. Menzer, 59.
6. Ellison, 9.
7. Author's recollections.
8. Ellison, 80.
9. Wilkinson, 33.
10. Ibid.
11. Ibid.
12. Ibid.
13. Ibid.
14. Wilkinson, 33–34.
15. Wilkinson, 35.
16. Ibid.
17. Ibid.
18. Ibid.
19. Ibid.
20. Richard Petty and William Neely, *King Richard I: The Autobiography of America's Greatest Auto Racer* (New York: Macmillan, 1996), 39–40.
21. Petty, 39.
22. Petty, 42.
23. Petty, 45.
24. Petty, 46.
25. Petty, 47.
26. Petty, 48.
27. Ibid.
28. Ibid.
29. Petty, 49.
30. Ibid.
31. *Charlotte Observer*, 17 October 2009.
32. Ibid.
33. "Louis Jerome 'Red' Vogt," Living Legends of Auto Racing, llor.com.
34. lloar.com/interviews.
35. Ibid.
36. "Louis Jerome 'Red' Vogt," lloar.com/garage.
37. Keith Parsons, "NASCAR's First Champion Car Owner Reminisces About Early Days," *Associated Press*, 10 June 2002. Neal Thompson, 16–17.
38. "Raymond Parks," livinglegendsofautoracing.com. "NASCAR," georgiaencyclopedia.org.

39. "Senate Resolution 443," legis.state.ga.us/legis/2005.
40. Keith Parsons, "NASCAR's First Champion Car Owner Reminisces About Early Days," *Associated Press*, 10 July 2002.
41. Peter Golenbock, *NASCAR Confidential* (St. Paul, Minnesota: MBI, 2004), 25.
42. Wilkinson, 19.
43. Bloys Britt and Bill France, *The Racing Flag: NASCAR—The Story of Grand National Racing* (New York: Pocket Books, 1965), 32.
44. Britt and France, Introduction.
45. Menzer, 85.
46. *Charlotte Observer*, 17 October 2009.
47. Ibid. *Daytona Beach Morning Journal*, 12 March 1940. *The Gainesville Sun*, 1 July 1940.
48. Hugh Ruppersburg and John C. Inscoe, *The New Georgia Encyclopedia* (Athens: University of Georgia Press, 2007), Internet edition, Sports and Recreation, NASCAR. "Rapid Roy, That Stock Car Boy," lyrics from Jim Croce's *Greatest Hits* album.
49. Menzer, 85.
50. "Lloyd Seay," visitnortheastgeorgia.com/lloydseay.
51. Neal Thompson, 169, 173, 190–191.

Chapter 4

1. "Robert 'Red' Byron," decadesofstockcarracing.com.
2. Henry "Smokey" Yunick, *Best Damn Garage in Town* (Daytona Beach, Florida: Carbon Press, 2001), 27–34.
3. Ben A. Shackleford, "Going National While Staying Southern: Stock Car Racing in America, 1949–1979," Ph.D. dissertation, Georgia Institute of Technology, December 2004, 85, 125, 159–60
4. Golenbock, 102–103.
5. Ibid.
6. Ed Hinton, "Smokey's Shop Was Hallowed Ground," 26 April 2011, espn.com.
7. smokey.com.
8. "That's Racin,'" Tom Higgins, 20 March 2006.
9. Craft, 18–19, 123–124.
10. *Charlotte Observer*, 3 January 2013.
11. Robert Edelstein, *Full Throttle: The Life and Fast Times of NASCAR Legend Curtis Turner* (Woodstock, New York: Overlook Press, 2003), 14–15. Neal Thompson, 61.
12. "Joe Weatherly," joeweatherly.ama-cycle.com.
13. Mike Smith, "Wendell Oliver Scott," Thunderplex, Street and Smith Sports Group. "Wendell Scott," Hall of Fame, Danville (Virginia) Museum of Fine Arts and History.
14. Fleischman and Pearce, 5.
15. Mike Fish, "Founding Father," 14 February 2002, CNN-SI.com.
16. Ibid.
17. Ibid.
18. Ibid.
19. Ibid.
20. Yunick, 137.
21. Yunick, 137–38.
22. Ibid.
23. Yunick, 279.
24. Fish, "Founding Father."
25. Ibid.
26. Bob Latford, *NASCAR: A Celebration* (London: Carlton Books, 2002), 2.
27. Fish, "Founding Father."
28. Ibid.
29. Mendel L. Rivers Papers, University of Charleston, Special Collections.
30. *Daytona Beach Morning Journal*, 20 October 1974. Kahn said he found this and another letter from France while cleaning out some of his files at home.
31. *Commerce News Today*, 5 September 2008. Speedwaymedia.com.
32. *Daytona Beach Morning Journal*, 20 October 1974.
33. Scott Oldham, "Good Ol' Boys Turn 50, *Popular Mechanics*, August 1998.
34. Menzer, 66–67.
35. Ibid.
36. Fleischman and Pearce, 5–6.
37. "Raymond Parks," garhofa.com.
38. Neal Thompson, 242.
39. Neal Thompson, 243.
40. Email to author from June Wendt, 11 January 2003.
41. lowesmotorspeedway.com/track. Menzer, 96. "O. Bruton Smith," referenceforbusiness.com/biography.
42. National Stock Car Racing Association, Inc., number E706606, Georgia Secretary of State's Office.
43. *Orlando Sentinel*, 4 June 2006. "Ayr Mount Historic Site," presnc.org.
44. Interview with Marjorie Flock, 26 August 2006, Buford, Georgia.
45. Ibid.
46. *Daytona Beach Sunday News-Journal*, 16 July 1974.

Chapter 5

1. Arthur R. Ashe, Jr., *A Hard Road to Glory* (New York: Warner Books, 1998), 230.
2. Suzanne Wise, Appalachian State University, 3 November 2009, email to author. pbs.org/forthegoldandglory. Brian Katen, "Full Throttle: Racing and Rodding in Southwest Virginia," Blue Ridge Institute and Museum, Ferrum College. Brian Donovan, *Hard Driving: The Wendell Scott Story* (Hanover, New Hampshire: Steerforth Press, 2008), 28. Todd Gould, *For the Gold and Glory: Charlie Wiggins and the African American Racing Circuit* (Bloomington: Indiana University Press, 2002), 49.
3. Gould, 13–14. racingforsuccess.com. Antonia Sekula, reference librarian, Speedway Public Library, Speedway, Indiana, 9 November 2009, email to author.
4. *The Afro-American*, 4 July 1925. Gould, 41.
5. Gould, 41–43.
6. pbs.org/forthegoldandglory.racingforsuccess.com.
7. Gould, 41–43.
8. Gould, 44–45.
9. Ibid.
10. Gould, 45–48.
11. pbs.org/forthegoldandglory.media.ford.com/article.
12. Ibid.
13. Ibid.
14. pbs.org/forthegoldandglory. Gould, 29, 47, 50, 71.
15. Gould, 44–45.
16. Ibid.
17. Gould, 60–67.
18. Ibid.
19. Ibid.
20. *Detroit Free Press*, 10 April 1950. Gould, 47.
21. Gould, 54.
22. Ibid.
23. M. William Lutholtz, *Grand Dragon: D. C. Stephenson and the Ku Klux Klan in Indiana* (West Lafayette, Indiana: Purdue University Press, 1990), 22–54.
24. pbs.org/forthegoldandglory.
25. Gould, 84.
26. Gould, 78–81.
27. Gould, 86–88.
28. Gould, 80, 85–86, 90–91.
29. pbs.org/forthegoldandglory.
30. Gould, 90–91.
31. *Indiana Monthly*, May 2003, 46.
32. Gould, 93.
33. Gould, 93–94.
34. Ibid.
35. Ibid.
36. Ibid.
37. Ibid.
38. pbs.org/forthegoldandglory.
39. Gould, 93–94.
40. Ibid.
41. pbs.org/forthegoldandglory.
42. Ibid.
43. Ibid.
44. Ibid. Author's 10 November 2009 telephone call to Crown Hill Cemetery.

45. Rajo Jack, bio by Larry L. Ball, Jr., 2007 inductee class in the Sprint Car Racing Hall of Fame.
46. Ibid.
47. Ibid.
48. Francis Quinn, 2006 National Sprint Car Hall of Fame.
49. Ibid.
50. Ibid.
51. Charlie Curreyer, West Coast Stock Car Hall of Fame, 2000.
52. Rajo Jack.
53. Patrick Sullivan, *Brick By Brick: The Story of Auto Racing Pioneer Joie Ray* (Fishers, Indiana: 2008), 20, 68–78.
54. Sullivan, 112–113, 147, 181.
55. Sullivan, 147. *Dayton Daily News*, 17 April 2007.
56. *Dayton Daily News*, 17 April 2007.
57. Email, 11-13-09, from Michael Flug, senior archivist, Chicago Public Library, to author. Ashe, 230–231.
58. *Jet*, 5 March 1952. pbs.org/forthegoldandglory.
59. "Andy Granatelli," Barbara E. Mathews, M.D., American National Business Hall of Fame, anbhf.org/pdf/granatelli. Also in 1947, operating on an advertising-promotional budget of $1,500, Granatelli drew 24,942 fans to a hot rod competition at Soldier Field.
60. Ibid.

Chapter 6

1. *Daytona Beach Morning Journal*, 11 February 1973.
2. *Daytona Beach Morning Journal*, 13 February 1973. thatsracin.com, 15 May 2003. Pierce, 98–100. Phil Smith, "Looking Back," *Speedway Scene*, 21 April 2008.
3. Ibid.
4. Neal Thompson, 230.
5. Neal Thompson, 230. Britt and France, 16.
6. Neal Thompson, 231.
7. Ibid.
8. Flock interview.
9. Georgia Secretary of State's Office, Business Name History, 17 May 2006. The National Stock Car Racing Association, Inc., was chartered March 25, 1947, and was not dissolved until January 15, 2001.
10. Neal Thompson, 230–231.
11. *Daytona Beach News-Journal*, 14 February 2002.
12. Ibid.
13. Pierce, 189. *Spartanburg Herald-Journal*, 31 July 1989.
14. Shackleford, 65.
15. Author's telephone call to NASCAR archivist Eddie Roach, 8 June 2008.
16. Shackleford, 66–67. Neal Thompson, 231.
17. Shackleford, 68.
18. Shackleford, 72, 74.
19. Shackleford, 70–71.
20. Neal Thompson, 231.
21. Shackleford, 72–78.
22. Shackleford, 67–86. Neal Thompson, 233–234.
23. Neal Thompson, 234.
24. Neal Thompson, 234–235.
25. Ibid.
26. Florida Secretary of State's office. Neal Thompson, 235.
27. Neal Thompson, 241–242.
28. Shackleford, 86.
29. Neal Thompson, 235.
30. Application for Certificate of Authority, Foreign Corporation, #8875, North Carolina Secretary of State. Certification of Incorporation of National Association for Stock Car Auto Racing, Inc.
31. Ibid.
32. Ibid.
33. Ibid.
34. Ibid.
35. Ibid.
36. Ibid.
37. Ibid.
38. Florida Department of State, Division of Corporations; Daytona Parts, Inc., document number 524263.
39. Application for Certificate of Authority, Foreign Corporation, #8875, North Carolina Secretary of State. Certification of Incorporation of National Association for Stock Car Auto Racing, 18 February 1948, Florida Secretary of State's Office.
40. Ibid.
41. Ibid.
42. Ibid.
43. Florida Department of State, Division of Corporations.

Chapter 7

1. foxnews.com/sports/2010/05/13.
2. *The Miami News*, 28 December 1947.
3. *St. Petersburg Times*, 9 February 1948.
4. *Daytona Beach Morning Journal*, 11 February 1948. Neal Thompson, 245–248.
5. Ibid.
6. *The Palm Beach Post*, 8 August 1948. Neal Thompson, 246–247.
7. Ibid.
8. Neal Thompson, 252–253.
9. Auto Editors, *Consumer Guide*, "1948 NASCAR Modified Recap." ultimateracinghistory.com/racelist.php?year=1948.
10. *Herald-Journal*, 11 April 1948.
11. Ibid.
12. *Herald-Journal*, 5 July 1948. Pierce, 106.
13. *Herald-Journal*, 30 and 31 May 1948.
14. *The Dispatch*, 1 March 1948. Golenbock and Fielden, 871.
15. *The Dispatch*, 3 June 1948.
16. *Billboard*, 19 June 1948.
17. Ibid.
18. *Herald-Journal*, 30 May 1948.
19. *Herald-Journal*, 29 June 1948.
20. Neal Thompson, 258. Eddie Samples, GerogiaRacingHistory.com, 9 April 2010.
21. Neal Thompson, 258.
22. Auto Editors, *Consumer Guide*, "1949 NASCAR Modified Recap." *Consumer Guide* is a product of Discovery Communications, founded by former North Carolina State University professor Marshall Brain in 1998. Among Discovery Communications' operations is television's Discovery Channel.
23. Samples. Neal Thompson, 258–263. *New York Times*, 26 July 1948. *Columbus Ledger-Enquirer*, 26 July 1948.
24. *Columbus Ledger-Enquirer*, 26 July 1948.
25. Neal Thompson, 261–262.
26. Ibid.
27. Ibid.
28. Ibid.
29. Neal Thompson, 258–263. Samples.
30. *The Palm Beach Post*, 8 November 1948. *Billboard*, 8 November 1947.
31. *Herald-Journal*, 5 October 1948. Golenbock and Fielden, 876.
32. *Herald-Journal*, 5 October 1948.
33. Neal Thompson, 268–269.
34. Ibid.
35. *Charlotte Observer*, 1 February 1998. *St. Petersburg Times*, 13 February 1998.
36. *Consumer Guide*, "1948 NASCAR Modified Standings." indianapolismotorspeedway.com.
37. Fleischman and Pearce, 6.
38. Neal Thompson, 274–275, 393.
39. Auto Editors, *Consumer Guide*, "1948 NASCAR Modified Recap."
40. Ed Hinton, *Daytona From the Birth of Speed to the Death of the Man in Black* (New York: Warner Books, 2001), 71.
41. Edelstein, 55.
42. ESPN.com, 12 April 2012.
43. Ibid.

Chapter 8

1. *Daytona Beach Morning Journal*, 11 February 1972.

2. Florida Department of State, Corporate Records, #173496.
3. *The Owosso Argus-Press*, 28 June 1948.
4. *The Owosso Argus-Press*, 28 July 1949.
5. *Daytona Beach Morning Journal*, 17 January 1949.
6. Ibid.
7. *The Miami News*, 21 January 1949.
8. *Palm Beach Post*, 23 January 1948.
9. *Herald-Dispatch*, 5 January 1949. *Consumer Guide*, "1949 NASCAR Strictly Stock Chronology."
10. *Reading Eagle*, 7 April 1949.
11. foxnews.com, "Speed-TV," 13 May 2010.
12. Eddie Samples, *Pioneer Pages*, March 1999. Jay Jarvis, *Georgia's Crime Doctor* (nc, 2009), 95.
13. Samples.
14. *Herald-Journal*, 19 March 1949.
15. *Reading Eagle*, 8 February 1949.
16. *Daytona Beach Morning Journal*, 17 March 1949.
17. Ibid.
18. Pierce, 119. bowmangrayracing.com/history.
19. bowmangrayracing.com/history.
20. *Daytona Beach Morning Journal*, 25 October 1948. *Pioneer Pages*, March 1999 article by Eddie Samples.
21. *Herald-Journal*, 16 March 1949.
22. Neal Thompson, 281–281. Pierce, 112. Mark D. Howell, *From Moonshine to Madison Avenue* (Bowling Green, Ohio: Bowling Green State University Popular Press, 1997), 22–23.
23. Neal Thompson, 280–281.
24. Ibid.
25. Neal Thompson, 287.
26. Yunick, 189.
27. Neal Thompson, 280–281. Howell, 22–23.
28. *Consumer Guide*, "1948 NASCAR Modified Results."
29. Neal Thompson, 281. Bob Zeller, *Car and Driver*, 4 June 2006.
30. Neal Thompson, 282.
31. Allen Madding, "Lakewood Speedway—Atlanta's Original Race Track," speedwaymedia.com.
32. *Herald-Journal*, 3 May 1968.
33. *Atlanta Journal-Constitution*, 5, 8, 13 June 1949.
34. Edelstein, 56.
35. Neal Thompson, 186.
36. Pierce, 112.
37. *The Milwaukee Sentinel*, 12 June 1953. *Daytona Beach Morning Journal*, 7 January 1953. *The Miami News*, 30 May 1953. Peter Golenbock and Greg Fielden, editors, *Stock Car Racing Encyclopedia* (New York: Macmillan, 1997), 402.
38. *The Dispatch*, 6 June 1949.
39. *The Daily Press* (Newport News, Va.), 15 March 2003.
40. Ibid.
41. Ibid. Neal Thompson, 292. Edelstein, 57–58.
42. Edelstein, 57–58. *The Daily Press*, 15 March 2003.
43. *The Daily Press*, 15 March 2003. *The Southeastern Missourian*, 22 September 1949. *Motorsports*, 18 June 2009.
44. *Daytona Beach Morning Journal*, 23 February 1963, 11 February 1973.
45. Auto Editors, *Consumer Guide*, "1949 NASCAR Strictly Stock Chronology." Neal Thompson, 299.
46. Auto Editors, *Consumer Guide*, "1949 NASCAR Strictly Stock Chronology."
47. Sidney Cruze, "They're Kicking Up Dust Again at the Orange Speedway," *Carolina Country*, January 2004. historicspeedwaygroup.org, Strictly Stock Race No. 3. The name of the speedway was changed in the 1950s.
48. *The Southeast Missourian*, 22 September 1949.
49. Ibid.
50. Auto Editors, *Consumer Guide*, "*1949* NASCAR Strictly Stock Standings."
51. Edgar Otto and Joann Biondi, *Ed Otto: NASCAR's Silent Partner* (Newburyport, Massachusetts: Costal 181, 2008), 67.
52. Ibid.
53. Certificate of Incorporation of National Association for Stock Car Auto Racing, Inc., 1.
54. *Bluefield Daily Telegraph*, 22 March 2009.
55. Ibid.
56. Ibid.
57. Auto Editors, *Consumer Guide*, "1949 NASCAR Strictly Stock Chronology and Standings."
58. Ibid.
59. Ibid.
60. Ibid.
61. aintree.co.uk/grand-national.

Chapter 9

1. *Daytona Beach Morning Journal*, 11 February 1973.
2. *Daytona Beach Morning Journal*, 4 February 1950. *The Miami News*, 6 February 1950. Auto Editors, *Consumer Guide*, "1950 NASCAR Grand National Results."
3. *Daytona Beach Morning Journal*, 4 February 1950. *The Miami News*, 6 February 1950.
4. *Daytona Beach Morning Journal*, 30 September 1950.
5. *Edmonton Journal*, 2 April 2010.
6. hemmings.com/clubs/roadraceslincoln.
7. Daryl Murphy, *Carrera Panamericana: History of the Mexican Road Race 1950–1954* (Bloomington, Indiana: Motorbooks International, 2008), 3–4.
8. Neal Thompson, 315–321.
9. Ibid.
10. Edelstein, 63–68.
11. Ibid.
12. Ibid.
13. hemmings.com/clubs/roadracelincoln. motortrend.com, Frank Markus, "The Legends of the Great Road Races Seminar," 11 March 2007.
14. Edelstein, 14–15. "King of the Wild Road, Curtis Turner," *Sports Illustrated*, 26 February 1968. Yunick, 284.
15. *Daytona Beach Morning Journal*, 5 February 1957.
16. Auto Editors, *Consumers Guide*, "1950 NASCAR Grand National Standings."
17. *The Reading Eagle*, 7 April 1950.
18. *The Item*, 5 February 1996. *Daytona Beach Morning Journal*, 22 August 1964.
19. *The Item*, 6 February 1996.
20. Ibid.
21. Ibid.
22. darlingtonracewayhistory.com. motorracingnetwork.com/tracks.
23. *Herald-Journal*, 23 May 1950.
24. *Daytona Beach Morning Journal*, 22 April 1964. *The Rock Hill Herald*, 13 September 1951.
25. Hinton, 76. *The Rock Hill Herald*, 13 September 1951. Neal Thompson, 323.
26. *Herald-Journal*, 30 August 1950.
27. Hinton, 77.
28. Ibid.
29. Edelstein, 83. Neal Thompson, 325.
30. Kim Chapin, "Get the Good Times Rolling," *Sports Illustrated*, 4 September 1972.
31. Ibid. *Daytona Beach Morning Journal*, 22 June 1982.
32. *New York Times*, 10 May 2008.
33. *The Item*, 6 February 1996.
34. *New York Times*, 10 May 2008.
35. *Gainesville Sun*, 13 February 1987.
36. *USA Today*, 5 May 2005. Neal Thompson, 326.
37. Auto Editors, *Consumer Guide*, "1950 Grand National Chronology."
38. Neal Thompson, 327.
39. Ibid.
40. Neal Thompson, 328.
41. *Congressional Record*, 5 August 1999, 19849–19850.
42. *Daily Press*, 3 September 1989.
43. Ibid.

44. *The Dispatch*, 3 October 1950. *Herald-Journal*, 10 December 1950.
45. Ibid.
46. Ibid. *Chicago Tribune*, 11 December 1950.
47. *Herald-Journal*, 7 November 1950.
48. Auto Editors, *Consumer Guide*, "1950 NASCAR Grand National Chronology."
49. Ibid.
50. Bob Zeller, *Car and Driver*, July 2003.
51. Ibid.
52. Fleischman and Pearce, 11–12. Golenbock and Fielden, 933–934.
53. *Daytona Beach Morning Journal*, 17 February 1951.
54. Golenbock and Fielden, 367, 379, 402.
55. *Detroit News*, 29 January 2001.
56. *Billboard*, 24 December 1949. Robert G. Hagstrom, *The NASCAR Way: The Business That Drives the Sport* (New York: Wiley, 1998), 47–48.
57. Ibid.
58. *The Dispatch*, 2 October 1950.
59. *Kentucky New-Era*, 6 July 1954. Auto Editors, *Consumer Guide*, "1951 NASCAR Grand National Chronology."
60. *Daytona Beach Morning Journal*, 22 August 1964.
61. Golenbock and Fielden, 933.
62. *Herald-Journal*, 3 September 1951.
63. *The Rock Hill Herald*, 13 September 1951.
64. Author's telephone conversation with Buzz Rose, 21 June 2010.
65. *Los Angeles Times*, 8 September 1952. *Milwaukee Sentinel*, 12 July 1952. *Milwaukee Journal*, 9 April 1955. *The Miami News*, 30 May 1953. *Chicago Tribune*, 23 November 1951.
66. hemmings.com/club/roadraces lincolns. Larry Edsall and Mike Teske, *Ford Racing Century: A History of Ford Motorsports* (Minneapolis: Motorbooks International, 2003), 62–65. Daryl Murphy, *Carrera Americana: History of the Mexican Road Race, 1950–1954* (Bloomington, Indiana: iUniverse, 2008), 58–59, 87.
67. Auto Editors, *Consumer Guide*, "1951 NASCAR Grand National Chronology." Golenbock and Fielden, 296.
68. Auto Editors, *Consumer Guide*, "1951 Grand National Results." Fleischman and Pearce, 12.
69. Fleischman and Pearce, 12–13.
70. *Daytona Beach Morning Journal*, 5 February 1951.
71. Golenbock and Fielden, 934.
72. "Evolution of Stock Cars," nascar.com, 24 March 2008.
73. Wilkerson, 38.
74. Ibid.
75. Jon Cullimore, *Trucking*, 18 April 2000. canadianracing.com. legendsofstockcarracing.com/buddy_shuman.
76. *The News and Courier*, 11 May 1952. *The Palm Beach Post*, 1 January 1953. *Daytona Beach Morning Journal*, 19 February 1958.
77. Ibid. Golenbock and Fielden, 914.
78. *Daytona Beach Morning Journal*, 25 August 1955.
79. *The Miami News*, 5 July 1952.
80. Brandon Reed, autoracing1.com/nascar, 26 December 2002. *The Rock Hill Herald*, 16 August 1952. Auto Editors, *Consumer Guide*, "1952 NASCAR Grand National Chronology."
81. *News and Courier*, 2 September 1952.
82. *Herald-Journal*, 15 February 1998.
83. *Herald-Mail*, 14 May 2007. Golenbock and Fielden, 934.
84. Fleischmann and Pearce, 13.

Chapter 10

1. Certificate of Incorporation of National Association for Stock Car Racing, Inc., 5–6, 8.
2. Otto and Biondi, 79–80. *Palm Beach Post*, 5 March 2006.
3. Otto and Biondi, 80.
4. *Daytona Beach Morning Journal*, 22 February 1958.
5. *Daytona Beach Morning Journal*, 5 February 1952.
6. *Daytona Beach Morning Journal*, 8 February 1952.
7. Ibid.
8. *The Palm Beach Post*, 10 February 1952.
9. Ibid.
10. *Daytona Beach Morning Journal*, 8 February 1952.
11. *Daytona Beach Morning Journal*, 20 March 1952.
12. Fleischman and Pearce, 11–12.
13. *Daytona Beach Morning Journal*, 4 November 1951.
14. *The Palm Beach Post*, 18 October 1953.
15. *The Palm Beach Post*, 16 October 1953.
16. *The Palm Beach Post*, 18 October 1953.
17. Ibid.
18. *Daytona Beach Morning Journal*, 22 October 1953.
19. Ibid.
20. Florida Department of State, Division of Corporations, Amendment, Certificate of Incorporation of the National Association for Stock Car Auto Racing, 26 October 1953.
21. *Daytona Beach Morning Journal*, 9 November 1957.
22. *Daytona Beach Morning Journal*, 5 November 1954.
23. *Daytona Beach Morning Journal*, 12 January 1955.
24. *Daytona Beach Morning Journal*, 22 March 1956.
25. Ibid.
26. *Time*, 12 April 1958.
27. Certificate, Florida Department of State, 29 March 1957.
28. Ibid.
29. *Daytona Beach Morning Journal*, 28 October 1957.
30. *Daytona Beach Morning Journal*, 8 November 1957.
31. Ibid.
32. Ibid.
33. Florida Department of State, Division of Corporations, document number 173496. *Daytona Beach Morning Journal*, 21 February 1958.
34. Wilkinson, 28.
35. Florida Secretary of State's Office. Brock Yates, *NASCAR Off the Record* (Minneapolis, Minnesota: Motorbook International, 2004), 190.
36. Peter C. Cook biography, The Hauenstein Center for Presidential Studies, Grand Valley State University. *News-Journal*, 1 April 1987.
37. *Ocala Star-Banner*, 1 June 1959. hauesteincenter.org/peter-cook-biography.
38. Mark Aumann, nascar.com, 4 February 2008. *Daytona Beach Morning Journal*, 26 February 1961, 8 December 1972.
39. Ibid.
40. Wilkinson, 29.
41. Ben Stewart, "Deep in The Heart of Dixie, *Popular Mechanics*, 1 October 2009. Mark Aumann, "How Daytona International Speedway Was Created," nascar.com, 4 February 2008.
42. *Daytona Beach Morning Journal*, 29 April 1958.
43. *The Miami News*, 16 November 1958.
44. Ibid.
45. *New York Times*, 2 November 1958.
46. *Daytona Beach Morning Journal*, 24 January 1959.
47. *Daytona Beach Morning Journal*, 29 April 1959.
48. *Daytona Beach Morning Journal*, 24 January 1959.
49. *Daytona Beach Morning Journal*, 7 February 1959.
50. *Herald-Journal*, 10 January 1988.

Chapter 11

1. *Roanoke Times*, 18 September 2003.

2. Hinton, 82–83.
3. *Daytona Beach Morning Journal*, 3 February 1953, 3 September 1955.
4. Fleischman and Pearce, 15–40. Golenbock and Fielden, 933–948.
5. *News-Journal*, 22 June 1958.
6. *Daytona Beach Morning Journal*, 11 February 1952. *Sarasota Herald-Tribune*, 11 February 1952.
7. *St. Petersburg Times*, 11 February 1952. *Sunday Herald*, 10 February 1952.
8. *Palm Beach Post*, 10 February 1952.
9. *Daytona Beach Morning Journal*, 10 February 1956.
10. Auto Editors, *Consumer Reports*, "1952 NASCAR Grand National Chronology."
11. Auto Editors, *Consumer Guide*, "1953 Grand National NASCAR Recap."
12. *The Palm Beach Post*, 11 July 1953.
13. Ibid.
14. Fleischman and Pearce, 13.
15. *The Pittsburgh Press*, 7 February 1953.
16. Ibid.
17. arcaracing.com.
18. Wilkinson, 45.
19. *Daytona Beach Morning Journal*, 19 February 1955.
20. Fleischman and Pearce, 12–15.
21. *The Palm Beach Post*, 22 February 1954. *The Tuscaloosa News*, 2 February 1954.
22. Jeffrey L. Rodengen, *Iron Fist: The Lives of Carl Kiekhaefer, Industrial Caesar of a Marine Industry Empire* (Ft. Lauderdale, Florida: Write Stuff Syndicate, 1991), 251.
23. *Herald-Journal*, 14 May 2007. Fleischman and Pearce, 10.
24. *The Sun*, 7 July 1953. *Herald-Mail*, 14 May 2007.
25. *The Palm Beach Post*, 22 February 1954. *Daytona Beach Morning Journal*, 22 February 1954.
26. *Daytona Beach Morning Journal*, 18 February 1954.
27. Golenbock and Fielden, 935.
28. *The Modesto Bee*, 25 August 1954.
29. Ibid.
30. *Rock Hill Herald*, 7 September 1954. darlingtonraceway.com.
31. *Sarasota Journal*, 15 August 1954. Yunick, 275.
32. Fleischman and Pearce, 14–15.
33. *Gettysburg Times*, 8 April 1955. Golenbock and Fielden, 935.

Chapter 12

1. *Milwaukee Journal*, 22 December 1994.
2. Ibid. *Daytona Beach Morning Journal*, 5 November 1983.
3. Rodengen, 247.
4. Rodengen, 247–248.
5. Rodengen, 250
6. Rodengen, 248–249.
7. Wilkinson, 38, 40.
8. *Daytona Beach Morning Journal*, 28 February 1955.
9. Wilkinson, 40.
10. Rodengen, 253.
11. *Daytona Beach Morning Journal*, 24 February 1955, 26 February 1955. *The Miami News*, 27 February 1956.
12. Ibid. *Daytona Beach Morning Journal*, 22 May 1956.
13. Ibid.
14. Wilkinson, 41. *News-Observer*, 5 March 2010.
15. Fleischman and Pearce, 15.
16. Rodengen, 254–255.
17. Ibid.
18. Rodengen, 255–256.
19. Ibid.
20. Rodengen, 247.
21. Rodengen, 261–263.
22. Ibid.
23. Hinton, 80.
24. *Herald-Journal*, 2 June 1955.
25. Golenbock and Fielden, 30.
26. *Hartford Courant*, 25 October 1954. *Milwaukee Sentinel*, 12 July 1953. *Lodi News-Sentinel*, 22 August 1955.
27. Edelstein, 99–100.
28. Ibid.
29. Ibid.
30. Fleischman and Pearce, 15–16.
31. *The Rock Hill Herald*, 25 April 1955.
32. *Daytona Beach Morning Journal*, 4 June 1957.
33. Golenbock and Fielden, 936937.
34. *The Rock Hill Herald*, 15 May 1962.
35. foxnews.com/sports.
36. Ibid.
37. *Daytona Beach Morning Journal*, 13 February 1956.
38. *Daytona Beach Morning Journal*, 13, 16 February 1956. MacLane, an accomplished musician and playwright, played the heavy who beat up Humphrey Bogart in *The Maltese Falcon* and shady contractor Pat McCormick in *The Treasure of the Sierra Madre*. imdb.com/name.
39. *Daytona Beach Morning Journal*, 16 February 1963.
40. *Daytona Beach Morning Journal*, 18 February 1956.
41. Ibid.
42. Ibid.
43. Ibid.
44. *Lakeland Ledger*, 12 March 1998.
45. Ibid.
46. *Chicago Tribune*, 30 April, 23 August 1951; 22 September 1952; 29 August 1953; 31 July 1954; 16 August 1968. *Post-Tribune*, 17 August 1988.
47. Ibid.
48. Wilkinson, 41.
49. Ibid. Fleischman and Pearce, 321. Rodengen, 271.
50. Rodengen, 260–261.
51. Ibid.
52. Rodengen, 259, 271.
53. *The Times-News*, 11 June 1956. *Reading Eagle*, 10 June 1956.
54. *Sarasota Herald-Tribune*, 21 November 1955.
55. *New York Times*, 5 July 1956.
56. Jim McLauren, *NASCAR's Most Wanted* (Washington, DC: Potomac, 2001), 193.
57. *Hartford Courant*, 6 August 1956. *New York Times*, 5 August 1956.
58. Golenbock and Fielden, 846.
59. *The Dispatch*, 15 October 1956.
60. *Daytona Beach Morning Journal*, 21 January 1956.
61. Hinton, 80–81.
62. Hinton, 81–82.
63. *Times-Daily*, 15 April 1953. *Desert News*, 9 November 1953. *Milwaukee Journal*, 6 December 1956.
64. bioguide.congress. *The Pittsburgh Press*, 12 July 1955. *The Spokesman Review*, 13 July 1955.
65. saferoads.org/federal2000/trafficaccidents/1899–2003.
66. *Milwaukee Journal*, 6 December 1956. *St. Petersburg Times*, 27 May 1956. *Times-Daily*, 28 December 1956.
67. *Los Angeles Times*, 1 September 1956.
68. *Lodi News-Sentinel*, 25 May 1956. *Chicago Tribune*, 26 May 1956.
69. Edelstein, 107–108.
70. Fleischman and Pearce, 16. foxnews.com/sports/2010/05/13/cup-origins.
71. Ibid. *Sarasota Herald-Tribune*, 16 November 1956.
72. *Herald-Journal*, 25 October 1956.
73. Fleischman and Pearce, 16, 321.
74. *Daytona Beach Morning Journal*, 4 July 1956.
75. *Sarasota Herald-Tribune*, 30 August 1956. *Milwaukee Journal*, 18 June 1957.
76. Fleischman and Pearce, 16–17.
77. *Daytona Beach Morning Journal*, 31 December 1956.
78. Petty, 149.
79. Petty, 149–150.
80. Fleischman and Pearce, 18.
81. *Circle Track*, February 2009. Pierce, 86. *News and Observer*, 28 March 2010.
82. *Circle Track*, February 2009.
83. Ibid.
84. *Daytona Beach Morning Journal*, 3 February 1957.

85. Ibid. *Daytona Beach Morning Journal*, 9 February 1957.
86. Rodengen, 265.

Chapter 13

1. *Daytona Beach Morning Journal*, 16 January 1955.
2. Ibid.
3. *Daytona Beach Morning Journal*, 12 February 1956.
4. Ibid.
5. Ibid.
6. *Daytona Beach Morning Journal*, 3 February 1957.
7. *The Robesonian*, 12 February 1957.
8. *Daytona Beach Morning Journal*, 17 February 1957.
9. Ibid. *Sarasota Herald-Tribune*, 19 December 1956.
10. *Daytona Beach Morning Journal*, 17 February 1957.
11. *Daytona Beach Morning Journal*, 1 May 1957.
12. Ibid.
13. Ibid.
14. Ibid.
15. Ibid.
16. *The Deseret News*, 22 January 1957.
17. Ibid.
18. Ibid.
19. *Daytona Beach Morning Journal*, 12 February 1957. Some of the automobile company executives who flew into Daytona Beach included Ed Cole, GM vice-president; F. C. Rerth, Ford vice-president; Edward Quinn, Chrysler president; M. C. Patterson, Dodge president; Jack Mansfield, Plymouth president; S. E. Knudsen, Pontiac vice-president, and Harley Earl, GM vice-president in charge of design.
20. *St. Joseph Gazette*, 13 February 1957. *New York Times*, 17 February 1957. *Daytona Beach Morning Journal*, 2, 16 February 1957. *St. Petersburg Times*, 16 February 1957.
21. *Daytona Beach Morning Journal*, 16 February 1957.
22. Ibid. *Daytona Beach Morning Journal*, 12 January 1957.
23. *Anderson Independent Mail*, 27 May 2009.
24. *The Lewiston Daily Sun*, 4 June 1957. *New York Times*, 5 June 1957.
25. saferoads.org/federal/2004/trafficfatalities1899-2003.pdf.
26. *Daytona Beach Morning Journal*, 7 June 1957.
27. Ibid.
28. Ibid.
29. *Herald-Journal*, 7 June 1957.
30. *The Dispatch*, 4 September 1957.
31. Yunick, 223.
32. Ibid.
33. Yunick, 223–224.
34. Yunick, 224.
35. Ibid.
36. *Daytona Beach Morning Journal*, 19 February 1957, 15 February 1973.
37. hamidcircus.com/about. *The Miami News*, 16 April 1966.
38. *Daytona Beach Morning Journal*, 9 February 1958.
39. Ibid.
40. Ibid.
41. Ibid.
42. Pierce, 45. *Daytona Beach Morning Journal*, 22 February 1963.
43. Edelstein, 166.
44. *Daytona Beach Morning Journal*, 23 February 1958.
45. Ibid.
46. Ibid.
47. Ibid.
48. Ibid.
49. Ibid.
50. fhwa.dot.gov/infrastructure/safety.
51. *Daytona Beach Morning Journal*, 23 February 1958.
52. *Daytona Beach Morning Journal*, 21, 24 February 1958.
53. Ibid.
54. Ibid.
55. *Reading Eagle*, 5 May 1958. *The Daytona Beach Sunday News-Journal*, 8 June 1958. *The Palm Beach Post*, 27 May 1958.
56. *Daytona Beach Morning Journal*, 29 May 1958.
57. *Reading Eagle*, 11 May 1958.
58. *The Palm Beach Post*, 27 May 1958. *Sarasota Herald*, 31 May 1958.
59. *Herald-Journal*, 31 August 1958.
60. *The Dispatch*, 4 June 1958. *The Daytona Beach Sunday News-Journal*, 8 June 1958.
61. *The Daytona Beach Sunday News-Journal*, 22 June 1958.
62. *Daytona Beach Morning Journal*, 5 July 1958. *The Daytona Beach Sunday News-Journal*, 29 June 1958.
63. *The Rock Hill Herald*, 30 August 1958.
64. *The Palm Beach Post*, 2 September 1958.
65. Ibid.
66. *The Loris Sentinel*, 9 July 1958.
67. Fleischman and Pearce, 18–19.

Chapter 14

1. *Daytona Beach Morning Journal*, 25 January and 10 February 1959.
2. Yunick, 274.
3. *Daytona Beach Morning Journal*, 17 February 1959.
4. Ibid. *News-Journal*, 9 February 1959.
5. *Daytona Beach Morning Journal*, 25 January 1959.
6. Yunick, 274.
7. Ibid. *Daytona Beach Morning Journal*, 10 February 1959.
8. *Daytona Beach Sunday News-Journal*, 10 February 1959.
9. *Daytona Beach Sunday News-Journal*, 12 February 1959.
10. Yunick, 274.
11. *Daytona Beach Sunday News-Journal*, 17 February 1959.
12. *Sarasota Herald-Tribune*, 12 February 1959.
13. *Daytona Beach Morning Journal*, 13 February 1959.
14. Ibid.
15. Ibid.
16. Ibid.
17. Ibid.
18. Ibid.
19. Ibid.
20. "1959 Daytona 500 Results," daytonainternationalspeedway.com.
21. *Daytona Beach Sunday News-Journal*, 13 February 1959.
22. Yunick, 274–275.
23. Ibid.
24. *Daytona Beach Morning Journal*, 31 January 1959.
25. *The Free Lance-Star*, 12 February 1958.
26. *Ocala Star-Banner*, 12 February 1959. *The Telegraph Herald* (International edition), 18 February 2001.
27. *Opelika Auburn News*, 11 February 2009.
28. *Daytona Beach Morning Journal*, 4 February 1959.
29. *Daytona Beach Morning Journal*, 31 March 1959. *Evening Independent*, 10 April 1959.
30. Ibid. motorsportshalloffame.com/bignotti. bowesfastseal.com.
31. *New York Times*, 8 April 1959. *The Milwaukee Journal*, 8 April 1959.
32. *Daytona Beach Morning Journal*, 18 November 1958.
33. *The Milwaukee Journal*, 8 April 1959.
34. *Daytona Beach Morning Journal*, 9 February 1959.
35. Ibid.
36. bleacherreport.com/articles.
37. Petty, 148.
38. *Reading Eagle*, 18 May 1959. *Daytona Beach Morning Journal*, 12 July 1970.
39. Auto Editors, *Consumer Guide*, "1959 Grand National Results."
40. *Rome News-Tribune*, 16 June 1959.
41. *Charlotte Observer*, 27 September 2005.
42. Ryan McGee, foxsports.com.
43. *Sarasota Herald-Tribune*, 27 June 1959. *Daytona Beach Morning Journal*, 1 July 1959.

44. *Daytona Beach Morning Journal*, 1 July 1959.
45. *Daytona Beach Morning Journal*, 8 July 1959. *The Tuscaloosa News*, 4 July 1959.
46. *New York Times*, 8 September 1959. *Herald-Journal*, 2 July 1959. *Daytona Beach Morning Journal*, 30 August 1959. *The Palm Beach Post*, 7 September 1959.
47. Fleischman and Pearce, 29–30.

Chapter 15

1. Edelstein, 121–122.
2. *Daytona Beach Morning Journal*, 26 February 1961.
3. S.S. Collins and Gavin D. Ireland, *Speedway: Auto Racing's Ghost Tracks* (Dorchester, England: Veloce, 2010), 143–144. Peter Schaefer, "A Look Back: Bowman Gray," nascar.com, 15 March 2011.
4. Edelstein, 128–134.
5. atlantamotorspeedway.com/media/history. *New Georgia Encyclopedia* (Athens: University of Georgia Press, 2007).
6. Ed Hinton, "Atlanta's Track Was Built in Wrong Place," espn.com.
7. Article of Incorporation of Charlotte Motor Speedway, 83634, North Carolina Secretary of State's Office. Edelstein, 120.
8. Articles of Amendment of Charlotte Motor Speedway, Inc., 94293, North Carolina Secretary of State's Office.
9. *Daytona Beach Morning Journal*, 14 February 1960.
10. *Daytona Beach Morning Journal*, 10 February 1960.
11. *The St. Petersburg Times*, 14 February 1960.
12. *Reading Eagle*, 14 February 1960.
13. *St. Petersburg Times*, 14 February 1960.
14. *Reading Eagle*, 14 February 1960.
15. *Daytona Beach Morning Journal*, 10 February 1960.
16. Ibid.
17. Ibid.
18. Yunick, 345.
19. Ed Hinton, "It's not rocket science ... or is it?" 30 June 2008, espn.com.
20. Ibid.
21. Yunick, 345.
22. *Charlotte Observer*, 23 November 2011.
23. Baker, 36.
24. Bob Zeller, *Motorsports*, 12 May 2010.
25. *Herald-Journal*, 2 April 1960.
26. Edelstein, 128–134.
27. Edelstein, 138, 141. *Herald-Journal*, 3 May 1968.
28. *Rock Hill Herald*, 10 June 1960.
29. Edelstein, 143.
30. Ibid.
31. *Herald-Journal*, 18 June 1960.
32. *Herald-Journal*, 16 June 1960.
33. *Herald-Journal*, 16 June 1960.
34. Edelstein, 144–145.
35. Edelstein, 146. *Daytona Beach Morning Journal*, 17 June 1960.
36. *Daytona Beach Morning Journal*, 17 June 1960.
37. *Daytona Beach Morning Journal*, 20 June 1960. *Rock Hill Herald*, 20 June 1960.
38. *Herald-Journal*, 21 June 1960.
39. *Daytona Beach Morning Journal*, 1 May 1961.
40. *Herald-Journal*, 12 July 1960.
41. Petty and Neely, 166.
42. Ibid.
43. Ibid.
44. *The Rock Hill Herald*, 4 July 1960.
45. Ibid.
46. Kathryn W. Kemp, *God's Capitalist: Asa Candler of Coca-Cola* (Macon, Georgia: Mercer University Press, 2002), 95–97.
47. *Herald-Journal*, 25, 28 June 1960.
48. atlantamotorspeedway.com/media/history.
49. *The Free Lance-Star*, 28 July 1960.
50. *Herald-Journal*, 31 July 1960. Petty, 167.
51. *Herald-Journal*, 31 July 1960.
52. *Ocala Star-Banner*, 6 September 1960.
53. Ibid. *Daytona Beach Morning Journal*, 27 August 1960. *Sarasota Journal*, 6 September 1960.
55. *Herald-Journal*, 11 August 1960.
56. Ibid.
57. *Daytona Beach Morning Journal*, 3 July 1960.
58. Ibid.
59. *Herald-Journal*, 13 October 1960. *Rock Hill Herald*, 20 June 1960.
60. Ibid.
61. Edelstein, 145–146.
62. *Ocala Star-Banner*, 18 October 1960.
63. Ibid. *Sarasota Herald-Tribune*, 16 October 1960.
64. *Daytona Beach Morning Journal*, 30, 31 October 1950. *Ocala Star-Banner*, 31 October 1960.
65. bristolmotorspeedway.com. Mark Aumann, "Nobody Could Imagine," nascar.com, 17 August 1961.
66. Aumann. federalreserve.gov/releases.
67. federalreserve.gov/releases.
68. Ibid. Autmann.
69. bristolmotorspeedway.com.
70. *The Free Lance-Star*, 31 July 1961.
71. *Daytona Beach Morning Journal*, 26 February 1961.
72. Ibid.
73. *Daytona Beach Morning Journal*, 8 November 1960.
74. Fleischman and Pearce, 31.

Chapter 16

1. *The Dispatch*, 24 March 1958.
2. Ibid.
3. *The Dispatch*, 4 March 1958. *Schenectady Gazette*, 13 September 1958. *New York Times*, 14 October 1958.
4. *Herald Journal*, 26 March 1957.
5. *The Dispatch*, 4 March 1957.
6. Yunick, 148.
7. *Herald-Journal*, 26 March 1957.
8. *The Dispatch*, 4 September 1957.
9. Edelstein, 113.
10. *The News and Courier*, 3 September 1957.
11. Ibid.
12. *Daytona Beach Sunday News-Journal*, 8 September 1957.
13. Ibid. *The Robesonian*, 11 September 1957.
14. *Daytona Beach Sunday News-Journal*, 8 September 1957.
15. Ibid.
16. Ibid.
17. *The Rock Hill Journal*, 30 August 1957.
18. *Herald-Journal*, 15 September 1957.
19. Ibid.
20. *The Dispatch*, 4 September 1957.
21. *The Dispatch*, 17 July 1957.
22. *Daytona Beach Morning Journal*, 23 February 1958.
23. *Daytona Beach Morning Journal*, 26 February 1961.
24. *The Times-News*, 21 February 1961.
25. Petty, 173–174.
26. Ibid.
27. Petty, 176.
28. Petty, 181.
29. Edelstein, 92–93. *The Sumter Daily Item*, 20 January 1964.
30. *The Lewiston Morning Tribune*, 27 February 1961.
31. *Charlotte Observer*, 2 February 2011.
32. *The Miami News*, 27 February 1961.
33. Ibid.
34. *Ocala Star-Banner*, *The Dispatch*, 27 February 1961.
35. *Daytona Beach Morning Journal*, 22 March 1961.
36. Ibid.

37. *Times-Herald,* 22 March 1961.
38. *Ocala Star-Banner,* 9 February 1961.
39. *Daytona Beach Morning Journal,* 9, 12, 21, 1961.
40. *The Robesonian,* 10 April 1961. *Daytona Beach Morning Journal,* 10 April 1961.
41. *Herald-Journal,* 16 April 1961.
42. Ibid.
43. Ibid. Otto and Biondi, 57.
44. *Herald-Journal,* 16 April 1961.
45. *Daytona Beach Morning Journal,* 11 April 1961.
46. Ibid.
47. *The Rock Hill Herald,* 7 May 1961.
48. *Sarasota Journal, Lawrence World Journal, New York Times,* 29 May 1961.
49. *Rock Hill Herald,* 29 May 1961.
50. *The Miami News,* 10 July 1961.
51. *Daytona Beach Morning Journal,* 1 July 1961.
52. Ibid.
53. Ibid.
54. Ibid.
55. Ibid.
56. *Daytona Beach Morning Journal,* 16 October 1961.
57. *Daytona Beach Morning Journal,* 26 March 1962.
58. *Ocala Star-Banner,* 11, 12 June 1962.
59. *Daytona Beach Morning Journal,* 11, 12 June 1962.
60. Ibid.
61. *Daytona Beach Morning Journal,* 13 June 1962. *The Dispatch,* 12 June 1962.
62. auto.howstuffworks.com.
63. Ibid. *St. Petersburg Times,* 24 September 1962.
64. *Daytona Beach Morning Journal, The Miami News,* 9 July 1963.
65. Ibid.
66. *The News and Courier,* 14 November 1963. *Herald-Journal,* 16 November 1963.
67. Ibid.
68. *Herald-Journal, The Sumter Daily Item,* 20 January 1964.
69. Yunick, 344.
70. Yunick, 343–344.
71. Ibid.
72. Edelstein, 204.
73. *Herald-Journal,* 2 May 1965.
74. *Daytona Beach Morning Journal,* 15 February 1965.
75. Ibid.
76. Ibid. *Herald-Journal,* 15 February 1965.

Chapter 17

1. *Anderson Daily Mail,* 27 May 2009.
2. *Daytona Beach Morning Journal,* 28 March 1961. *Herald-Journal,* 28 March 1961.
3. Ibid.
4. Peter Golenbock and Greg Fielden, *The Stock Car Racing Encyclopedia* (New York: Macmillan, 1997), 42.
5. *Daytona Beach Morning Journal,* 11, 27 February 1961.
6. *Herald-Journal,* 12 April 1961.
7. *The Sumter Daily Item,* 19 April 1961.
8. Edelstein, 156–157.
9. Ibid.
10. Edelstein, 160–161.
11. Edelstein, 161–162.
12. Ibid.
13. *Dayton Beach Morning Journal,* 12 July 1961.
14. *Herald-Journal,* 10 August 1961. Edelstein, 168–169.
15. 29 United States Code, 186 (Taft-Hartley Act Sec. 302).
16. Edelstein, 169. William N. Thompson, *Gambling in America* (Santa Barbara, California: ABC-CLIO, 2001), 122. President John F. Kennedy signed the Wire Act into law in September 1961.
17. Edelstein, 167–168. *Herald-Journal,* 10 August 1961. *Daytona Beach Morning Journal,* 10 August 1961. Otto and Biondi, 64.
18. Petty, 180.
19. *The Sumter Daily Item,* 11 August 1961.
20. Ibid.
21. *The Charlotte Observer,* 11 August 1961.
22. Ibid. *Sarasota Herald-Tribune,* 2 August 1957. *St. Petersburg Times,* 19 December 1956.
23. Ibid.
24. Edelstein, 169.
25. *Daytona Beach Morning Journal,* 10 August 1961.
26. Ibid.
27. uaw.org/page/uaw-history.
28. Edelstein, 170.
29. *Chicago Tribune,* 26 October 2001.
30. Edelstein, 170–171.
31. Ibid.
32. Ibid.
33. *Daytona Beach Morning Journal,* 11 August 1961.
34. *The Miami News,* 12 August 1961.
35. *Charlotte Observer,* 12 August 1961.
36. Hinton, 96.
37. Ibid.
38. Ibid.
39. *Daytona Beach Morning Journal,* 12 August 1961.
40. Pierce, *Real NASCAR,* 218.
41. *Charlotte Observer,* 13 August 1961.
42. *Daytona Beach Morning Journal,* 12 August 1961.
43. Ibid.
44. *Daytona Beach Morning Journal,* 12 August 1961. *Charlotte Observer,* 13 August 1961.
45. *Charlotte Observer,* 13 August 1961.
46. nflpa.com/about-us. nbapa.com/about-us. mblpa.com.
47. *Daytona Beach Morning Journal,* 12 August 1961.
48. *Charlotte Observer,* 13 August 1961.
49. *Daytona Beach Morning Journal,* 10, 11 August 1961.
50. Golenbock, *NASCAR Confidential,* 96.
51. Ibid.
52. Ibid.
53. *Daytona Beach Morning Journal,* 21 August 1958.
54. *Charlotte Observer,* 13 August 1961.
55. *Daytona Beach Morning Journal,* 10 August 1961.
56. Ibid.
57. Edelstein, 175–176.
58. Edelstein, 177.
59. *Daytona Beach Morning Journal,* 14 August 1961. *Milwaukee Sentinel,* 15 August 1961.
60. Ibid.
61. *The Milwaukee Journal,* 22 August 1961. *Daytona Beach Morning Journal,* 19 October 1961.
62. *Daytona Beach Morning Journal,* 29 August 1961. *The Tuscaloosa News,* 29 August 1961.
63. *Herald-Journal,* 27 August 1961. *Daytona Beach Morning Journal,* 5 September 1961.
64. Ibid. *New York Times,* 5 September 1961.
65. Golenbock, 99.
66. Golenbock, 98.
67. Edelstein, 177. A January 12, 2010, email from Volusia Circuit Clerk Barbara Long's office said no record of the complaint existed because Florida court records were destroyed five years after final adjudication of the legal action.
68. Edelstein, 177–178.
69. Ibid.
70. Edelstein, 182–185.
71. Ibid.
72. Ibid.
73. Ibid.
74. Ibid.
75. *The Sumter Daily Item,* 29 November 1961.
76. Otto, 94.
77. *Herald-Journal,* 3 May 1968.
78. Ibid.
79. *Daytona Beach Morning Journal,* 1 February 1962.
80. *The News and Courier,* 20 March 1963.

81. *Star-News*, 29 July 1963. *Daytona Beach Morning Journal*, 28 July 1963. *The News and Courier*, 30 August 1963. *Ocala Star-Banner*, 3 September 1963.
82. *The Dispatch*, 23 May 1964.
83. Ibid. *The Milwaukee Sentinel*, 25 May 1964.
84. *The St. Petersburg Times*, 25 May 1964. *The Palm Beach Post*, 3 July 1964. *The Milwaukee Sentinel*, 25 May 1964.
85. *The Montreal Gazette*, 30 May 1964. *Reading Eagle*, 2 July 1964.
86. Golenbock, 134–137.
87. *The Miami News*, 26 May 1964.
88. *Daytona Beach Morning Journal*, 20 June 1964.
89. Yunick, 286–287.
90. *The Palm Beach Post*, 3 July 1964. *Daytona Beach Morning Journal*, 6 July 1964.
91. *Gadsden Times*, 3 July 1964.
92. *Sumter Daily Item*, 10 July 1964.
93. Ibid.
94. *The St. Petersburg Times, Free Lance-Star, Eugene Register Guard*, 23 September 1964.
95. *Reading Eagle*, 18 January 1965.
96. Hinton, 140–141.
97. Hinton, 140
98. *Reading Eagle*, 18 January 1965.

Chapter 18

1. Edelstein, 186–187.
2. Ibid.
3. Ibid.
4. Ibid.
5. Edelstein, 177–178.
6. Edelstein, 191.
7. Ibid.
8. *The News and Courier*, 3 September 1962.
9. Ibid.
10. Edelstein, 196–197.
11. Ibid.
12. Edelstein, 207.
13. Edelstein, 207.
14. Edelstein, 207–209.
15. Ibid.
16. *Daytona Beach Morning Journal*, 16 February 1965.
17. NASCAR Grand National Results for 1961, Racing-Reference.info.com.
18. Edelstein, 211–212.
19. *Daytona Beach Morning Journal*, 16 May 1965.
20. Edelstein, 212.
21. Ibid. *Daytona Beach Morning Journal*, 26 October 1964.
22. Edelstein, 211–212. *Consumers' Guide*, "NASCAR 1965 Results," "1965 NASCAR Grand National Recap."
23. Edelstein, 212.
24. *Sumter Daily Item*, 14 August 1965.
25. *Sumter Daily Item*, 6 July, 14 and 25 August 1965.
26. Ibid. Edelstein, 213.
27. *The Dispatch*, 2 August 1965. *Herald-Tribune*, 2 August 1965.
28. *Sumter Daily Item*, 17 August 1965.
29. *Herald-Journal*, 13 August 1965.
30. *Sumter Daily Item*, 14 August 1965.
31. *Herald-Journal*, 13 February 1965.
32. *Herald-Journal*, 31 August 1964. Edelstein, 220.
33. *Kingsport Post*, 7 October 1965.
34. Golenbock, 145.
35. Edelstein, 220.
36. Ibid. *The News and Courier*, 14 September 1965.
37. Edelstein, 221.
38. Edelstein, 221–223.
39. Golenbock and Fielden, 945.
40. *St. Petersburg Times*, 8 September 1965. *Daytona Beach Morning Journal*, 14 September 1965. *Sarasota Herald-Tribune, Sarasota Journal*, 18 October 1965. *Herald-Journal*, 21 October 1965.
41. *Herald-Journal*, 21 October 1965.
42. *The News and Courier*, 30 October 1965.
43. Edelstein, 228–233.
44. Ibid.
45. *Herald-Journal*, 31 October 1965. Edelstein, 232–233.
46. Ibid.
47. Edelstein, 228–234.
48. Ibid.

Chapter 19

1. (Raleigh) *News and Observer*, 29 September 1903. Wilkinson, 115.
2. "Old 97," Blue Ridge Institute and Museum.
3. *Star-News*, 19 October 1988. *Charlotte News-Observer*, 22 September 2009.
4. Wilkinson, 117.
5. *Star-News*, 19 October 1988.
6. Wilkinson, 117.
7. Ibid. Donovan, 36.
8. Donovan, 39.
9. *The Free Lance-Star*, 22 July 1977.
10. *The Toledo Blade*, 24 December 1990. Smith, *American Racing Classics*.
11. Donovan, 44–46.
12. Ibid.
13. Ibid.
14. Petty, 203–204.
15. Tom Cotter, Al Pearce, *Holman-Moody: The Legendary Race Team* (St. Paul, Minnesota: MBI, 2002).
16. *The Toledo Blade*, 24 December 1990.
17. Ibid.
18. Ibid.
19. Donovan, 39.
20. Donovan, 40.
21. *The Free Lance-Star*, 22 July 1977.
22. Donovan, 40.
23. Donovan, 42.
24. *The Free Lance-Star*, 22 July 1977.
25. Mike Smith, "Oliver Wendell Scott," *American Racing Classics*, Vol. 3, 1994.
26. Ibid.
27. *The Free Lance-Star*, 22 July 1977.
28. Donovan, 51.
29. Ibid.
30. Donovan, 57–58.
31. Donovan, 60–61.
32. Ibid.
33. Donovan, 61–62.
34. *Star News*, 19 October 1988. *Virginia Pilot*, 25 December 1990.
35. *Herald-Journal*, 3 January 1959.
36. *Richmond Times-Dispatch*, 28 July 2001.
37. Golenbock and Fielden, 374.
38. Donovan, 102–103.
39. Yunick, 100.
40. Golenbock and Fielden, 374, 453.
41. *Star-News*, 19 October 1988.
42. Golenbock and Fielden, 374.
43. Ibid.
44. Golenbock and Fielden, 433.
45. Donovan, 127–128.
46. Golenbock and Fielden, 734, 943.
47. Donovan, 128–134. *The Toledo Blade*, 24 December 1990.
48. *The Florida Times-Union*, 17 June 2007.
49. Donovan, 128–134.
50. Ibid.
51. Donovan, 134–135.
52. *Charlotte Observer*, 5 February 2011.
53. Cotter, 120.
54. Fleischman and Pearce, 201.
55. Wilkinson, 119.
56. Ibid.

Chapter 20

1. *Prescott Evening Courier*, 12 June 1962. *Toledo Blade*, 14 June 1962.
2. Ibid. Fleischman and Pearce, 323–424.
3. 1962, 1963 NASCAR Grand National Results, racing-reference.info.com. Goldenbock and Fielden, 941–942.

4. *Daytona Beach Morning Journal*, 16 February 1965.
5. Golenbock, 145.
6. *Reading Eagle*, *Herald-Journal*, *The Milwaukee Journal*, 1 March 1965.
7. Edelstein, 211–212.
8. *Daytona Beach Morning Journal*, 16 May 1965.
9. *Times-Daily*, 13 June 1965. *The Dispatch*, 18 June 1965. *Sarasota Herald-Tribune*, 11 April 1965.
10. *The Palm Beach Post*, 6 June 1965.
11. *Rome News-Tribune*, 16 June 1965.
12. *St. Petersburg Times*, 8 September 1965. *Daytona Beach Morning Journal*, 14 September 1965. *Sarasota Herald-Tribune*, *Sarasota Journal*, 18 October 1965. *Herald-Journal*, 21 October 1965.
13. *Herald-Journal*, 21 October 1965.
14. *Daytona Beach Morning Journal*, 14 December 1965.
15. *Daytona Beach Morning Journal*, 16 December 1965.
16. *Herald-Journal*, 18 December 1965.
17. *Daytona Beach Morning Journal*, 8 January 1966.
18. *Herald-Journal*, 19 May 1966.
19. Ibid.
20. *Herald-Journal*, 20 February 1966. Yunick, 265–266.
21. Yunick, 265–266.
22. Ibid.
23. *Herald-Journal*, 25 February 2001. *Daytona Beach Morning Journal*, 15 December 1966.
24. *Ocala Star Banner*, 28 February 1966.
25. *Daytona Beach Morning Journal*, 28 February 1966. *Modesto Bee*, 27 February 1966.
26. NASCAR Grand National Results, 1963, Racing Reference.info.
27. *Gadsden Times*, 11 May 1966.
28. Ibid.
29. Ibid.
30. *Daytona Beach Morning Journal*, 19 October 1964.
31. Ibid.
32. *Herald-Journal*, 18 December 1965.
33. *Herald-Journal*, 17 April 1966. *Rome News Tribune*, 18 April 1966.
34. *The Rock Hill Journal*, 7 April 1966. *Rome News Tribune*, 18 April 1966.
35. *The Rock Hill Herald*, 7 April 1966.
36. *Tuscaloosa News*, 23 April 1966.
37. Ibid.
38. *Herald-Journal*, 23 April 1966.
39. *Sarasota Herald-Tribune*, 25 April 1966.
40. Cotter, 111–112.
41. *Herald-Journal*, 19 June 1966.
42. *The Sumter Daily Item*, 23 June 1966.
43. *The News and Courier*, 8 August 1966.
44. Tom Jensen, *Cheating* (Phoenix, Arizona: David Bull, 2002).
45. *Charlotte Observer*, 8 March 2012.
46. Ibid.
47. Jensen, 94.
48. *Charlotte Observer*, 8 March 2012.
49. Ibid.
50. Ibid. NASCAR Grand National Results, 1966, Racing Reference-Info.com.
51. Jenson, 94–95.
52. *The Times News*, 5 September 1966.
53. *Charlotte Observer*, 26 September 1966. *Herald-Journal*, 29 September 1966.
54. *Herald-Journal*, 29 September 1966.
55. Ibid.
56. Ibid.
57. *The Robesonian*, 30 September 1966.
58. *The Milwaukee Journal*, 30 September 1966.
59. *Pittsburgh Post-Gazette*, 31 October 1966.
60. *Herald-Journal*, 31 October 1966.
61. Ibid.
62. *Star-News*, 27 October 1972. *Herald-Journal*, 4, 6 March 1966.
63. Edelstein, 157–158.
64. Ibid.
65. Ibid.
66. *Herald-Journal*, 31 October 1966.
67. Golenbock and Fielden, 946. Fleischman and Pearce, 36–37.
68. *The Sumter Daily Item*, 20 March 1967. *Daytona Beach Morning Journal*, 28 December 1966.
69. *The Rock Hill Herald*, 17 January 1967.
70. *Herald-Journal*, 27 April 1967.
71. *Daytona Beach Morning Journal*, 22 January 1967.
72. *The Sun* (British Columbia), and *Free Lance-Star*, 21 January 1967. *Eugene Register-Guard*, 26 January 1967.
73. *Daytona Beach Morning Journal*, 25 January 1967.
74. *Daytona Beach Morning Journal*, 17 February 1967.
75. *Gadsden Times*, 25 February 1967. *Herald-Journal*, 2 April 1967.
76. Edelstein, 254.
77. *Daytona Beach Morning Journal*, 9 February 1967. *The Norwalk Hour*, 25 February 1967.
78. *Reading Eagle*, 28 February 1967.
79. Ibid.
80. Yunick, 267.
81. *St. Petersburg Times*, 27 February 1967.
82. Cotter, 119.
83. Ibid.
84. Yunick, 268.
85. *Gadsden Times*, 22 March 1967. *Herald-Journal*, 25 March 1967.
86. *The Free Lance-Star*, 28 March 1967. *Gadsden Times*, 22 March 1967.
87. *Rome News-Tribune*, 12 March 1967.
88. Yunick, 268.
89. Edelstein, 255.
90. Yunick, 268.
91. Edelstein, 255.
92. *Daytona Morning Journal*, 18 June 1967.
93. Yunick, 268–269.
94. Edelstein, 257.
95. *The Morning Herald*, 3 April 1967. *The Tuscaloosa News*, 3 April 1967.
96. *Daytona Beach Morning Journal*, 1 April 1967.
97. Golenbock and Fielden, 946.
98. *The Times-News*, 5 May 1967. *The Dispatch*, 24 April, 11 May 1967.
99. Golenbock and Fielden, 946.
100. Jensen, 16.
101. *Daytona Beach Morning Journal*, 12 April 1967.
102. *Daytona Beach Morning Journal*, 18 April 1967.
103. Ibid.
104. *Daytona Beach Morning Journal*, 29 April 1967.
105. *Daytona Beach Morning Journal*, 13 June 1967.
106. Ibid.
107. *Herald-Journal*, 10 April 1967.
108. Ibid.
109. *Herald-Journal*, 18 June 1967.
110. *Daytona Beach Morning Journal*, 18 June 1967.
111. *St. Petersburg Times*, 5 July 1967.
112. *Lawrence Journal-World*, 1 September 1967.
113. *The Dispatch*, 18 October 1967.
114. *Schenectady Gazette*, 7 November 1967.
115. *Ocala Star-Banner*, 14 November 1967.
116. Fleischman and Pearce, 37. Golenbock and Fielden, 946.

Chapter 21

1. *Tri-Cities Herald*, 29 September 1967.
2. *Daytona Beach Morning Journal*, 5 February 1968.

3. Yunick, 269.
4. Yunick, 270.
5. Ibid.
6. Yunick, 270–271.
7. Ibid.
8. Ibid. Bob Bolles, "Smokey Yunick's Legendary 1967 Chevelle, A Technical Expose of the Most Innovative Stock Car Ever," *Circle Track*, 4 August 2010.
9. Bolles.
10. Yunick, 271–272.
11. *Daytona Beach Morning Journal*, 5 February 1968.
12. *Daytona Beach Morning Journal*, 11 February 1968.
13. Yunick, 272. *The Sumter Daily Item*, 7 February 1968. Golenbock and Fielden, 947.
14. *Herald-Journal*, 24 February 1968.
15. Ibid.
16. *Daytona Beach Morning Journal*, 26 February 1968. *Times Daily*, 26 February 1968.
17. *Daytona Beach Morning Journal*, 21, 24 February 1969.
18. *Daytona Beach Morning Journal*, 26 February 1968.
19. *Herald-Journal*, 3 May 1968. *Modesto Bee*, 17 June 1969. *Times Daily*, 17 July 1969.
20. *Modesto Bee*, 17 June 1969. *Daytona Beach Morning Journal*, 4 February 1969.
21. Ibid.
22. *Daytona Beach Morning Journal*, 19 July 1968.
23. *Daytona Beach Morning Journal*, 4 February 1969.
24. Ibid. *Herald-Journal*, 19 September 1969.
25. *St. Petersburg Times*, 13 March 1969. *Daytona Beach Morning Journal*, 23 February 1969.
26. *St. Petersburg Times*, 13 March 1969. *Toledo Blade*, 23 February 1969.
27. *Daytona Beach Morning Journal*, 23 February 1969. Foxsports.com.
28. *The Pittsburgh Press*, 23 February 1969.
29. *The Fort Scott Tribune*, 7 May 1970.
30. Fleischman and Pearce, 40. Stephen C. Smith, "Something Just Wasn't Right," *Car and Driver*, October 2008. Michael Sirocco, *Jacksonville Times-Union*, "Athletes of the Century: Yarbrough Dominated His Era," 2000 (no day or month).
31. Smith, "Something Just Wasn't Right."
32. Ibid.
33. Ibid.
34. David McGee, *Tales of the Bristol Speedway* (Charleston, South Carolina: History Press, 2011), 41.
35. McGee, 42.
36. bristolmotorspeedway.com/news_media/history. Golenboch, 41.
37. *Charlotte Observer*, 19 July 2009.
38. Ibid.
39. Ibid.
40. Ibid.
41. Ibid.
42. *Daytona Beach Morning Journal*, 23 January 1970.
43. Ibid.
44. Fleischman and Pearce, 38–40.

Chapter 22

1. Victor Flock, 2-24-2011, email to author.
2. Ibid.
3. *The Dispatch*, 5 September 1957. Yunick, 313–314.
4. Yunick, 314.
5. Ibid.
6. Ibid.
7. *The Anniston Star*, 1 May 1994.
8. Ibid. 2-24-2011 Victor Flock email to author.
9. *Herald-Journal*, 12 February 1968.
10. Ibid.
11. *The Anniston Star*, 1 May 1994.
12. Yunick, 314.
13. *Gadsden Times*, 9 June 1968, 9 August 1969. *Times Daily*, 3 February 1953, 18 April 1954.
14. Ibid.
15. Pierce, 323.
16. *Rock Hill Herald*, *The Sumter Daily Item*, *Hartford Courant*, 20 November 1968. *The Evening Independent*, 21 November 1968.
17. *Daytona Beach Morning Journal*, 5 July 1968.
18. *St. Petersburg Times*, 3 September 1968.
19. *The Miami News*, 23 October 1968.
20. *Gadsden Times*, 3 May 1967.
21. Ibid.
22. "International Motorsports Hall of Fame," Encyclopedia of Alabama.org. motorsportshalloffame.com.
23. Pierce, 267.
24. *Daytona Beach Morning Journal*, 30 June 1971.
25. *Daytona Beach Morning Journal*, 22 February 1969.
26. Ibid.
27. *Daytona Beach Morning Journal*, 28 July 1968.
28. *Gadsden Times*, 28 August 1969.
29. csc.noaa.gov/hes/docs/poststorm/H-CAMILLE. *The Milwaukee Journal*, 18 August 1969. *Gadsden Times*, *The Palm Beach Post*, 9 August 1969.
30. *Herald-Journal*, 13 September 1969.
31. Ibid.
32. *St. Petersburg Times*, 20 August 1969.
33. Ibid.
34. Ibid.
35. *Modesto Bee*, 20 August 1969.
36. Ibid.
37. Ibid.
38. *The Tuscaloosa News*, 20 August 1969.
39. *Gadsden Times*, 14 September 1969.
40. *Herald-Journal*, 10 September 1969. Pierce, 268.
41. *Charlotte Observer*, 23 November 2011.
42. *Gadsden Times*, 14 September 1969.
43. *The Sumter Daily Item*, 16 September 1969.
44. Ibid.
45. Ibid.
46. Ibid.
47. *Herald-Journal*, 10 September 1969.
48. *Daytona Beach Morning Journal*, 17 September 1969.
49. *Herald-Journal*, 19 September 1969.
50. *The Sumter Daily Item*, 16 September 1969.
51. *Herald-Journal*, 12 September 1969.
52. Edward Minter, 12-13-2012 interview with the author. *Trains, The Magazine of Railroading*, 6 November 2008. *The Bridge*, August 2008, Vol. 22, No. 2, 4.
53. Minter interview. *The Bridge*, August 2008, Vol. 22, No. 2, 4.
54. Raymond E. Robertson, "Chemical Properties of Asphalt and Their Relationships to Pavement Performances," Strategic Highway Research Program, National Research Council, 1991.
55. *The Sumter Daily Item*, 16 September 1969.
56. *Herald-Journal*, 12 September 1969.
57. Ibid.
58. Pierce, 272.
59. Ibid.
60. Ibid.
61. Lazarus, 153.
62. Ibid.
63. *Gadsden Times*, 14 September 1969.
64. *The Sumter Daily Item*, 16 September 1969. *The Tuscaloosa News*, 15 September 1969. *Gadsden Times*, 14 September 1969.
65. Golenbock and Fielden, 152.
66. *Gadsden Times*, 14 September 1969. *Tuscaloosa News*, 15 September 1969.

67. *Tuscaloosa News*, 15 September 1969.
68. *The Sumter Daily Item*, 16 September 1969.
69. Ibid.
70. *Herald-Journal*, 15 September 1969.
71. *The Free Lance-Star*, 17 September 1969.
72. Ibid.
73. *The Sumter Daily Item*, 16 September 1969.
74. *The Dispatch*, 24 September 1969.
75. *Daytona Beach Morning Journal*, 25 September 1969.
76. *The Dispatch*, 24 September 1969.
77. *Daytona Beach Morning Journal*, 25 September 1969.
78. Ibid.
79. talladegasuperspeedway.com.

Chapter 23

1. Golenbock and Fielden, 933–948.
2. *Daytona Beach Morning Journal*, 4 January 1970.
3. *Daytona Beach Morning Journal*, 4 January 1970.
4. *The Dispatch*, 7 January 1970.
5. *The Milwaukee Sentinel*, 29 January 1970.
6. Ibid.
7. *Herald-Journal*, 20 February 1970.
8. *Daytona Beach Morning Journal*, 17 February 1970. research.stlouisfed.org.
9. *Daytona Beach Morning Journal*, 17 February 1970.
10. *The Fort Scott Tribune*, 7 May 1970.
11. *Daytona Beach Morning Journal*, 13 April 1970.
12. *Herald-Journal*, 3 March 1970. *Daytona Beach Morning Journal*, 4 March 1970.
13. *The Sumter Daily Item*, 3 March 1970. *Herald-Journal*, 3 March 1970.
14. *Herald-Journal*, 9 March 1970.
15. *Herald-Journal*, 3 March 1970.
16. *The Dispatch*, 20 March 1970. *Herald-Journal*, 22 March 1970. *The Robesonian*, 23 March 1970. *The Day*, 30 March 1970.
17. *The Palm Beach Post*, 30 March 1970.
18. *Rome News-Tribune*, 13 April 1970.
19. *The Tuscaloosa News*, 10 April 1970. *Montreal Gazette*, 13 April 1970. *The Owosso Argus-Press*, 11 April 1970. *Reading Eagle*, 12 April 1970. *The Rock Hill Herald*, 9 April 1970.
20. *The Tuscaloosa News*, 10 April 1970. *The Palm Beach Post*, 9 August 1970.
21. *The Sumter Daily Item*, 19 May 1970.
22. Ibid.
23. *The Palm Beach Post*, 25 May 1970. *Times-Daily*, 25 May 1970.
24. Ibid.
25. Hinton, 113–114.
26. *The Palm Beach Post*, 19 April 1970.
27. *Herald-Journal*, 19 April 1970.
28. *The Owosso Argus-Press*, 11 May 1970.
29. *Herald-Journal*, 9 May 1970.
30. *Herald-Journal*, 8 June 1970.
31. Ibid.
32. Fleischman and Pearce, 327.
33. Ibid.
34. Ibid.
35. *Herald-Journal*, 19 October 1970. *Waycross Journal-Herald*, 1 August 1970. *Times Daily*, 3 August 1970. *Herald-Journal*, 19 October 1969. *USA Today*, 14 June 2010.
36. *Park City Daily News*, 27 July 1970. *Gettysburg Times*, 30 July 1970.
37. *Herald-Journal*, 3 August 1970.
38. Ibid.
39. Ibid.
40. Auto Editors, *Consumers' Digest*, "How Stuff Works, NASCAR," Restrictor Plates.
41. *The Palm Beach Post*, 9 August 1970.
42. *Schenectady Gazette*, 17 August 1970.
43. Ibid.
44. *The Rock Hill Herald*, 20 August 1970.
45. Jensen, 112.
46. *Herald-Journal*, 17 August 1970. Golenboch and Fielden, 948–949.
47. *Herald-Journal*, 22 August 1970.
48. *Herald-Journal*, 1 September 1970. *Times-News*, *Times Daily*, 8 September 1970.
49. Edelstein, 292.
50. Edelstein, 292.
51. Edelstein, 294–295.
52. Yunick, 284.
53. Yunick, 284–285.

Chapter 24

1. *Herald-Journal*, 20 November 1970.
2. *Daytona Beach Morning Journal*, 17 February 1971.
3. *The Palm Beach Post*, 20 November 1970. Golenbock and Fielden, 948–949.
4. *The Robesonian*, 20 December 1970.
5. Ibid.
6. Ibid.
7. *Daytona Beach Morning Journal*, 20 December 1970.
8. *Waycross Journal-Herald*, 1 August 1970. *The Owosso Argus-Press*, 22 December 1970. *USA Today*, 12 June 2010. *Herald-Journal*, 19 October 1969.
9. Peter Golenbock, *Miracle: Bobby Allison and the Saga of the Alabama Gang* (New York: St. Martin's Press, 2006), 114–115.
10. *Chicago Tribune*, 15 April 1965. *New York Times*, 15 September 1967.
11. *Daytona Beach Morning Journal*, 1 January 1971.
12. *Gadsden Times*, 17 December 1970.
13. Ibid.
14. Ibid.
15. Ibid.
16. *Daytona Beach Morning Journal*, 20 December 1970.
17. *Daytona Beach Morning Journal*, 20 June 1957, 11 February 1971.
18. *Daytona Beach Morning Journal*, 11 February 1971.
19. *Herald-Journal*, 2 August 1971.
20. *Daytona Beach Morning Journal*, 10 February 1971.
21. Robert Jones, "No Recession for Mr. Petty," *Sports Illustrated*, 22 February 1971.
22. Ibid.
23. *The Palm Beach Post*, 15 February 1971.
24. *The Sumter Daily Item*, 4 February 1971.
25. *The Tuscaloosa News*, 14 February 1971.
26. *Daytona Beach Morning Journal*, 13 February 1971.
27. *The Morning-Record*, 15 February 1971.
28. Ibid.
29. Jones, "No Recession for Mr. Petty."
30. *Daytona Beach Morning Journal*, 20 February, 26 February 1971.
31. *Los Angeles Times*, 28 February 1971. Ryan McGee, espn.com, 23 February 2008.
32. *Herald-Journal*, 5 August 1971.
33. *The Dispatch*, *The Rock Hill Herald*, *The Montreal Gazette*, 1 March 1971.
34. *The Dispatch*, *Herald-Journal*, 15 March 1971.
35. *The Dispatch*, 16 February 1971.
36. *Star-News*, 17 February 1971. *Atlanta Journal Constitution*, 22 February, 14 July 1990.
37. *Times-Daily*, 27 March 1971.
38. Ibid.
39. *Herald-Journal*, 4 April 1971.
40. Ibid.
41. *The Times-News* (Henderson-

ville, North Carolina), 13 July 1973. "Jackie Steward," formula1.com/teams.
  42. *The Sumter Daily Item*, 3 May 1971.
  43. Ibid.
  44. Ibid.
  45. *Daytona Beach Morning Journal*, 17 May 1971. *Herald-Journal*, 4 May 1971.
  46. *Daytona Beach Morning Journal*, 17 May 1971.
  47. *The Tuscaloosa News*, 23 May 1971. *The Robesonian*, 17 May 1971.
  48. Ibid.
  49. *Daytona Beach Morning Journal*, 29 May 1971.
  50. *Daily News*, 30 May 1971.
  51. *The Times News*, 31 May 1971.
  52. *Toledo Blade*, 12 June 1971.
  53. Ibid.
  54. Ibid.
  55. *Herald-Journal*, 1 July 1971.
  56. Ibid. *Schenectady Gazette*, 2 July 1971. *The Morning Record*, 3 July 1971.
  57. *Daytona Beach Morning Journal*, 5 July 1971.
  58. Ibid.
  59. *Herald-Journal*, 1 August 1971.
  60. Ibid.
  61. Ibid.
  62. Ibid.
  63. *Herald-Journal*, 8 August 1971.
  64. *Herald-Journal*, 2 August 1971.
  65. *The Portsmouth Times, Tuscaloosa News*, 23 August 1971.
  66. *Herald-Journal*, 5 August 1971.
  67. *Herald-Journal*, 5 August 1971.
  68. *Daytona Beach Morning Journal*, 28 August 1971. *Herald-Journal*, 27 August 1971. *Gadsden Times*, 27 August 1971.
  69. *Herald-Journal*, 27 August 1971. *Daytona Beach Morning Journal*, 28 August 1971. *The Times-Herald*, 11 January 1972.
  70. *Herald-Journal*, 3 September 1971.
  71. Ibid.
  72. Ibid.
  73. Ibid.
  74. Ibid.
  75. TimesNewsweekly.com (Ridgewood, New York), 11 December 2008.
  76. Ibid.
  77. *The St. Petersburg Times*, 24 April 1970. Hinton, 115.
  78. *Herald-Journal*, 7 September 1971.
  79. Ibid.
  80. *Herald-Journal*, 27 September 1971.
  81. *Sarasota Herald-Tribune*, 11 October 1971. *Herald-Journal*, 8 October 1971.
  82. *Daytona Beach Morning Journal*, 29 September 1971.
  83. *The Palm Beach Post*, 25 October 1971.
  84. Ibid.
  85. *The Free Lance Star*, 9 November 1971.
  86. Ibid.
  87. *The Tuscaloosa News*, 13 December 1971.
  88. Fleischman and Pearce, 41.
  89. Jim McFarland, *Stock Car Racing*, 12 August 2010. Yunick, 256.

Chapter 25

  1. *Daytona Beach Morning Journal*, 2 July 1972.
  2. *Herald-Journal*, 13 January 1972.
  3. *Bryant Times*, 18 January 1972.
  4. Ibid.
  5. Ibid.
  6. Ibid.
  7. *Los Angeles Times*, 24 January 1972.
  8. *Daytona Beach Morning Journal*, 24 January 1972.
  9. *The Evening Independent*, 24 January 1972.
  10. *Daytona Beach Morning Journal*, 18 February 1972. *The Windsor Star*, 18 February 1972.
  11. Ibid.
  12. *Sumter Daily Item*, 19 February 1972. *Herald-Journal*, 21 February 1972. *Times-Daily*, 21 February 1972.
  13. *Times-Daily*, 21 February 1972.
  14. *Gadsden Times*, 19 February 1972.
  15. *The Rock Hill Herald*, 9 March 1972.
  16. Ibid.
  17. *Herald-Journal*, 25 March 1972.
  18. Smith, "Something Just Isn't Right." *The Florida Times-Union*, 25 June 2011.
  19. Ibid.
  20. Ibid.
  21. Smith, "Something Just Isn't Right."
  22. Ibid.
  23. *The Robesonian*, 27 March 1972.
  24. *The Times-News*, 15 April 1972.
  25. *Rome News-Tribune*, 24 April 1972.
  26. *The Evening Independent*, 16 May 1972. *The Washington Post*, 16 May 1972.
  27. *The Palm Beach Post*, 11 April 1972.
  28. *Herald-Journal, Sunday Times-Sentinel, Star News, Tuscaloosa News*, 8 May 1972.
  29. Ibid.
  30. Ibid.
  31. *Herald-Journal, Tuscaloosa News*, 8 May 1972.
  32. *Rome News-Tribune*, 9 May 1972.
  33. *Herald-Journal*, 26 May 1972. *Milwaukee Journal-Sentinel*, 15 April 2002.
  34. *Herald-Journal*, 26 May 1972.
  35. Ibid.
  36. Ibid.
  37. Ibid.
  38. *Sarasota Herald-Tribune*, 12 April 1972
  39. *Daytona Beach Morning Journal*, 2 July 1972.
  40. *Daytona Beach Morning Journal*, 4 December 1971.
  41. Ibid.
  42. *Daytona Beach Morning Journal*, 9 December 1971.
  43. *Daytona Beach Morning Journal*, 4 December 1971.
  44. *Daytona Beach Morning Journal*, 16 January 1972.
  45. Ibid.
  46. Ibid.
  47. *Daytona Beach Morning Journal*, 9 December 1971, 11 January 1972.
  48. *Daytona Beach Morning Journal*, 2 July 1972.
  49. Ibid. *Daytona Beach Morning Journal*, 3 July 1972.
  50. *Star-News*, 5 July 1972.
  51. *The Evening Independent, The Argus-Press*, 7 August 1972.
  52. *Herald-Journal*, 5 September 1972.
  53. Ibid.
  54. *Times-Daily*, 11 September 1972.
  55. Ibid.
  56. Ibid.
  57. Ibid.
  58. Fleischman and Pearce, 54.
  59. *Times-Daily*, 9 October 1972. *Gadsden Times*, 9 October 1972.
  60. *Star-News*, 13 November 1972.
  61. Fleischman and Pearce, 52–53.

Chapter 26

  1. *Daytona Beach Morning Journal*, 13 January, 11 February 1973.
  2. *Daytona Beach Morning Journal*, 20 January 1973. allpar.com, American Motors.
  3. *Daytona Beach Morning Journal*, 20 January 1973. *The Sumter Daily Item, The Dispatch*, 20 January 1973. Golenbock and Fielden, 192.
  4. *Daytona Beach Morning Journal*, 11 February 1973.
  5. *Kentucky Speedway, LLC v. National Association for Stock Car Auto Racing, Inc., et al.* Case No. 2–05-CV-138, filed April 20, 2007, United States District Court, Eastern District of Kentucky, Northern Division at Covington.
  6. Ibid. *Sarasota Herald-Tribune*, 18 February 1973.

7. *The Times-News, Daytona Beach Morning Journal*, 19 February 1973.
8. *Lakeland Ledger*, 26 March 1973.
9. *The Dispatch*, 26 March 1973. *The Robesonian*, 12 March 1973.
10. *The Times-News*, 19 March 1973.
11. *Gadsden Times*, 18 March 1973. *Herald-Journal*, 17 March 1973.
12. *The Rock Hill Herald*, 14 February 1973.
13. *The Lewiston Daily Sun*, 16 April 1973.
14. *The Sumter Daily Item*, 17 April 1973.
15. Ibid.
16. *Herald-Journal*, 16 April 1973. Hinton, 129.
17. *The Bladen Journal*, 10 May 1973. *Sarasota Herald-Tribune*, 7 May 1973.
18. Ibid. *The Dispatch*, 7 May 1973. *The Rock Hill Herald*, 7 May 1973. *The Pittsburgh Press*, 6 May 1973.
19. *Herald-Journal*, 5 May 1973.
20. Ibid.
21. *Herald-Journal*, 14 April 1973.
22. *Herald-Journal, The Times-News*, 14 May 1973.
23. *Herald-Journal*, 28 May 1973.
24. *Herald-Journal*, 5 July 1973.
25. *The Times News*, 7 July 1973.
26. *Herald-Journal*, 4, 5 July 1973.
27. Ibid.
28. Ibid.
29. *The Tuscaloosa News*, 9 July 1973.
30. *Herald-Journal*, 13 August 1973.
31. Ibid. *The Lewiston Daily Sun, Rock Hill Herald*, 13 August 1973.
32. *The Free Lance Star*, 14 August 1973.
33. Fleischman and Pearce, 342. *Lakeland Ledger*, 13 August 1973.
34. *Herald-Journal*, 13 September 1973.
35. Ibid.
36. Golenback and Fielden, 200.
37. Tom Higgins and Steve Waid, *Brave in Life: Junior Johnson* (Phoenix, Arizona: David Bull, 1999), 104. *The Tuscaloosa News*, 13 October 1973.
38. Jenson, 107. *Star-News*, 11 October 1973.
39. *Herald-Journal*, 17 1973.
40. *The Times-News*, 8 October 1973.
41. Higgins and Waid, 107. *The Tuscaloosa News*, 13 October 1973.
42. Ibid.
43. *Herald-Journal*, 19 October 1973.
44. *Herald-Journal*, 9 October 1973.
45. *The Times-News*, 8 October 1973.
46. Jensen, 108.
47. Higgins and Waid, 108. *Herald-Journal*, 9 October 1973.
48. Jensen, 109. Higgins and Waid, 108.
49. *Herald-Journal*, 17 October 1973.
50. Higgins and Waid, 108.
51. Higgins and Waid, 108.
52. *The Tuscaloosa News*, 13 October 1973.
53. *Herald-Journal*, 19 October 1973.
54. *News and Courier*, 22 October 1973. *The Dispatch*, 20 October 1973.
55. *News and Courier*, 22 October 1973. Fleischman and Pearce, 56.
56. Fleischman and Pearce, 56.
57. *Gadsden Times*, 9 November 1973. Fleischman and Pearce, 57.
58. *St. Petersburg Times*, 21 December 1973.
59. *Gadsden Times*, 30 November 1973. *Lakeland Ledger*, 6 January 1974.

Chapter 27

1. *Herald-Journal*, 16 February 1974.
2. Ibid.
3. *Lakeland Ledger*, 17 February 1974.
4. Ibid.
5. Ibid.
6. *Daytona Beach Morning Journal*, 13 February 1974.
7. Ibid.
8. Ibid.
9. *Daytona Beach Morning Journal*, 16 February 1974.
10. *Herald-Journal*, 4 May 1974.
11. *Daytona Beach Morning Journal*, 9 February 1974.
12. *The Dispatch*, 11 January 1974.
13. *St. Petersburg Times*, 18 February 1974.
14. Ibid.
15. Golenback and Fielden, 297–298.
16. Fleischman and Pearce, 345.
17. *The Anchorage Daily News*, 19 February 1974.
18. *Daytona Beach Morning Journal*, 20 March 1974.
19. *The Palm Beach Post*, 26 January 1974.
20. *The Dispatch*, 16 March 1974. *The Evening Independent*, 18 March 1974.
21. *Herald-Journal*, 23 March 1974. *Daytona Beach Morning Journal*, 17 March 1974. Matt McLaughlin, "50 Years of NASCAR," www.racersreunion.com, 25 November 2012.
22. *Herald-Journal*, 23 March 1974.
23. Ibid.
24. *Gadsden Times*, 23 March 1974.
25. *Star-News*, 7 April 1974.
26. *Lakeland Ledger, The Tuscaloosa News*, 21 April 1974.
27. *The Milwaukee Sentinel*, 22 April 1974.
28. *Herald-Journal*, 9 May 1974.
29. Ibid.
30. *The Victoria Advocate*, 23 May 1974.
31. *The Sumter Daily Item, Gadsden Times*, 15 May 1974.
32. *Gadsden Times*, 15 May 1974.
33. *Star-News*, 17 May 1974.
34. *Star-News*, 27 April 1974.
35. Ibid.
36. *Toledo Blade*, 14 June 1974.
37. *The Times-News*, 27 May 1974.
38. Ibid.
39. *Lakeland Ledger*, 6 May 1974.
40. Ibid.
41. *The Tuscaloosa News*, 23 June 1974.
42. *Herald-Journal*, 17 June 1974.
43. Ibid.
44. Ibid.
45. Ibid.
46. *Lakeland Ledger*, 2 July 1974.
47. Ibid.
48. *The Modesto Bee*, 5 July 1974.
49. Ibid.
50. *Herald-Journal*, 29 July 1974
51. Fleischman and Pearce, 349.
52. *The Victorian Advocate, The Sumter Daily Item*, 5 August 1974.
53. *Daytona Beach Morning Journal, Ocala Star-Banner*, 18 August 1974.
54. *Ocala Star-Banner*, 18 August 1974.
55. *Spokesman Review*, 16 August 1974.
56. *Milwaukee Journal*, 12, 17 August 1974.
57. *Times Daily*, 12 August 1974.
58. *Spokesman Review*, 16 August 1974.
59. *The Dispatch*, 22 November 1974. *The Evening Independent*, 28 November 1974. *The News-Dispatch*, 26 November 1974.
60. *Daytona Beach Morning Journal*, 4 November 1974.
61. *The Times-News*, 7 November 1974.
62. Fleischman and Pearce, 58.

Bibliography

Ashe, Arthur R., Jr. *A Hard Road to Glory: A History of the African American Athlete*. New York: Warner Books, 1988.

Bechtel, March. *He Crashed Me So I Crashed Him Back: The True Story of the Year the King, Jaws, Earnhardt, and the Rest of NASCAR's Feudin', Fightin' Good Ol' Boys Put Stock Car Racing on the Map*. New York: Little, Brown, 2010.

Bonkowski, Jerry. *Trading Paint: 101 Great NASCAR Debates*. Hoboken, New Jersey: John Wiley and Sons, 2010.

Britt, Bloys, and Bill France. *The Racing Flag: NASCAR—The Story of Grand National Racing*. New York: Pocket Books, 1965.

Brown, Allan E. *History of America's Speedways, Past and Present*. Comstock, Michigan: America's Speedways, 1984.

Center, Bill, editor. *NASCAR: The Thunder of America*. New York: HarperCollins, 1998.

Clarke, Liz. *One Helluva Ride: How NASCAR Swept the Nation*. New York: Villard Books, 2008.

Coffey, Frank, and Joseph Laden. *America on Wheels: The First 100 Years*. Los Angeles: General Publishing Group, 1996.

Collins, S.S., and Gavin D. Ireland. *Speedways: Auto Racing's Ghost Tracks*. Dorchester, England: Veloce, 2009.

Cotter, Tom, and Al Pearce. *Holman-Moody: The Legendary Racing Team*. St. Paul, Minnesota: MBI, 2002.

Donovan, Brian. *Hard Driving: The Wendell Scott Story*. Hanover, New Hampshire: Steerforth Press, 2008.

Edelstein, Robert. *Full Throttle: The Life and Fast Times of NASCAR Legend Curtis Turner*. New York: Overlook Press, 2005.

Ellison, Betty Boles. *Illegal Odyssey: 200 Years of Kentucky Moonshine*. Bloomington, Indiana: 1st Books Library, 2003.

Fleischman, Bill, and Al Pearce. *Inside Sports: NASCAR Racing*. Detroit, Michigan: Visible Ink, 1998.

Flowers, Raymond, and Michael Wynn Jones. *One Hundred Years of Motoring: An RAC Social History of the Car*. London: McGraw-Hill, 1981.

Garner, Joe. *Speed, Guts and Glory: 100 Unforgettable Moments in NASCAR History*. New York: Warner, 2006.

Gittelman, Steven H. *Willie K. Vanderbilt II: A Biography*. Jefferson, North Carolina: McFarland, 2010.

Golenbock, Peter. *American Zoom: Stock Car Racing from the Dirt Tracks to Daytona*. New York: John Wiley and Sons, 1993.

_____. *The Last Lap: The Life and Times of NASCAR's Legendary Heroes*. New York: Macmillan, 1998.

_____. *NASCAR Confidential: Triumph and Tragedy in America's Racing Heartland*. St. Paul, Minnesota: Motorbooks International, 2004.

Golenbock, Peter, and Greg Fielden. *The Stock Car Racing Encyclopedia: The Complete Record of America's Most Popular Sport*. New York: Macmillan, 1997.

Gould, Todd. *For the Gold and Glory: Charlie Wiggins and the African-American Racing Circuit*. Bloomington: University of Indiana Press, 2002.

Higgins, Tom, and Steve Waid. *Junior Johnson: Brave in Life*. Phoenix, Arizona: David Bull, 1999.

Hinton, Ed. *Daytona: From the Birth of Speed to the Death of the Man in Black*. New York: Warner Books, 2001.

Hogstrom, Robert G. *The NASCAR Way: The Business That Drives the Sport*. New York: Wiley, 1998.

Howell, Mark D. *From Moonshine to Madison Avenue*. Bowling Green, Ohio: Bowling Green State University Popular Press, 1997.

Hunter, Don, and Al Pearce. *The Illustrated History of Stock Car Racing: From the Sands of Daytona to Madison Avenue*. Minneapolis, Minnesota: Motorbooks International, 1998.

Jensen, Tom. *Cheating: An Inside Look at the Bad Things Good NASCAR Winston Cup Racers Do in Pursuit of Speed*. Phoenix, Arizona: David Bull, 2002.

Kemp, Kathryn W. *God's Capitalist: Asa Candler of Coca-Cola*. Macon, Georgia: Mercer University Press, 2002.

Latford, Bob. *NASCAR: A Celebration*. London: Carlton Books, 2002.

Lazarus, William P. *The Sands of Time: Celebrating 100 Years of Racing at Daytona*. Champaign, Illinois: Sports Publishing, 2004.

Lutholtz, M. William. *Grand Dragon: D. C. Stephenson and the Ku Klux Klan in Indiana*. West Lafayette, Indiana: Purdue University Press, 1991.

MacGregor, Jeff. *Sunday Money: Speed! Lust! Madness! Death! A Hot Lap Around America with NASCAR*. New York: HarperCollins, 2005.

Martin, J.A., and Thomas E. Saal. *American Automobile Racing: The Milestones and Personalities of a Century of Speed*. Jefferson, North Carolina: McFarland, 2004.

McGee, David. *Tales of Bristol Motor Speedway*. Charleston, South Carolina: History Press, 2011.

Menzer, Joe. *The Wildest Ride, Or How a Bunch of Good Ol' Boys Built a Billion-Dollar Industry Out of Wrecking Cars*. New York: Simon & Schuster, 2001.

Murphy, Daryl E. *Carrera Panamericana: History of the Mexican Road Race, 1950–54*. Bloomington, Indiana: Motorbooks International, 2008.

Nye, Douglas. *The United States Grand Prix and Grand Prize Races, 1908–1977*. Garden City, New York: 1978.

Pettifer, Julian, and Nigel Turner. *Automania: Man and the Motor Car*. London: Guild, 1984.

Playle, Ron. *The Iowa State Fair in Vintage Postcards*. Charleston, South Carolina: Arcadia, 2006.

Petty, Richard, and William Neely. *King Richard I: The Autobiography of America's Greatest Auto Racer*. New York: Macmillan, 1986.

Pierce, Daniel S. *Real NASCAR: White Lightning, Red Clay and Big Bill France*. Chapel Hill: University of North Carolina Press, 2010.

Quattlebaum, Julian K. *The Great Savannah Races*. Athens: University of Georgia Press, 1985 (1957).

Radruch, Don. *Dirt Track Auto Racing 1919–1941: A Pictorial History*. Jefferson, North Carolina: McFarland, 2004.

Rodengen, Jeffrey L. *Iron Fist: The Lives of Carl Kiekhaefer*. Fort Lauderdale, Florida: Write Stuff Syndicate, 1991.

Ruppersburg, Hugh, and John C. Inscoe, editors. *The New Georgia Encyclopedia Companion to Georgia Literature*. Athens: University of Georgia Press, 2007.

Sullivan, Patrick. *Brick by Brick: The Story of Auto Racing Pioneer Joie Ray*. Fiskers, Indiana: American Scene Press, 2008.

Thompson, Neal. *Driving with the Devil: Southern Moonshine, Detroit Wheels, and the Birth of NASCAR*. New York: Crown, 2006.

Thompson, William N. *Gambling in America: An Encyclopedia of History, Issues and Society*. Santa Barbara, California: ABC-CLIO, 2001.

Tuthill, William R.. *Speed on Sand*. Ormond Beach, Florida: Ormond Beach Historical Trust, 1978.

White, Gordon Eliot. *Lost Race Tracks: Treasures of Automobile Racing*. Hudson, Wisconsin: Iconografix, 2002.

Wilkinson, Sylvia. *Dirt Tracks to Glory: The Early Days of Stock Car Racing as Told by the Participants*. Chapel Hill, North Carolina: Algonquin Books, 1983.

Yates, Brock. *NASCAR Off the Record*. Minneapolis: Motorbooks International, 2004.

Yunick, Smokey. *Best Damn Garage in Town: The World According to Smokey*. Daytona Beach, Florida: Carbon Press, 2001.

Periodicals

The Afro-American
American Motorists
American Racing Classics
Billboard
The Bridge Car and Driver
Carolina Country
Circle Track
Congressional Record
Consumer Guide
Indiana Monthly
Journal of Southern History
LookMotor World Wholesale
Motorsports
Popular Science Monthly
Sports Illustrated
Sports Scene
Time
Trains, The Magazine of Railroading

Newspapers

Anchorage Daily News
Anderson Daily Mail
Anniston Star
Argus Press
Atlanta Journal-Constitution
Bladen Journal
Bluefield Daily Telegraph
Bryant Times
Charlotte News
Charlotte Observer
Chicago Tribune
Columbus Ledger-Enquirer
The Daily Press
The Day
Daytona Beach Morning Journal
Daytona Beach News-Journal
Daytona Beach Sunday News-Journal
Desert News
Detroit Free Press
The Dispatch
Edmonton Journal
Eugene Register-Guard
Evening Independent
Florida Times-Union
The Fort Scott Tribune
Free-Lance Star
Gadsden Times

Gainesville Sun
Gettysburg Times
Hartford Courant
Herald and Courier
Herald-Journal
Herald-Mail
Indianapolis Star
The Item
Jacksonville Times-Union
Kentucky New Era
Kingsport Post
Lakeland Ledger
Lawrence World Journal
Lewiston Daily Sun
Lewiston Morning Tribune
Lodi News-Sentinel
Los Angeles Times
Miami News
Miami Sun
Miami Sun News
Milwaukee Journal
Milwaukee Sentinel
Modesto Bee
Montreal Gazette
The Morning Herald
The Morning Record
New York Times
Norwalk Hour
News and Observer (Raleigh)
News-Journal
Ocala Star-Banner
Opelika Auburn News
Orlando Sentinel
Owosso Argus Press
Palm Beach Post
Pampas Daily News
Park City Daily News
Pittsburgh Post-Gazette
Pittsburgh Press
Portsmouth News
Post-Tribune
Prescott Evening Courier
Reading Eagle
Richmond Times-Dispatch
Roanoke Times
The Robesonian
Rock Hill Herald
Rome News-Tribune
St. Joseph Gazette
St. Petersburg Times
Sarasota Herald
Sarasota Herald-Tribune
Sarasota Journal
Schenectady Gazette
The Southeast Missourian
Spartanburg Herald-Journal
Spokesman Review
Star-News
Sumner Daily Item
The Sun
The Telegraph Herald

Times-News
Times-Daily
Toledo Blade
Tri-Cities Herald
Tuscaloosa News
USA Today
Washington Post
Waycross Journal-Herald
Wilmington Star
Windsor Star
Victoria Advocate

Internet Sources

aintree.co.uk/grandnationalamericangrandprizeraces.com
arcaracing.com
atlantamotorspeedway.com/media/history
bioguide.congress.gov
bleacherreport.com/articles
bluebird-electric.net/Campbell
bowmangrayracing.com/history
bristolmotorspeedway.info.com
brooklandsracing.co.uk
buzzmckim.com
cnn-si.com
darlingtonraceway.com/history
decadesofstockcarracing.com
encyclopediaofalabama.org
flaglermuseum.us.org
floridamemory.com
foxnews.com/sports
garhofa.com
georgiaencyclopedia.org
georgiaracinghistory.com
hamidcircus.com
hemmings.com
historicspeedwaygroup.org
indianapolismotorspeedway.com
joeweatherly.ama-cycle.com
legendsofstockcarracing.com
lihistory.com
lowesmotorspeedway.com
measuringworth.com
motorracingnetwork.com
nascar.com
pbs.org/forthegoldandglory
prenc.org
racingcampbells.com
racingforsuccess.com
racing-reference.info.com
referenceforbusiness.com
smokey.com
speedwaymedia.com
talladegasuperspeedway.com
thatsracin.com
theselvedgeyard.wordpress.com
vanderbiltcupraces.com
visitnortheasterngeorgia.com
volusia.org/history/speed

Index

••••••

AAA Stock Car Champion 100, 160, 163, 177–178, 184, 191
ABC-TV 206, 208, 222, 227
Acme 10
Adcox, Grant 248
Aero Commander 211
Africa 34
African Americans, as race drivers 40
Agajanian, J. C. 190
Aintree Racecourse 71
Airline Auto Service 31
Akron, Ohio 235
Alabama 27–28, 58, 80, 193, 210–211, 225, 248
Alabama 500 202–203, 205, 207–208
Alabama Gang 216, 218, 226
Alabama Industrial Bonds 196
Alabama International Motor Speedway 195–197, 199, 204, 207, 229, 237, 239
Alabama League of Municipalities 184
Albuquerque, New Mexico 235
ALCO 8
Aldrin, Buzz 192
Aleutian Islands 34
Alexander, J. W. 154
Alfa Romeo 73, 185
Alhambra, California 81
Ali, Muhammad 216
Allen, James A. 12
Allen, Johnny 129, 133–134, 142, 192
Allen, Ted 19
Allgood, Eddie 166, 168
Allison, Bobby 183, 186, 192, 198–199, 201, 206–207, 215, 217–230, 232–233, 235–237, 240, 239, 241–241, 245–249, 250–251
Allison, Donnie 2, 198, 200–201, 207, 213, 218–220, 226, 232, 245, 247
Alpines 185
Alvarez, Bernard 178
Alzheimer's Disease 120
Amateur Division 137

AMC: Javelin 186, 220; Matador 235, 248–250
America 500 164, 178–180, 206, 223, 243
American Automobile Association (AAA) 2, 7, 9, 14–15, 19–21, 38–42, 44–47, 49, 57, 63–65, 67, 73–75, 79–82, 91, 97, 99–100, 111–112
American Baseball Guild 151
American Challenge Cup 143
American Competition Committee for United States (ACCUS) 186, 203, 223, 145
American Giants 42
American Motorcycle Association 138, 152, 174
American Motorist 14
American Motors 236
American Power Boat Association 106
American Raceways, Inc. 208–209, 246
American Racing Association 47
American Speedster 14
American Stock Car Racing Association 40
Amick, George 121–123, 222
Anderson, Jack 143
Anderson, Woodrow 33
Andretti, Mario 174, 182–183
Annadale, Virginia 141
Anniston, Alabama 196
The Anniston Star 195
Anti-Trust law suit 235
Apperson Jackrabbit 5
Arizona 80, 100
Arkansas 15
Armstrong, Jack 181
Armstrong, Neil 192–193
Army Air Force 34
Arness, James 137
Arrington, Bobby 232
Asbury, Herbert 27
Ascot Speedway 190
Asheboro, North Carolina 29, 150, 152, 155, 249

Asheville Citizen 151
Asheville-Weaverville Speedway 104, 139, 152–153, 186, 190, 192, 223
Assari, Alberto 105
Associated Press 2, 139, 150, 154, 182, 198–199, 215, 221, 226, 228, 233, 238, 241
Atkins, Virginia 24
Atlanta, Georgia 11, 18, 24, 28–29, 31–34, 38, 40–41, 49, 56–57, 64–65, 73, 81, 93, 97–98, 105, 124–125, 130–131, 140–141, 156, 173, 178, 182, 195–196, 207, 209–210, 217, 223, 228, 242, 245–246
Atlanta Automobile Club 130
Atlanta Constitution 38
Atlanta 500 133, 141, 157, 182–183, 207, 217, 228
Atlanta Gospel Chorus 44
Atlanta International Raceway (AIR) 130–133, 140, 142, 145, 161, 173, 177–178, 180, 183, 186, 190, 217, 221, 246–247
Atlanta Journal-Constitution 121
Atlanta Motor Speedway 32
Atlanta Motordrome 15
Atlanta Stock Car Club 56
Atlantic City, New Jersey 113
Atlantic Ocean 115
Atlantic States Racing Association 38
Augusta, Georgia 126, 173
Augusta International Speedway 142
Austin, Ray 211
Austin Mini Coopers 185
Auto-Polo 21
The Automobile 10
Automobile Club of America (ACA) 2, 9, 15
Automobile Competition Committee for the United States (ACCUS) 7, 91, 248
Automobile Manufacturers Association (AMA) 172, 176
Automobile Racing Club of America (ARCA) 93, 160–161, 181, 202

273

Index

B-17 Flying Fortress 34
B-24 34
B-25 34
B-29 34
Bagby, Garland 124–125, 130
Bahamas 228
Bailee, H. H. 230
Bainbridge, Ohio 81
Baker, E. G. "Cannonball" 49, 52, 67, 132
Baker, Elzie "Buck" 6, 31, 36, 57, 65, 67, 75, 81–82, 95, 98, 100, 102, 104, 113, 117, 120, 126, 131, 134, 135, 142, 147–148, 170, 202, 228, 230–232
Baker, Elzie, Jr. "Buddy" 198, 201–202, 207, 210–211, 215–224, 229–230, 233–240, 247, 250
Bank of the Big Island 129
Banks, Henry 121, 140, 173
Bannon, Roy 60–61
Barber, Kioda 43
Barber-Wanock Ford Special 42–43
Barkheimer, Bill 56, 131
Barnes, Hugo 45
Barnes Special 45
Batista, Fulgenico 6
Batson, Neal 217
Battle of the Bulge 33
Batty, Frank 10
Baughman, Bob 211
Beach-road course races 18, 20, 22–23, 35, 37, 56, 60, 64, 68, 72, 74, 81, 85, 92, 94, 97–98, 102–103, 108, 110–111, 116
Beach speed trials 15
Beam, Herman 107
Beauchamp, Johnny 90, 129, 138
Beck Special 43
Beebe, Leo C. 174
Beer 50
Belgium 33
Bell, Bert 131, 148
Benzes 10
The Best Damn Garage in Town 37
Bethlehem Steel 89
Bettenhausen, Gary 248
Bettenhausen, Tony 97, 118, 182
Bignal, Al 60
Bignolli, George 121
Bill France Enterprises 63, 65, 68
Bill France Racing, Inc. 63, 70, 88
Biloxi, Mississippi 104
Binford, Thomas W. 121, 139, 190
Birmingham, Alabama 58–59, 89, 184, 201
Bisher, Truman 130
Black, Charles 209
Blackburn, Bunky 191
Blair, Bill 59, 68, 70
Blanche 145
Blaylock, John 131
Blouch, John 119
Blue Island, Illinois 103
Blue Laws 79, 195
Bluebird 19
Bluff City, Tennessee 239
Blunt, David 141
Blunt, Jack 125

Board tracks 18, 20
Boca Ciega Bay, Florida 88
Boca Raton, Florida 84, 86
Boggs, David 226
Bolles, Bob 188
Bolster, John 8
Bonneville Salt Flats 65, 105, 223
Bookmaking 114
Boone, North Carolina 192
Bootleg cars 28
Bootlegger 500 217
Bootleggers 29, 32, 67, 72
Bottoms, William 41, 43
Boule Valve Special 45–46
Bourque, William 13
Bowes, Robert M., II 121
Bowes Seal Fast Special 121
Bowman Gray Stadium 35, 49, 65, 74, 87, 125, 137, 142, 148–150, 154–155, 162, 167, 169, 183, 199
Boyd, Bill 125
Brasington, Harold 74–76, 78–81, 125, 148, 163–164
Bremer, Arthur H. 228
Briarcliff course 2, 8
Brickhouse, Richard 202
Bridal Veil, Oregon 73, 239
Briggs, Walter 89
Brinegar, Claude S. 89
Bristol, Tennessee 133, 156, 203, 223
Bristol Motor Speedway 173, 182, 190, 192, 236, 239, 246
British Royal Air Force 57
Britt, Bloys 32, 182, 200, 228
Broady, J. A. 165
Brodack, Bill 225
Brookings, Edward 196
Brooklands 13, 16
Brooklyn, Michigan 198, 208, 219, 223, 248
Brooklyn, New York 15
Brooks, Dick 206, 208, 210, 215, 218, 236–237, 239
Brooks, Glen 20
Brotherhood of Professional Base Ball Players 151
Broward Speedway 64
Brownsville, Kentucky 78, 236
Bruce-Brown, David 12
Bruner, Johnny 129, 133, 142, 178, 249
Bryan Station, Texas 193, 223–233
Bryon, Georgia 223
Buddy Shuman Award 113, 126
Buellton, California 237
Buffalo, New York 133
Buffalo Civic Stadium 79
Buick 10, 11, 13–15, 64, 67, 99, 102
Bullard, David 146
Bulldozers 128
Burchman, Bob 245
Burma 34
Burman, Bob 8, 13, 15
Burrell, T. M. 152
Burris, Carl 169
Butler, A. J. 79
Butler, D. Gordon 79
Byers, Ralph 131
Byron, Robert "Red" 6, 31–32, 34–35, 49, 51, 57, 59–61, 64–69, 73, 76–79, 92

Cabarrus Memorial Hospital 157
Cadillacs 67, 76
Cagle, Clarence 90
Calhoun County, Alabama 196
California 15, 28, 31, 41, 56, 78, 80–81, 100, 131, 169, 211
Call, Willie Clay 31
Cameron, Paul A. 240
Cameron's Speedster 5
Camp Butner, North Carolina 167
Campbell, Malcolm 16, 19
Canada 81, 93, 95, 114, 151
Canadian Club 164
Canate, Frank 93
Candler, Asa G. 130
Candler Field 130
Canfield, Ohio 75
Cannon, Bill 119
Capital City 500 233
Capone, Al 44
Carden, Billy 59–60, 64–66
Carolina Atlantic Timber Corporation 161
Carolina Country 68
Carolina 500 206–207, 217, 227, 236, 244
Carolina Speedway 20
Carrera Panamericana 72, 76
Carrier, Larry 133–134, 192, 203
Carruthers, California 235
Carson, Bill 44, 46
Carson, William 43
Carter, David 250
Cassidy, John 203
Castles, Neil "Soapy" 193, 219
Cedar Rapids, Iowa 226
Cedarburg, Wisconsin 96
Central Labor Union 23, 152
Central States Auto Racing Association (CSARA) 38, 63, 75, 81
Century races 108
Chain gang 30
Champion, Bill 201
Champion spark plugs 99, 113, 126
Chandler, A. B. "Happy" 165
Chapel Hill, North Carolina 226
Chapman, J. Root 118–119
Chapter 10 Bankruptcy 155
Charlie's Grill & Hi-Hat Club 22
Charlotte, North Carolina 20, 23, 29, 30, 36, 49, 64–65, 72, 76, 93–94, 99, 105–106, 124, 130–131, 133, 140–141, 146–147, 150, 155, 157, 160, 164–165, 167, 176, 199, 203, 207, 211, 223, 228, 230, 242–243, 245
Charlotte Fairgrounds 39
Charlotte Memorial Hospital 156
Charlotte Motor Speedway 103, 128, 132, 134, 140, 145–146, 152, 155–157, 160–162, 173, 177, 180, 183, 186, 190, 192, 217, 221, 223, 224, 238, 240, 245, 247
Charlotte News 6, 146
Charlotte Observer 39, 51, 140, 148, 150–151, 159, 161, 171, 179

Index

Charlotte Red Cross 156
Charlotte Speedway 7, 65–68, 74
Chatham Artillery 10
Chattanooga, Tennessee 56, 59, 64, 129, 226, 245, 248
Cheating 178, 242
Chevrolet 27, 36, 100–102, 106, 111, 114, 120, 123, 126, 134, 170, 172–174, 177, 180–183, 186, 188–190, 225–226, 228, 236, 238–241, 245–246–249; Camaro 186, 196, 202, 220, 223; Chevelle 174–175, 177–178, 181–183, 187–189; Corvette 110
Chevrolet, Arthur 43
Chevrolet, Gaston 43
Chevrolet, Louis 13–15
Chevrolet Special 46
Chicago, Illinois 9, 42–45, 48, 108, 121, 147, 174
Chicago Colored Speedway Association 41, 43
Chicago Defender 41–43
Chicago Whip 45
Childress, Richard 202, 233, 236, 243, 250
Chillicothe Federal Prison 116
China 34
Chitwood, Joey 185
Chop Shop 103
Christian, Sarah 57, 67–68
Christiansburg, Virginia 201
Chrysler 67, 80, 96–99, 101–102, 106, 110, 115, 161, 164, 172–174, 176–178, 180–183, 185–191, 203, 205, 213–214–215, 219–221, 238
Churchill Downs 13
Cincinnati, Ohio 87, 154
Cincinnati, Indianapolis & Western Railroad 41
Circle Track 188
Civil War 26–27
Civilian Conservation Corps 36
Clement-Bayards 10
Clements, Jap 13
Clemson University 181
Cleveland, Ohio 45
Closed circuit speed record 118
CNN-SI 37–38
Cobb, Tom 87, 184
Coble, Kermit 184
Coca-Cola 118, 130
Coca-Cola 600 191
Codding, C. C. 20
Coleman, J. C. 186
College Station, Texas 222–223
Collins, Bob 181
Colorado 15, 165
Colored Speedway Association (CSA) 41–46
Columbia, South Carolina 102, 176, 185, 189, 223
Columbia, Tennessee 232, 239
Columbus, Georgia 58, 64, 175
Columbus Speedway 59–60
Colvin, Bob 80, 136, 139–140, 143, 152, 161–163, 172, 180–181, 236
Comet 191
Concord, North Carolina 56, 60, 135, 139, 170

Concord Motor Speedway 39
Concrete track walls 7
Congress 26–27
Conklin, Millard 19, 22
Connecticut 40, 52, 80–81
Connolly, John 228
Connor, Roy Pat 73
Consumer Guide 61
Contest Board 19, 21, 39, 80
Convertible Division 63, 70, 74, 90–91, 101, 103–104, 110–111, 115, 117, 135, 137, 146, 154
Cook, Howard 168
Cook, Jim 206
Coombs, Charlie 72, 125
Coombs, Jack 125
Corbin, Kentucky 83, 94
Corsicana, Texas 73
Costa Mesa, California 157
Courtwright, Billy 79
Cowcatchers 28
Crane, George 14
Cravens, J. B. 155
Crawford, Jimmy 226
Crisler, Al 68, 72, 77–78
Crittenden Memorial Hospital 104
Croce, Jim 33
Crowe, Mrs. Fred 24
Crowley, John 163
Crown Hill Cemetery 46
Cruze, Sidney 68
CT Corporation 53
Cuban cigars 50
Cummings, Bill 46
Cunningham, George 36, 140, 150–151, 159–160
Cup Champion 229
Cureyer, Charlie 47
Cutting 50 14
Cypress Gardens, Florida 98

Dahlonega, Georgia 28
Daily Press 68
Dallas Cowboys 88
Dallas Morning News 29
Dallas Texans 214
Dalton, Dean 249
Dalton, Frances 166
Danville, Virginia 59, 165, 168
Danville Fairgrounds Speedway 166

Darlington, South Carolina 74–76, 81–82, 112–114
Darlington Raceway 35, 78–81, 88, 93–95, 100–101, 106–107, 116–117, 122–123, 125, 131–132, 134, 136–137, 139–140, 142, 145, 148, 152, 154, 156, 160–161, 163–165, 169, 172–173, 177, 179, 181, 183, 186, 190–191, 195–196, 200, 208, 211, 218, 221–223, 228, 232, 236–237, 247
Darracqs 10
Dart 186
Davis, Bill "Slick" 60
Davison, Donald 14
Dawson County, Georgia 31, 33
Dawsonville, Georgia 24, 65
Dayton, Ohio 45, 121

Daytona Beach, Florida 1, 5–8, 23–24, 34, 38–40, 48–49, 52, 54–57, 64–65, 68, 77, 84–90, 92, 94, 96–100, 102, 105, 109–114, 118, 120–121, 133–136, 138–140, 148, 152, 157, 168, 178, 184, 187, 189, 196–197, 201–203, 206, 208, 214, 219–220, 223, 225, 228, 231–232, 235, 239, 241
Daytona Beach Boat Works 36
Daytona Beach Chamber of Commerce 22
Daytona Beach Elks Club 20–21
Daytona Beach Junior Chamber of Commerce (Jaycees) 22
Daytona Beach Morning Journal 16, 21, 23, 38, 68, 87, 109–111, 114, 123, 131, 176, 190, 213, 235, 244
Daytona Beach Municipal Airport 87
Daytona Beach News-Journal 22, 40
Daytona Beach Race and Recreational Facilities District (DBR-RFD) 87–88, 184, 231
Daytona Beach Racing Association 22
Daytona Beach Racing Club 18
Daytona Beach Speedway Association 18
Daytona Beach-Volusia County Racing Association 19
Daytona Beach-Volusia County Speedway 87
Daytona 500 90, 118, 120, 123–124, 126, 132, 137–139, 142, 147, 161, 172, 174, 181–182, 187–191, 206, 209, 215, 221, 226, 235–236, 244–245
Daytona: From the Birth of Speed to the Death of the Man in Black 61
Daytona International Speedway 7, 88, 114, 118, 121, 126, 130, 143, 145, 149, 153, 160–161, 180–181, 183–184, 186, 188–189, 216, 219, 226, 231–232, 246, 249–251
Daytona International Speedway Corporation 63, 88–89, 134, 157
Daytona Parts, Inc. 54
Daytona Plaza 125
Daytona Speed Week 81, 85–86, 93, 102, 109, 118, 126, 145, 162, 175, 181, 226, 228, 235, 246
Dedham, Massachusetts 206
Deep Gap, North Carolina 205
Democratic National Committee 228
Denton, North Carolina 163
de Palma, Ralph 11, 15, 100
de Paolo, Peter 100, 106
Department of Justice 149
DeSoto 168
de Soto, Jack 47
Detroit, Michigan 12, 45, 51, 63, 80, 89, 106, 109–112, 114–115, 126, 166, 172, 182, 187, 199, 208–209, 213
Detroit Festival of the Great Lakes 80
Detroit Tigers 89
Devies, Bill 201

Index

Dewitt, Lindsay 163, 217, 226
Dial, Gerald 197
Dieringer, Darel 178–179, 236
Dietrick 10
Dillinger, John 46
Disney, Walt 194
Disney World 194
The Dispatch 80
Distilling, illegal 26
District of Columbia 41
Diversified Financial Services 209
Dixie 81
Dixie 300 130
Dixie 400 173, 177–178
Dixie 500 209, 220–221, 228, 250
Dixie Racing Circuit 41, 166–167
Dixiecrat 38
Dodge 101–102, 106, 172, 175, 178–181, 194, 200, 202, 206–207, 215–215, 219, 225–226, 228, 233, 235, 238, 244, 246–247, 249
Dog Track Speedway 175
Dolan, Dick 76
Donlavey, W. C. "Junie" 244
Donohue, Mark 235
Donovan, Brian 167–170
Dover, Delaware 223
Dover, Massachusetts 191
Dover, New Jersey 59
Drag Racing Division 91
Dreamland Ballroom and Café 43
Dreamland Derby 43
Driving with the Devil 39
Drummond, Buck 168
Dublin, Georgia 206
DuBois, Pennsylvania 211
Duesenberg 16, 43, 108
Dunaway, Glenn 57, 68
Dunningham, Harry 42
Durham, North Carolina 146
Duval, John 44
Dwyer, Carson 40
Dye, Ronnie 173
Dye, Wayne 173

Eagle, Pop 101
Eaker, Verlin 226
Earl, Harley 89, 139
Earl, Henry A. 42–42, 45–46
Earles, H. Clay 40, 50, 70, 107–108, 139, 150, 152–153, 203
Earnhardt, Dale 74, 95, 121, 163
Earnhardt, Ralph 141, 169
East Point, Georgia 226
Eastaboga, Alabama 194, 196–197
Eastaboga Air Field 195
Ebony 48
Ebony Lounge 49–50, 115
Economaki, Chris 61
Ecuador 211
Edelstein, Robert 61, 73, 136, 146–147, 154, 159, 161, 163–164, 180
Eden, North Carolina 167
Edward Knowles Rayson Trophy 35
Edwardsville, Indiana 193
Eighteenth Amendment 26–27
Eisenhower, Dwight D. 115
El Paso, Texas 73
Elder, Jake 210

Elder, Ray 235
Elkhart Lake Road Course 103
Ellerbe, North Carolina 186, 233
Ellington, C. D. "Duke" 146
Ellington, Charles E. "Hoss" 240
Ellinor Village Country Club 110, 125
Ellis, Fred 13–14
Ellis, Tommy 223
Elmhurst, Illinois 138, 179
Elmore, "No Brains" Tommy 19–20
Empire 1911C 14
The Encyclopedia of Alabama 197
Endurance races 24
Eno River 58, 69, 78
Entry Forms 205
Epcot Center 194
Epton, Joe 72, 119, 133, 135, 137, 142, 170, 209, 231
Esquire 32
Etheridge, Jack 31, 65
Eubank, Joe 57, 59, 80, 102, 131
Eubank, Owen 184
Europe 34, 165
Evansville, Indiana 42
Experimental cars 109

Fairfax, Virginia 205
Fairgrounds Speedway 131
Farmer, Charles "Red" 216, 226, 232
Farr, Marion "Bubba" 126
Farrell, Gil 16, 18, 23
Federal Bureau of Investigation 37; Identification Division 37
Federal Reserve 133
Federal Wire Act 147
Federation Internationale de l'Automobile (FIA) 7, 91, 121, 139, 174
Federation of Professional Athletes (FPA) 147–148, 150–152, 155, 159–160, 198
Fees 92
Fenger, Harlan 121
Fiat 10–11, 16
Firecracker 250 123, 130, 141, 196
Firecracker 400 142, 157, 177, 185, 219, 238–239, 248–250
Firecracker 500 238
Firestone 99, 163, 174, 187, 189, 199
First Baptist Church 157
Fish, Mike 37
Fisher, Carl 12–14
Flagler-Bunnell Airport 126
Fleischer, Lawrence 198, 204
Fleishman, Bill 20–21, 38
Fletcher, Sam 88, 163
Flock, Bob 28–29, 32, 57–61, 64–68, 70, 73–74
Flock, Carl 28
Flock, Ethel 28, 68
Flock, Lee Preston 27
Flock, Marjorie 40, 50, 194
Flock, Reo 28
Flock, Tim 28–29, 32, 34, 59, 61, 67–68, 72–74, 81–82, 92–94, 97–100, 102–104, 111, 148, 150, 153–156, 159–160, 162, 215
Flock, Truman "Fonty" 24, 28, 31–32, 40, 49–50, 56–57, 60, 65, 67–68, 70, 74, 81–81, 92, 98–99, 102–103, 136–137, 193–196
Flock, Victor 194
Flock brothers 6–7, 31, 57
Flock family 27–29
Florence, South Carolina 81, 136
Florida 19, 21, 41, 66, 81, 146–147
Florida Democrat Party 228
Florida Fish and Game 89
Florida Secretary of State 6
Florida Speedways 56
Florida Supreme Court 231
Flowe, W. Owen 128
Foley, Dick 120
Fond du Lac, Wisconsin 107
For the Gold and Glory: Charlie Wiggins and the African American Racing Circuit 45
Ford 30–31, 35, 67–68, 100–102, 104–105, 110–117, 138, 141, 154, 156, 166–168, 171, 174–175, 177–181, 183, 186–191, 203, 205, 207–208, 211, 213–214, 218, 221, 225–226, 238, 247, 249; Model A 45, 47; Model T 18, 42, 47; Mustang 186, 220, 223; Thunderbird 126
Ford, Benson 111
Ford, Henry II 172, 176
Ford Lister 143
Ford Motor Company 159, 172, 174, 176, 188, 202
Ford Proving Grounds 89
Ford Racing 163
Formula One 105, 218
Fort Benning 59
Fort Knox 225
Fort Lauderdale, Florida 64–65
Fort Wayne, Indiana 88, 225
Foster, Billy 180
Foster, Jim 116, 129, 132–133
Fourth of July 80
Fox, Ray 37, 101, 106, 126–127, 140–141, 181
Fox News 102
Foyt, A.J. 121, 157–158, 173, 182–183, 205, 215–218, 226, 228–229, 245–246, 251
France, Anne 18, 23, 36, 38, 53, 61, 136, 235
France, Betty Jane 235
France, James C. 53, 55, 225, 235
France, William Clifton 18, 38, 54–55, 88, 157, 161, 171, 202, 225, 228, 229–230, 232, 235–238, 241–245, 247, 251
France, William Henry Getty "Bill" 2–3, 6–7, 18, 20–24, 31–40, 49–82, 84–96, 99–102, 105, 108–109, 111–116, 118–129, 133–136, 138–142, 144–148, 150–157, 159, 161, 163, 168–169, 171–177, 179, 181–182, 184–190, 192–200, 202–206, 208–209, 211, 213–214, 216, 218–221, 225–226, 228–230, 232, 235, 243, 245, 251
Frank Christian 58
Frankfort, Kentucky 201
Frankfurt, Germany 126

Frasson, Joe 222, 226, 237, 249
Fredericksburg, Virginia 166
Fredericksburg Speedway 167
French, Claude 47
Friel, Norris 137, 175, 178
Fronda Fairgrounds Speedway 59
Frontenac-Ford 42–43
Frontenac Motor Plant 43
Fuller 1911 14
Funk, Frank 23

Gadsden Times 195, 199, 226
Gaines, Wilbur 48, 51
The Gainesville Sun 33
Galfe, Bob 86
Gallan, Tom 49
Gambling 151
Gardena, California 81, 107, 117
Gardner, Slick 237
Garner, James 74, 124
Garnes, Tom 236
Garrison, Wilton 39
Gaston, Dewey "Rajo Jack" 47
Gaston, Ruth 47
Gazaway, Bill 188, 207, 209, 231, 240–242, 244, 249
General Motors 89, 115, 127, 172, 214
Georgeson, Benny 64
Georgia 15, 34, 25, 29, 31, 58, 50, 66, 81
Georgia Automobile Racing Hall of Fame 31, 39
Georgia Bureau of Investigation 64
Georgia Encyclopedia 33
Georgia Gang 33
Georgia Hussars 10
Georgia Tech 51
Germanton, North Carolina 111, 136
Germany 27
Glotzbach, Charlie 193, 198, 200, 206, 209–210, 219, 222, 225, 240–241, 249
Godfrey, Dewey 129
Goins, A. C. 155, 161
Gold and Glory Sweepstakes 42–46, 48
Golden Gloves 201
Golden Valley, Minnesota 237
Goldsmith, Paul 111–112, 115, 136, 142, 160, 177
Golenbock, Peter 152
Goodman, Bernie 131
Goodyear 187, 198, 200, 225, 247
Gordon, Cecil 193, 201, 224, 239, 251
Gould, Todd 45
Grace Steamship Lines 89
Graham, George 42
Graham Fronty-Ford 45
Granatelli, Andy 48, 226
Grand American Racing Association (GARA) 161–162
Grand American series 220–221
Grand National Champion 28, 31, 99, 107, 113, 131, 134, 143, 145, 180, 191, 193, 212, 219, 224
Grand National Division 58, 71–74, 79–82, 85–86, 90–92, 94–95, 98–101, 103–108, 111–113, 115–117, 122–123, 125, 127, 129, 131–132, 135, 137–139, 141–143, 147, 150, 153–154, 156–158, 161, 164–165, 169–170, 172–174, 176–177, 180, 185–186, 189, 191, 193, 198, 204–212, 214–216, 219–220, 222–223, 225, 228–229, 234, 236, 242, 245
Grand National Division Rookie of the Year 169
Grand National East 223
Grand National West 223
Grand Prix 57, 72, 181, 218
Grand Prix Mercedes 12
Grand Prize Races 2–3, 10–11, 25, 113, 139
Grand Rapids, Michigan 94
Grand Touring Series 201–202
Grand Turismo 143
Granger, Gene 143, 169, 170, 189, 200–201, 203, 208, 218, 221, 223, 225, 230, 237, 240, 242, 245
Granite 128
Grant, George 9
Gray, Bowman, Jr. 214
Gray, Henley 201
Great Bend, Kansas 68
Great Depression 25, 45
The Great Savannah Races 10
Green, George 126
Green Belt, Maryland 140
Greensboro, North Carolina 58–60, 68, 100, 122, 134
Greensboro News and Record 40
Greenville, South Carolina 57, 133, 142, 176, 192, 223
Greenville-Pickens Speedway 57, 182
Greenwood, Indiana 47
Grennel, Warren 125
Gretna, Virginia 168
Griffin, John 161, 211
Griffin, Charlie 131
Grimsley, Tennessee 27
Gulf States Auto Association 38
Gunsmoke 137
Gurney, Dan 143, 157, 159–160, 192
Gwyn Staley 400 228, 247

Habering, Harold E. 137–138
Halifax, Florida 108
Hall, Lee Roy 38
Hall, Roy 23–24, 32–33, 39
Hamburg, New York 70
Hamid, George 113, 116
Hamid, George, Jr. 113, 116
Hamilton, Frank E., Jr. 154–155
Hamilton, Pete 191, 198, 206–208, 211, 215, 217, 219–220
Hampton, Georgia 125
Hanford, California 81
Hankinson, Ralph 21, 113, 139
Hannon, Malcolm 41–43
Hardwick, James L. 195, 248
Harlan, Iowa 90, 122
Harman, Butch 233
Harris, Gayther "Runt" 166
Harroun, Ray 15
Hartford, Johnny 206
Hartsfield International Airport 130
Harvard University 8
Harvey, Charles 66

Harvey, Pat 66
Hassler, Joanne 226
Hassler, Raymond "Friday" 226–227
Haugdahl, Sig 16, 19, 21–22
Hawaii 93
Hawkins, Alvin 40, 49, 65, 76, 78, 125, 162, 169, 182
Hawkins, Joe 182
Hawthorne Speedway 43
Hays, John J. 68
Haywood, Tommy 98
Heidelberg, Pennsylvania 81
Heidelberg Speedway 70
Helch, Peter 12
Helms, Jimmy 173
Henderson, North Carolina 69
Hendricks, Ray 166
Hepburn, Ralph 47
Herald-Journal 106, 116, 128–129, 132, 139, 242, 245
Herbert, Tom 126
Hersey, Skimp 24, 39
Hickory, North Carolina 100, 106, 185
Hickory Speedway 35, 139, 161, 223
Higgins, Jack 56
Higgins, Tom 122, 177–178, 192–193, 208, 240, 242
High Commissioner 131–132
High Point, North Carolina 59, 104, 167, 177, 203
Highway A1A 19, 56
Hill, Harold 64
Hill climbs 15, 24
Hilliard, W. H. 11
Hillsborough, North Carolina 58–59, 68, 78–79
Hillsborough Speedway 136, 139
Hinton, Ed 13, 35, 61, 75, 100, 105, 125, 149–150, 157–158, 237
Historic Speedway Group 58
Hoar, Steve 162
Hobby, Gene 69
Hobby Division 91, 137
Hoffa, Jimmy 7, 145, 151, 154
Hoffman, Bob 242
Holcomb, Harry 13
Holiday Inn 192
Holland, Bill 79
Holloway, W. G., Jr. 89
Hollywood 102
Holman, John 106, 156–157, 178–179, 218
Holman-Moody 127, 156, 160, 162, 167, 171, 177, 183, 210, 213, 220
Horse Shoe, North Carolina 224
House, A. J. 14
House Armed Forces Committee 38
Householder, Ron 219
Houston, Texas 223, 230
Howard, Richard 155, 160–161, 163, 180, 183, 190, 192–193, 203, 207, 211, 217, 225, 240–241, 245, 247
Hub City Speedways 57, 64–65
Hudson 67–68, 81, 92, 95, 235; Commodore 65; Hornet 52, 78, 168
Hueytown, Alabama 183
Hunter, Jim 37–38, 228

Index

Huntersville, North Carolina 201, 202, 225
Hupmobile 18
Hurricane Camille 2, 198
Hurricane Racing Association 48
Hurtubise, Jim 177
Hutcherson, Dick 177, 186
Hutchin, Sonny 223
Hyatt, Clint 162
Hyde, Henry 78, 219–220, 225, 229, 235, 238–240, 244
Hylton, James 180, 186, 193, 198, 200–201, 205, 208, 211, 220, 224, 226, 232, 236–237, 240

I Dream of Jeannie 102
Illinois 15, 45, 81
India 34
Indian River Gold Cup 107
Indiana 44, 49
Indiana Billiards Parlor 42
Indiana State Fairgrounds 41–41, 44, 46
Indianapolis, Indiana 10–11, 38, 41–43, 75, 121, 243
Indianapolis 500 14, 16, 41–43, 46, 61, 65, 67, 74, 104, 121, 139, 218, 226
Indianapolis Motor Speedway 8, 13, 90
Indianapolis Recorder 45
Indianapolis Star 13–14, 45, 181
Indianapolis Times 45
Inman, South Carolina 180
Inside Sports Magazine NASCAR Racing 20
Insole, Jimmy 235
Insurance 113
International Motor Contest Association (IMCA) 19, 38
International Motorsports Hall of Fame 196
International Speedway Corporation (ISC) 21, 55, 61, 63, 89, 202, 225, 235
International Stock Car Racing Association 38
Iowa 15
Ireland, Innes 181
Irish Green Jaspers 10
Irwin, Tommy 126
Isaac, Bobby 31, 177, 192, 202, 207–208, 211, 215, 217–220, 223, 225, 227–229, 232, 236, 238–240, 245–246, 249
Isaac, Patsy 227
Isaac, Rhonda 227
Isaac, Robin 227
Isabeck, Alvin 136
Isle of Hope 11
Islip, New York 223
Isotta-Fraschini 10
Italas 10

J. Walter Thompson Advertising Agency 110
Jack Kochman's Thrill Shows 67
Jackson 14
Jackson, Gov. Edward 44
Jackson, Walker 125

Jackson, Mississippi 88
Jackson 30 14
Jacksonville, Florida 20, 37, 60, 81, 191, 227
Jacksonville Speedway 170–171
Jaguars 88
James, Bill 45
Janey, Acey 128
Jarrett, Ned 126, 133–134, 145, 149, 155–156, 158, 163, 166, 169–170, 177–180
Jefferies, William "Wild Bill" 41–43, 45
Jekyll Island Club 10
Jenkins, Chales 59–60
Jensen, Tom 178, 242
Jersberger, Joe 47
Jet 48
Joe Weatherly Stock Car Museum 143, 163
Johncock, Gordon 187
Johns, Bobby 126–127, 129, 131, 133–134, 141
Johnson, Gordon 182
Johnson, Jack 43
Johnson, Joe Lee 129, 131
Johnson, Robert Glen 26, 105
Johnson, Robert Glen, Jr. "Junior" 26, 31–32, 35–36, 93, 98, 100, 105, 118, 122, 126–127, 129–130, 133, 138, 140–141, 153, 156, 164, 177–179, 189, 101, 208, 211, 213–214, 219, 222, 225–226, 228, 236, 240–242, 247, 249
Johnson City, Tennessee 107, 126
Jolliff, Homer 14
Jones, Delmar 64
Jones, Parnelli 15, 157, 159, 185, 190, 205
Jones, Possum 131
Jonesboro, Tennessee 226
Judge, Judy 34, 154, 156
Judge, William 37

Kagle, Red 140
Kahn, Bernard 20–21, 38, 49, 68, 72, 84–85, 108–110, 112, 114–115, 126, 131–132, 136, 174, 176, 184, 197, 213, 230–232, 235, 244–246
Kaiser 67, 70, 168
Kannapolis, North Carolina 81, 141
Kansas 21
Keech, Ray 16
Keller, Al 102
Kellum, Charles 14
Kelly, Ollie 44
Kelly, Walter 44
Kelly-Morris Circus 146
Kendell, Donald 89
Kennedy, Lesa France 61
Kennedy, Robert F. 147, 154
Kentucky 147, 198
Kentucky Department of Transportation 201
Kentucky Speedway 235
Keokuk, Iowa 45, 179, 186, 202
Keselowski, Ron 229
Kiekhaefer, Carl 96–104, 106–107, 111, 114

Kimberly, Don 117
Kincaid, Tom 13
King, Bud 83
King, Clarence 211
King, Harold 76, 173
Kingston Speedway 223
Kite, Harold 72
Kitty Hawk, North Carolina 193
Knight, Alfred 56, 64
Knochman, Jack 59
Knox 8, 14
Knox Giant 13
Knudsen, Semon "Bunkie" 174–175, 183, 188
Kokomo, Indiana 44
Korean Conflict 79, 87, 105
Korkett, Bill 108
Krauskopf, Nord 219–220, 225, 236, 238, 240, 244, 247
Ku Klux Klan 44
Kuchler, L. A. "Lin" 174, 179, 182, 188, 202–203, 205, 207, 220, 223, 231, 234, 239, 242, 244, 251

L. C. Newton Trucking Company 236
Labor Day 75, 80–81, 94, 117, 123, 177–178
Lake Lloyd 89, 121, 126
Lake Lure 150
Lake Superior 159
Lakeview Speedway 57–59, 74
Lakewood Speedway 33, 38, 56, 60, 66, 70, 74, 79, 105, 122, 130, 163
Lamar Life Insurance Company 88, 134
Lambertville, New Jersey 116
Lancaster Speedway 95
Lancia 11
Landis, Kenesaw Mountain 131
Landover, Maryland 217
Langhorne, Pennsylvania 45, 59, 66, 72
Langhorne Speedway 21, 69, 83, 135
Langley, Elmo 126, 193, 198, 201, 217, 220, 224
Laramie, Wyoming 201
LaRue, William S. 88
Latford, Bob 37–38
Laurel, Maryland 18, 228
Lawing, Houston 68–70, 74–75, 79, 209, 231
Lawson, Curry 125
Lazarus, William 21, 202
Leaksville, North Carolina 169
Legion Ascot Racing Team 47
Lehi, Arkansas 104
Leighton, Mel 41
Leland, F. W. 10
Le Mans, France 105, 226
LeMay, Curtis 195
Lenoir, North Carolina 239
Lester, Art 125, 131
Leuegh, Pierre 105
Lewis, Paul 129
Lewiston Daily Sun 22
Lexington, North Carolina 57, 59
Lifetime ban 160, 162
Liggett and Myers 214

Index

Lincoln Speedway 95
Lincolns 67–68
Linder, Dick 70
Littlejohn, Joe 6, 23–24, 40, 49, 53, 55–57, 59, 64–66, 113, 130, 145, 181, 185
Litz, Deacon 44
Liverpool, England 71
Lloyd, Saxton 19, 22, 87–89
Lockenkemper, Jim 110
Lockhart, Frank 16, 18
Lockhart, Frank, Memorial Race 24
Lockport, New York 70
Locton, David B. 216
Logan, Gary 248
London, England 181
Long, Bernard 24
Long Beach, California 77
Long Boat Key, Florida 163
Long Island, New York 8
Long Island Motor Parkway 8
LoPatin, Lawrence 190, 198, 200, 202, 208–210, 214, 216–217, 245–246
Lorenzen, Fred 138, 140–144, 157, 163, 167, 172, 175, 177–183, 207, 210–211, 215, 217–218, 221–222, 229, 232–233
Los Angeles, California 10, 47, 190, 216
Los Angeles Rams 209, 214
Los Angeles Times 105
Los Angeles Times 500 251
Louisiana 15, 146–147
Louisville, Kentucky 80, 104
Lovett, Fred 149
Lowell, Massachusetts 9, 15
Lozier 10–11
Lund, DeWayne Louis "Tiny" 122–123, 142, 179, 189
Lutz, Florida 153
Lynchburg, Virginia 129, 166, 167
Lynwood, California 117
Lynyrd Skynyrd 191
Lyons Special 44
Lytle, Herbert 10

M & M Special 45
MacLane, Barton 102
MacLeod, Mac 74
Macon, Georgia 59, 64, 223
MacTavish, Don 191
Mad Dog IV 153
Madison Square Garden 21
Mahon, Fred 57, 59
Major League Baseball (MLB) 48, 131, 151, 165
Malone, Art 153
Malta, New York 23
Mansfield, Ohio 185
Mansgrover, Bobby 201
Mantz, Johnny 77–79, 81
Manufacturers' Control Association 9
Mapleton, Georgia 59
Marcum, John 56, 93
Marcus, Dave 201, 218, 227, 236, 238–239
Marietta, Georgia 72

Marion, Milton 20
Marion County, Indiana 44
Marlin, Clifton "Coo Coo" 232, 230, 245, 247
Marmon 15, 42
Marshall, George P. 148
Marshall Teague Memorial Trophy 123
Martinsville, Virginia 29, 106–108, 113, 200, 232
Martinsville Motor Speedway 70, 73–74, 139–140, 150, 152–153, 160, 173, 177, 179, 190, 203, 223, 225, 237
Mason, George H. 146
Mason jars 118
Matthews, Barbara E. 48
Matthews, Edwin "Banjo" 6, 83, 138, 141–142, 156, 213, 242, 245
May, Lysle 63
Mayle, Jon 228–229
Maynard, Troyer 216
Mayne, Roy 200–201, 237
Maynor, Henry 93
McCahill, Tom 109, 120
McCain, Ross 143–144
McCarter, Jeffrey 193
McConnell, Fred 82
McCulla, William 10
McDonald, "Mad" Marion 6
McDonald, Ward 168
McDuffie, J. D. 201, 239, 249
McDuffie, Paul 131
McGovern, George 228
McGriff, Hershel 73
McHugh, Clint 104
McIlvaine, James L. 146
McKim, Buz 19
McLemore, Henry 19
McLemore, Morris 196
McQuagg, Sam 175, 177
McQueen, Steve 216
M. E. Whitmore Dodge 69
Measured Mile 107, 109–110
Mechanix Illustrated 109, 120
Memorial Cemetery 157
Memorial Day 79, 116
Memorial Stadium 108, 126
Memphis, Tennessee 104, 112
Memphis-Arkansas Speedway 104
Mercury 103, 110–111, 114, 142, 172, 178, 180, 189, 192, 207, 215, 218, 220–221, 226, 239, 246–249; Cougar 185–186
Mercury outboard motors 96–98, 107
Merrell, Earl 191
Merrell, Jane 109
Merz, Charlie 13
Mexican road race 77, 81, 92, 97
Mexico City, Mexico 73
Meyer, Louie 47
MGs 88
Miami, Florida 83, 131, 133, 202, 211
Miami Dolphins 113
Miami News 24, 89, 196
Michener, H. 10
Michigan 45, 80, 202, 248

Michigan International Speedway 210
Michigan State Fairgrounds 80
Mid-Carolina Auto Racing Association 162
Middlebrook, Bill 72
Midget Division 91
Midget races 126
Midland, Georgia 59
Midwest Association for Racing Cars (MARC) 56, 93
Midwest Dirt Track Racing Association (MDTRA) 47
Miller, Bert 13
Miller, Donald 248
Miller, Weyman 64
Miller High Life 500 216
Miller Motor Speedster 47
Mills, John 111
Milton, "Terrible" Tommy 16, 20
Milwaukee, Wisconsin 48, 97, 99, 228
Milwaukee Journal 22
Mines Field 47
Minneapolis, Minnesota 226
Minneola, New York 21
Minnesota 16, 42
Minter, Edward 201
Miss America 137
Miss Southern 500 137
Mission Hills, California 235
Mississippi 198
Mississippi River 81, 205
Missouri 68
USS *Missouri* 38
Mitchell, Gene 250
Mizell, Herbert 215
Mobile, Alabama 81, 169
Modified division 51, 56, 61–63, 66, 70, 81, 85, 90–93, 98, 100, 108, 115, 126, 138, 146, 169
Moir, Harry 89
Moneypenny, Charles 89
Monroe, North Carolina 64–65
Monza, Italy 105, 118–119
Moody, Lloyd 20, 22
Moody, Ralph 102, 104, 167, 171, 179, 182
Moonshine 27, 34, 49, 67, 118, 165
Moonshiners 25–27, 67
Moore, Bob 164
Moore, Carl 133–134, 192
Moore, Lee 189
Moore, Walter "Bud" 66, 101–102, 115, 143, 153, 177–180, 185, 189, 192, 225, 239–240, 247, 249
Mooresville, Indiana 41
Moran, Charles J. 130
Morgan, Bob 141
Morgan, Henry 146
Morgan, William J. 113, 139
Morris, D. N. 155
Morris, Rodney 45
Morris-Thornton Construction 197
Morristown, New Jersey 94
Morrisville, North Carolina 226
Morton, Clayton 170
Motor Holding Company 2, 9
Motor State 400 219, 248
Motor Trend 500 205

Motordromes 5
Mt. Airy, North Carolina 160
Moyers, Russ 231
Moyoch Speedway 175
Muhlman, Max 6, 146
Mundy, Frank 32, 49, 59, 67, 81, 102
Murchison, Clint 88–89
Murchison, Clint, Jr. 88
Murchison, John 88
Murphy, Danny 22
Murphy's Law 128
Music City 420 238
Myers, Billy 111, 136
Myers, Bobby 136
Myrtle Beach, South Carolina 222

Nally, G. B. 146
Naman, Don 250
Nance, Allen 146
Napier Bluebird 16
NASCAR: A Celebration 37
NASCAR Confidential 152
NASCAR Hall of Fame 93
NASCAR Insurance 194
NASCAR Racing Commission 142
Nash 73, 76, 96
Nash-Hudson 115
Nash-Kelvinator 235
Nashville, Tennessee 131, 223, 240
Nashville Fairgrounds Speedway 238
National 10, 13
National Association for Stock Car Automobile Racing (NASCAR) 2, 6–7, 19, 21, 28, 31, 34–38, 47, 51–74, 76, 78, 80–82, 84, 85–89, 91, 92–96, 98–100, 104–107, 109–111, 113–116, 118–123, 127, 129–132, 135, 137, 139–140, 142–143, 145, 147–151, 153–155, 157–163, 165, 167–176, 178–179, 181–184, 187–192, 194–203, 205–210, 213–216, 219–225, 227–228, 230–233, 235–244, 247–249, 251
National Auto Racing League 40
National Basketball Association (NBA) 151, 198
National Business Hall of Fame 48
National Championship Stock Car Circuit (NCSCC) 38–39, 57, 79
National Football League (NFL) 87, 131, 148
National Football League Players Association (NFLPA) 148, 151
National 400 133, 141, 157, 173
National 500 211, 221, 223, 228, 23, 240
National Guard 102
National Hot Rod Association 126
National Hunt Horse Race 71
National Motor Speedway Association 43
National Motorsports Commission 243
National Motorsports Press Association Hall of Fame 163
National Racing Corporation (NRC) 55
National Safety Council 112, 114
National Speed Sport News 84

National Sports Syndicate 41
National Stock Car Racing Association (NSCAR) 23, 39, 40, 50, 56, 59, 64–67, 73, 79
National Timber Sales 125
Nazareth, Pennsylvania 174, 182
Neal, Bob 168
Negre, Ed 201
Nelson, J. T. 146
Nelson, Norm 98, 102, 160, 177
Neuberger, Richard L. 105
Neusetter, M. 10
New England Stock Car Racing Association (NESCAR) 56
New Jersey 15, 40, 66, 100, 113, 133, 169
New Smyrna Beach Yacht Club 110
New York 15, 24, 49, 59, 74, 169
New York Times 1, 8, 13, 15, 105
New Yorker Bar and Grill 20
Newby, Arthur 12
Newport, New York 223
Newport, Rhode Island 8
Newport, Tennessee 106, 239
News-Star 248
Newton, North Carolina 126
Newtown Square, Pennsylvania 235
Niagara Falls, Ontario 81
Nichels, Ray 179, 202, 218
Niver, Dotti 86
Nix, Walt 217
Nixon, O. L. 226
Nixon, Richard M. 37, 89, 138, 235
Norfolk, Virginia 135
Norman, Whitey 169
North Africa 36
North Carolina 23, 29, 32, 39–41, 49–50, 57–58, 81, 100, 106, 147, 150, 193, 234
North Carolina Motor Speedway 163, 206, 217
North Carolina Secretary of State's Office 2, 53
North Wilkesboro, North Carolina 40, 79, 81, 103, 157, 199, 203, 208, 223, 227
North Wilkesboro Speedway 49, 58, 107, 125, 127, 152–153, 160–161, 184, 186, 190, 225, 228, 236, 247
Northern, Glen 63
Northern 500 114, 116
Northwestern University 206
Norwalk, California 206
Norwood, North Carolina 211
Novi Special 118
Numbers operation 20, 23
Nunis, Sam 21, 50, 56, 59–60, 66, 70–71, 74, 79–80, 113–116, 122, 139, 181
Nye, Doug 12

Oak Hill, Florida 146
Oakboro, North Carolina 64
Oakland, California 47, 94
Oakland Speedway 47
Oberboltzen, Madge 44
Occoneechee (Orange) Speedway 40, 58–59, 68, 74, 78

Odell, Don 133
Office of Price Administration 36–37
Ohio 15, 45, 74, 93
Oklahoma City, Oklahoma 104
Oklahoma State Fairgrounds 104
Old 97 165
Old Dominion 500 142, 178, 223
Oldfield, Berna Eli "Barney" 8
Oldham, Ellis 167
Olds, Ransom Eli 16, 18
Oldsmobile 36, 57–58, 67–68, 70, 73, 80, 82, 112–113
O'Leary, Col. M. J. 10
Oliver, Summer "Red" 46
Olivia, North Carolina 78, 83
Omphoy, Irving 180
Ona, West Virginia 220, 223, 229–230
Ontario, California 190, 218, 223
Ontario Speedway 216
Opoe, R. G. 134
Orange City, Florida 21
Oregon 105
Orlando, Florida 34, 98
Ormond Beach, Florida 5, 15, 22, 49, 118, 139
Oshkosh, Wisconsin 96
Osleski, Bob 153
Ossinsky, Louis 6, 49, 53–55, 67, 84–85, 87, 122, 154–155, 215, 244
Ottinger, L. T. 239
Otto, Edward 40, 56, 82, 84, 87, 99, 131, 155
Oval tracks 5, 8
Owens, Everett "Cotton" 6, 32, 57, 65–66, 127, 129, 131, 138–139, 173–174, 178–179, 183, 185, 226, 246
Owens, John 43
Owens, Robert 73
Owensboro, Kentucky 229
Owosso, Michigan 63
Owosso Motor Speedway 63

Pacillos, Paul 75
Packard 5, 115
Packard, Sammy 49–51
Pagan, Eddie 117
Page, Lenny 133
Palm Beach, Florida 228
Pan American Highway 72
Panch, Marvin 101, 107, 113, 131, 138, 142, 154, 156–157, 173, 178
Panhard 8, 15
Pappis, Eddie 68, 92–93
Pardue, Jimmy 157
Pari-mutuel betting 114, 146, 211
Paris, France 91
Parks, Raymond 6, 23–24, 31–35, 39–40, 49–50, 53, 55, 66, 70, 73, 76, 92
Parks-Vogt 33
Parsons, Benny 207, 226, 233, 236, 238–239, 243, 246–247, 250–251
Parsons, Johnny 79
Paschal, Charles 201–203
Paschal, Jim 67, 177, 183
Passino, Jacque 163
Pathé News 42

Index

Patterson, J. Lewis 146
Patterson, Johnny 83
Paul Revere Race 185, 196
Pearce, Al 20–21
Pearl Harbor, Hawaii 24
Pearson, David 131, 140–142, 164, 173–175, 177–180, 182–183, 189, 191–192, 198–199, 206–208, 210–211, 213, 215, 218–219, 225, 228–229, 232–233, 235–240, 243, 246–251
Pee Dee River 76
Peekskill, New York 123
Peking to Paris race 72
Pennsylvania 15, 42, 66, 72, 74, 93, 95
Penske, Roger 235, 249
Pepsi-Cola 89
Permatex 300 191
Petersburg, Virginia 239
Petty, Elizabeth 122–123, 135
Petty, Julian 29–30
Petty, Lee 29, 67, 70, 81, 83, 90, 93–95, 98–100, 104, 106, 112–113, 116–117, 122–123, 126–127, 129–130, 135, 137–138, 143, 147, 149, 177, 206, 209, 225
Petty, Maurice 123
Petty, Richard 29–30, 58, 107, 122–123, 126, 128–130, 133–134, 138, 158, 161, 164, 166–167, 170, 173, 175, 177–180, 182–184, 186, 189, 191–193, 198–208, 210–211, 215–226, 228–229, 232–237, 239–243, 245–251
Philadelphia, Pennsylvania 9–10, 34, 235
Philip Morris 214
Phillips, Benny 240
Phillips, J. Richard 125
Phoenix, Arizona 133, 137
Pickett, Wilburn 202
Pickle, Ronald 157
Piedmont 29
Piedmont-Interstate Fairgrounds 57, 64–65, 94, 145
Pierce, Daniel S. 20, 67, 114, 196–197
Pierce, Richard 45
Pikes Peak 159–160
Pistone, Tom 122, 126, 129, 136, 161
Pittsburgh, Pennsylvania 70, 93
Pittsburgh Press 99, 233
Plantation 151, 205
Plumbers and Fitters Local 487 152
Plymouth 58, 70, 77–78, 83, 114, 130, 143, 157, 163, 173, 175, 177, 179–180, 183, 206–208, 211, 215–216, 219–220, 225, 233, 238; Barracuda 173, 186
Pocono, Pennsylvania 250
Points Fund 92
Polson, Maurice 168
Pompano Race Track 56
Pond, Lennie 239, 247, 251
Pontiac 35, 105, 111, 114, 127, 132, 134, 136, 138, 140–142, 154, 156, 161, 172, 188; Firebird 186, 202
Poole, Al 10

Pool's Creek Reservoir 38
Porsche 185
Porterville, California 210
Powell, George 167
Prest-O-Lite 13, 113
Price, Talmage 206
Priddy, Cotton 104
Prince, Jack Shillington 5, 18, 134
Princess Issesa Hotel 85, 125
Proctor, Eddie 193
Professional Drivers Association (PDA) 198–199, 202–205, 220, 232, 245
Prohibition 5, 27, 32, 44
Pronger, Bob 103
PT boat 181
Public Broadcasting System (PBS) 46
Purcell, Pat 100, 113–116, 120, 122, 127, 129, 131, 133, 143, 145, 149–150, 152, 162, 174
Pure advertising law 110
Pure Oil 76, 89, 92, 99
Purolator 99, 239–240
Purolator 500 251
Purse(s) 2, 50, 57, 64–71, 75, 80–81, 85, 90–94, 98, 111, 113, 116–117, 123, 129, 175, 181, 180, 202, 206–207, 216, 219, 223, 237, 246, 251
Purser, C. D. "Smokey" 20, 22–24, 31, 114, 151
Purvis, Sam 19

Quarterson, Ralph 93
Quattlebaum, Dr. Julian K. 10
Quinn, Francis 47
Quisenberry, Jim 49

Rabin, William R. 147
The Racing Flag: NASCAR—The Story of Grand National Racing 32
Rajah Temple 182
Raleigh, North Carolina 29, 82, 99, 107, 113, 250
Raleigh 250 117
Ramsey, Sherman 74–75
Randleman, North Carolina 29, 90, 175, 209
Rathmann, Dick 82, 121
Rationing stamps 37
Ray, Joie 47–48
Raymond, Paul 90
Rayson, Theodore 57
Rayson Memorial race 56
Reading, Pennsylvania 64–65, 102, 182
Reading Eagle 15
Reagan, President Ronald 38
Real NASCAR: White Lightning, Red Clay and Big Bill France 20, 67, 196
Rebel 300 101, 139–140, 146, 161, 173, 183
Rebel 400 208, 218, 228
Rebel 500 236, 246–247
Reconstruction 26
Red Springs, North Carolina 131, 192
Redneck 25
Reece, Charlie 21–22

Reed, Evelyn 24
Reed, Jim 102, 123
Reese, Mabel Norris 120
Reliability contests 15
Renaults 10
REO Speedwagon 5
Restrictor plates 210, 215, 219, 221, 238
Revenue agents 26, 30–31
Revolutionary War 105
Rhinelander, Wisconsin 121
Rhode Island 49–50
Rice, Sam, Jr. 107
Richards, Bob 49
Richmond, Virginia 223, 244
Richmond Fairground Speedway 135, 166, 168–169, 186, 233
Richter, Les 209, 214
R. J. Reynolds Tobacco Company 7, 36, 214–215, 218–220, 223, 237
Riley, Raymond 166–167
River-Ocean Development Corporation 88
Rivers, Mendel 38
Riverside, California 7, 47, 143, 170, 180, 190, 205, 223, 225–226, 235, 243, 246, 250
Road course 5, 107, 143
Roadster Division 51, 63, 70
Roanoke, Virginia 146, 152, 160, 211
Robbin, Marty 229
Roberts, Doris 170
Roberts, Glenn "Fireball" 7, 32, 76, 78, 98, 102–104, 107–108, 116–117, 120, 123, 126, 129–133, 138–139, 142, 147–148, 150, 152, 154–158, 166, 170, 173–175, 197, 249
Robinson, Bill 121
Robinson, Jackie 48, 165
Robinson, Robert N. 155
Rochester, New York 81
Rock Hill Speedway 100
Rockford, Illinois 48
Rockingham, North Carolina 163–164, 178–180, 183, 186, 200, 203, 206–207, 211, 217, 223, 227, 233, 241–243
Rocky Point, North Carolina 202
Rodenger, Jeffery L. 96, 99
Rogers, Jackie 241
Rogers, Johnny 59
Rogers, R. M. 177, 182
Rohn, Ronnie 170
Rolls-Royce 19
Roman Coliseum 13
Root, J. Chapman 118–119, 121
Roper, Jim 68
Rose, Buzz 81
Rose, Mauri 47, 61, 100
Rose Bowl 13
Roseman, North Carolina 59
Ross, Earl 248
Royal Flying Corps 16
Rubber barrier wall 7
Rubber fuel cell 7
Ruby, Lloyd 196
Rucker, William 41–43
Ruester, Ray 231

Rutherford, Johnny 143
Ruttman, Tony 142

Sache, Earl 105
Sagalowsky, Louis 42
St. Albans, New York 19
St. Augustine, Florida 24
St. Clair Shores, Michigan 111, 177
St. Louis, Missouri 16, 42, 153
St. Petersburg Times 105
Salisbury, North Carolina 23
Sall, Bob 131
Salsman, George 10
Samples, Edward 40, 49, 56–60, 64–67, 72–73, 79–80
San Diego, California 157
San Mateo, California 94, 103
Sanders, Bob 154
Sandy Springs, Georgia 82, 134, 168
Sarasota Herald-Tribune 177
Sargent, Jack "Long Shot" 41–42
Sauers, "Lucky" 59
Savannah, Georgia 2, 10, 139, 191
Savannah Automobile Club 10
Savannah Cup 11
Scenicano, Ralph 125
Schilling, Oscar E. 41
Schneider, Frankie 116
Schoolfield, Hank 137, 162
Scott, Franklin 168
Scott, Ramo 202, 232, 237, 245
Scott, Wendell 31, 36, 164–166, 167–172, 182, 186, 189, 206, 217, 237–239, 250
Scott, Wendell, Jr. 168
Seabreeze High School 118
Seaford, Delaware 236
Seagraves, Ralph 214
Sears, John 186, 201
Sears' Motor Buggy 5
Seay, Lloyd 6, 24, 31
Sedan Division 185–186
Segrave, Henry O'Neal de Houne 16
Seifert, Bill 201, 206, 222, 227
Seminole Speedway 34
Shackleford, Ben A. 51, 53
Shade tree mechanics 27
Sharder Field 167
Shaw, Ben 19
Shaw, Wilbur 79
Sheek, Dan, Jr. 47
Shelton, Henry 27
Shepard, Alan 154
Sherman, Henry A. 93
Shew, James W. 31
Shield's Special 42
Short Track Division 91
Shuman, Louis Grier "Buddy" 6, 30–31, 39, 47, 52, 57–59, 61, 64–67, 72–73, 79–80, 82, 100, 106, 118
Simplex 10
Sisco, David 240
Skeen, Buren 163, 173
Skelton, Betty 110
Skyland, North Carolina 206
Sluder, Gene 152
Sluyter, Howard 88–89
Smith, Charles 151
Smith, Chester L. 99

Smith, Ebenezer "Slick" 76
Smith, G. D. 146
Smith, Gene 45
Smith, Hoke 10
Smith, Jack 32, 57, 64, 66–67, 76, 82, 98, 127, 129–131, 133–134, 139, 168, 170
Smith, Jen 41
Smith, Larry 239
Smith, Lloyd 125
Smith, Ollen Bruton 39, 56, 64, 66, 79–80, 100, 103, 113, 124–125, 128, 130, 132, 146, 153, 211, 245
Smothers, Jimmy 226–227
Snowden, Bill 56–57, 59, 65
Snowden, William 24
Soldiers Field 48
Somberg, Seymour I. 146
Sommers, Sam 191
Sosbee, Gober 6, 31–32, 39, 57, 59–60, 64, 68, 76
South Bend, Indiana 45
South Boston, Virginia 223
South Boston Speedway 141
South Carolina 36, 38, 41, 74–76, 78–79, 81, 147, 154, 186, 195, 218, 227, 240
South Carolina Stock Car Racing Association (SCSCRA) 56–57, 60
Southeastern 500 192, 246
Southeastern International Dragway 173
Southern 500 76, 79, 95, 100, 106, 112, 114, 116–117, 122–123, 131, 136–137, 140, 143, 156, 194, 196, 211, 221–222, 232
Southern Railroad 165
Southern Runabout Cup 10
Southland Speedway 82
Spanguello, Leo 89
Spartanburg, South Carolina 21, 23–24, 49, 57, 80, 82, 94, 126, 140, 185, 195, 206, 217, 240
Spartanburg Herald-Journal 189, 200, 203
Spartanburg Municipal Arena 181
Spaulding, Paul G. 116
Speed Age 49
Speedway Park 57
Speedway Stock Car Championship 14, 113
Spencer, G. C. 201, 226
Sports Car Division 91
Sports Club of America (SCA) 185, 214
Sports Illustrated 74, 218
Sportsman Division 63, 70, 81–82, 93, 95, 98, 100, 107, 115, 126, 168–169, 191, 206, 222, 240, 248
Stacy, Nelson 142, 154
Stafford Motors 57
Staley, Enoch 6, 40, 49–50, 72, 105, 125, 135, 152–153, 192
Staley, Gwyn 102, 135, 208
Stamford Park Raceway 82
Stansell, Rex 82
Star-News 169
Starkey Speedway 152
Stephens, Jim 123

Stepp, Ray 152
Sterns 10
Stevenson, D. C. 44
Stewart, Jackie 218
Still 105
Stock Car Auto Racing Society (SCARS) 39
Stock car races/racing 1–2, 7–8, 10, 26, 49, 63–66, 95, 105, 111, 214
Stock cars 5–6, 8
Stoddard-Dayton 15
Story, Nelson 141
STP 226
Strange, Louis 9–10, 13–14
Streamline Hotel 49
Streeter, William 49
Strictly Stock Division 51, 58, 63–64, 66–67, 69–70, 76
Stroppe, Bill 103
Stuart, Virginia 216
Studebaker 103–104
Sturgis, Ray 89
Stutz Black Hawk Special 16
Sullivan, Pat 48
Sumar 118
Sumter, South Carolina 162, 200, 237
Sumter Daily Item 201, 218
Sunbeam 16
Super speedways 123
Surry, England 13
Susequehanna Speedway 95
Sweatland, Charles 131
Syracuse, New York 103

Talladega, Alabama 2, 34, 58, 184, 190, 195, 197, 201, 203, 205–206, 214, 216, 218, 221, 223, 239, 245, 248, 250
Talladega County, Alabama 196
Talladega 500 210, 232
Tallahassee, Florida 20
Tampa, Florida 154
Tanber, George J. 195
Tar Heel Speedway 175
Tarr, Donald F. 202
Taunton, Massachusetts 104
Taylor, Bernie 121
Taylor, Harvey 24
Taylor, Joe 131
Teague, Marshall 6, 49, 52–53, 55–57, 62, 64–67, 72, 76, 79–81, 99, 100, 118–119, 121–122
Teague, Mitzi 118–120, 123
Teague, Patricia 118, 123
Teamsters Union 145, 147–154, 245
TelePrompTer Corporation 181
Tennessee 124, 133, 193, 198
Terre Haute, Indiana 119
Texas 15, 218, 222
Texas 500 193, 233
Texas Speedway 233
Thomas, Dick 104
Thomas, Herb 67, 76, 78, 81, 83, 93, 95, 98–99, 100, 102, 106, 113, 136
Thomas, Jabe 201
Thomas Flyer 10
Thompson, Arthur B. "Speedy" 64–67, 98, 102, 106, 113, 133, 135, 137, 162

Index

Thompson, Bruce 23
Thompson, Jimmy 76, 131
Thompson, Neal 23, 39, 50, 53, 61, 65, 76–77
Thompson, Roscoe 60, 65, 67, 141, 162
Thompson, Tommy 80
Thoroughbred Racing 147
Thurman, Senator Strom 38, 78
Tides 84–85
Tiedeman, George 10
Tiedeman Trophy 11
Tiller, Travis 249
Time 218
Timing Device 137
Timmonsville, South Carolina 122, 189
Tinley Park, Illinois 118
Titusville, Florida 107
Titusville-Cocoa Speedway 107
Tobacco Bowl 169
Toledo, Ohio 93
Toledo Blade 219, 248
Tone, F. W. 10
Tooms, T. A. 183
Torzeski, Nick 147–148, 151
Trailways 36
Trans-America Series 185, 192
Transporters 27
Trauffi, Piero 73
Treadmill, Margaret 24
Trenton, New Jersey 59, 113
Trenton 500 113
Trenton Speedway 113, 116, 122
Trey of Hearts Special 44
Triangle, Virginia 249
Trippers 27, 31, 67
Trivett, E. J. 201, 205
Troy, Michigan 229
Tucker, Ben 58
Tucker, Tommy 218
Turner, Ann 61
Turner, Curtis 6–7, 31–32, 36, 60–61, 64, 66–67, 72–74, 76–78, 81, 88, 92, 100–104, 106, 112, 114, 123–126, 128–133, 135–137, 140, 143, 146–156, 159–164, 169, 171, 177–183, 185, 188–189, 198, 211–212, 215, 222, 238, 245
Turner, Darrell 128
Turner, Pat 197
Turner Investments 146
Tuscaloosa News 242
Tuthill, William 40, 49, 52–53, 55, 65, 67, 84, 85–87, 145
Tyner, Roy 131, 192
Tyrone, Pennsylvania 117
Tyson, J. H. 9

Underhill, Henry 72
Union Oil 89, 189
United Auto Workers 149
United Press 19, 110, 119, 154, 172
United States 65, 82, 91, 93, 95, 105, 145
United States Automobile Club (USAC) 49, 67, 73, 98, 116, 118, 121, 137, 139, 141, 157–161, 173–176, 180, 183, 190, 211, 214, 224, 226, 229, 236, 249

United States District Court 196
United States District Court, Middle District of Florida 37
United States Motorcycle Association 144
United States Senate 78
United States Stock Car Racing Association 40
United States Stock Car Racing Club 49
United States Weather Service 85
United Steel Workers of America 151
University of Florida 132
Unser, Al 189, 218
Unser, Bobby 196, 235
Upper Peninsula of Michigan 159
U.S. Air Force 200
U.S. Army 36, 72, 79, 96, 126, 156, 165
U.S. Marshals 37
U.S. Navy 36, 96, 154
Utah 223
Utsman, John A. 239

Vancouver, Washington 47
Vanderbilt, Cornelius 2
Vanderbilt, William K. "Willie K." 1–2, 8, 14, 17, 113
Vanderbilt Cup Races 3, 8–11
Vandiver, Jim 202, 226–227, 238
Van Zant, Ronnie 191
Vatican City 13
Vermillion, R. M., Jr. 131
Vernon, New York 79
Victoria, British Columbia 180
Victory Dinners 85, 92, 113, 125
Vietnam 206
Villa Park, Illinois 217
Vincent, Arnold 88, 215, 231
Vincent, C. A., Jr. 184
Virginia 29, 41, 58, 68, 81, 141, 198, 240
Virginia 500 107, 139, 150, 177
Vogt, Jerome "Red" 6, 18, 31–35, 39–40, 49, 51–53, 55, 57, 64, 120
Volstead Act 27
Volunteer 500 134, 192, 239
Volusia Circuit Court 154, 215
Volusia County, Florida 7, 23–24, 54, 88, 134, 231–232, 251
Volvo 185
Vukovich, Bill 104–105

Wagner, Louis 11
Waid, Steve 240, 242
Walker, Otis 29
Wallace, Barney 135, 222, 237
Wallace, Bobby 44, 46
Wallace, George 38, 195–196, 228
Wallace, Lurleen 196–197
Walnut Gardens Speedway 41, 44–46
Walthall, William 42
Waltrip, Darrell 208, 229, 236, 238, 240, 243, 245, 248, 250–251
Ward, William 195
Warren, Dan 86
Warren, Leon "Al" 45

Washington, George 196
Washington, D.C. 18, 75, 147, 235
Washington Redskins 148
Waters, Dick 241
Watkins Glen, New York 107
Waukegan, Wisconsin 48
Wausau, Wisconsin 227
Wawak, Bobby 217
Waynesboro, Virginia 168
Weatherly, "Little" Joe 7, 36, 100–102, 104, 106, 110–111, 124, 128, 131, 138, 140–143, 156, 160, 164, 165, 168, 173, 179–180, 196
Weaver, Nelson 140
Weaverville, North Carolina 81, 94, 151, 192
Weaverville Speedway 107, 182
Webb, Elsie J. 203, 205, 207
Weber, A. G. 214–215
Wellborn, Bob 100, 102, 128–120, 141
Wendt, June 39
West, James 14
West Middlesex, Pennsylvania 93
West Palm Beach, Florida 83, 84, 86
West Palm Beach Speedway 86
West Virginia 198
Westchester County, New York 9
Westcott F 14
Western Carolina 500 151
Western District of North Carolina 155
Western 500 226, 235, 246
Western Research Institute 201
Westmoreland, Hubert 68, 76–78
Whaley, Cliff 37
Wheaton, Mary 126
Wheeler, Frank 12
Wheelmen 27, 31
Whiskey 26, 50; illegal 5, 29, 30–32, 67, 77, 127
White, Al 129
White, Don 170
White, Jack 70
White, Rex 130–134, 142, 148
White Triplex 16
Wichita Falls, Texas 196
Wickersham, Rob 163
Widenhouse, Bill 102
Wiggins, Charlie 41–47
Wiggins, Lawrence 46
Wiggins, Roberta 42–44
Wiggins Special 43–46
Wild hogs 100
Wiley, Jack 153
Wilkes County, North Carolina 31
Wilkes Hotel 40
Wilkinson, Sylvia 32, 81, 88–89, 93, 165
Williams, Buckshot 40
Williams, DeVere 218
Williams, Eustice 41
Williams, LaRue 251
Williams, Peachtree 28
Williams, Raymond 226
Willow Springs, California 107
Wilmington, North Carolina 248
Wilson, Woodrow "Woodie" 169
Wilson, North Carolina 106
Wilson Speedway 122

Index

Wimbledon 13
Winchester, Indiana 23
Winchester, Kentucky 94
Window nets 143
Wingfield, Robert B. 154–155
Winston Cup 7, 205, 208, 238, 240, 243, 245–246, 248, 251
Winston Cup Grand National Championship 243, 251
Winston 500 191, 214, 218–219, 222, 229, 237–238, 248
Winston Grand National 220–221, 224–225, 232–233, 235, 237
Winston-Salem, North Carolina 35, 49, 67, 99, 136, 148, 150, 153, 162, 168–169, 175, 182, 202, 220
Winston-Salem Auditorium 182
Winston-Salem State University 65
Wisconsin 45, 81, 96–97, 100, 105
Wisconsin Special 14, 19
Witte, Norman 75, 81
Wohlfiel, Johnny 63
Wolfe, Joe 64–65, 102, 120

Wolford, John 129
Womack, H. Muse 88–89
Womack Asphalt Paving 88
Wood, Leonard 66, 160, 163–164
Wood, Glen 66, 142, 163–164, 169, 216, 221–222, 239, 246, 249
Wood Brothers 163–164, 213, 221, 244, 249
Wooden tracks 5
Woods, Ernest 94
Woolford, Dave 219, 248
World Championships 218
World 600 128–131, 133, 140, 146, 177, 207, 219, 229, 247–248
World War I 12, 15, 19
World War II 6, 24, 34, 36, 63, 66, 96, 181, 214, 229
Wright, Chuck 236
Wright Brothers 193
Wyoming 15

Yankee 400 210
Yankee Stadium 13

Yarborough, Cale 123, 164, 177, 179, 182–183, 189, 192–193, 198, 201, 206–208, 210–211, 213, 215–217, 236–243, 245–251
Yarbrough, LeeRoy 2, 181–182, 189, 191–191, 198–200, 208, 210–211, 213, 222, 226–228, 232
Yarbrough, Minnie 228
Yonkers, New York 83
Young, Buddy 201, 205–206
Young, Frank A. 42, 45
Young, George 251
Yunick, Henry "Smokey" 6–7, 34–35, 37, 66, 74, 95, 107, 112–116, 119–120, 123, 126–127, 131, 135–138, 143, 153–154, 157, 169, 173, 175–178, 181–185, 187–189, 194–197, 211–212, 224, 226, 236, 239, 241

Zanesville, Ohio 233
Zier, Patrick 248

www.ingramcontent.com/pod-product-compliance
Lightning Source LLC
Chambersburg PA
CBHW081543300426
44116CB00015B/2730